COUNSELING and
PROFESSIONAL IDENTITY

Becoming a Skilled Counselor

Richard D. Parsons
Naijian Zhang

West Chester University of Pennsylvania

Los Angeles | London | New Delhi
Singapore | Washington DC

Los Angeles | London | New Delhi
Singapore | Washington DC

FOR INFORMATION

SAGE Publications, Inc.
2455 Teller Road
Thousand Oaks, California 91320
E-mail: order@sagepub.com

SAGE Publications Ltd.
1 Oliver's Yard
55 City Road
London, EC1Y 1SP
United Kingdom

SAGE Publications India Pvt. Ltd.
B 1/I 1 Mohan Cooperative Industrial Area
Mathura Road, New Delhi 110 044
India

SAGE Publications Asia-Pacific Pte. Ltd.
3 Church Street
#10–04 Samsung Hub
Singapore 049483

Acquisitions Editor: Kassie Graves
Editorial Assistant: Elizabeth Luizzi
Associate Editor: Maggie Stanley
Digital Content Editor: Lauren Habib
Production Editor: Eric Garner
Copy Editor: Gretchen Treadwell
Typesetter: Hurix Systems Pvt. Ltd.
Proofreader: Susan Schon
Indexer: Sheila Bodell
Cover Designer: Candice Harman
Marketing Manager: Lisa Brown
Permissions Editor: Adele Hutchinson

Printed in the United States of America

Library of Congress Cataloging-in-Publication Data

Parsons, Richard D.

Becoming a skilled counselor / Richard D. Parsons, Naijian Zhang.

p. cm.—(Counseling and professional identity)

Includes bibliographical references and index.

ISBN 978-1-4522-0396-6 (pbk.)

1. Counseling. 2. Helping behavior. 3. Counselor and client. 4. Human services. 5. Social service. I. Zhang, Naijian. II. Title.

BF636.6.P368 2014

361'.06—dc23

2012045692

This book is printed on acid-free paper.

SUSTAINABLE FORESTRY INITIATIVE

Certified Chain of Custody
Promoting Sustainable Forestry
www.sfiprogram.org
SFI-01268

SFI label applies to text stock

13 14 15 16 17 10 9 8 7 6 5 4 3 2 1

Contents

Chapter 9: Care for the Counselor   273

Chapter 10: The Unfolding Professional Identity   293

Editors' Preface

Introduction to the Series
Counseling and Professional Identity

Becoming a Skilled Counselor is a text that introduces the basic information and fundamental skills required of all who are beginning their journey toward their development as professional helpers. As is obvious, one text—or one learning experience—will not be sufficient for the successful formation of your professional identity and practice. The formation of both this professional identity and practice will be a lifelong process—a process that we hope to facilitate through the presentation of this text and the creation of our series: *Counseling and Professional Identity.*

Counseling and Professional Identity is a fresh, new, and pedagogically sound series of texts targeting counselors-in-training. This series is *not* simply a compilation of isolated books matching that which is already in the market. Rather each book, with its targeted knowledge and skills, is part of a larger whole. The focus and content of each text serves as a single lens through which counselors can view their clients, engage in their practice, and articulate their own professional identity.

Counseling and Professional Identity is unique not just in the fact that it "packages" a series of traditional texts, but that it provides an integrated curriculum targeting the formation of the readers' professional identity and efficient, ethical practice. Each book, within the series, is structured to facilitate the ongoing professional formation of the reader. The materials found within each text are organized to move readers to higher levels of cognitive, affective, and psychomotor functioning, resulting in assimilation of the materials presented into both their professional identity and approach to professional practice. While each text targets a specific set of core competencies (cognates and skills)—competencies identified by the Council for Accreditation of Counseling and Related Educational Programs (CACREP) as essential to the practice of counseling (see inside front cover)—each text in the series will also emphasize each of the following:

1. Assimilation of concepts and constructs provided across the text found within the series, thus fostering the reader's ongoing development as a competent professional

2. Blending of contemporary theory with current research and empirical support

3. Development of procedural knowledge with each text employing case illustrations and guided practice exercises to facilitate the readers ability to translate the theory and research discussed into professional decision making and application

4. Need for and means of demonstrating accountability

5. Fostering of the reader's professional identity and with it the assimilation of the ethics and standards of practice guiding the counseling profession

We are proud to have served as coeditors of this series, feeling sure that each will serve as a significant resource to readers and their development as professional counselors.

Richard D. Parsons, PhD

Naijian Zhang, PhD

Authors' Preface

Becoming a Skilled Counselor

Having a desire to assist or to help another may be ingrained in one's DNA—however the ability to be of assistance, to truly be a helper, requires more than a desire and a caring heart. Competent helpers possess and exhibit certain personal qualities or dispositions and specific knowledge and skills. Parents, for example, when confronted with their child's 102-degree fever will certainly be moved to "help." Regardless of the strength of their desire to help, without the knowledge and skill necessary to address the issue at hand, their desire to help will, at best, be inadequate and at worse detrimental.

Helping when performed in the absence of the required knowledge and skills is not only inadequate but, when provided by one who presents as a "professional" may prove to be both unethical and illegal. *Becoming a Skilled Counselor* serves as *one* step toward the development of the knowledge and skills essential to the role of helper and the process of helping. Specifically, this text provides an understanding of the essentials of the counseling relationship, the dynamic of the helping process, and the nature of the theories and research guiding selection and employment of interventions.

Becoming a Skilled Counselor is a book designed to address specific competencies identified by the Council for the Accreditation of Counseling and Related Educational Programs (CACREP) as essential to developing an understanding of the processes of counseling and the development of a counselor's professional identity (see Table AP.1).

Table AP.1 CACREP 2009 Standards Addressed				
	1. PROFESSIONAL ORIENTATION AND ETHICAL PRACTICE	5. HELPING RELATIONSHIPS	7. ASSESSMENT	8. RESEARCH AND PROGRAM
Chapter 1		5a 5b 5g		
Chapter 2				
Chapter 3		5b 5c		
Chapter 4		5c		
Chapter 5		5c		
Chapter 6		5c 5d		8e
Chapter 7		5g	7b	
Chapter 8	1a 1d 1e	5g		8e
Chapter 9	1a 1b 1f 1g 1h 1i	5a 5c 5d 5g		
Chapter 10		5b 5c 5d		
Chapter 11		5b 5c 5d		
Chapter 12		5b 5c 5d		

Specifically the goals of this text are to complete the following:

1. Provide the reader with a view of the goals of counseling to include wellness and prevention.

2. Assist the reader's identification of personal motives for becoming a counselor, one's own personal state of wellness, and life adjustments which may be needed when becoming a counselor.

3. Highlight counselor characteristics and behaviors that influence helping processes.

4. Review essential interviewing and counseling skills.

5. Describe counseling theories and models that serve as models for conceptualizing client issues and treatment planning.

6. Review research supporting professional practice and treatment selection.

7. Highlight the need for the employment of measures of accountability.

This text includes extensive discussion and attention given to the specific nature of the helping relationship and the dynamics of the process of helping. As suggested previously, you will be introduced to the unique attitudes and skills required of the effective helper and become familiar with the contemporary theory and research which is used to guide case conceptualization and treatment planning. However, beyond the didactics of the book, the reality highlighted throughout this text, and each text within the series, is that helping another human being at a time when he or she needs our support involves much more than theory or skill application. Serving in the role of counselor is an experience of deep personal responsibility and satisfaction. It is in the blending of your heartfelt desire to help, with your increasing knowledge and skill about the counseling profession and practice, that you will become a true and competent counselor.

MORE THAN THE ACQUISITION OF INFORMATION

Unlike those enrolled in training programs in other "nonhelping" disciplines, those engaging in training as professional helpers need to approach their readings and their training with the intent of moving beyond simple information acquisition to the assimilation of that information into their identity as a professional; this assimilation also applies to the values these trainees employ to guide the applications of this knowledge and skill. To this end, this book, as with the other books within the series, has been structured in a way to promote the reader's assimilation and personalization of the material presented and the development of higher levels of learning, including the ability to value what is presented.

The chapters are designed to include case illustrations, practical exercises, and thoughtful suggestions for future direction. This approach is offered in hopes that you will gain:

1. *Cognitive clarity.* It is important to not only read the material presented, but reflect on the material and discuss the concepts described with your teachers, classmates, or colleagues. The goal should be to move from simply understanding to assimilating the theories, the constructs, and the concepts presented into your developing professional identity and an approach to helping.

2. *Behavioral clarity.* You are invited to practice the skills described by completing the exercises, modeling, and role playing, and also requesting corrective feedback from your teachers, classmates, or colleagues. While this practice probably won't make it perfect, it will certainly lead to improvement.

3. *Affective clarity.* Finally, as you will soon discover, helping is not a sterile, formulaic process. It is an awesome, demanding, and potentially rewarding experience that will touch you deeply. It is important as you continue to develop your professional identity and professional practice to clarify your feelings associated with being a helper, identifying those feelings which are facilitative and those which may be inhibitory to your helping endeavors.

ONE CAVEAT

The very nature of a book—with its static, two-dimensional presentation of life—severely limits the accurate and complete depiction of the helping process—a process that is *personal* and *dynamic*.

The information found within this text is presented in nice, linear, and logical steps. This is done because it supports the goals of explanation and knowledge acquisition. However, life is neither linear nor always logical—a point highlighted by the cases presented in Part III.

It is important to remember that the steps and skills described are presented in an artificially static state and that in reality they are employed in a dynamic, intertwined, and spiraling state of reflective practice. As such, we caution you that as you read through the upcoming chapters *not* to minimize the complexity of the human condition, nor the awesomeness of both the experience and responsibility of being a counselor.

The profession in which you are engaging has both a noble history and a valued future, and its health relies on the ethical, competent participation of members—like you.

Acknowledgments

Many researchers and theorists provide the foundation for the material to be discussed, however the real substance and "life" of the book has been extracted from the many courageous clients and supportive colleagues with whom we have been privileged to work. The illustrations presented throughout the book reflect a composite of the various individuals with whom we have worked. All the names and significant identifying information about the actual cases have been modified in order to insure confidentiality.

While our names appear as authors on this work, we would be remiss if we didn't acknowledge all those who have helped us in the process. A special thank you goes to each of the following who so graciously reviewed our project and provided valuable suggestions which have made this final manuscript something of which we, and we hope they, are proud. These include: Phu D. Hoang, Texas A&M International University; Geoffrey G. Yager, University of Cincinnati; Sandra Loew, University of North Alabama; James R. Verhoye, Metropolitan State University; Allan A. Morotti, University of Alaska Fairbanks; George I. Mamboleo, Alabama A&M University; Patricia K. McIntyre, Rosemont College; Susan Temperato, Canisius College; Lorraine J. Guth, Indiana University of Pennsylvania; DeDe Wohlfarth, Spalding University; Cheryl Ramey, Eastern Kentucky University; Margaret Carlock-Russo, Hofstra University; Linda Barley, York College, CUNY; Peggy Brooks, Massachusetts College of Liberal Arts; Rolanda Bell, University of Phoenix; and Dorothy Durband, Texas Tech University.

While the aforementioned provided guidance in regard to the content found within this text, it was the special gift and talent of Gretchen Treadwell who, as copy editor, turned our thoughts, our content, into the reader-friendly copy you now hold in your hands.

Finally, we would be remiss if we did not say a very special thank you to Kassie Graves, senior acquisitions editor; Maggie Stanley, associate editor; Elizabeth Luizzi, editorial assistant; and Eric Garner, production editor at SAGE Publications who not only kept us focused and on time, but also provided the much needed support throughout the development of this text.

This book is dedicated to our students, our clients, and our colleagues who have helped us better understand the helping process and the dynamics of change.

Counseling: A Process and a Profession

Counseling, as the upcoming chapters will explicate, is both a dynamic, intentional helping process as well as an established and ever-evolving profession. Prior to discussing the specific knowledge and skills essential to becoming an effective, ethical counselor it is important for all entering the profession to understand the essence of both the process and the uniqueness of the profession. Chapter 1 highlights the unique knowledge, skills, and process that make counseling unique from other forms of day-to-day helping. Chapter 2 then details the elements intentionally employed within a counseling process to facilitate understanding and achieving desired outcomes.

Counseling: Helping as a Professional Practice

Counseling—more than lending a helping hand

INTRODUCTION

On more than one occasion, each of the authors has been politely challenged by a student who truly questions the need and value in having to take a course on the fundamentals of helping, or the requirement to read a text such as *Becoming a Skilled Counselor.* One such student, Lydia, presented the concern stating,

> I hope this doesn't sound obstinate but I'm wondering why we need a course on the fundamentals of helping. I mean isn't helping just common sense? I mean hasn't everyone in the class provided help to someone at sometime? Helping seems to be something we all do naturally.

Lydia's question is not only valid, but also extremely valuable. Training experiences in counseling differ from other courses or training experiences where the goal is basically to promote understanding of the concepts presented. Becoming a counselor *demands* moving beyond simply understanding the information being presented in order to pass a test or satisfy a course requirement to valuing the information as essential to one's professional identity and practice. Whether presented by a professor or found within a textbook or research article, the theories, principles, concepts, and constructs that provide our discipline's foundation must be processed not as passive students but as developing professionals. Asking questions to gain clarity of understanding is only part of our responsibility as developing professionals. We need to seek evidence of the validity of these concepts and their utility to our own practice and promotion of our profession as counselors. It is essential that we challenge that which is presented by asking questions such as, "Why should we know this?" and "What should this or will this do for me as a professional counselor if we are to move from simple understanding to valuing and assimilating what we are taught?" Our profession and, more important, the people who entrust us with their concerns demand such questions.

In this initial chapter, you will not only discover what distinguishes counseling as a form of professional helping from the natural, unprofessional form of helping most of us have experienced, but also begin to see what it takes to become a professional within the profession of counseling. Specifically, after reading this chapter you will be able to do the following:

Helping is not just helping

- Describe the elements that distinguish professional counselors from their lay, nonprofessional counterparts.
- Describe what is meant by *professional identity*.
- Identify the unique characteristics of an effective, expert professional counselor.
- Describe the impact of training on the effectiveness of a professional counselor.

HELPING AS A NATURAL HUMAN EXPERIENCE

As noted previously, Lydia's question regarding what appears to be a natural human trait—to help—was quite insightful. The desire to help seems to be engrained within our DNA. Research has demonstrated that babies are innately not only sociable but also helpful to others. Biologists also see in humans a natural willingness to help (Tomasello, 2009). Research (e.g., Constantine, Myers, Kindaichi, & Moore, 2004; Hoogasian & Lijtmaer, 2010; Patterson & Memmott, 1992) has demonstrated that many of us are *natural helpers* to whom people turn in times of difficulty. These *natural* helpers provide informal, spontaneous assistance, which is embedded in everyday life—so much so that their value is often not recognized (Israel, 1985).

Research on these natural or indigenous helpers (see Constantine, Myers, Kindaichi, & Moore, 2004; Hoogasian & Lijtmaier, 2010) demonstrates that many employ effective skills of helping. Natural helpers appear to be effective, in part, because they are part of the community and not only possess knowledge that is meaningful to those seeking help but are also able to communicate with similar language and cultural values.

According to Patterson and Memmott (1992), these natural helpers assist others by *facilitating* (i.e., listening, encouraging, focusing on strengths, suggesting alternatives, etc.), *doing* (giving advice or material help, making decisions for others, or using persuasion and influence, etc.), or *facilitating-doing* (i.e., providing social support services for others). These natural helpers may compensate for their lack of formal training by being sensitive, empathic good listeners who have good judgment and expertise in solving certain types of problems. Further the evidence supporting their effectiveness led one noted counselor, Robert Carkhuff (1968), to declare that ". . . evidence indicates that with or without training and/or supervision the patients of lay counselors do as well or better than the patients of professional counselors" (p. 117). Needless to say, such a statement created quite a stir among professional counselors.

Given the previously noted research on the "naturalness" of helping, it would appear that Lydia's question is even more valid and deserving of an answer. If helping and the ability to help are natural, why do we need a course or a text covering the skills of helping?

It is certainly true that many elements, found in professional helping, are also present in our own nonprofessional helping encounters. For example, if we were to analyze a time when we provided help to a friend we may discover that the helping took place in the context of a *trusting relationship,* one in which the friend in need willingly and freely *shared his or her story* of concern or vision of desired goals. And when effective, it was most likely because we, who were attempting to provide help, not only heard what our friend shared, but *truly understood the message*—the story. These elements of trust, disclosure, and understanding appear universal in all helping encounters, whether the helping occurs in the context of a friendship or a more professional encounter.

Albeit these abilities may come naturally for some of us, each of us can increase our knowledge and skills of when and how to employ them. It is this need to gain knowledge of the elements of helping along with the skills to employ that knowledge that argues for the value of a course or a text on the essentials of counseling. But the value of such a course or text lies beyond the value of training in these general elements of helping. The conditions of helping which we may have employed or encountered in our own experiences of helping or being helped—conditions such as trusting, sharing, and understanding—are not the only, nor are they the sufficient, elements defining professional helping or professional counseling. As you will see, helping as a profession entails much more than simply offering a friendly, understanding ear.

COUNSELING AS A HELPING PROFESSION

Professional counselors intentionally construct with their clients a helping process that is very different from the lay helper's conversation with his friends. More specifically, helping as a profession differs from that provided by a lay nonprofessional helper along four dimensions: (1) the formality of helping, (2) professional helping's expanded goals, (3) the process of helping, and (4) the characteristics of the helper. Each of these dimensions is discussed in detail in the subsequent sections.

The Formality of Professional Helping

While there are many variations among the way counselors approach their professional duties, all ethical professional counselors are obligated to approach helping with a set of standards and guidelines (e.g., standards and guidelines of American Counseling Association [ACA], American Mental Health Counselors Association [AMHCA], American Psychological Association [APA], and American School Counselor Association [ASCA]). In addition to these standards or guidelines of practice, the professional counselor understands the fundamental nature of helping, the processes employed, and the rights and responsibilities of one operating as a professional. These standards and common structures the professionals employ distinguish them from their lay-counterparts.

Professional helping is structured

Unlike lay helping which can be spontaneous, informal, and reciprocal with the roles of helper and helpee being fluid and changing within the exchange, there is a fundamental structure to professional helping which maintains the distinction of the roles being assumed as well as the expectations of what will and will not go on within the helping encounter.

It is not difficult to imagine that a friend may seek out your help and assistance. This can happen anywhere and at any time. For example, you may find yourself approached within your home, or on the beach, or as you are walking with a friend to and from class. During these times you could be wearing anything you feel comfortable wearing, even shorts or pajamas, and you may choose to sit, slouch, or lie in a position that is comfortable to you. The language employed during the exchange may include slang, possible vulgarity, and both parties may find themselves "fighting" for talk time. This is the informality that characterizes a nonprofessional relationship.

The professional counselor, however, will not be so informal. The professional counselor will look and act *professionally*. The formal structure of helping is evident in that most professional helping occurs in a designated location, with designated, if not scheduled, times. Professional helping, again with an appreciation for the various settings and clientele a professional counselor may see, will often employ a referral process, a mechanism for scheduling appointments, paperwork to document the work being done, and, when called for, procedures for the collection of fees for service. But perhaps the most distinctive element to professional helping is the distinctive roles being assumed. Professional counselors recognize that they are engaged in this process for the benefit of their clients (Seligman & Reichenberg, 2010). Unlike lay helpers who may want to switch back and forth in the roles of helper and helpee, professionals maintain their objectivity and focus on the needs of the client. Further, unlike informal helping wherein the exchange between the parties can go at length and without direction, professional counselors engage in *intentional communication*—seeking data they feel is necessary to the helping process and sharing information they feel is helpful. Random, purposeless discussion or simple small talk has no real place in a professional helping exchange. From the first hello to a final goodbye, the professional counselor is purposeful with communications, and that purpose is the helping of the client. Exercise 1.1 will help you further distinguish between the structural elements of professional helping and the informality of the lay-helping encounter.

goal sets.

 Exercise 1.1

IDENTIFYING NATURAL HELPERS WITHIN THE COMMUNITY

At times of stress and distress or when confronted with a significant life decision people often find themselves gravitating to a special friend or person within the community in order to seek this person's support and consult.

Directions: Your task is to interview your friends, family, or colleagues in order to achieve the following:

1. Identify a person to whom they would turn if confronted with any of the situations listed below.

2. Identify the characteristics of the identified person that appear to be the factors contributing to his or her attractiveness as a natural helper.

For example, an individual may seek the comfort from a friend of 20 years when confronted with the death of a spouse. The friend is sought out because she is nonjudgmental, trustworthy, and has exhibited the ability to listen and to be both sensitive and objective.

Life Issue	Natural Helper	Characteristics/Traits of Attraction
Experiencing a loss of a loved one	_____ _____ _____	_____ _____ _____
Making a commitment to a relationship (e.g., marriage proposal)	_____ _____ _____	_____ _____ _____
Dropping out of school or quitting a job	_____ _____	_____ _____

(Continued)

(Continued)

Life Issue	Natural Helper	Characteristics/Traits of Attraction
Being confronted with a serious medical diagnosis	_____ _____ _____	_____ _____ _____
Considering a job offer that would require relocation away from family and friends	_____ _____ _____	_____ _____ _____
Feeling unsure whether to remain in a relationship	_____ _____ _____	_____ _____ _____
Feeling guilty for doing something and unsure whether to confess it	_____ _____ _____	_____ _____ _____
(Add one of your own life decisions here.)	_____ _____ _____	_____ _____ _____

Professional helping has ethical and legal implications

A core element to the structure of professional helping is that counselors, as professionals, are mandated to adhere to guides of professional practice and the laws enforcing such adherence.

The term *professional counselor* connotes a minimum standard of education and practice and, with that, the expectation of competence to help. Assuming the role of professional places the counselor in a position of accepting and assuming the ethical and legal ramification for embracing that title and presenting as a professional. Professional counselors must understand and abide by the codes of ethics of the profession and the local, state, and federal laws governing practice (Parsons, 2001). It is essential that those entering the profession know, understand, assimilate, and value these standards and laws governing practice.

As professionals, counselors adhere to standards of practice that are good for the public, and the profession. These standards help to (1) clarify counselors' ethical responsibilities, including the primary responsibility to respect the dignity and to promote the welfare of clients, (2) support the mission of the profession, (3) establish principles to guide best practice of counselors, and (4) serve as a guide for promoting the values of the profession (ACA, 2005). Beyond embracing the ethics of the profession, the counselor as a professional must abide by the laws and responsibilities governing that professional practice.

Counselors have a fiduciary duty to those they serve and are required to act in ways that are in the best interest of the client. The professional counselor makes decisions and takes actions that are motivated by client need and client best interest—not personal needs. Violation of such a fiduciary duty is not only a violation of one's professional ethic but may be a legal transgression and opens the professional counselor to legal action (see Exercise 1.2).

Exercise 1.2

THE COUNSELOR AND THE LAW

Counselors understand that professional standards of practice are guidelines for ethical practice. However, the law mandates many of the decisions counselors make in their practice.

Directions: The following are just a few areas in which your state may have mandates or laws governing a counselor practice and practice decision. It is important, as you enter your professional training that you become aware of these. Your task is to investigate each of the following and discuss its implication to your future practice and practice decision with your colleagues or classmates.

1. *Hanging a "shingle."* Can anyone in your state call oneself a "counselor" and charge for service? Are there minimum requirements to legally declaring oneself as a professional counselor?

2. *Confidentiality.* Is there a legal difference between confidentiality and privilege? Do professional counselors in your state have privilege?

3. *Responsibility.* When are counselors required, by law, to break confidentiality?

4. *Age of consent.* What are the laws governing confidentiality for clients who are 14 to 16 years or older? Do they vary given the issue being confronted, for example, pregnancy? AIDS? Drug addiction? Abortion?

(Continued)

(Continued)

5. *Abuse.* What, if any, is the legal responsibility when a counselor suspects that a client is being abused? Does that vary with age, for example, a child versus an elderly person?

6. *Practice location.* Can a counselor licensed to practice in one state provide professional services to a client in another state using the Internet?

7. *Records.* What are the laws governing a counselor's (1) maintenance of client records, (2) access to those records, and (3) disclosure of records to the courts? Are professional counselors required to meet Health Insurance Portability and Accountability Act, or HIPPA, standards?

The Expanded Goals of Professional Helping

While it may seem obvious that the goal of all "helping" is to help no matter if the helping is professional or nonprofessional, what may not be obvious is that the way a professional counselor defines what is helpful may be quite different than as defined by a lay, nonprofessional help giver. These differences are apparent when we view the way professional counselors approach their understanding of the problem, their expectation of change, and the depth and breadth of goals that are set.

Understanding the Problem

In most nonprofessional encounters, the helper draws upon her own experience with similar situations and problems as the reference point for understanding the experience presented by the helpee. For example, you may have been in a situation where you were upset or very concerned about the loss of a relationship, or upset upon hearing bad news and had a friend who suggested that he knew "exactly how you feel." For most of us, the experience of pain is uniquely ours. The concerns we have are our concerns and the anxieties we encounter are truly personal experiences. The phrase "I know exactly how you feel" not only misses the mark but can sometimes make the helpee seem as uncaring and dismissing.

Professional counselors understand that they may have similarly experienced the end of a loving relationship or the reception of bad news, but these events were experienced in a very unique way and they are unique to each counselor and as such they truly do *not* know how this helpee feels. It is difficult for any professional counselor to keep personal experiences out of the equation and in some cases these experiences are very useful as long as the counselor can maintain the awareness that experiences of the counselor are not the same as that encountered by the helpee.

Professional counselors want to step out of their own experience as a reference point and step into the experience and perspective of the helpee. The training professional counselors receive allow them literally to step into the experience of the helpee so that there is a complete understanding of what the helpee is trying to share.

Healthy boundary

For the professional counselor, the only way that the phrase "I know exactly how you feel" has validity is when the counselor could actually step into the helpee's world and experience life and these points of concerns from the lived experience of that helpee. It would be as if the counselor could factually leave his own experience, memories, and values and step inside of the helpee, embracing the experiences, memories, values, and meaning found within. Skills such as attending and actively listening to both the words and feelings of the helpee's message can facilitate the counselor's ability to join in and thus fully understand what the helpee is disclosing (McClintock, 1999). These are skills that one begins to acquire in a course or text on the essential or fundamentals of counseling, but will continue to mature and develop throughout the professional life of a professional counselor.

Expectation of Change

Another point of difference between lay helping and that offered by the professional counselor rests in the goals and reasons for engagement. Typically the lay helper is invited into the helping process because the helpee is experiencing a problem or concern and is seeking advice and direction. For the lay helper, the goal of the helping exchange may be simply to provide the helpee with a supportive ear, or suggestions or information. More often than not, the nonprofessional helper hopes to assist the helpee move out of the position of discomfort or concern and often seeks to accomplish this by way of advice or solution giving. The lay helper is truly the "answer person."

Professional counselors—unlike their lay counterparts—*are not in the business of answer giving.* For the professional counselor, the primary goal is to empower the client so that he can adjust to life situations and demands. The operative word in the previous statement is *empower.*

A counselor's job is *not to fix* the client, even though many seeking help request or even demand such fixing. As a professional, a counselor assists individual clients, families, or even groups to develop and employ those personal resources needed to achieve their goals.

Unlike the lay helper who may feel the path to helping is by providing advice and giving answers and directing the helpee as to what to do, the professional counselor employs her understanding of the research and theory in psychology, human development, and mental health to develop and use strategies to empower clients to clarify their own goals and use their own resources to achieve those goals. Further, the professional counselor sees beyond the goal of removing the immediate source of concern or pain in order to assist the helpee in the path of personal growth and development of wellness. As such, the professional counselor—while hoping to relieve the clients distress—has set his or her focus on facilitating change in the client's thinking, feeling, acting, or interpersonal relationships (Orlinsky, Ronnestad, & Willutzki, 2004). Change is the essential purpose of professional helping, and without change on the part of the client, professional helping becomes empty, worthless, and meaningless. The professional helper hopes and expects not only to assist the client in moving away from the current distress but to do so in a way that will prevent return to that distress. This is certainly the case for the counselor depicted in Case Illustration 1.1.

CASE ILLUSTRATION 1.1

HAVEN'T WE BEEN HERE BEFORE?

As noted in text, professional helpers—counselors—are interested not just in helping to resolve a client's current concerns or help them achieve their goals but attempt to do so in a way that will prevent return to that condition of distress. The brief exchange that follows took place between a counselor at the university counseling center and a sophomore with whom the counselor had previously worked. The exchange illustrates the counselor's attempt at expanding the focus of the discussion in hopes of identifying ways to resolve both the current issue and reduce the possibility of its reoccurrence.

Lindsey:	(tearfully) I can't believe this. I'm a wreck after breaking up with Carlos and no one cares. I mean I changed my status on Facebook to single and Charlene, Robert … even Jamal all posted sarcastic comments … like, "really … again." I can't believe them. They are supposed to be my friends.
Counselor:	So, your friends knew about your ending the relationship with Carlos. Was the only response you received their postings on Facebook?
Lindsey:	Well, no … not really.
Counselor:	Not really?
Lindsey:	Well, I broke up with him Sunday night and those guys all came to my room and let me cry on their shoulders.

Counselor:	Oh, so they were supportive initially but then posted comments on Facebook, and was that upsetting and confusing to you?
Lindsey:	Upsetting—yeah really! Really embarrassing. But I know what they meant. I seem to do this a lot.
Counselor:	Do … what a lot?
Lindsey:	Get into and then out of relationships. Jamal says I'm like one of those circular doors in an office building. He's always teasing me.
Counselor:	So, I hear that you were upset with the ending of your relationship with Carlos and are now embarrassed that your friends are "teasing" you on Facebook, but I'm wondering if it is possible that your friends are trying to get you to look at this pattern.
Lindsey:	Pattern?
Counselor:	Well it appears that you have been jumping in and out of relationships quite frequently and your friends, while maybe being somewhat sarcastic, seem to be suggesting that this is not the best way to go.
Lindsey:	Well, they are not just suggesting; they have been all over me about "needing a boy" in my life.
Counselor:	Perhaps this is something you and I could look at … I mean this "needing a boy" in your life.

Thus, a major distinction between the lay helper and a professional counselor is that the latter operates with a goal of helping that extends beyond that which was presented to include the facilitation of change and personal growth in the client, with the end result being a client who is more independent and capable of navigating his own life challenges (Orlinsky, Ronnestad, & Willutzki, 2004).

The Process of Professional Helping

While a good lay nonprofessional helper calls upon her extensive experience and interpersonal skills to comfort and assist a helpee in distress, the professional counselor understands and calls upon expanded resources, including reliable strategies and intervention which have been found within the art and science of the profession. Further, the professional counselor is aware that the purpose of interaction is to provide assistance to the client. As such the professional counselor employs professional skills and objectivity to maintain the focus of the helping dynamic on the client.

Expanded Resources

When presented with a question, problem, or concern, lay helpers search their own experiences with similar situations or perhaps their own developed model of problem solving to begin to craft an intervention or recommendation for the helpee. This is certainly true for the professional counselor as well. However, unlike lay helpers, professional counselors draw on an expanded database for solution formulation. Professional counselors do not restrict the search to their own specific experiences or problem-solving models.

Counseling as a profession rests squarely on the science of psychology and principles of human development. As such, the professional counselor has, through training, gathered knowledge about normal and abnormal human development, the factors contributing to each, and the strategies that have proved to be effective for the promotion of wellness and the remediation of pathology. It is this expansive database of research and theory that serves as the resource employed by the professional counselor in his formulation of helping strategies (see Exercise 1.3). It is a database that leads to increased effectiveness and clearly distinguishes the trained professional counselor from the untrained lay helper.

Exercise 1.3

EXPANDING YOUR INTERVENTION DATABASE

Many professional counselors call upon their own problem-solving skills and experience in order to formulate helpful interventions, but it is essential and ethically responsible for professional counselors to know and employ those strategies and interventions which have been documented, by way of research, to be effective.

Directions: Below you will find a number of typical issues clients may bring to a professional counselor. Your task is to generate an intervention based on your own intuition or experience and then search the literature to identify a specific intervention that has been demonstrated to be effective. Is the evidence-based strategy similar to the one you generated? The first row provides a model for the exercise.

Presenting Problem or Issue	Personally Derived Intervention	Empirically Supported Intervention
A fifth grade student is not doing his homework.	Make a rule that he can't play his video game until his homework is completed.	Olympia et al. (1994). Using student-managed interventions to increase homework completion and accuracy. *Journal of Applied Behavior Analysis, 27,* 85–99.
A client is terrified to speak in public and as part of his job he has to give presentations in front of clients.	*practice from a small scale* ___ *process why terrifying in public.* ___	___ ___ ___ ___ ___ ___
A client is having recurring nightmares and can't sleep after having seen an animal accidentally hit and killed by a car.	*verbal process* ___ *create safety nets.* ___ ___	___ ___ ___ ___ ___
The client just lost her job and is feeling depressed and hopeless about her life and her future.	*grief & loss* ___ ___ ___ ___	___ ___ ___ ___ ___

Reliable Techniques and Strategies

A professional counselor is also different from a lay helper in terms of skills and models used in the helping process. A lay helper does not have any scientifically based knowledge or skills and learned models to use when helping a friend. In contrast to the lay helper, the professional counselor has mastered multiple sets of helping skills and models.

These skills and models are scientifically sound and reliable. With knowledge of the research supporting specific strategies and intervention techniques, professional counselors will engage in what has been termed *evidence-based practice* (Kazdin, 2008). Professional counselors employ their knowledge of this research along with their identification of the client's needs, values, and preference to guide their professional decisions and craft helpful interventions. It is in the competent application of this science within the helping process that lends to the increased effectiveness of the professional counselor. Further it is in blending this science of helping with the art of being a counselor which serves as a major distinction between the professional counselor and the nonprofessional help giver. Exercise 1.3 helps with the development of this distinction.

Use of Formal Interventions

Intervention is a crucial part in the helping process, and professional counselors often use scientifically tested interventions both in sessions and outside counseling sessions. For example, when a helpee is depressed, the professional counselor would use interventions such as "confront the client's acting-out behaviors as avoidance of the real conflict with unmet emotional needs" (Jongsma, Peterson, & McInnis, 1996, p. 51) and "teach and reinforce positive cognitive messages that facilitate the growth of client's self-confidence and self-acceptance" (p. 52). A lay nonprofessional helper would not be able to employ these or the other interventions that can only be gained professional training. As such, the lay helper is most often left only with the offering of opinions or advice, or the utterance of platitudes such as "everything will be okay." Sadly, such platitudes or simple advice giving are ineffective.

The Focus of the Helping Process

Unlike the lay helper who may in the process of helping a friend, and who joins that friend in the sharing of personal information and the seeking of mutual support, the professional counselor deliberately maintains the focus of the exchange on the helpee and the helpee's issues of concern. Personal disclosures when provided by the professional counselor are done with the intent of strengthening the helping relationship or providing the client with an insight that would prove beneficial. The self-disclosures for the professional counselor, unlike the ones for the lay helper, are not to be self-serving; rather, they are used as a helping strategy. Case Illustration 1.2 highlights the distinction between the lay and professional helper when invited to share personal information.

CASE ILLUSTRATION 1.2

HAVE YOU EVER HAD A BAD BREAKUP?

This case highlights the distinction between the lay and professional helper when invited to share personal information.

Directions: As you read the following illustrations, think about how you would approach this client.

Scenario 1: The client is extremely upset, distraught about being "dumped" by his girlfriend.

> Client: This is horrible—I can't go on. She was leading me along the whole time. She didn't care. I don't know what I can do without her. Can you understand what I am saying? This hurts a lot. I mean … have you ever gone through a breakup like this?

	Intentions/Goals	*Response*
Helper	To provide comfort and demonstrate care and concern	Yes, I have and I know how horrible it feels. It took me months to get over my divorce. I can imagine how upset and confused you are. I mean when I was served with the papers I felt like somebody had slammed me with a board. I didn't expect it—it seemed so unfair. I know what you are going through … it is horrible.
Professional counselor	(1) To demonstrate she is listening (2) To demonstrate an understanding of the client's emotional experience (3) To affirm her willingness to be of help while maintaining the focus on the client	William, I can see that this breakup came as a terrible shock and that you are not only hurt, but feeling lost and confused as if you are not sure anyone could understand what you are going through. I do want to understand and be of help so perhaps you could tell me a little more about what happened and how you feel.

The counselor in Case Illustration 1.2 is not trying to be secretive or illusive. Rather the counselor hopes to convey understanding and concern while at the same time refocus the interaction on the client, because the purpose and intent of the interaction is on assistance to the client rather than a mutual sharing of experience. This refocusing on the client is a hallmark of a professional helping.

THE CHARACTERISTICS OF A PROFESSIONAL COUNSELOR

It is clear that in order to be a competent and effective professional counselor, one must master factual knowledge and specific practice related to scientifically developed skills (Hill & Kellems, 2002; Hill & Lent, 2006; Hilsenroth, Defife, Blagys, & Ackerman, 2006; Kivlighan, 1989; Kivlighan, 2010; Multon, Kivlighan, & Gold, 1996; Schottler, Oliver, & Porter, 2005), but it may not be so obvious that to be an effective professional counselor one needs to develop and exhibit a number of personal traits or characteristics which, in total, further distinguish the professional counselor from the lay helper. These traits include: (1) self-awareness, (2) values and disposition which are facilitative to the helping process, (3) employment of procedural knowledge and forward thinking, and (4) the unfolding of a professional identity.

Self-Awareness

Professional counselors value self-awareness as an element necessary for efficient and ethical practice (Hansen, 2009). Professional counselors are aware of their strengths and limitations and they allow that awareness to serve as a guide to their professional decisions. For example, when confronted by a client whose concerns and needs exceed the knowledge and skill of the counselor, the effective counselor will seek super-vision and or referral in response to that client's needs. But self-awareness goes beyond recognition of the limitations to our knowledge and skills (Pedersen, 2003). Effective, ethical counselors are also aware of their personal motivations, values, worldviews, and biases, and the potential impact these may have on their professional interactions and decisions (Collins, Arthur, Wong-Wylie, 2010; Sink & Yillik-Downer, 2001). Perhaps most important, professional counselors are fully aware that they serve as an instrument within the helping relationship, one which can either be effective in facilitating their helpees' growth or when ineffective, hindering their helpees' development.

Personal Motivation

Effective counselors are aware of their own motivations for becoming helpers as well as the motivations that guide their practice decisions in regards to any one client, at any one time.

Being a counselor is both a powerful role and an awesome responsibility. Counselors need to be aware of their own needs and desires in order to insure that it is *not* their personal needs but the needs and desires of their clients that serve as motivation for their practice decisions. Case Illustration 1.3 highlights the importance of this need for self-awareness.

CASE ILLUSTRATION 1.3

THE LONELY COUNSELOR

The following exchange occurred between a client, Kate, who had recently moved into the area, taking on an exciting yet stressful position and a counselor who lacked awareness of his own personal motives and needs and how these might impact the relationship with this client.

As part of her commitment to self-growth, Kate sought out a counselor in order to help her develop stress-management strategies. The counselor to whom her HR department referred her had recently been divorced and is feeling lonely and isolated.

Kate:	The job is great—very exciting and challenging but a bit stressful, at least as I'm getting started. I'm finding that I am spending 60 to 70 hours a week working.
Counselor:	That does sound a bit demanding, even exhausting.
Kate:	Yeah, but that's a good thing, not the exhaustion but the amount of time I'm spending at work. I mean I'm new in the area and haven't had a chance to meet people so if I wasn't occupied with work I probably would just be in my apartment feeling lonely or something … so work keeps me occupied.
Counselor:	So you are not in a relationship at the current time, are you?
Kate:	Boy I wish (laughing). No, I haven't been in relationship for quite a while.
Counselor:	So even before coming here you weren't with anyone, were you?

Kate:	No, not really. I've been pretty career focused, not much time for anything else.
Counselor:	Career focused—that can be a bit isolating. Wouldn't you want to be dating?
Kate:	I guess. But I'm okay with it …. I'm not sure why you are asking?
Counselor:	Oh, it's just, well, I know how lonely it can be without a meaningful connection, it's not fun being alone at night or on weekends.
Kate:	(a little uncomfortable) Yeah, it's okay. As I said, I'm really busy with work right now and I guess that's what I was hoping to talk about … you know, some ways to manage the stress of a new job …and things like that.

Counter transference

Clearly, the counselor's own issues bled into the interaction in such a way as to not only direct him to off-task discussion, but also made the client feel uncomfortable.

It is important for the effective counselor to engage in an ongoing process of self-reflection and clarification of personal needs, values, and motives while engaging in the helping process. Exercise 1.4 asks you to reflect on the motives that have stimulated your interest in becoming a professional counselor. As you reflect on these motives, identify both the possible positive and negative effects such motives may have on the helping process and helping outcomes.

Exercise 1.4

PERSONAL MOTIVES

Being a counselor is a very powerful and responsible position. Often clients come to counseling hurt and vulnerable, and counselors need to be clear that their motives are honorable and protective of the client. It is thus important to identify the motives that not only have led you to this profession, but also served as the energizing forces behind your practice decisions at any one moment with any one client.

Directions: Below you will find a number of reasons a person may be attracted to the role of counselor. Each offers something positive and something potentially negative to the counseling relationship. Your job is to identify potential positive and negative impacts afforded by each.

Counselor Motivation	Possible Positive Impact	Possible Negative Impact
Desire to more fully understand the human condition	_urb._	_asking unnecessary things_
Wish to help others	_motivated_	_dangerous when not knowing what to do._
The status acquired by becoming a part of a profession		
A curiosity about why people do certain things		
A desire to better understand oneself		
The freedom to be one's own boss		
Being a "people" person		
Provision of a good way to make money		
Feeling a sense of power and control		
Enjoyment for puzzles and problem solving		
(Other/your motives)		
(Other/your motives)		
(Other/your motives)		

Cultural Framework and Worldview

Effective counselors understand that their view of life, and more specifically their view of a helpee and a helpee's problem, is highly influenced by their own world or cultural viewpoint (Sue & Sue, 2008; Vontress, 2003). To be an effective counselor, one must become aware of his own cultural framework and the way it biases his attitudes, values, worldviews, behaviors, and approach to helping (Arredondo, Tovar-Blank, & Parham, 2008). While some may suggest that counselors need to be value-free and totally objective in their view of each client, the truth is that such total objectivity is not possible. We enter a helping relationship as we enter all relationships: full of personal expectations, biases, and values. Further, as with any of our encounters, these expectations, biases, and values can and will influence our interactions if gone unchecked. The competent counselor is aware of this worldview and accompanying values and biases, and is thus positioned to take steps to insure that these worldviews, values, and biases do not influence practice decisions.

Exercise 1.5 highlights the potential danger when counselors are unaware of their biased worldview. The counselors depicted in Exercise 1.5 have strong biases. Your task is therefore to identify potential helpee characteristics or helpee-presenting concerns for which each counselor may experience professional decisions made ineffective because of the influence of personal bias filtering into the process.

Exercise 1.5

POTENTIAL IMPACT OF BIASED WORLDVIEW

Directions, Part I: For each of the following situations, identify how the specific life experiences may have biased the counselor. In addition, identify a presenting concern or a particular set of helpee characteristics that elicit strong, nonprofessional, and biased responses for the counselor.

1. Counselor A is a female who was abandoned as a child and has been independent and self-supportive since the age of 17.

2. Counselor B has been married 13 years and recently was told by his spouse that she was leaving him for another woman, having come to acceptance of her lesbian sexual orientation.

3. Counselor C is an adult child of a very strict, Christian fundamentalist minister.

4. Counselor D is an alcoholic, sober for 3 years, and a strong supporter of 12-step programs.

Directions, Part II: For each of the following helpee-presenting concerns, identify a counselor's values that may interfere with the ability to provide effective counseling.

1. Helpee A presents with depression after having been caught cheating on her husband.

2. Helpee B is a pedophile.

3. Helpee C has anger management issues and has been court ordered to counseling for wife abuse.

4. Helpee E is in conflict about coming out (in regard to his homosexual orientation) to his parents.

Exercise 1.6 invites you to begin the process of increasing your awareness of your worldview, values, and biases as they may come to play in your professional decision making. Being aware of our worldviews, values, and biases as they operate within our helping relationships is not a one-time process. Professional counselors will reflect on their decisions while working with a client to make sure that they not only reflect what is known as best practice for the profession but also what appears to be in line with the way that they typically work with a client. A dramatic variation from a counselor's typical procedure or routine may be a strong indication that something other than the helpee's issues may be at play.

Exercise 1.6

CLARIFYING PERSONAL WORLDVIEW, VALUES, AND BIAS

Directions: The following issues may tap a strong value, attitude, or belief. Identify your own views of each of the following and consider how those views may serve or hinder your helping of any one particular client. You may find it beneficial to do this exercise with a colleague or classmate.

(Continued)

(Continued)

1. Single parenthood

2. Chastity before marriage

3. Monogamy in marriage

4. Right to life

5. End of life decisions—not to employ artificial means of maintaining life

6. Recreational drug usage

7. Civil unions

8. Transgender orientation

9. Use of medication to treat psycho-emotional issues

10. Spousal abuse

Facilitative Values and Disposition

The effective counselor exhibits specific attitudes or dispositions and values that have been demonstrated to be facilitative to the helping process. Helping does involve the application of strategies and techniques. However, the employment of these interventions, strategies, or techniques occurs within the context of a relationship and the outcomes of this helping are most often affected by the nature of the relationship and the personal attributes of the counselor facilitating that relationship. Carl R. Rogers, in his 1951 publication on the person-centered counseling approach, first suggested the three primary facilitative conditions. Subsequent research has identified these facilitative conditions to be associated with successful outcomes of helping (Orlinksy, Grave, & Parks, 1994; Tepper & Hass, 2001). These three conditions are:

1. *Genuineness.* The ability to be real, transparent, and role free. The counselor who is genuine openly has the feelings and attitudes that are flowing within at any one moment.

2. *Empathy.* The intellectual identification with or the vicarious experiencing of the feelings, thoughts, or attitudes of another. It is the ability to lay aside personal views and values in order to enter another's world without prejudice.

3. *Unconditional positive regard.* A condition beyond caring for the helpee, to valuing and prizing the helpee in a total rather than a conditional way.

These conditions are presented only briefly here, and they, along with other counselor dispositions found to be facilitative to the helping process, are discussed in great detail in Chapter 3.

Procedural Knowledge and Forward Thinking

As you progress through your training, you will most certainly acquire much more factual knowledge about the human condition. In addition to this increase in your declarative knowledge (i.e., factual information), you will also begin to employ procedural knowledge, that is, the ability to know what to do under what specific types of conditions. Case Illustration 1.4 highlights the application of such procedural knowledge when confronted with the simple presentation of a client on first visit.

CASE ILLUSTRATION 1.4

TO SHAKE OR NOT TO SHAKE

A professional counselor understands that counseling involves intentional communication. A professional counselor asks questions or chooses to reflect and summarize a client's disclosures with the *intent* of facilitating the helping process. Such intentional responding requires the counselor to listen, observe, and reflect on what these data imply about the client and the process of counseling. The following is a brief look "inside" one counselor as he processes client disclosures and selects responses to facilitate the helping relationship and process.

Counselor:	(opening the door) Welcome, Mr. Anderson?
Mr. Anderson:	Yes, good morning Dr. Banks.
Counselor:	(reaching out his hand to shake) Please come in and …

(Counselor notices the nervousness in Mr. Anderson's voice, difficulty making eye contact, and the handkerchief held in his right hand.)

Counselor Reflection

The client seems very anxious. I wonder if he is perspiring and his hand is damp. He may be uncomfortable with my outreached hand and the invitation to shake.

Counselor Decision

Counselor makes a gentle sweeping motion pointing away from the client toward the couch.

Counselor: Make yourself comfortable on the couch.

Effective counselors have the ability to approach situations with a greater awareness of what to do if a particular condition exists. Thus the counselor in Case Illustration 1.4 was able to make the appropriate on-the-spot decision to resist attempting to shake hands with the client, perceiving the subtle signs of anxiety and discomfort. This is the result of using procedural knowledge.

Procedural knowledge allows counselors to connect disparate areas of knowledge, facilitating their ability to make more discriminating judgments about the information being presented and the best response to provide (Chi, Glasser, & Farr, 1988). Research has shown that effective counselors employ greater procedural knowledge when compared to less effective novices (Chi, Glasser, & Farr, 1988; Etringer, Hillerbrand, & Claiborn, 1995).

Case Illustration 1.5 demonstrates this *if . . . then* procedural approach wherein the counselor attempts to help the client recognize his own personal responsibility in the situations being discussed.

CASE ILLUSTRATION 1.5

SELECTIVE USE OF REFLECTION

As noted previously, the counselor is engaged in intentional communication, selecting responses to the client's disclosure that the counselor feels will facilitate the helping process. Most counselors-in-training will learn to listen and be able to reflect the explicit and implicit message shared by the client. However, as illustrated in this case exchange, the effective counselor understands that such reflection is not indiscriminate. The effective counselor considers the if I do this, then this may be the outcome. The effective counselor reflects that which he feels will serve the helping relationship and the process in which he is engaged.

Joey:	He's always on my case.
Counselor:	Always?
Joey:	Yeah … like today. I come into class and I am 2 minutes late and he gives me this look.

At this point the counselor could reflect Joey's entire statement, "So you are two minutes late and he gave you a look" or the counselor could focus on the teacher's response and state: "… so he gave you a look." But if the hypothesis is that Joey needs to take more responsibility for his actions, then the counselor may be selective and purposeful in the reflection stating, " So you came to class 2 minutes late …"

Counselor:	So, you came to class 2 minutes late?
Joey:	Yeah, but, I had an excuse … I had to go to my locker. I am not the only person who comes late sometimes. I know, I got to get it together, but….

The counselor's choice of material to reflect served the purpose of refocusing the discussion on the client, as opposed to the teacher, or the school rules.

In addition to using procedural knowledge, the effective professional counselor engages in forward reasoning. The professional counselor gathers information from the client and uses knowledge of the current research and counseling theories to develop a concept of not only what is going on but what needs to happen in order to move the client from where she is to where she wishes to be (Gick, 1986). The effective professional counselor, unlike the lay counterpart, has learned and has become adept at this forward thinking, selecting relevant client data to process and use to plan an approach to helping. The effective professional counselor uses these data to develop an individual case formulation, that is, a set of "hypotheses about the causes, precipitants, and maintaining influences of a person's psychological, interpersonal, and behavioral problems" (Eells, 2002, p. 815). This case formulation provides a succinct, flexible, and appropriately comprehensive account of clients' concerns and the steps needed to move them to their desired goals. The ability to engage in case formulation is one of the characteristics that differentiates the expert counselor from the novice or lay helper (Cummings, Hallberg, Martin, Slemon, & Hiebert, 1990; Hillerbrand & Claiborn, 1990; Kivlighan & Quigley, 1991). Consider the case of Cynthia in Exercise 1.7.

Exercise 1.7

CASE FORMULATION: A LOOK AT COUNSELOR REFLECTIONS

The professional counselor attempts to process the client information and disclosure through counseling theory and research as a way of understanding the origins of the problem, the goals of the counseling, and the processes that may move the client from *what is* to *what is desired*.

Directions: Review the brief case description and develop your responses to the questions presented in the following table. You may find it useful to discuss your observations and conclusions with a classmate or colleague.

Cynthia: Initial Referral

The referral sheet provided only minimum information. The client was a 35-year-old woman currently going through a divorce after 10 years of marriage, with no children. She has worked as a pharmacist for the past 11 years and complained to her boss that she was having trouble focusing on work given the stress of the divorce.

Data Collected Within the Session

The client described that she has lost 15 pounds in the past 3 weeks and is unable to sleep (difficulty getting to sleep and staying asleep). The client stated that she has difficulty getting to work since she simply thinks, "why bother." Further, the client shared that she has had problems with concentration and in fact has caught herself placing incorrect medications or incorrect amounts in prescription bottles that she is filling. When asked about suicidal ideation, the client noted that she is horrified about being the only person in her family ever to have gone through a divorce and that she is not sure she can face her family. She noted that while she sometimes "wishes" she would just disappear, her faith and the realization of the impact that hurting herself would have on her parents prevent her from ever thinking about killing herself.

Step	*Questions to Address*	*Data From Client Disclosure*
Step 1. Identifying the presenting concern	What does the client say his or her problems or concerns are?	_____ _____ _____

Step	Questions to Address	Data From Client Disclosure
Step 2. Making sense of these data	a. What factors contributed to this current situation?	_____ _____
	b. What might these data suggest about the client's feelings, thoughts, actions, and interpersonal relationships?	_____ _____ _____ _____ _____ _____
	c. What strengths or resources does the client bring to this situation?	_____ _____ _____
Step 3. Identifying where to, and how	a. What are the goals and objectives for the counseling?	_____ _____
	b. What steps would you take to move the client toward these goals?	_____ _____ _____

Professional Identity

Finally and perhaps most important, the primary difference between the professional counselor versus the nonprofessional or lay helper rests in the fact that the professional counselor embraces an *identity* as a professional and as a member of a unique profession—counseling.

The issue of professional identity of counseling has long been discussed in the counseling literature (Auxier, Hughes, & Kline, 2003; Gale & Austin, 2003; Goodyear, 1984; Hill, 2004; Leinbaugh, Hazler, Bradley, & Hill, 2003; Ramsey, Cavallaro, Kiselica, & Zila, 2002; Swickert, 1997). The issue is one but impacting the profession at two different levels.

At the macrolevel, the American Counseling Association (ACA) has posited that developing a shared professional identity for counseling is critical to the future of this profession (ACA, 2009). As a profession, counseling has a rich history that depicts its uniqueness among professions serving the mental health and well-being needs of its consumers. It is a uniqueness that needs to be promulgated and embraced by all within the profession.

Unlike other professions addressing the mental health needs of its consumer, counseling is unique in that its goals go beyond addressing issues of pathology and providing intervention for those with mental health challenges, and expand to include goals of promoting wellness, personal growth, education, and career development (ACA, 1997). Counseling is a profession, which serves normal functioning populations as well as those with pathology. It is unique in emphasizing the use of a *wellness model* of service, targeting clients' current level of well-being and assisting them to reach optimal levels of well-being (Witmer & Granello, 2005). Rather than treating emotional challenges as pathological, counselors see these as part of a process of living, part of the human condition, and basic concerns that must be addressed in order to facilitate progression to the next stage of one's life. Thus as a profession, counseling is unique in mission, philosophy, service, and points which must be understood and valued by each member of the profession as the foundation for the development of one's own professional identity.

At the microlevel of each individual counselor, the development of professional identity as a counselor serves as a cognitive frame of reference to determine one's counseling role and responsibility (Brott & Myers, 1999). Counselors are not friends, loved ones, nor confessors to their clients, but they have developed identities with competency and view themselves as professionals employing and reflecting the art and science of counseling. *Counselor professional identity* is the integration of professional training with personal attributes in the context of a professional community (Nugent & Jones, 2009).

This *professional identity* is the counselor's view of self as a professional along with the competency to perform within that professional role. The counselor's professional identity develops while assimilating the knowledge of the profession along with the skills and attitudes that are essential to successful practice. As the counselor increasingly integrates the knowledge that serves as the foundation for the discipline and practice of counseling along with the standards of ethical practice shared by those within the profession and articulated by the professional organizations into his view of self as counselor, professional identity will take form. According to Reisetter and colleagues (2004), professional identity is the view of self as a professional plus competence as a professional, resulting in congruence between personal worldview and professional view.

This process will continue to unfold as you progress through your training and move on through your professional career. Exercise 1.8 invites you to reflect on this emerging professional identity with a process that you may want to revisit throughout your training.

Exercise 1.8

EMERGING PROFESSIONAL IDENTITY

As noted within the text, a counselor's *professional identity* is the integration of professional training with personal attributes in the context of a professional community. This professional identity is the counselor's view of self as a professional along with the competency to perform within that professional role.

Directions: While it is not expected that as a beginning student you would have achieved the following competencies, the list may serve as a useful tool to mark the development of your professional identity as you proceed through your training.

Aspects of Professional Identity— Council for Accrediting of Counseling and Related Educational Programs (CACREP) Standards	*Current State of Development (0 = yet to begin, 5 = mastered and integrated)*	*Plan for Future Development*
1. Professional Identity—Studies that provide an understanding of all of the following aspects of professional functioning:	_____ _____ _____	
1a. Describe the history and philosophy of the counseling profession, including significant factors and events.	_____ _____ _____	
1b. Discuss professional roles, functions, and relationships with other human service providers.	_____ _____ _____	
1c. Demonstrate technological competence and computer literacy.	_____ _____	
1d. Identify professional organizations, primarily ACA, its divisions, branches, and affiliates, including membership benefits, activities, services to members, and current emphases.	_____ _____ _____	

(Continued)

(Continued)

Aspects of Professional Identity—Council for Accrediting of Counseling and Related Educational Programs (CACREP) Standards	Current State of Development (0 = yet to begin, 5 = mastered and integrated)	Plan for Future Development
1e. Describe professional credentialing, including certification, licensure, and accreditation practices and standards, and the effects of public policy.		
1f. Discuss public and private policy processes, including the role of the professional counselor in advocating on behalf of the profession.		
1g. Practice advocacy processes needed to address institutional and social barriers that impede access, equity, and success for client.		
1h. Describe ethical standards of ACA and related entities, and applications of ethical and legal consideration in professional counseling.		
2. Social and Cultural Diversity—Studies that provide an understanding of the cultural context of relationships, issues, and trends in a multicultural and diverse society related to such factors as culture, ethnicity, nationality, age, gender, sexual orientation, mental and physical characteristics, education, family values, religious and spiritual values, socioeconomic status and unique characteristics of individuals, couples, families, ethnic groups, and communities including all of the following:		

Aspects of Professional Identity— Council for Accrediting of Counseling and Related Educational Programs (CACREP) Standards	Current State of Development (0 = yet to begin, 5 = mastered and integrated)	Plan for Future Development
2a. Describe multicultural and pluralistic trends, including characteristics and concerns between and within diverse groups nationally and internationally.	_____ _____ _____ _____	
2b. Demonstrate attitudes, beliefs, understandings, and acculturative experiences, including specific experiential learning activities.	_____ _____ _____ _____	
2c. Utilize individual, couple, family, group, and community strategies for working with diverse populations and ethnic groups.	_____ _____ _____ _____	
2d. Describe counselors' roles in social justice, advocacy and conflict resolution, cultural self-awareness, the nature of biases, prejudices, processes of intentional and unintentional oppression and discrimination, and other culturally supported behavior that are detrimental to the growth of the human spirit, mind, or body.	_____ _____ _____ _____ _____ _____ _____ _____	
2e. Utilize theories of multicultural counseling, theories of identity development, and multicultural competencies.	_____ _____ _____ _____	
2f. Discuss ethical and legal considerations.	_____	

(Continued)

(Continued)

Aspects of Professional Identity— Council for Accrediting of Counseling and Related Educational Programs (CACREP) Standards	Current State of Development (0 = yet to begin, 5 = mastered and integrated)	Plan for Future Development
3. Human Growth and Development— Studies that provide an understanding of the nature and needs of individuals at all developmental levels, including all of the following:		
3a. Identify individual and family development and transitions across the lifespan.		
3b. Utilize theories of learning and personality development.		
3c. Describe human behavior, including an understanding of developmental crises, disability, exceptional behavior, addictive behavior, psychopathology, and situational and environmental factors that affect both normal and abnormal behavior.		
3d. Utilize strategies for facilitating optimum development over the life span.		
3e. Identify ethical and legal considerations.		
4. Career Development—Studies that provide an understanding of career development and related life factors, including all of the following:		
4a. Describe career development theories and decision-making models.		

Aspects of Professional Identity— Council for Accrediting of Counseling and Related Educational Programs (CACREP) Standards	Current State of Development (0 = yet to begin, 5 = mastered and integrated)	Plan for Future Development
4b. Utilize career, avocational, educational, occupational, and labor market information resources, visual and print media, computer-based career information systems, and other electronic career information systems.	_____ _____ _____ _____ _____ _____	
4c. Describe a career development program planning, organization, implementation, administration, and evaluation.	_____ _____ _____	
4d. Identify interrelationships among and between work, family, and other life roles and factors including the role of diversity and gender in career development.	_____ _____ _____ _____ _____	
4e. Discuss career and educational planning, placement, follow-up, and evaluation.	_____ _____ _____	
4f. Identify assessment instruments and techniques that are relevant to career planning and decision making.	_____ _____ _____	
4g. Utilize technology-based career development applications and strategies, including computer-based career guidance and information systems and appropriate world wide websites.	_____ _____ _____ _____ _____	

(Continued)

(Continued)

Aspects of Professional Identity— Council for Accrediting of Counseling and Related Educational Programs (CACREP) Standards	Current State of Development (0 = yet to begin, 5 = mastered and integrated)	Plan for Future Development
4h. Discuss career counseling processes, techniques, and resources, including those applicable to specific populations.		
4i. Identify ethical and legal considerations.		
5. Helping Relationships—Studies that provide an understanding of counseling and consultation processes, including all of the following:		
5a. Describe counselor and consultant characteristics and behaviors that influence helping processes including age, gender, and ethnic differences, verbal and nonverbal behavior and personal characteristics, orientations, and skills.		
5b. Demonstrate an understanding of essential interviewing and counseling skills so that the student is able to develop a therapeutic relationship, establish appropriate counseling goals, design intervention strategies, evaluate client outcome, and successfully terminate the counselor–client relationship. Studies will also facilitate student awareness so that the counselor client relationship is therapeutic.		
5c. Apply counseling theories that provide the student with a consistent model(s) to conceptualize client presentation		

Aspects of Professional Identity— Council for Accrediting of Counseling and Related Educational Programs (CACREP) Standards	Current State of Development (0 = yet to begin, 5 = mastered and integrated)	Plan for Future Development
and select appropriate counseling interventions. Student experiences should include an examination of the historical development of counseling theories, and exploration of affective, behavioral, and cognitive theories, and an opportunity to apply the theoretical material to case studies. Students will also be exposed to models of counseling that are consistent with current professional research and practice in the field so that they can begin to develop a personal mode of counseling that maintains appropriate professional boundaries.		
5d. Apply a systems perspective that provides an understanding of family and other systems theories and major models of family and related interventions. Students will be exposed to a rationale for selecting family and other systems theories as appropriate modalities.		
5e. Use a general framework for understanding and practicing consultation. Student experiences should include an examination of the historical development of consultation, an exploration of the stages of consultation and the major models of consultation, and an opportunity to apply the theoretical material to case presentations. Students will begin to develop a personal model of consultation.		

(Continued)

(Continued)

Aspects of Professional Identity—Council for Accrediting of Counseling and Related Educational Programs (CACREP) Standards	Current State of Development (0 = yet to begin, 5 = mastered and integrated)	Plan for Future Development
5f. Integrate technological strategies and applications within counseling and consultation processes.		
5g. Discuss and practice ethical and legal considerations and behavior.		
6. Group Work—Studies that provide both theoretical and experiential understandings of group purpose, development, dynamics, counseling theories, group counseling methods and skills, and other group approaches, including all of the following:		
6a. Identify principles of group dynamics, including group process components, developmental stage theories, group members' roles and behaviors, and therapeutic factors of group work.		
6b. Discuss group leadership styles and approaches, including characteristics of various types of group leaders and leadership styles.		
6c. Describe theories of group counseling, including commonalities, distinguishing characteristics, and pertinent research and literature.		
6d. Practice group counseling methods, including group counselor orientations and behaviors, appropriate selection criteria and methods, and methods of evaluation of effectiveness.		

Aspects of Professional Identity—Council for Accrediting of Counseling and Related Educational Programs (CACREP) Standards	Current State of Development (0 = yet to begin, 5 = mastered and integrated)	Plan for Future Development
6e. Describe approaches used for other types of group work, including task groups, psycho-educational groups, and therapy groups.		
6f. Identify professional preparation standards for group leaders.		
6g. Describe and practice ethical and legal considerations and behavior.		
7. Assessment Studies—Studies that provide an understanding of individual and group approaches to assessment and evaluation, including all of the following:		
7a. Integrate historical perspectives concerning the nature and meaning of assessment.		
7b. Apply basic concepts of standardized and nonstandardized testing and other assessment techniques including norm-referenced and criterion-referenced assessment, environmental assessment, performance assessment, individual and group test and inventory methods, behavioral observations, and computer-managed and computer-assisted methods.		
7c. Apply statistical concepts, including scales of measurement, measure of central tendency, indices of variability, shapes and types of distributions, and correlation.		

(Continued)

(Continued)

Aspects of Professional Identity— Council for Accrediting of Counseling and Related Educational Programs (CACREP) Standards	Current State of Development (0 = yet to begin, 5 = mastered and integrated)	Plan for Future Development
7d. Use reliability (i.e., theory of measurement error, models of reliability, and the use of reliability information).		
7e. Use validity (i.e., evidence of validity, types of validity, and the relationship between reliability and validity).		
7f. Incorporate age, gender, sexual orientation, ethnicity, language, disability, culture, spirituality, and other factors related to the assessment and evaluation of individuals, groups, and specific populations.		
7g. Apply strategies for selecting, administering, and interpreting assessment and evaluation instruments and techniques in counseling.		
7h. Apply an understanding of general principles and methods of case conceptualization, assessment, and/ or diagnoses of mental and emotional status.		
8. Research and Program Evaluation— Studies that provide an understanding of research methods, statistical analysis, needs assessment, and program evaluation, including all of the following:		
8a. Describe the importance of research and opportunities and difficulties in conducting research in the counseling profession.		

Aspects of Professional Identity—Council for Accrediting of Counseling and Related Educational Programs (CACREP) Standards	Current State of Development (0 = yet to begin, 5 = mastered and integrated)	Plan for Future Development
8b. Define research methods such as qualitative, quantitative, single-case designs, action research, and outcome-based research.		
8c. Use technology and statistical methods in conducting research and program evaluation, assuming basic computer literacy.		
8d. Identify principles, models, and applications of needs assessment, program evaluation, and use of findings to effect program modifications.		
8e. Review research to improve counseling effectiveness.		
8f. Describe ethical and legal considerations.		

CHALLENGES ENCOUNTERED ON THE ROAD TO BEING A PROFESSIONAL: RECOGNIZING ONE'S RESPONSIBILITY

The opening to this chapter pointed to research that supported the notion that people appear to have the desire to help one another ingrained in their collective DNA. Further, the discussion highlighted the research pointing to the effectiveness of those who appear to have the ability to serve as so-called natural helpers. However, as professional counselors, we need not only to know how to help another, but to do so in a way that reflects positively on our profession.

The American Counseling Association's (2005) *Code of Ethics,* Section C (p. 9) details the responsibilities of a professional counselor. As depicted within the code, these responsibilities challenge each and every counselor not only to serve those in need, but also to take up the mantel of the profession advocating for wellness and developing our best practices.

While your introduction to counseling as a profession may be beginning with this text, and this chapter, as you soon will discover, your road to being a professional counselor is unending both in terms of responsibility and satisfaction. For the professional counselor, the acquisition of a degree, a certification, or a license is not an end; rather these are but markers along a path of being a professional. You will be challenged to maintain your professional competence, expand your knowledge and skills related to helping, advocate for those in need of wellness, represent and promote your profession, and take care of yourself. These are not merely good ideas—these are mandates of your profession's standards of ethical practice.

Maintaining Professional Competence

As a professional counselor you will be expected to practice " . . . in a nondiscriminatory manner within the boundaries of professional and personal competence . . ." (ACA, 2005, p. 9). Throughout your professional career you will be challenged not only to practice within the boundaries of your training and expertise, but also continue to monitor your effectiveness and take those steps needed to insure your continued professional growth and development.

Employing Best Practice

Counselors have a responsibility to the public to engage in counseling practices that are based on rigorous research methodologies. According to the ACA (2005) *Code of Ethics,* counselors use techniques and procedures that are grounded in theory or empirical research (sec. C.6.e). While ours is a relatively new profession, the scientific bases for our practices are expanding exponentially. It will be your duty— your challenge—to stay up with that research and engage in training and supervision so that you can incorporate those emerging techniques within your practice.

Advocating for Improved Quality of Life

A counselor's desire to help should not be restricted to the client standing at her office door. Counselors, unlike others working within the field of mental health, are concerned for prevention and wellness and not just remediation and intervention. As such, counselors advocate to promote change that results in improved quality of life and the removal of barriers to the provision of counseling services. This call to advocacy challenges each counselor to be active not just with individuals and groups, but at institutional and societal levels as well. As a professional counselor you will be challenged to move beyond your comfort levels to truly attempt to make the world a healthier place.

Fostering Improvement of Counseling as a Practice and Profession

As professionals, counselors are not only responsible to those they serve but also are called to engage in those activities that foster the development and improvement of their own profession. As such, you will be challenged to become active members within your local, state, and national associations. Through your membership and participation within these associations, you will be able to foster the development and improvement of counseling and advocate for the profession and its delivery of service. This involvement need not be delayed until the point of your graduation. Counseling associations seek and value student participation and membership.

 Taking Care of Self

Being trained in the principles of mental health and wellness does *not* make counselors immune from life stressors nor their detrimental effects. In fact, serving as a counselor can be both challenging, stress-filled, and under some conditions, can lead to counselor burnout. It is not unusual for counselors to experience emotional depletion as a result of working long hours in isolation dealing with people in pain and in crisis. Under these conditions it is not unusual for burnout to occur, especially when the counselor begins to develop a sense of inefficiency and helplessness. Under these conditions the counselor will experience *compassion fatigue,* that is, a state of emotional, mental, and physical exhaustion (Smith, Jaffe-Gill, & Segal, 2008).

As a graduate student or a new professional, you may have neglected self-care. Late hours studying, catching meals on the run, and multitasking are not prescriptions for self-care. Your challenge now and later once in professional practice is to engage in self-care activities to maintain and promote your emotional, physical, mental, and spiritual well-being. In caring for self, you will be better positioned to care for others and meet your professional responsibilities.

COUNSELING KEYSTONES

- Helping seems to be perfectly natural; however, being a "perfect" or at least effective counselor need not be natural and can be developed through training.
- Helping is more than advice giving; it is a unique process that requires both knowledge and skill.
- Helping involves an interpersonal process using helpee resources to facilitate movement toward some specific outcome.
- Being a professional helper brings with it both ethical and legal responsibilities.
- Defining one as a professional implies: (1) the possession of unique knowledge and skills; (2) the adherence to a standard of ethical practice; and (3) the

assimilation of one's professional skills, knowledge, and affiliations into a professional identity that serves as a framework for practice.

- Counselors, in contrast to other mental health professionals, operate within and from a wellness model.
- Research supports the value of training as a means for increasing the effectiveness of a counselor and counseling.
- As professionals, counselors are challenged to take those steps necessary to provide best-practice service to their clients, advocate for clients and their profession, and engage in those activities that insure their own health and well being.

ADDITIONAL RESOURCES

Reading

Lister, J. L. (1969). *Characteristics of the modern school counselor.* Retrieved from www.ascd.org /ASCD/pdf/journals/ed_lead/el_196903_lister.pdf

Web Resources

Ethics
American Counseling Association
www.counseling.org/Resources/CodeOfEthics/TP/Home/CT2.aspx
American School Counselor Association
http://asca2.timberlakepublishing.com//files/EthicalStandards2010.pdf

Professional Development
American Counseling Association
www.counseling.org/Resources/ProfessionalDevelopment/TP/Home/CT2.aspx
American School Counselor Association
www.schoolcounselor.org/content.asp?pl=325&sl=129&contentid=129

Statement of Ethical Principles and Standards
American College Student Personnel Association
www2.myacpa.org/statement-of-ethical-principles-and-standards

Vision, Mission, Statement, Goals, and Structure
American College Student Personnel Association
www2.myacpa.org/visionmissiongoals

REFERENCES

American Counseling Association. (1997). *ACA governing council minutes* (Summer, 1997). Alexandria, VA: Author.
American Counseling Association (2005). *ACA code of ethics.* Alexandria, VA: Author.

American Counseling Association. (2009). *20/20 statement of principles advances the profession.* Retrieved from www.counseling.org/PressRoom/NewsReleases.aspx?AGuid=4d87a0ce-65c0 –4074–89dc-2761 cfbbe2ec

Arredondo, P., Tovar-Blank, Z. G., & Parham, T. A. (2008). Challenges and promises of becoming a culturally competent counselor in a sociopolitical era of change and empowerment. *Journal of Counseling and Development, 86,* 261–268.

Auxier, C. R., Hughes, F. R., & Kline, W. B. (2003). Identity development in counselors-in-training. *Education and Supervision, 43*(1), 25–38.

Brott, P. E., & Myers, J. E. (1999). Development of a professional school counselor identity: A grounded theory. *Professional School Counseling, 2*(5), 339–348.

Carkhuff, R. R. (1968). Differential functioning of lay and professional helpers. *Journal of Counseling Psychology, 15*(2), 117–126.

Chi, M. T. H., Glasser, R., & Farr, M. J. (Eds.). (1988). *The nature of expertise.* Hillsdale, NJ: Lawrence Erlbaum.

Collins, S., Arthur, N., & Wong-Wylie, G. (2010). Enhancing reflective practice through multicultural counseling in cultural auditing. *Journal of Counseling & Development, 88,* 340–347.

Constantine, M. G., Myers, L. J., Kindaichi, M., & Moore, J. L. (2004). Exploring indigenous mental health practices: The roles of healers and helpers in promoting well-being in people of color. *Counseling and Values, 48*(2), 110–125.

Cummings, A. L., Hallberg, E. T., Martin, J., Slemon, A., & Hiebert, B. (1990). Implications of counselor conceptualizations for counselor education. *Counselor Education and Supervision, 30,* 120–134.

Eells, T. D. (2002). Formulation. *Encyclopedia of Psychotherapy, 1,* 815–822.

Etringer, B. D., Hillerbrand, E., & Claiborn, C. D. (1995). The transition from novice to expert counselor. *Counselor Education and Supervision, 35,* 4–17.

Gale, A. U., & Austin, B. D. (2003). Professionalism challenges to professional counselors collective identity. *Journal of Counseling & Development, 81*(1), 3–10.

Gick, M. L. (1986). Problem-solving strategies. *Educational Psychologist, 21,* 99–120.

Goodyear, R. K. (1984). On our journal's evolution: Historical developments, transitions, and future directions. *Journal of Counseling & Development, 63,* 3–8.

Hansen, J. (2009). Self-awareness revisited: Reconsidering a core value of the counseling profession. *Journal of Counseling & Development, 87*(2), 186–193.

Hill, N. R. (2004). The challenges experienced by pre-tenured faculty members in counselor education. *Counselor Education and Supervision, 44,* 135–146.

Hill, C. E., & Kellems, I. S. (2002). Development and use of the helping skills measure to assess client perceptions of the effects of training and of helping skills in sessions. *Journal of Counseling Psychology, 49*(2), 264–272.

Hill, C. E., & Lent, R. W. (2006). A narrative and meta-analytic review of helping skills training: Time to revive a dormant area of inquiry. *Psychotherapy: Theory, Research, Practice, Training, 43*(2), 154–172.

Hillerbrand, E. T., & Claiborn, C. D. (1990). Examining reasoning skill differences between expert and novice counselors. *Journal of Counseling & Development, 68*(6), 684–691.

Hilsenroth, M. J., Defife, J. A., Blagys, M. D., & Ackerman, S. J. (2006). Effects of training in short-term psychodynamic psychotherapy: Changes in graduate clinician technique. *Psychotherapy Research, 16*(3), 293–305.

Hoogasian, R., & Lijtmaer, R. (2010). Integrating Curanderismo into counselling and psychotherapy. *Counselling Psychology Quarterly, 23* (3), 297–307.

Israel, B. A. (1985). Social networks and social support: Implications for natural helper and community level interventions. *Health Education Quarterly, 1,* 12, 65–80.

Jongsma, A. E., Jr., Peterson, L. M., & McInnis, W. P. (1996). *The child and adolescent psychotherapy treatment planner.* New York: John Wiley & Sons.

Kazdin, A. E. (2008). Evidence-based treatment and practice: New opportunities to bridge clinical research and practice, enhance the knowledge base, and improve patient care. *American Psychologist, 63,* 146–159.

Kivlighan, D. M. (1989). Changes in the counselor intentions and response modes and in client reactions and session evaluations after training. *Journal of Counseling Psychology, 36,* 471–476.

Kivlighan, D. M. (2010). Changes in trainees' intention use and volunteer clients' evaluations of sessions during early skills training. *Psychotherapy: Theory, Research, Practice, Training. 47*(2), 198–210.

Kivlighan, D. M., & Quigley, S. T. (1991). Dimensions used by experienced and novice group therapists to conceptualize group process. *Journal of Counseling Psychology, 38,* 415–423.

Leinbaugh, T., Hazler, R., Bradley, C., & Hill, N. R. (2003). Factors influencing counselor educators' subjective sense of well-being. *Counselor Education and Supervision, 43*(1), 52–64.

McClintock, E. (1999). *Room for change: Empowering possibilities for therapists and clients.* Needham Heights, MA: Allyn & Bacon.

Multon, K., Kivlighan, D., & Gold, P. (1996). Changes in counselor adherence over the course of training. *Journal of Counseling Psychology, 43,* 356–363.

Nugent, F. A., & Jones, K. D. (2009). *Introduction to the profession of counseling* (5th ed.). Upper Saddle River, NJ: Pearson.

Orlinsky, D. E., Grave, K., & Parks, B. K. (1994). Process and outcome in psychotherapy. In A. E. Bergin & S. L. Garfield (Eds.), *Handbook of psychotherapy and behavior change* (pp. 257–310). New York: Wiley.

Orlinsky, D. E., Ronnestad, M. H., & Willutzki, U. (2004). Fifty years of psychotherapy process-outcome research: Continuity and change. In M. J. Lambert (Ed.), *Bergin and Garfield's handbook of psychotherapy and behavior change* (pp. 307–389). New York: John Wiley & Sons.

Parsons, R. (2001). *Ethics of professional practice.* Needham Heights, MA: Allyn & Bacon.

Patterson, S. L., & Memmott, J. L. (1992). Patterns of natural helping in rural areas: Implications for social work research. *Social Work Research & Abstracts, 28,* 22–28.

Pedersen, P. B. (2003). Increasing the cultural awareness, knowledge, and skills of culture-centered counselors. In F. D. Harper & J. McFadden (Eds.), *Culture and counseling: New approaches* (pp. 31–46). Boston: Allyn & Bacon.

Ramsey, M., Cavallaro, M., Kiselica, M., & Zila, L. (2002). Scholarly productivity redefined in counselor education. *Counselor Education and Supervision 42*(1), 40–57.

Reisetter, M., Korcuska, J. S., Yexley, M., Bonds, D., Nikels, H., & McHenry, W. (2004). Counselor educators and qualitative research: Affirming a research identity. *Counselor Education and Supervision, 4,* 2–16.

Schottler, T., Oliver, L. E., & Porter, J. (2005). Defining and evaluating clinical competence: A Review. *Guidance & Counseling, 20*(2), 46–55.

Seligman, L., & Reichenberg, L. (2010). *Theories of counseling and psychotherapy.* Boston: Pearson.

Sink, C. A., & Yillik-Downer, A. (2001). School counselors' perceptions of comprehensive guidance and counseling programs: A national survey. *Professional School Counseling, 4,* 278–288.

Smith, M., Jaffe-Gill, E., & Segal, J. (2008). *Preventing burnout: Signs symptoms, causes, and coping strategies.* Retrieved from http://helpguide.org/mental/burnout_signs_symptoms.htm

Sue, D. W., & Sue, D. (2008). *Counseling the culturally diverse: Theory and practice* (5th ed.). New York: Wiley.

Swickert, M. L. (1997). Perceptions regarding the professional identity of counselor education doctoral graduates in private practice: A qualitative study. *Counselor Education and Supervision, 35,* 218–229.

Tepper, D. T., & Hass, R. F. (2001). Verbal and nonverbal communication of facilitative conditions. In C. E. Hill (Ed.), *Helping skills: The empirical foundation* (pp. 211–223). Washington, DC: American Psychological Association.

Tomasello, M. (2009). *Why we cooperate.* Cambridge, MA: MIT Press.

Vontress, C. E. (2003). On becoming an existential cross-cultural counselor. In F. D. Harper & J. McFadden (Eds.), *Culture and counseling: New approaches* (pp. 20–30). Boston: Allyn & Bacon.

Witmer, J. M., & Granello, P. F. (2005). Wellness in counseling education and supervisions. In J. M. Witmer & P. F. Granello (Eds.), *Counseling for wellness: Theory, research and practice* (pp. 261–271). Alexandria, VA: American Counseling Association.

Chapter 2

Counseling: The Practice of Facilitating Change

I hate myself and so does everyone else.

INTRODUCTION

The opening comment, posed by our anonymous client—a comment implying a deep sense of sadness and maybe even hopelessness—calls for a response. But what type of response? For example, "I hate myself and so does everyone else" might elicit a disconfirming response such as "That's not true" or an inquiry such as "Why do you hate yourself?" or even a self-disclosing response such as "Yeah, I know what you mean. I've felt that way." The question, of course, is which, if any, is the correct response?

As you consider your response to the question, take a moment to identify the basis upon which you selected your response. What were you trying to accomplish through that particular response? Were you responding to your curiosity and asking for more detail? Were you attempting to clarify your confusion by asking, "Who is everyone?" Or, were you merely attempting to join in the conversation by offering a self-disclosure such as "Yes, I know how that feels"? As a professional counselor, your response needs to be purposeful and goal directed, with the goal and purpose being to help this client.

In order to select a helpful response, a counselor needs to understand the nature of a helping relationship and the elements necessary for the unfolding of the helping process and consider how any one response will contribute to this helping. The current chapter provides an overview to the helping process, the elements entailed in its development, and the skills essential to the nurturance and care of a helping relationship and the facilitation of the helping process. Specifically, after reading this chapter you will be able to do the following:

- Explain what is meant by the phrase, *counseling is an intentional process of change.*
- Describe the various elements of the counseling process.
- Identify specific counselor skills and dispositions that facilitate the process of counseling.

COUNSELING: AN INTENTIONAL PROCESS OF CHANGE

Counseling is a professional relationship that empowers diverse individuals, families, and groups to accomplish mental health, wellness, education, and career goals (ACA, 2010). It is a process that promotes change—be it in the form of healing or growth. Counselors serve as agents of that change with our mission being to empower people for positive change (Cameron, 2007; Davis & Osborn, 2000; Ivey & Bradford-Ivey, 2006; Maag et al., 2009; Selekman, 2010). As such, counselors engage with the client in a purposeful and intentional way using skills to facilitate change (Ivey & Authier, 1978; Ivey & Rollin, 1972; Schmidt, 1984). Exercise 2.1 will help you begin to become more aware of *intentionality* and how it may engage during a counseling interaction.

The strategies or techniques employed by a counselor in part makes up the *what* of counseling, whereas the *why* behind that *what* is the counselor's intention

---

Exercise 2.1

WHERE AM I GOING?

Directions: This is an exercise that you may want to revisit at the end of the chapter as well as later, as you progress through the text. The goal is to help you begin to consider what it is you would hope to attain by making a comment or a response to a client. As such, it may be helpful to do this exercise with a colleague or classmate in order to gain another perspective. The task is to read the descriptions that follow and then complete the following parts:

1. Identify two ways in which you could respond.

2. Identify what immediate change in the client or the conditions of the moment that you would like to see occur.

3. Identify which of the two previously described responses (in Number 1) you would select (intentionality) in order to best achieve the outcome desired (in Number 2).

EXAMPLE: ALFRED

Client Presentation

Alfred is an 8-year-old child who was sent to the school counselor's office by his third-grade teacher. According to the teacher, Alfred punched Alicia during silent reading time. Alicia is a student who sits in front of Alfred. Alfred enters the counseling office and immediately starts to sob. This is the first time Alfred has seen the counselor and it is the first time Alfred has ever been in trouble.

Potential Counselor Responses

  a. To remain silent and allow Alfred to cry until he is ready to initiate conversation
  b. To reflect the observational data by saying: "Alfred, it appears you are really upset about being sent to the counselor by Mrs. Willis?"

Immediate Change Desired

The counselor would like Alfred to stop crying and feel safe enough to begin to share his perspective on what happened in class.

Counselor Choice of Response

Counselor chose to move his chair a little closer to Alfred, and while leaning slightly forward, stated, "Alfred, I'm sorry you are so upset, about being sent down to talk with me . . ."

CASE 1: RAUL

Client Presentation

Raul is a 29-year-old construction worker who was mandated by the courts to see a court appointed counselor because of being arrested for domestic violence. Raul entered the counselor's office, ignored the counselor's extended gesture of welcome

(Continued)

(Continued)

(hand held out to shake), and literally flopped in the chair, stating, "How long is this crap going take?"

Potential Counselor Responses

Immediate Change Desired

Counselor Choice of Response

CASE 2: MITCHELL

Client Presentation

Mitchell is a 67-year-old retired minister. Mitchell has recently married a woman 22 years his junior. Mitchell's intake reveals his reason for coming to counseling was because of the concern he is feeling in regards to his erectile dysfunction and his concern about the impact on his new marriage. Mitchell came into the counselor's office, with his head down, and sat in the seat, crossing both his arms and legs as he pushed back into the chair. Mitchell began the session by apologizing to the counselor: "I'm sorry to take up your time with such a ridiculous issue. I mean at 67 I know sexual drive and function begins to waiver. I guess I should just accept I'm old. Maybe it was a mistake to marry Rebecca. It's not fair to her."

Potential Counselor Responses

Immediate Change Desired

Counselor Choice of Response

CASE 3: SAKURA

Client Presentation

Sakura is a 20-year-old college senior. She is about to graduate and has had multiple job offers. Her problem was that the job she desired would require her relocation out of state. Sakura is a first generation Japanese-American and the first in her family to graduate from college. Sakura feels a commitment to stay at home with her parents and support them. She is very upset and believes that she cannot take her dream job. Sakura desires to be able to take the job without feeling guilty, and feels as if she is hurting her parents.

Potential Counselor Responses

Immediate Change Desired

Counselor Choice of Response

(Miller, 1997). The counselor's intention is the cognitive component that mediates the type of response or intervention selected at any one moment of the counseling (Hill & O'Grady, 1985). This characteristic of professional counselors to be able to select their helping behaviors and choose specific strategies with a clear purpose and direction has been referred to as a counselor's level and degree of intentionality (Ivey, 1994; Purkey & Schmidt, 1987; Schmidt, 1984).

In the opening of this chapter we encouraged you to not only consider your response to our anonymous client's comment but also to consider the reason behind your choice of response. This rationale behind your selection is what is meant by intention (Fuller & Hill, 1985). Being aware of your intentions as you work with a client is important, because research has found a relationship between a counselor's intention and her helpful process (Elliot, 1979; Fuller & Hill, 1985; Kivlighan, 1990).

Consider Case Illustration 2.1 as it highlights the intentionality behind the counselor's response.

It is clear that the counselor in Case Illustration 2.1 had many ways in which he could choose to respond. His choice was to interrupt the client in midsentence and provide her with a suggestion as to how he would like to proceed.

While we are unable to determine what his specific intent was, we can assume that at some level, his response was in service of his desire to engage in a counseling process and to be of help to this client. Perhaps he simply felt that gaining control and giving some structure to the interaction would be more helpful to the client than simply allowing her to continue to freely and somewhat randomly disclose. This intent and desire to help facilitate the desired change in and for the client should serve as the impetus behind all of our actions as counselors.

But to select and employ actions that are intended to facilitate the achievement of the change desired requires that a counselor's decision at any one moment be guided by his understanding of the elements of counseling necessary to the facilitation of change along with an understanding of how to best engage these elements to insure their effectiveness.

ELEMENTS OF THE COUNSELING PROCESS

Before beginning the discussion of the elements of the counseling process, a caveat is in order.

A Caveat

It is almost commonplace to discuss the counseling process as involving *stages*. While the number of stages which have been proposed have varied in number

CASE ILLUSTRATION 2.1

OPTIONS

The following took place during the initial meeting between Mrs. Jenkins and her counselor. As Mrs. Jenkins entered the office, she immediately begins to speak in a somewhat hurried and disjointed manner.

> Mrs. Jenkins: I'm so glad you could see me . . . do I sit here or does it matter? I guess in the counselor's office everything matters (giggles). It's been really a couple of pretty rough—not that I haven't had tough times before—oh my god I sound like such a whiner. So what do we do? How do we start, I'm really eager . . .

At this point, the counselor has many options in terms of how he may respond. He could remain silent and allow her to continue. He could invite her to share more about what is making this a tough time, or he could even challenge her self-evaluation as a whiner.

> Counselor: Mrs. Jenkins, excuse me for interrupting you, but it would help me if perhaps we could take just a moment to gather some basic information and then I could tell you a little about what I do and suggest how we might proceed.

from three (Egan, 2010) to five (Corey, Schneider-Corey, & Callanan, 2007) or even six and more (Brammer & MacDonald, 2002), they generally include labels such as the relationship building stage, the diagnostics and assessment (or problem defining) stages, the goal setting stage, and then acting and termination stages.

We have deliberately chosen to describe the helping process not in terms of stages, but in terms of *elements*. The choice of terminology is not merely one of word preference.

The use of the word *stage* or *phase*, while potentially a useful tool for textbooks and classroom can be misleading if it leads one to conclude that the counseling process occurs in a predictable, sequential style moving through clearly delineated stages of development. This is not the case. Counseling is dynamic.

As an analogy consider the process of making cake batter. It is possible that the recipe calls for inserting flour into the bowl, then water, and eggs and butter; this occurs in a series of clearly defined and articulated steps defining which goes first and which follows. In this case, one could conclude that batter making occurs in a series of distinct, sequential steps or stages. But, consider an alternate recipe—one that requires the baker to be more interactive with the ingredients. In this situation, the baker adds the ingredients in varying portions and at varying times and intervals depending on a judgment of the color, texture, and consistency of the developing batter. In this case, the ingredients are added and blended dynamically—with the inclusion of any ingredient determined not by a prescribed formula, but by the unfolding nature of the batter and the judgment of the baker. In this situation, the batter making is dynamic not static, interactive and not stage bound.

Counseling is a dynamic process. It is a process in which the counselor is an active agent—targeting specific elements for inclusion and intentionally employing specific skills as determined by the unfolding nature of the interaction and the goals desired. Counseling is not a process in which the counselor does A before B and then goes on to doing C. Rather, as a dynamic process, counseling moves back and forth engaging all the elements of counseling, with the amount of emphasis given to any one of these elements determined by the uniqueness of the people involved and the issues and goals targeted. So, as discussion of the elements found within the counseling process proceeds, it is important to keep in mind this dynamic flow and not assume a nice, clean, distinct sequential staging.

The Elements

Counseling, as depicted in the American Counseling Association (2005) *Code of Ethics* is a process in which

counselors and their clients work jointly in devising integrated counseling plans that offer reasonable promise of success and are consistent with abilities and circumstances of clients. Counselors and clients regularly review counseling plans to assess their continued viability and effectiveness, respecting the freedom of choice of clients. (sec. A.1.c)

An analysis of this statement will provide some insight into the types of elements found in the counseling dynamic. However, prior to this discussion, completing Exercise 2.2 may assist in developing an anticipation of what is to follow.

Exercise 2.2

THE ELEMENTS OF THE COUNSELING DYNAMIC

Directions: As with Exercise 2.1, this may be an exercise that you want to revisit multiple times as you proceed through the text. The goal is to begin to identify the specific types of knowledge and skills a counselor would need to possess and employ in order to facilitate the counseling relationship and the movement toward desired change. As you review each of the following, identify the knowledge and skill that may be required of the counselor in order to achieve each of the descriptions.

Description	*Counselor Knowledge*	*Counselor Skill*
Counselor and clients work jointly . . .	Example: How to initiate and maintain a relationship	Example: The ability to make the client feel safe
Devise integrated counseling plans . . .	————————	————————
Devise plans that offer a reasonable promise of success . . .	————————	————————
Devise plans that are consistent with abilities and circumstances of the client . . .	————————	————————
Assess the plans' viability and effectiveness . . .	————————	————————
Respect the client's freedom of choice . . .	————————	————————

- . . . *work jointly.* If we consider the initial phrase in the ACA definition, "counselors and clients work jointly," we can appreciate that one element in this process of counseling is the development and maintenance of a working relationship between counselor and client. Working together requires the counselor to engage those conditions or elements that *support* and encourage open communication and foster mutual motivation to work together. While clearly a very important element to the overall dynamic and process of counseling, it is important to note that as is true for each of the elements found within the counseling process, this creation of a working relationship is not the end point or ultimate goal of counseling—it is simply an ingredient or element contributing to the formation, maintenance, and outcome of this process called counseling.

- *... devise integrated, individual counseling plans.* As we continue with our review of the description of the counseling process as presented by the American Counseling Association, we find the motive for counselor and client engagement. The counselor and client come together in order to ". . . devise integrated, individual counseling plans." Accomplishing this task of developing integrated, individual counseling plans requires that the client's story—including an identification of the client's concerns, desired goals, and resources—needs to be shared and understood. The effective counselor is able to employ those communication skills that facilitate client self-disclosure and support counselor understanding. Together, the counselor and client are transported to greater understanding of the client and increased awareness of how to facilitate the change desired.

- *... plans ... with reasonable promise.* Finally, according to the ACA description, counseling is a helping process that has a " . . . reasonable promise" of facilitating the client's movement from her presenting concern(s) to a resolution and achievement of the client's goals. The details of the client's story along with an awareness of the client resources, counseling theory, and research, provide the raw materials from which the counselor crafts the plans for facilitating change and goal achievement. This is a collaborative process with both the client and counselor reflecting on the *what is,* the *what is desired,* and the possible paths available to move in the desired direction. While often it is this element—an action element—that is most often labeled counseling, but as should be obvious, acting without accurate knowledge of the client and the clients issues and resources would be foolhardy and most likely ineffective. Building a collaborative relationship, and understanding the depth and breadth of the client's story, is just as essential to the successful counseling outcome as is the creative plans which are laid in place for the client to follow. This is a point that many novice counselors fail to appreciate and as a result often rush too rapidly into suggesting strategies and encouraging action.

The elements of working together, exploring together, and acting together along with the specific knowledge and skills necessary to successfully engage each element serve as the matter for in-depth review in the chapters to come. However, each has been presented in brief in the following sections.

Before we begin, however, we must once more reiterate our caution. While each element will be the focus of a specific chapter, this singular focus is employed merely as an editorial tool to help in the explanation of the component. It is hoped that the case illustrations will help you see the element in action—as it intertwines with the other elements—to give life and direction to the helping process.

Working Jointly

The element of "working jointly" requires the formation and maintenance of a very unique relationship—a helping relationship. The creation of this relationship is an important element contributing to the ultimate outcome of the counseling (Castonguay, Constantino, & Grosse Holtforth, 2006; Lambert & Barley, 2001) but it is not, in and of itself, an end goal—nor is it the sufficient condition for helping (Cailhol et al., 2009; Kelley, Bickman, & Norwood, 2010).

The relationship between counselor and client exists in service of the achievement of the goals established. As such, the unique needs of the participants and the specific goals they hope to achieve gives direction to the nature of the relationship and the form of interaction. Case Illustration 2.2 details the interactions between a counselor and two different clients. The illustration highlights the way the uniqueness of the client along with the intended goals gives form to the relationship and the counselor's choices. As you review the exchange, see if you can identify the unique way the counselor attempts to engage each client in the helping relationship. Following the exchange the counselor describes her intent and the strategies she used to facilitate the development of each relationship.

The decisions a counselor makes with the intent of facilitating the formation, deepening, and maintenance of a helping relationship are like any other action the counselor takes and are employed only to the extent that it effectively moves the counseling process in the desired direction. Building this relationship is not the goal of counseling. It is simply one of the elements contributing to the effectiveness of the overall counseling process. As such, a counselor would do well to understand the nature of this relationship and master the skills necessary to develop and maintain a relationship that facilitates goal attainment.

The helping relationship is at its core a human encounter, a social exchange, and as such is affected by those conditions that affect all human interaction. Conditions such as the physical environment in which the encounter occurs, the language and values shared by the participants, and even the norms or rules guiding the interaction all need to be considered as forces affecting the unfolding of this human encounter, this social exchange.

CASE ILLUSTRATION 2.2

CREATING CONDITIONS FOR WORKING JOINTLY

Both of the following client–counselor exchanges occurred during the first session. Following the presentation of the two illustrations, the counselor provides her reflections on what she intended and how she was attempting to go about it.

Illustration 1

Rachael is a newly married, 32-year-old female for whom this is her first experience with counseling. Rachael suggested to the counselor during their phone conversation that she wanted to discuss "something very personal and embarrassing."

Rachael:	Do I need to sit anywhere in particular (nervously laughing)?
Counselor:	Rachael, it is very nice to meet you. Please sit anywhere you would like. There are no assigned seats (smiling). Make yourself comfortable.
Rachael:	I'm not sure that's possible (nervously laughs). This is hard—I've never gone to a counselor before. I'm not sure what I'm supposed to do. I'm a pretty private person.
Counselor:	Rachael, thank you for sharing that and I can imagine it is hard if this is a totally new experience for you. I can hear the nervousness in your voice. We are not in a hurry and there really isn't any "suppose to dos."
Rachael:	That's good to hear.
Counselor:	Perhaps we could start with just some general information. The packet of material that you were given describes some of the nature of my practice and how I approach issues such as record keeping and confidentiality. Are there any questions?

Rachael:	(looking down) Oh, I am really sorry . . . I have that packet here . . . but, but . . . I didn't really get a chance to look at it.
Counselor:	(very calmly) Rachael, that's fine. Remember there are no have tos (smiling). Sometimes all of this information can be overwhelming and truthfully a bit confusing. We can go over all that in a moment but how about if we begin by reviewing the information you provided just so I can check to see that I have it correctly.
Rachael:	Okay (noticeably calmer).
Counselor:	Wonderful. I have your mailing address as . . .

Counselor Reflection

Rachael presented anxiously. Her anxiety seemed to stem from two issues. First, she suggested that she is a private person and not one who freely discloses. Second, this is her first encounter with a counselor and she is unsure of what is expected or what will happen. Her response to not reviewing the packet of information seems to suggest that she is concerned with "doing it right" or at least not offending. Given these assumptions on my part, I decided that Rachael needed to experience me and the exchange as nonjudgmental, safe, and one which will unfold at a pace comfortable for her. I attempted to achieve these conditions by focusing the exchange on factual, nonemotive information and when she demonstrated self-reproach or anxiety, I tried to reflect in a supportive, nonjudgmental way.

Illustration 2

Taryn is married with two grown children, and the younger one has just gotten married. Taryn, after talking with her husband, decided she wanted to get back into the work force and was considering a couple of different avenues to pursue. She thought that the objective perspective of a counselor might be helpful.

| Taryn: | (extending her hand and shaking vigorously) Dr. Carlson, I am so happy to meet you. I've heard a lot of good things about you and I am really excited about getting to work. |
| Counselor: | Well, Taryn, thank you for that. Please have a seat. |

Taryn:	I'm not sure if this will help, but I have printed out an information sheet; you know, name, rank, phone number, insurance, etc. (handing the sheet to the counselor).
Counselor:	Well, you certainly came prepared (smiling and looking over the information sheet).
Taryn:	Not sure if I'm prepared but I'm eager to start.
Counselor:	That's great. I just need one thing—your social security number; also I would like to ask you if you had any questions about information in the "Welcome to My Practice" packet, anything about the HIPPA requirements, or the details of my practice?
Taryn:	No, thank you. It was very clear and I understand the limits to confidentiality as well as your scheduling and fee policies. I signed the form (handing the form to the counselor).
Counselor:	Well, thank you. Taryn, perhaps you could tell me about your decision to come to counseling?

Counselor Reflection

Taryn presented as a very self-assured, confident, take-charge woman. She came to the session well prepared and took responsibility to review and reflect upon the information describing my practice and ethical standards. As such, I felt that a more direct-task focus was called for and I tried to move the relationship in that direction by directly asking for the missing data (i.e., social security number) and rapidly moving into inviting her to share her concerns/or goals.

As Chapter 3 details, counseling is more than a mere social exchange and the counseling relationship is much more than a typical social encounter. Counseling is unique in that it is also a professional relationship (Jennings & Skovholt, 1999; Walitzer, Dermen, & Conners, 1999). Counselors need to understand and embrace what a *professional relationship* entails and possess the knowledge and skills needed to foster the development of this professional quality.

As a professional relationship, the rules that guide the nature of the counseling interaction and even the roles expected of those involved are prescribed in the ethics and standards of professional practice. For example, unlike most informal exchanges, the counseling relationship is one defined as *confidential* in which the role of one participant, the counselor, is to promote the dignity and welfare of the other member, the client (ACA, 2005, sec. A.1.a). In Exercise 2.2, we saw the counselor taking steps to define the relationship as *professional* and inform- ing the clients of the unique conditions of this professional relationship by both presenting printed information and, in the case of Rachael, proceeding to review this information together. This characteristic of counseling as being a professional relationship demands that the counselor know and employ those skills needed to create and maintain the ethical and legal boundaries to the counseling relationship.

The third and final dimension to the counseling relationship is that it is formed for a prescribed purpose and goal. Counseling exists in order to facilitate change for one of its participants, the client. As such, counselors must possess the knowl- edge and skills necessary to keep the unfolding relationship focused on the needs and goals of the client. As you will most likely experience, this is not always an easy task. It can be quite difficult working with an individual in need who may wish for a more mutual, co-equal social relationship. The effective, professional counselor has the knowledge and skills necessary to maintain the appropriate pro- fessional boundary and refocus all discussion on the unique needs and goals of the client. Case Illustration 2.3 provides a brief look at one counselor's strategy for maintaining his helping focus.

The specific knowledge and skill necessary to effectively create and maintain the helping relationship—as a social encounter, a professional relationship, and a client-focused dynamic—are presented in detail in the following chapter, Chapter 3.

Discovering the Client: Needs, Goals, and Resources

As previously described, counselors and their clients work jointly in order to devise plans that are individually tailored and reflect the abilities and circumstances of the client. For such plans to be developed and to have a reasonable chance for success, the counselor needs to develop a full, complete understanding of the client and the client's story.

The counselor attempting to unravel the client's story in all of its depth and breadth will use those skills necessary to help the client to share his story. This is not, however, a process of encouraging random disclosure. This discovery, like all of counseling, is purposeful. The counselor employs skills that support her intention of assisting the client to more fully understand and articulate the depth and breadth of her concerns as well as, together with the client, their envisioned

CASE ILLUSTRATION 2.3

TELL ME, DOC.

The following exchange took place during the fifth session between the counselor and the client. The client presented a high degree of insecurity and social anxiety. The focus of the counseling has been on assisting the client to identify specific thoughts and beliefs that seem to be contributing to his creation of his social anxiety and helping the client learn to debate these thoughts and replace them with more rational, data-supported thoughts.

Dean:	Doc, I blew it again.
Counselor:	Dean, I'm not sure what you mean you blew it. Could you tell me what happened?
Dean:	Well I was trying to make small talk with Ellen, at work, and I think in my excitement I actually may have spit a little on her . . . you know like just a little moisture. But I'm sure I sprayed. She must think I am such a weirdo. I bet everybody at work knows and will just start avoiding me. This is horrible. I mean, I don't know, is this something that has happened to you, spitting like that?
Counselor:	When you say "spitting,"' you mean that in your excitement some of your saliva, like a droplet, came out?
Dean:	Yeah . . . you've done that, right?
Counselor:	You know Dean, I'm wondering if it would be productive to reflect on past encounters and see if it ever happened to you. Have you ever been in a conversation with someone and the person accidentally propelled some spit?
Dean:	Yeah, I was just rippin' on my brother for that, recently. He was getting excited during an Eagles game and turned to me after an unbelievable play

and said "Did you see that?" He drenched me. I said, "Say it don't spray it" and he laughed.

Counselor: So let me see if I understand. Your brother, in his excitement, kind of "sprayed you" and your response was just to tease him?

Counselor Reflection

I chose to ignore Dean's inquiry into my own experience not because I haven't had an experience like that or that it would be wrong about sharing it, but because my experience with Dean is that when he feels insecure, and potentially "reject-able," he looks for affirmation and normalization from others. I anticipated that my disclosure may get him off the hook and we would miss an opportunity to work it through cognitively. So I chose, and honestly lucked out, to get him to focus on an experience where he was the recipient. My hope was that we could use his reaction, which in this case was to use humor, as a counterpoint to his projection of how his coworkers would respond. This fit into our approach and goal of clarifying his cognitive distortions.

preferred state. Specifically, the client and counselor engage in this process of discovery in order to do the following:

- Develop an understanding of the depth and breadth of the client's concerns.
- Identify the desired state or wished for future condition.
- Enumerate the client's resources and personal challenges as they may affect the achievement of the desired goals.

This purposeful exploration is evident in the brief exchange found in Case Illustration 2.4.

As is evident by this brief exchange, it is not unusual that a client may present very vague, generalized expressions of concern. It is also possible that the concerns that are initially identified as the so-called problem may be but a symptom or reflection of a larger issue. Thus while helping to narrow the concerns from the general statement of not being able to "make it" to issues of managing her finances and social life, the counselor engaging in exploration will want to look for issues that may be lying beneath the surface. For example, is it possible that these specifics are only examples of a larger issue of the client's insecurity and dependency on others?

CASE ILLUSTRATION 2.4

I JUST CAN'T MAKE IT

The following exchange occurred midway through the first session between Liz and her counselor. Liz is a married woman who was told by her husband that he is filing for divorce.

Liz:	He just came home and told me he was done—it was over. What am I going to do? I can't make it without him.
Counselor:	I can see how upset you are. It sounds like it really was a shock.
Liz:	It's devastating . . . I mean I don't know what I am going to do?
Counselor:	Liz, you sound overwhelmed—confused and very anxious about the future but I'm wondering what you mean when you say that you can't make it without him.
Liz:	I've been married for 26 years—you know, a "Mrs." for most of my life . . . how am I going to make it? I mean what do I do for money . . . where am I going to live . . . how about our friends (crying). I just can't make it without him.
Counselor:	Make it without him? Financially? Socially?
Liz:	(calming) That's really not it. I know things will be fine financially; I already do all the budgeting and the house is paid for. No it's not that. I have a wonderful support group. It just feels so unreal that I will no longer be a married woman.
Counselor:	I am sure it feels unreal. Only having been told 4 days ago, you still haven't had time to get your mind around it.
Liz:	It's just so scary. I will have to start over again with so many things . . .

| Counselor: | I am sure there are things that you will have to learn and do on your own, but clearly you have skills and resources that will help you, including your experience with the house budget and most important your friends and family who will support you through this difficult time. |
| Liz: | I'm fortunate that way . . . they have been great. But what are they going to think about me . . . I mean . . . I don't know . . . I just feel like such a loser . . . |

Counselor Reflection

Liz's disclosure that she felt as if she couldn't make it without her husband was somewhat confusing to me, given that she presented as an emotionally mature, bright, and socially competent woman. This disclosure did not seem to match my observations.

It was my intention to help her move from a broad, vague conceptualization of her concern that "I can't make it without him," to a more concrete, specific identification of those areas or issues. Further, in her current emotional upheaval she was unable to reconnect with her personal and social resources that she could draw on during this difficult transition. My reflections were employed to help her make that connection.

Liz's last statement, however, suggests there may be more to this picture than that which is being presented. I have questions, which I would like to test out—issues such as whether Liz is overly dependent on the evaluations of others; does her sense of value depend solely on the approval of others, etc.

This process of exploration and discovery with the hope of gaining clarity is far from an easy process. It is, however, a process that is facilitated by the timely application of the knowledge and skills described in the upcoming chapters.

A Plan, a Strategy, and Then Action

As the client's story unfolds the counselor will be privy to a vast array of client data including such things as current concerns, history of these concerns, family background, present stressors, and so forth. Counseling, as previously noted, is an intentional process. As such, the data the counselor gathers is collected specifically for its value in providing both the counselor and the client understanding of the nature of the current situation, the factors supporting these issues, and the possible steps that can be taken to facilitate the client's desired change.

Case Conceptualization

The counselor, through a process of case conceptualization (Eells, 2002) will organize these data and develop hypotheses about the causes, precipitants, and maintaining factors coming to play in this client's psychological, interpersonal, and behavioral problems. In addition to helping the client and counselor draw conclusions about what caused and maintains the presenting concerns, case conceptualization helps the counselor link the client's presenting concerns to a plan for addressing those concerns.

Gaining the knowledge and skills required for case conceptualization can be a challenge for many novice counselors (Caspar, Berger, & Hautle, 2004). Repeated and deliberate practice have been cited as integral components in the development and mastery of therapeutic and case conceptualization skills (Caspar et al., 2004). Exercise 2.3 provides an opportunity to practice engaging in elementary case conceptualization.

Exercise 2.3

A STAB AT CASE CONCEPTUALIZATION

While the process of case conceptualization is difficult and requires much more training and experiencing than we would expect you may have had up to this point, it is useful, even at this early stage of your formation, to begin the process of developing initial impressions and working hypotheses. As you do, it is important to try to keep your hypotheses to data presented, watching for your own personal bias, or judgments.

Directions: The following information was acquired during the initial session with the client, Alexia. The material is presented in segments and you will be directed to develop working hypotheses as you proceed through the case.

Information

Alexia is a 24-year-old, single female who is living on her own and running her own home-and-office cleaning business. The business has been a success, financially, but it has occupied all of Alexia's time and energy. She came to counseling complaining of needing a "boyfriend" and wondered what was wrong with her, because all her friends are engaged or going with someone. Alexia described that other than for the last 2 years when she was working to start her business, she has always had a boyfriend. In fact, she noted that she can't remember not ever having a boyfriend, going back to her middle school years, "probably seventh grade."

Working Hypotheses (example)

1. Given her successful self-owned business, one might conclude that Alexia appears to be a self-motivated person.

2. Alexia is feeling as if one missing element in her life is the presence of a relationship.

3. It appears that her concern about a boyfriend may be less a matter of seeking an intimate relationship as it is fitting in with her friends.

Theme (connecting to previous information) (example)

1. Given her history of so-called boyfriends, and concerns about her friends' engagements, is it possible a person who places a lot of value on being accepted by others may even be seeking external validation of her personal worth by belonging?

Information

Alexia disclosed that her mom and dad were divorced when she was very young (8 years old) and that her mom, while never remarrying, had a number of live-in boyfriends as Alexia was growing up.

Working Hypotheses (keep the hypotheses tied to the actual information presented)

Theme (connecting to previous information)

Information

Alexia reported that her first sexual experience occurred while she was in ninth grade. She noted that she started dating a senior and that relationship ended after he

(Continued)

(Continued)

found out that she had cheated on him (sexually) with a college freshman. Alexia admitted that she was "out-of-control" sexually throughout her high school years. Her promiscuity was a concern to her mom and she took Alexia to see a therapist. Alexia only went twice to that therapist, reporting that she just wasn't ready.

Working Hypotheses (keep the hypotheses tied to the actual information presented)

Theme (connecting to previous information)

Information

Alexia explained that her concern about having a boyfriend had little to do with any sexual needs. She noted that she really desired a meaningful relationship. She envied her friends who seemed to be with people who were "best friends." She shared her serious doubt that she would ever find anyone who would want her, other than for sex.

Working Hypotheses (keep the hypotheses tied to the actual information presented)

Theme (connecting to previous information)

While the hypotheses drawn in Exercise 2.3 needed further evidence for support, they provide an initial focus for the conversation. In working with Alexia, the counselor would want to test the hypotheses by way of posing specific questions, providing tentative interpretations, or simply listening for specific data that would confirm or negate the hypotheses. The response of the counselor as he tests these hypotheses could be viewed as interventions, in that each may help the client gain better insight as to the nature of this current issue and potential underlying patterns, as well as lay the foundation for a more defined set of action steps that will help move the client in her desired direction.

The Treatment Plan

Integrating these data into a consistent view of the client's main issues provides the base for developing a coherent plan for change (Eells, 1997; Shaw & Dobson, 1988). This plan of change may target goals ranging from reduction of client symptoms, improvement of functioning, increasing client insight, or prevention of relapse (Sim, Gwee, & Bateman, 2005).

The treatment plan serves as a guideline for achieving the changes the client desires. As a reflection of the counselor's respect for the client's right to self-determination, treatment plans are developed collaboratively, with the client and counselor acting together. The treatment plan outlines goals and objectives as well as the specific strategies, techniques, and action steps to be taken to achieve these.

As the counselor and client focus on this element of acting together they will begin to

- Identify a number of alternatives or solutions to the concerns presented.
- Select, implement, and evaluate a strategy to be employed.
- Assist the client in moving toward increased independence and self-reliance.

As discussed in Chapter 6, there are a number of strategies to call upon in the process of acting together. However, for this brief overview, it is sufficient to point out that the strategies or approaches employed need to *offer reasonable promise of success and are consistent with abilities and circumstances of clients* (ACA, 2005, sec. A.1.c).

The Organic and Dynamic Nature of Helping

The introduction of these strategies, techniques, and action steps may lead one to conclude that the real work of counseling has now begun. But as previously highlighted, the elements of working and discovering together also constitute the "real work" of counseling. And like the other elements, the inclusion of treatment strategies or action plans is done with an appreciation for the organic, dynamic nature of helping.

The preliminary data gleaned as a result of coming and exploring together served as the basis from which the counselor engages in strategies and action steps intended to move the process forward. As more client data is revealed, the conceptualization of the case will be recast and with it a concomitant change in the treatment plan. This organic and interactive dynamic among the elements found in counseling can be observed in operation in Case Illustration 2.5. It is this organic, dynamic nature of the counseling process that serves as the base for our delineation of *elements* earlier in this chapter. Like the expert baker, the effective counselor introduces elements of working together, discovering together, and acting together all throughout the relationship.

CASE ILLUSTRATION 2.5

THE ORGANIC NATURE OF THE COUNSELING PROCESS

The exchange that follows took place during the initial session between the counselor and William, a 47-year-old single male who has just lost his house in foreclosure.

William:	I really can't take it anymore. This is all too much for anyone.
Counselor:	It sounds like you are really feeling overwhelmed and hopeless.
William:	It is hopeless. Look, it's not just having my house foreclosed; I haven't worked in 26 months, my fiancée ended our engagement, my parents are ashamed of me—I'm just a loser. I can't do it anymore. There's nothing that is going to help.
Counselor:	William, I am very sorry to hear about the end of your engagement and the financial difficulties you are experiencing, but you came to counseling and for that I am grateful. But I wonder what could

	happen as a result of you and me getting together that may help you believe it was worthwhile coming?
William:	Turn back the clock—make it like it used to be!
Counselor:	Actually, that is really a good idea. I don't mean turn back the clock but I wonder if we take a look at a time in the recent past when things were a little better, a little more manageable—you know, a time when you were working and had the financial resources to pay your mortgage and the social skills to meet and develop meaningful relationships. Maybe it would help us understand a little more about you and the skills that you bring to this situation.
William:	What skills?
Counselor:	Well, clearly there was a time, not so long ago, when you were able to seek and gain employment, manage your finances, and even develop a meaningful relationship?
William:	Yeah, but I don't have any of those things now.
Counselor:	I do understand that, and I can hear how sad and concerned you are about these losses. But I wonder, were these losses evidence of you being a loser or were some other conditions or elements involved?
William:	I know you are right. It wasn't my fault the company went under, and I did keep the house afloat well beyond what most people thought I could. Even my fiancée's decision was not all completely about me. She had concerns about getting married given the health problems her mom was having. But man this really sucks.
Counselor:	Yes it does, but maybe you and I working together can begin to identify steps that can be taken to make it a little less so?

As we review the exchange in Case Illustration 2.5, the fluid engagement and dynamic interaction between the elements become clear. The counselor's supportive and nonjudgmental responses and demeanor contributed to the development of the helping relationship as well as facilitated the client's ability to explore and share his story. Further, the counselor's selective responding helped the client clarify his concerns and in so doing helped to reframe these concerns from those initially felt to be overwhelming and unmanageable to something that, while difficult, was clearly within his ability to cope. In this brief, introductory exchange we can see the elements of relationship building, story sharing, and intervention—all contributing to changes in this client's feelings and view of his life condition.

Presenting counseling as a dynamic process allows us to expand our perspective on the nature of change and the goals of counseling. While we can certainly see how helping clients achieve their goals would qualify as achieving the change desired, it may be a little less clear and easy to realize that helping clients better understand the depth and breadth of their presenting concern is also meaningful change. Placing change along a continuum will allow us to appreciate that the counselor can make significant impact in the client's life from the moments of the first hello through to the final goodbye.

CHANGE: MOVEMENT ALONG A CONTINUUM

Previously baking served as an analogy for the reflective attention and intentionality a counselor should employ when engaging in the helping process. Just as the baker, attending to her batter, may adjust the amount and timing of the inclusion of specific ingredients in response to the unfolding texture of the batter, so too must the counselor differentially attend to elements supporting the relationship, strategies that facilitate the client's telling of his or her story, and the introduction of strategies of change. Counseling is a process that is not only influenced by the nature of the concerns presented, the goals desired, and the model or approach employed by the counselor, but also by where a client may be on a continuum of change.

A Continuum of Change

Researchers suggest that individuals engaged in the process of change, whether that occur within a helping relationship or outside of one, move through a series of stages and that their movement can be facilitated by the inclusion of specific processes (e.g., McConnaughy, DiClemente, Prochaska, & Velicer, 1989; McConnaughy, Prochaska, & Velicer, 1983; Prochaska, 1991; Prochaska, DiClemente, & Norcross, 1992; Prochaska & Velicer, 1997).

The most common conceptualization of this continuum depicts five stages of change that are problem-specific and "represent specific constellations of attitudes, intentions, and/or behaviors that are relevant to an individual's status in the process of change" (Prochaska & DiClemente, 1992, p. 185). Within this model, the concept of stages represents both a period of time as well as a set of tasks or processes needed for movement to the next stage (p. 160).

As noted earlier, these stages of change occur whether the person is in a formal helping relationship or is attempting to achieve change on one's own. Exercise 2.4 is a multipart exercise and may help you personalize the material that follows. It is suggested to complete Part I of Exercise 2.4 before proceeding, and then return to the text until our prompt for Part II of this exercise.

Counselor Interventions Along the Continuum of Change

The concept of a continuum of change helps counselors to see behavioral change as more than an end-state action when the counseling goal has been attained. Counselors with the perspective that change occurs along a continuum tailor their intervention to facilitate movement across that continuum and observe changes even when the end state, the final goal, has yet to be achieved. The five targets for change to be discussed are: (1) precontemplation, (2) contemplation, (3) preparation, (4) action, and (5) maintenance (Prochaska & DiClemente, 1992).

Precontemplation

Clients in the *precontemplation stage* are characterized by a lack of recognition that a problem exists. The initial stage of change is actually one in which the client most likely has no intention to change. While others may see the need for the client to change, the client himself appears either in denial or simply oblivious to that need. Consider the case of a student who was sent to the counselor's office by a teacher or a marriage partner who clearly does not understand why his spouse is so upset about his drinking. While both parties may in fact be exhibiting problematic behavior, such as the student's failure to complete assignments and the alcohol dependence of this spouse, the motivation to change is other-generated, rather than intrinsic to the client. As such, the focus for counseling and the interventions employed would need to target the clients' lack of awareness or ownership of the problem and not the problem, itself (see Case Illustration 2.6). Counselors aware of a continuum of change understand that while their counseling may not be addressing the identified issues of concern, real helping, real counseling, real intervening, or real action is occurring as the counselor employs intentional strategies to elevate the client's awareness and ownership of the identified area of concern.

Exercise 2.4

EXPERIENCE WITH CHANGE

Most people, at one time or another, have set goals for personal improvement. These may include things such as losing weight, stopping smoking, exercising, and so forth. The experience we have had in moving from becoming aware of a need or interest in a desired change through the achievement of our goals reflect the stages of change that are discussed in this chapter.

Directions: In order to personalize the material, the following exercise is presented in multiple parts. You will be instructed to return to the exercise at varying points within the text.

Part I: Identification of Personal Goal for Change

Step 1. Identify one goal for personal change that you may have set and have been successful in achieving. This could be anything ranging from saving money, stopping smoking, returning to school, or improving upon some personal quality.

Step 2. Describe how you became aware of the value of setting and achieving this goal. Was it the result of another person's input, for example, your doctor or significant other? Was it the result of some personal experience, for example, feeling ill or frustrated or being unable to participate in some activity?

Part II: Contemplation

Step 1. How long have you been thinking about doing something about this goal?

Step 2. What happened to facilitate your movement from thinking to doing?

Part III: Preparing for Action

Step 1. Using the goal identified in Part I, specify how long it was between your awareness of needing or wanting to make a change, and the first preliminary steps you took to change.

Step 2. What were the initial steps that you took that indicate you were investing in change? Did you start reading about the goal or plans for achieving the goal? Did you buy some equipment? Did you make a commitment to a friend? Did you try it out, or pilot it?

Part IV: Action

Step 1. Once you were committed to achieving your goal, what specific plan or steps did you take to insure success?

Step 2. How did you develop or select this specific plan? Did you consult with another? Did you do research? Did you use trial and error?

Part V: Maintenance

Given that you were successful in achieving this goal, what steps have you taken, or will you take, to maintain this change?

CASE ILLUSTRATION 2.6

INCREASING CLIENT AWARENESS AND OWNERSHIP

The client is a 16-year-old male who is a gifted athlete but who is failing most of his classes. He was sent to the counselor's office by his English teacher.

Michael:	I know what you are going to say—I get it—Mrs. Antonio is all bent out of shape about my English grades.
Counselor:	Well, Mrs. Antonio is concerned . . .
Michael:	(interrupting) Really not a problem, I got it under control. Look, and I don't want to sound like I have a big head or anything, but you know I'm being recruited by a ton of Division I schools, so I just need to pass with Ds and do well this season. So really there is no problem here.
Counselor:	Michael that sounds good, but I wonder if you consider the fact that all Division I programs by NCAA rule can only admit students that have given evidence that they have a reasonable chance of succeeding.

Michael:	So?
Counselor:	Well, currently you are in danger of failing all of your major subjects and getting Ds in the others. I'm not sure what we would point to that is evidence that you can succeed in college, even though I believe if you ever decided to do what needs to be done you would do well.
Michael:	Well I can take care of that next semester after the season over.
Counselor:	Well, we may have another problem. You may have seen in the student handbook that we do have an academic eligibility policy.
Michael:	No. What's that?
Counselor:	Well, the policy states that any student who is failing three or more classes or has a grade point average of less than 1.75 will not be able to participate in extracurricular activities. Michael, you are failing four and your GPA is 1.55.
Michael:	What are you saying? I can't play football?
Counselor:	Well, if the season were starting today you would not be allowed to participate . . . but we have 5 weeks and according to your teachers it is just a matter of you completing your assignments.
Michael:	That's a lot of work.
Counselor:	I can imagine it may be, but if you are interested maybe you and I can figure how to get it done.
Michael:	I would appreciate it if you could—I can't blow this.

Regardless of whether Michael in Case Illustration 2.6 was in denial or simply being oppositional, it is clear that the initial concerns over his academic performance were those of his teacher and not his. Any attempt to strategize about ways to improve his grades would most likely be unsuccessful until the motivation for this change was his. The counselor in this situation was wise to focus his attention on those things that were important to Michael, like his football. Elevating Michael's awareness of the connection between his current behavior and the possible negative impact on his playing football helped to arouse his interest and motivation for engaging in the counseling.

In this case, as is true for most cases in which the client enters at the precontemplative stage, the counselor may find that the use of processes that raise the client's awareness and ownership of the issues as well as provide some immediate relief would be of value.

Contemplation

In the *contemplation stage,* clients may recognize that they have a problem and even begin to consider various solutions. The client in this stage is both aware and desirous of change but has not yet made a serious commitment to take action. Clients could literally be in this stage of contemplation, without action, for years (DiClemente, Prochaska, & Gibertini, 1985).

Our student Michael, for example, may begin to embrace the fact that he has a problem once he becomes aware that he may miss out on the opportunity to play football at a Division I school. With this awareness, he may even admit that he is not performing up to his ability and truthfully espouse his need to and interest in doing better. But, as with all clients in the contemplation stage, Michael may find it difficult to actually engage in those actions necessary to insure passing. Perhaps your own experience with change parallels that of Michael. To further reflect on this, you can now return to Exercise 2.4 and complete Part II.

A counselor working with this student would be ill advised to focus her interventions on the issue of assignment completion. The interventions chosen for a client at this point in the change process are those that help the client see the benefits of change and take steps to reduce the costs of that change. For example, a counselor can facilitate movement to the next stage by breaking the steps to be taken down into smaller units, units of minimal cost and maximal payoff. For example, it may be useful to have Michael talk with his teachers and get a list of the missing assignments, or even identify, along with his counselor, peers who could be of assistance in understanding the assignments. Setting these small steps as goals and thus reducing the amount of effort required, while not resulting in increased assignment production, positions the client to move to the next stage of change, the preparation stage.

Preparation

As the client moves into the *preparation stage* of change, he moves from merely thinking about doing something to actually taking small steps in the direction of change. If you return to Exercise 2.4, responding to Part III will help highlight this point.

The challenge at this point, however, is that some clients, while motivated to change, may not really know how to proceed or may experience inhibitory anxiety about their ability to change or the impact of such change. When this is the case, the action and intervention of counseling turn from achieving the terminal goal to addressing these needs of skill and knowledge acquisition and anxiety reduction. For example, perhaps Michael really doesn't know how to complete the assignments and it is this lack of understanding that serves as the barrier to his performance. Having Michael seek clarification from the teacher or, if less threatening, engage a peer who has been successful in doing the assignments, may be the interventions needed at this stage.

Action

While identified as an element of *action,* it should be obvious that real action, real intervention, and real change have happened all along the continuum. The action stage is one in which the now motivated and committed client is ready and able to address the concerns presented and the goals desired.

What the client and the counselor choose to do during this stage will most likely be determined by the nature of the client's concerns and goals, as well as the counselor's operating framework or theory of counseling (e.g., solution focus, behavioral, cognitive, etc.). However, in a generic way, the counselor at this stage serves as a consultant assisting the client to become more autonomous and to take control over her life. In reviewing your own action step (see Exercise 2.4, Part IV), was there a person or resource that you used as a consultant?

Maintenance

For many counselors, having assisted the client to achieve his or her goal is the signal that the counseling has reached a point of termination. Reaching one's goal is desirable and a clear indication of significant change, from the *what was* to the now *what is.* However, reaching the goal is only one aspect of change. The counselor and client need to strategize about ways to maintain the progress—the success they made. It is in developing an effective maintenance strategy that the change becomes permanent.

When change has taken place and new patterns are becoming established, it is time to implement strategies of *maintenance.* The final stage of change has as its goals the consolidation of gain, generalization of these changes, and relapse prevention (McConnaughy et al., 1983). For many, this stage is given only lip service and as a result the changes attained are not retained.

Prochaska and Norcross (1994) stressed the need for clients to be aware of the possible cognitive, behavioral, emotional, and environmental pitfalls that can get in the way of successful action. Thus effective counselors will employ strategies that facilitate the maintenance of the changes established, such as providing clients with an education of the relapse dynamic and encouragement for continued actions necessary to prevent relapse of symptoms (Gorski & Miller, 1982). Exercise 2.4, Part V invites you to reflect on your own maintenance plan.

The Fluidity of Stages

Counselors using a continuum of change for their frame of reference understand that not all people enter counseling at the same stage of change. As such, they approach the counseling process identifying where the client is on the continuum and developing strategies to facilitate the client's movement toward a desired end point. They also understand that while this continuum is presented as a series of stages, stages that are a linear sequencing of steps toward a goal, that in practice, clients often exhibit a spiraling or cycling back and forth across these stages as they move toward their desired end point. As clients spiral into various stages of change, the counselor needs to adjust the focus of their interventions.

CHALLENGES ENCOUNTERED: COUNSELING IS NOT FORMULAIC

The gift of writing a textbook is that we as authors can describe counseling in its most ideal state. We can use examples that always work and present clients who are always the most cooperative. This works in textbooks but is not an honest reflection of the reality counselors experience day-to-day in their professional life. Counseling is not always neat and tightly packaged. Clients are not always cooperative. And the best-laid plans of the professional counselor often fall short of their mark. This is why effective counselors understand the elements of counseling and are able to adjust their approach while engaged with a client. A couple of examples may help to highlight the fact that in counseling "one size does *not* fit all!"

Working With Children

Children are a unique population and textbooks often describe most theories and skills in a way that applies to adult clients. When working with children, counselors must be cognizant of the needs and challenges that this unique population holds in the counseling process. First, children may not see any need for treatment because almost all children in counseling are referred by their parents, teachers, school administrators, or physicians. Because of the forceful nature of the referral, children oftentimes view counseling as punishment. Such a view most likely results in uncooperative behaviors in the helping process. Second, children may not understand the informed consent because all the standards and rules are made by adults and from adults' perspective and most of them are beyond the comprehension of children. This may cause some challenges for the counselor, confidentiality in particular. For example, whether the counselor should share the content of the counseling with parents, teachers, or school administrators can be an issue. Third, children may have difficulty expressing themselves and not respond to many of the counselor's skills developed based on adult clients. As we all know, many children do not have sufficient words to express themselves and they tend to use a lot of their emotions to cope with whatever situations they encounter. Counselors who are used to traditional counseling approaches and techniques developed based on adult clients may therefore face challenges working with children. Finally, children are emotional and can be either uncooperative with or dependent on the counselor. Subsequently, they are more delicate than adults and need a lot of patience and understanding; many counselors who are accustomed to traditional counselor methods and skills may feel this as a challenge.

So, when working with children, counselors may want to make adjustment to their counseling methods, styles, and techniques, for example, using small chairs to match children's level to avoid talking down to them, letting them play or draw while talking with them, using simple words and short sentences, avoiding broad open questions, and constantly employing the listening skills of paraphrasing and summarizing (Ivey, Ivey, & Zalaquett, 2010). For instance, to gather information from children the counselor may employ one of the most popular counseling techniques for children—picture drawing (Srebalus & Brown, 2001). Once the pictures are completed, the children are asked to tell about their pictures. Other methods such as play therapy (e.g., Landreth, 2002) or role play (e.g., Rogers & Evans, 2006) can also be used while counseling children.

Counseling Clients With a Multicultural Background

Helping clients with a multicultural background can be challenging for many counselors, and in particular, counselor-in-training because these clients come for help with a different worldview and cultural background from those of the counselors. The difference between counseling minority clients and clients with the American mainstream cultural background has been extensively discussed in the field of counseling profession. As such becoming multicultural competent is one of the ethical standards for professional counselors (e.g., ACA, 2005; CACREP, 2009).

The subject of counseling clients with a multicultural background can be broad and extensive, which is beyond the scope of this book. However, there are some major elements that are essential for counselors effectively helping clients with a multicultural background. These elements may include worldviews, values, and acculturation.

Worldview refers to "an individual's perception of the world based on his or her experiences as well as the socialization processes of the person in interaction with members of his or her reference group (e.g., culture, country)" (Gladding, 2001, p. 128). *Values* are described as follows:

> Values can be defined as concepts or beliefs that function as guiding principles in counselors' lives (personal values), in selecting and evaluating their own professional behavior (professional values), in judging clients' choices and behaviors (mental health values), and in ascertaining the outcome of counseling. (Consoli, Kim, & Meyer, 2008, p. 182)

Acculturation is the process of change that occurs when two cultures come in contact with each other (Redfield, Linton, Herskovits, 1936).

These elements, including many others not addressed here, are important to consider when helping multicultural clients because all theories and techniques used to implement these theories are developed from a Western worldview and Western cultural values. For example, when counselors value autonomy and independence, they may espouse these values by affirming them in the client's behaviors while challenging the client's stance if this stance is not grounded on autonomy and independence (Consoli et al., 2008). Moreover, a counselor who values egalitarianism would affirm this value and promote the establishment of an equal relationship in the counseling process. However, this value may contradict the value of a client who comes expecting a hierarchical relationship. The following is an example of how a White male counselor's worldviews and values are different from those of his Asian-American client.

Counselor:	Hello, Lin (looking into the client's eyes and offering his hand to the client).
Lin:	How do you do, Mr. Johnson? (hesitates but shakes hand with Dr. Johnson anyway)
Counselor:	Come on in and sit down.

Lin:	Thank you, Mr. Johnson (moves one of the two chairs which face each other a little bit sideway and then sits down).
Counselor:	(moves the other chair and then sits down facing the client squarely) You may call me Steve.
Lin:	(looks down and remains silent)
Counselor:	Hi again Lin?
Lin:	hmm . . . (being silent)

What issues do you see in this initial interaction? Consider the following:

- "Hello, Lin" is very informal which is considered lacking respect in a formal contact from an Asian cultural perspective. Also, a stranger using a woman's first name shows little respect or a lack of sensitivity in some Asian cultures.
- Looking into the woman's eyes or having direct eye contact is viewed as rude and impolite in most of the Asian cultures.
- Shaking a woman's hand in the first encounter is not acceptable among many Asians.
- "Come on in and sit down" is viewed as informal and impolite from many Asian-Americans' viewpoints.
- "You may call me Steve" from a Western viewpoint, shows the counselor trying to be equal and attempting to promote an egalitarian relationship with his client Lin. However, it is not common and disrespectful for a woman from Eastern cultures to address a stranger by his first name (attributed to the value of a hierarchical relationship).
- The counselor moves his chair and then sits down facing the client squarely. Although this approach is endorsed in many counseling textbooks, using it with some Asians, Asian-American clients, or minority clients is inappropriate and impolite (according to the worldview of some Asian-Americans).
- "Hi again Lin" shows that the counselor has no awareness of the client's formal interactive style.

In this example, it is apparent that the counselor does not have multicultural awareness and knowledge. He espouses his Western worldviews and values in the counseling process.

Here we must emphasize that not all Asian-Americans exercise Asian cultures or hold an Eastern worldview. As counselors, we need to keep in mind that acculturation determines multicultural clients' attitude toward counseling (Gim, Atkinson, & Kim, 1991) and also our approach when working with multicultural clients. Some multicultural clients were born in the United States and may have acculturated to the mainstream culture and adopted a Western worldview while others may continue to practice their own cultures and function based on their cultural values. Assessing multicultural clients' acculturation level is crucial in the helping process when counselors work with multicultural clients, and racial/ethnic clients in particular.

To effectively help clients with a multicultural background, counselors must be sensitive and responsive to the needs and the experiences of the clients. To do so, counselors must increase their multicultural self-awareness and knowledge. Possessing knowledge about the clients' cultures is not sufficient to be competent multicultural counselors. The counselors must be able to apply the knowledge to their understanding of the clients. Furthermore, the counselors need to show respect for their clients; be genuine, empathic, and understanding of their clients; communicate empathy, respect, and genuineness to their clients; accept their clients as individuals; allow their clients to explore their own values; and help their clients work out individual solutions. All of these are core qualities that may transcend culture (Sue & Sue, 2008). In addition, the counselors may discuss the racial and ethnic differences between themselves and their clients (Zhang & Burkard, 2008) and assess their clients' acculturation level when appropriate. More important, counseling is intentional and the counselors must clearly communicate to their clients what will happen in the counseling process and how the clients can benefit from the experience.

Working With Reluctant or Resistant Clients

While this, and other similar texts, present case illustrations that appear to move smoothly and effectively through the process of counseling, this is not always the case in the real world. Despite the best efforts that the counselors have put into the helping process clients often fail to respond to the interventions employed. It is not unusual to experience a client, perhaps one who is mandated to come to counseling, or one who, for a variety of personal reasons, may be unwilling or only minimally willing to cooperate. These clients may fail to act on or participate in the counseling process. Often counselors identify such reluctance as *resistance.*

Counseling professionals have defined resistance as "any behavior that moves a client away from areas of discomfort or conflict and prevents the client from developing" (Gladding, 2001, p. 104), or "a process of avoiding or diminishing the self-disclosing communication requested by the interviewer because of its capacity to make the interviewee uncomfortable or anxious" (Pope, 1979, p. 74). It is also described as the "push-back from clients when they feel they are being coerced" (Egan, 2007, p. 184). A resistant client often appears unwilling to seek help and opposed to change. A resistant client may take the initial steps to seeking help, but once engaged, fails to follow through, avoiding the painful process that the change demands. Based on these definitions, resistance can be both external (e. g., coercion) and internal (e.g., fear or vulnerability) in terms of the client's negative reaction to the helping relationship.

For example, clients who are mandated by the court or correctional facilities and clients who are forced to the helping process by third-party referrers—such as spouses, parents, teachers, school administrators, or supervisors—may feel coerced and thus present resistance to counselors' prescribed interventions. These clients perceive that counseling is done to them and do not believe that they have a need to seek help; they likely believe that their right has not been respected so they resent those who refer them. Consequently they bring this resentment into the counseling process (Egan, 2010).

Some clients may also become resistant when they feel uncertain about what will happen to them. These clients may fear failure and taking risks, or feel shame because they believe that seeking help from someone means admitting weakness or losing face. When clients have fear of failure and taking risks, they have no knowledge of the change that occurs in the counseling process and often set high expectations for success or perceive change as a risk; for instance, through resistance clients would have control of the session and prevent from discussing and confronting painful topics and intense negative feelings. Other clients may become resistant when they see they would lose attention from their counselors and the therapeutic relationship if they get better, or when they have a difference from their counselors in terms of the degree of change desired (Egan, 2010). Some clients may even present as reluctant as an extension of their cultural experiences or values. This would be the case with an African American client who is resistant as a result of a "healthy cultural paranoia" (Boyd-Franklin, 2003) or cultural mistrust (Terrell & Terrell, 1981), or the Asian-American client who is reluctant due to feeling embarrassed or afraid of losing face by disclosing personal secrets to a stranger.

In order to help the resistant client, the counselor must acknowledge the resistance as a natural and therapeutic response of the client to helping. The counselor needs further to understand the reasons behind the client's resistant behavior with the guidance of various theoretical frameworks on conceptualization of resistance (Watson, 2006). When resistance occurs, counselors should take a look at their own contribution to the client's resistant behavior and not just employ outward thinking that all resistance originates from the client (Brammer & MacDonald, 2002). Other strategies in working with resistant clients may include:

- Educating the client about the counseling process
- Using the Socratic method of questioning to defuse the client's resistance

- Providing the client with choices and freedom in the counseling process
- Fostering collaboration and cooperation between the counselor and the client
- Reviewing the pros and cons of changing or not changing
- Providing empathy for the resistance
- Discussing the case conceptualization with the client
- Speaking the client's language
- Maximizing the use of client self-direction
- Gently persisting when clients subtly avoid (Newman, 1994)

It is no easy task to work with reluctant and resistant clients and master all the nuts and bolts of helping. To conclude this chapter, we want to make clear that although we have and will emphasize the precision and rigor of counseling and its integrated nature of art and science, no counselor is perfect. As you walk through your way of becoming a professional counselor, you will, like many other professional counselors, encounter challenges and make mistakes. It is these challenges and mistakes that will help you grow in this unfolding learning and becoming process.

COUNSELING KEYSTONES

- Counselors engage with the client in a purposeful and intentional way, using skills to facilitate change.
- The intent and desire to help facilitate the desired change in and for the client should serve as the impetus behind all counselor actions.
- Counseling is a dynamic process. It is a process in which the counselor is an active agent—targeting specific elements for inclusion and intentionally employing specific skills as determined by the unfolding nature of the interaction and the goals desired.
- Working together requires the counselor to engage those conditions or elements that support and encourage open communication and foster mutual motivation to work together.
- For the counselor and client to *devise integrated, individual counseling plans,* the client's story—including an identification of concerns, desired goals, and resources—needs to be shared and understood.
- The counseling relationship is a social encounter, a professional relationship, and a client-focused dynamic.
- Case conceptualization helps the counselor and client draw inferences about what caused and maintains the presenting concerns. It also helps the counselor link the client's presenting concerns to a plan for addressing those concerns.

- Counseling is a process that is not only influenced by the nature of the concerns presented, the goals desired, and the model or approach the counselor employs, but also by where a client may be on a continuum of change.

ADDITIONAL RESOURCES

Adams, L. G., & Paxton, M. (2011). Counseling children and youth in times of crisis: Understanding child development and building rapport. *Child Law Practice, 30,* 49–58.

Consoli, A. J., Kim, B. S. K., & Meyer, D. M. (2008). Counselors' values profile: Implications for counseling ethnic minority clients. *Counseling and Values, 52,* 181–197.

Glauser, A. S., & Bozarth, J. D. (2001). Person-centered counseling: The culture within. *Journal of Counseling and Development, 79,* 142–147.

Kottman, T., & Stiles, K. (1990). The mutual storytelling technique: An Adlerian application in child therapy. *Individual Psychology: The Journal of Adlerian Theory, Research & Practice, 46*(2), 148–157.

McClintock, E. (1999). *Room for change: Empowering possibilities for therapists and clients.* Needham Heights, MA: Allyn & Bacon.

Muscat, A. C. (2005). Ready, set, go: The transtheoretical model of change and motivational interviewing for "fringe" clients. *Journal of Employment Counseling, 42*(4), 179–191.

Newman, C. F. (1994). Understanding client resistance: Methods for enhancing motivation to change. *Cognitive and Behavioral Practice, 1,* 47–69. Retrieved from www.nwlcbttraining.net/documents/101213NewmanResistanceinCBT.pdf

REFERENCES

American Counseling Association. (2005). *ACA code of ethics.* Alexandria, VA: Author.

American Counseling Association (2010) Resources. Retrieved from http://www.counseling.org/Resources/

Boyd-Franklin, N. (2003). *Black families in therapy: Understanding the African American experience* (2nd ed.). New York: Guilford Press.

Brammer, L. M., & MacDonald, G. (2002). *The Helping relationship: Process and skills* (8th ed.). Boston: Allyn & Bacon.

Cailhol, L., Rodgers, R., Burnand, Y., Brunet, A., Damsa, C., & Andreoli, A. (2009). Therapeutic alliance in short-term supportive and psychodynamic psychotherapies: A necessary but not sufficient condition for outcome? *Psychiatry Research, 170*(2–3), 30, 229–233.

Cameron, H. (2007). A descriptive account of the literature. *Counselling & Psychotherapy Research, 7*(4), 245–249.

Caspar, F., Berger, T., & Hautle, I. (2004). The right view of your patient: A computer assisted, individualized module for psychotherapy training. *Journal of Clinical Psychology, 41*(2), 125–135.

Castonguay, L. G., Constantino, M. J., Grosse, & Holtforth, M. (2006). The working alliance: Where are we and where should we go? *Psychotherapy: Theory, Research, Practice, Training, 43*(3), 271–279.

Consoli, A. J., Kim, B. S. K., & Meyer, D. M. (2008). Research and theory: Counselors' values profile: Implications for counseling ethnic minority clients. *Counseling and Values, 52,* 181–197.

Corey, G., Schneider-Corey, M., & Callanan, P. (2007). *Issues and ethics in the helping professions* (8th ed.). Belmont, CA: Brooks/Cole.

Council for Accreditation of Counseling and Related Educational Programs (2009). *CACREP accreditation manual.* Alexandria, VA: Author.

Davis, T. E., & Osborn, C. J. (2000). *The solution-focused school counselor: Shaping profes practice.* Philadelphia: Taylor & Francis.

DiClemente, C. C., Prochaska, J. O., & Gibertini, M. (1985). Self-efficacy and the stages change of smoking. *Cognitive Therapy and Research, 9*(2), 181–200.

Egan, G. (2007). *The skilled helper* (8th ed.). Boston: Allyn & Bacon.

Egan, G. (2010). *The skilled helper* (9th ed.). Boston: Allyn & Bacon.

Eells, T. D. (Ed.). (1997). *Handbook of psychotherapy case formulation.* New York: Guilford Press.

Eells, T. D. (2002). Formulation. In M. Hersen & W. Sledge (Eds.), *The encyclopedia of psycho-therapy* (pp. 815–822). New York: Academic Press.

Elliott, R. (1979). How clients perceive helper behaviors. *Journal of Counseling Psychology, 26,* 285–294.

Fuller, F., & Hill, C. E. (1985). Counselor and helpee perceptions of counselor intentions in relation to outcome in a single counseling session. *Journal of Counseling Psychology, 32,* 329–338.

Gim, R. H., Atkinson, D. R., & Kim, S. J. (1991). Asian American acculturation, counselor ethnicity and cultural sensitivity, and ratings of counselors. *Journal of Counseling Psychology, 38,* 1–6.

Gladding, S. T. (2001). *The counseling dictionary.* Upper Saddle River, NJ: Prentice Hall.

Gorski, T. T., & Miller, M. (1982). Counseling for relapse prevention. Independence, MO: Independence Press.

Hill, C. E., & O'Grady, K. E. (1985). List of therapist intentions illustrated in a case study and with therapists of varying theoretical orientations. *Journal of Counseling Psychology, 32*(1), 3–22.

Ivey, A. E. (1994). *Intentional interviewing in counseling* (3rd ed.), Pacific Grove, CA: Brooks/Cole.

Ivey, A. E., & Authier, J. (1978) Microcounseling: Innovations in interviewing, counseling, psycho-therapy, and psychoeducation (2nd ed.). Oxford, UK: Charles C Thomas.

Ivey, A. E., & Bradford-Ivey, M. (2006). *Intentional interviewing and counseling: Facilitating client development in a multicultural environment* (6th ed.). San Francisco: Brooks/Cole.

Ivey, A. E., Ivey, M. B., & Zalaquett, C. P. (2010). *Intentional interviewing & counseling* (7th ed.). Belmont, CA: Brooks/Cole.

Ivey, A. E., & Rollin, S. A. (1972). A behavioral objective curriculum in human relations: A com-mitment to intentionality. *Journal of Teacher Education, 23*(2), 16–165.

Jennings, L., & Skovholt, T. M. (1999). The cognitive, emotional, and relational characteristics of master therapists. *Journal of Counseling Psychology, 46*(1), 3–11.

Kelley, S. D., Bickman, L., & Norwood, E. (2010). Evidence-based treatments and common factors in youth psychotherapy. In B. L. Duncan, S. D. Miller, B. E. Wampold, & M. A. Hubble (Eds.), *The heart and soul of change: Delivering what works in therapy* (2nd ed., pp. 325–355). Washington, DC: American Psychological Association.

Kivlighan, D. M. (1990). Relation between counselors' use of intentions and clients' perception of working alliance. *Journal of Counseling Psychology, 37,* 27–32.

Lambert, M. J., & Barley, D. E. (2001). Research summary on the therapeutic relationship and psy-chotherapy outcome. *Psychotherapy: Theory, Research, Practice, Training, 38*(4), 357–361.

Landreth, G. (2002). *Play therapy: The art of the relationship* (2nd ed.). New York: Brunner-Routledge.

McConnaughy, E. A., DiClemente, C. C., Prochaska, J. O., & Velicer, W. F. (1989). Stages of change in psychotherapy: A follow-up report. *Psychotherapy: Theory, Research, Practice, Training, 26*(4), 494–503.

McConnaughy, E. A., Prochaska, J. O., & Velicer, W. F. (1983). Stages of change in psychotherapy: Measurement and sample profiles. *Psychotherapy: Theory, Research, Practice, Training, 20,* 368–375.

Miller, M. J. (1997). Counselor intentionality: Implications for the training of beginning counselors. *Counseling and Values, 41*(3), 194–203.

Newman, C. F. (1994). Understanding client resistance: Methods for enhancing motivation to change. *Cognitive and Behavioral Practice, 1,* 47–69.

Pope, B. (1979). *The mental health interview.* New York: Pergamon.

Prochaska, J. O. (1991). Prescribing to the stage and level of phobic patients. *Psychotherapy: Theory, Research, Practice, Training, 28*(3), 463–468.

Prochaska, J. O., & DiClemente, C. C. (1992). The transtheoretical approach. In J. C. Norcross & M. R. Goldfried (Eds.), *Handbook of psychotherapy integration* (pp. 300–334). New York: Basic Books.

Prochaska, J. O., DiClemente, C., & Norcross, J. (1992). In search of how people change: Applications to addictive behaviors. *American Psychologist, 47,* 1102–1114.

Prochaska, J. O., & Norcross, J. C. (1994). *Systems of psychotherapy: A transtheoretical analysis* (3rd ed.). Pacific Grove, CA: Brooks/Cole.

Prochaska, J. O., & Velicer, W. (1997). The transtheoretical model of health behavior change. *American Journal of Health Promotion, 12,* 38–48.

Purkey, W. W., & Schmidt, J. J. (1987). *The inviting relationship: An expanded perspective for professional counseling.* Englewood Cliffs, NJ: Prentice Hall.

Redfield, R., Linton, R., & Herskovits, M. (1936). Memorandum on the study of acculturation. *American Anthropologist, 37,* 149–152.

Rogers, S., & Evans, J. (2006). *Playing the game? Exploring role play from children's perspectives.* Philadelphia: Taylor & Francis.

Schmidt, J. J. (1984). Counselor intentionality: An emerging view of process and performance. *Journal of Counseling Psychology, 31,* 383–386.

Selekman, M. D. (2010). Collaborative strengths-based brief therapy with self-injuring adolescents and their families. *Prevention Researcher, 17*(1), 18–20.

Shaw, B. F., & Dobson, K. S. (1988). Competency judgments in the training and evaluation of psychotherapists. *Journal of Consulting & Clinical Psychology, 56,* 666–672.

Sim, K., Gwee, K. P., & Bateman, A. (2005). Case formulation in psychotherapy: Revitalizing its usefulness as a clinical tool. *Academic Psychiatry, 29,* 289–292.

Srebalus, D. J., & Brown, D. (2001). *A guide to the helping professions.* Needham Heights, MA: Allyn & Bacon.

Sue, D. W., & Sue, D. (2008). *Counseling the culturally diverse: Theory and practice* (5th ed.). Hoboken, NJ: John Wiley & Sons.

Terrell, F., & Terrell, S. L. (1981). An inventory to measure cultural mistrust among Blacks. *Western Journal of Black Studies, 5,* 180–184.

Walitzer, K. S., Dermen, K. H., & Conners, G. J. (1999). Strategies for preparing clients for treatment: A review. *Behavior Modification, 23*(1), 129–151.

Watson, J. C. (2006). Addressing client resistance: Recognizing and processing in-session occurrences. *VISTAS 2006 online.* Retrieved from http://counselingoutfitters.com/Watson.htm

Zhang, N., & Burkard, A. W. (2008). Client and counselor discussions of racial and ethnic differences in counseling: An exploratory investigation. *Journal of Multicultural Counseling and Development, 36*(2), 77–87.

Part II

The Elements and Dynamics of Counseling

Part II reviews and illustrates the dynamic of the counseling process along with the elements of this process. The elements of the counseling process and dynamic presented within the chapters include: the counseling relationship, client issues, goal setting, counseling interventions, accountability, and professional identity. Chapter 3 explores the counseling relationship and the skills necessary to the development and maintenance of the counseling relationship, and the concept of working alliance is presented and discussed in detail. Chapter 4 deals with the identification of the skills necessary to facilitate client disclosure and understanding of the issues a client brings to counseling. This chapter also discusses strategies on how to help clients move from their current situation to their desired situation. Listening, attending, and communication skills necessary to make this process effective are included. Chapter 5 focuses on the process and value of goal setting. The rationale of goal setting is presented and the characteristics of effective goals are illustrated. In addition, challenges and considerations of setting effective goals are reviewed. Chapter 6 covers the process of helping clients move from their current state of concern to what each client desires as a preferred state. The major elements in this process include intervention planning, the use of theory and research to guide the intervention planning, goal achievement, and counselor competence to successful intervention. The chapter also outlines an *atheoretical* model of change. Chapter 7 highlights the ethical mandate and practical value of employing assessment and measures of accountability in counseling. Finally, in Chapter 8, professional identity unfolds. Four major components are included: (1) the reason to establish a professional identity, (2) the elements contributing to professional identity, (3) the assessment of the counselor's unfolding professional identity, and (4) the continuing development of the counselor's professional identity.

Chapter 3

The Counseling Relationship

A Unique Social Encounter

Is helping what you do to another . . . or with the other?

INTRODUCTION

For many, the thought of helping another is envisioned as a process of doing something for or to another person as would be the case of a neighbor lending a hand with a fallen tree or perhaps assisting another with pushing his car out of a snow drift. For the professional counselor, helping is not an act *done to* another person. Helping, when it takes form in counseling, is a shared process, in which a counselor and a client work together in facilitating the change desired (ACA, 2005, sec. A.1.c).

As a shared process, the nature and quality of the relationship between the counselor and the client influence its effectiveness. It is this counseling relationship and its uniqueness that serve as the focus of the current chapter.

This counseling relationship is neither ephemeral nor mystical but a social exchange that can be analyzed in concrete elements, which can be taught and employed by counselors-in-training. As such, the current chapter begins to outline the *what, why,* and *how* of this very unique relationship. Specifically, after reading this chapter you will be able to do the following:

- Describe the core elements found within a counseling relationship that make it a unique social encounter.
- Explain what is meant by working alliance.
- Describe the qualities of a counselor that support the creation and maintenance of a working alliance.

- Discuss the specific counselor communication skills that help create and maintain a working alliance.
- Describe strategies to be employed by counselors when working with the client who presents a challenge to the development and maintenance of the counseling relationship.

COUNSELING: MORE THAN A SOCIAL ENCOUNTER

The relationship between a counselor and a client or a helper and a helpee is unique among human encounters. The helping relationship is not just an artifact of two people coming together over a common concern, but rather it is one of the most important components found within the helping process and contributing to the success of its outcome.

Unlike other social encounters where the relationship serves as a medium or context within which the "work" is done, the relationship in counseling is more than the mere context of work; instead, it *is* an essential part of the work being done (Norcross & Wampold, 2011). For example, while the bedside manner of a physician is valuable in creating conditions in which the medicine or the cure can be delivered, the bedside manner is typically not considered to be the medicine. Similarly, in counseling, the unique quality of the helping relationship has been demonstrated to be an active and valuable contributor to the helping outcome (e.g., Martin, Garske, & Davis, 2000; Norcross, 2002; Zuroff & Blatt, 2006). The relationship between the counselor and the client is a hub of communications and "the foundation of the therapeutic enterprise" (Teyber, 1997, p. 16).

The Counseling Relationship: Intentionally Created and Purposively Directed

Professional helping found between a counselor and a client involves a unique form of conversation or dialogue. This dialogue is unique in that it is focused upon the concerns, wishes, wants, and experiences of just one member, the client. In this dialogue, the client explores difficult situations, missed opportunities, uncertain feelings, or challenging choices with the counselor. Such disclosure and personal explorations require that the client feels safe and comfortable with the counselor and the counseling setting (Brammer & MacDonald, 1999). Clearly, without the client's honest, open disclosure and willing receptiveness to the feedback from the counselor little change could be expected. It is in hopes that the counselor intentionally creates the counseling relationship in which conditions are developed and maintained to support such open dialogue.

Setting the Stage

The conditions of *relationship building* begin with the initial greeting. For clients entering counseling for the first time, questions and concerns regarding the person of the counselor and the nature of the process of counseling can be quite anxiety provoking. It is important that the counselor initiate steps to make sure that both the physical and social context are ones that ease the client's initial anxieties and concerns.

Counselors, for example, are aware that the physical setting plays an important role in the creation of the expectations of privacy, confidentiality, and even emotional intimacy. As such, it is important, when possible, to engage with the client in a setting that is comfortable, free from interruption, and guarantees the needed privacy. But the influence of physical setting to both the sense of comfort and safety for the client and the progress of the interaction goes beyond providing for confidentiality and privacy. The appearance, layout, and things a counselor places within the office affect the client and the counseling dynamic. Factors such as room temperature, lighting, displays on the walls, and furniture arrangement can impact the client and the counseling dynamic. For example, while studying the effects of lighting and decoration on client's self-disclosure, Miwa and Hanyu (2006) found that dim lighting worked best for most clients. As for décor, such as pictures and other forms of decorations, the rule of thumb is for décor to reflect the professional nature of the counselor and counseling. Professional licenses, degree certificates, and honors or award plaques of counseling practice may be displayed on the walls to demonstrate qualifications so as to gain trustworthiness of clients and thereafter influence the client change (Heppner & Dixon, 1981; Rothmeier & Dixon, 1980).

In addition to decorations, the type and arrangement of the furniture within the office can also affect the relationship of counselor and client. For comfort, the chairs selected should reflect the counselor's view on equality of counselor and client. If the counselor's chair is bigger, it may signal an elevated status or power for the counselor and prove intimidating for the client. Finally, one of the most overlooked aspects of interpersonal communication is the use of distance—the arrangement of physical space surrounding the people that occupy that space. The proximity of people to one another when they interact and the configuration of work areas send a message that affects people in different ways. Because different individuals within and between cultures seem to define the use of physical space differently, it may be useful for the counselor to allow the client to choose where to sit in the office and then sit down and ask the client for sitting-distance adjustment.

In addition to creating the physical environment conducive to the formation and maintenance of this unique relationship, the counselor needs to establish the social conditions necessary for supporting the process in which the client and counselor are about to engage. The creation of this psychological environment begins with the very first greeting from the counselor to the client. Some may ask what difference it can make when you say hello to someone at the first time meeting. In casual social interaction, it may have little effect on individuals' later interaction, but in counseling the first greeting to a client from a counselor can be significant because of client cultural difference and psychological experience, as initially discussed in Chapter 2. For example, it may not be appropriate for a male counselor to shake hands with a female client who practices the traditional Asian culture or Middle Eastern culture because handshaking between men and women is forbidden in such cultures.

Case Illustration 1.4, To Shake or Not to Shake, in Chapter 1 is a perfect example of clients with psychological issues who may not feel comfortable being touched. The counselor, at the very first meeting, attempted to reach out to shake his client's hand but immediately noticed that his client was very nervous, making no eye contact and the handkerchief held in his right hand. His instant reflection was therefore that his client may be very anxious, feeling uncomfortable with his outreached hand and his invitation to shake. To avoid making his client uncomfortable, he made a gentle sweeping motion pointing away from the client toward the couch.

But as noted previously, counseling is not just a social encounter, governed by the norms or mores of a culture. To create a safe and comfortable environment for clients to change, counselors need to not only greet the client and establish a warm, accepting environment but also set the conditions of counseling and educate or *enculturate* the client into the rules, roles, and responsibilities of counseling. As such, counselors will inform the clients about some of the major characteristics of counseling, which may include the distinction between counseling and typical social encounters, the defining of the counselor role, the client role, confidentiality, the agency rules, and the proceedings in the counseling process.

One major topic at the very first counseling session may include counselor self-introduction. This happens first because in later sessions counselors may not have any chance to tell their clients about themselves except some necessary and appropriate self-disclosures that are purely therapeutic in purpose. The content of the self-introduction can be the counselor's professional identity such as degree(s) and license obtained, professional training, and counseling experiences. Some counselors may even ask their clients if the clients have any questions for them. The counselors may use their clinical judgment to keep the self-introduction short in length and within a limited amount of time.

Clients unfamiliar with counseling may enter the relationship with questions and concerns about what is expected, what is allowed, and what will most likely transpire within this counseling relationship and dynamic. Research has demonstrated that clients' expectations can affect many of the important aspects of counseling including the degree to which the client will disclose and the nature of those disclosures (e.g., Barich, 2002). Clients who, for example, are unsure about the degree to which the information shared will be held in confidence may be quite selective in their disclosures. So the concept of confidentiality and its role as an element of ethical practice are shared during the first session, and such sharing of confidentiality with clients as a critical point will be highlighted throughout the counseling relationship.

While the specifics of the type of additional information shared may vary as a function of the setting (e.g., school, private practice, clinic); client (e.g., age, competence); or nature of the presenting concern (e.g., suicidal risk, drugs/alcohol), what is needed in all counseling situations is for the counselor to provide enough information about the nature of the relationship in which the client is soon to be engaged so that the client can provide *informed consent.* This process will be developed further in upcoming chapters.

This is not only a practical step in facilitating the client's engagement in the counseling process but it is an ethical requirement and in many states a legal mandate.

The American Counseling Association's (2005) *Code of Ethics,* for example, states:

> Clients have the freedom to choose whether to enter into or remain in a counseling relationship and need adequate information about the counseling process and the counselor. Counselors have an obligation to review in writing and verbally with clients the rights and responsibilities of both the counselor and the client. Informed consent is an ongoing part of the counseling process, and counselors appropriately document discussions of informed consent throughout the counseling relationship. (sec. A.2.a)

The types of information required for such informed consent is found in Table 3.1. This information, while verbally explained to the client, may also be placed in writing and presented to the client as a reference.

Table 3.1   American Counseling Association (ACA) *Code of Ethics* (2005)

Section A: The Counseling Relationship

A.2.a. Informed Consent

Clients have the freedom to choose whether to enter into or remain in a counseling relationship and need adequate information about the counseling process and the counselor. Counselors have an obligation to review in writing and verbally with clients the rights and responsibilities of both the counselor and the client. Informed consent is an ongoing part of the counseling process, and counselors appropriately document discussions of informed consent throughout the counseling relationship.

A.2.b. Types of Information Needed

Counselors explicitly explain to clients the nature of all services provided. They inform clients about issues such as, but not limited to, the following: the purposes, goals, techniques, procedures, limitations, potential risks, and benefits of services; the counselor's qualifications, credentials, and relevant experience; continuation of services upon the incapacitation or death of a counselor; and other pertinent information. Counselors take steps to ensure that clients understand the implications of diagnosis, the intended use of tests and reports, fees, and billing arrangements. Clients have the right to confidentiality and to be provided with an explanation of its limitations (including how supervisors and/or treatment team professionals are involved); to obtain clear information about their records; to participate in the ongoing counseling plans; and to refuse any services or modality change and to be advised of the consequences of such refusal.

Standard of Practice Two (SP-2): Disclosure to Clients. Counselors must adequately inform clients, preferably in writing, regarding the counseling process and counseling relationship at or before the time it begins and throughout the relationship.

This principle of educating the client to the uniqueness of the relationship and dynamic of counseling is so important that it should be applied even when the client may be too young to provide legal consent. In this situation, the counselor should explain the nature of the relationship, especially around the issues of boundaries and confidentiality, and seek to gain the client's assent.

Assent is a term used to express willingness to participate in counseling by persons who are by definition too young to give informed consent but who are old enough to understand the process in which they are about to engage. Assent by itself is not sufficient, however. If assent is given, informed consent must still be obtained from the subject's parent or guardian.

THE *WHAT, WHY* AND *HOW* OF A WORKING ALLIANCE

Once the counselor explains, and the client understands, the general structure of the counseling relationship and dynamic, the counselor needs to begin to move the focus of the relationship to the client and the client's concerns. The counselor employs specific communication skills to move the relationship from the arena of a simple social exchange to one that now fosters the client's disclosure and the facilitation of the counselor's understanding of the client's issues of concern, goals, and resources.

The *What:* Characteristics of a Working Alliance

For the work of counseling to prove effective, the counselor and client must engage in what has been termed a *working alliance.* This alliance is characterized by an honest give-and-take of information and the client's willingness to risk and become somewhat vulnerable when sharing personal information with the counselor. The goal in creating such a working alliance is for the client's concerns, in all their depth and breadth, to be shared and understood in order for meaningful and achievable goals to be established, and initial processes for attaining these goals identified and owned by both the counselor and client.

Although there is no one commonly agreed-upon definition of this working alliance, it is typically conceptualized as collaboration between an agent of change—the counselor—and the client (Horvath & Greenberg, 1994). Constantino and his colleagues (2002) defined the alliance as the " . . . interactive, collaborative elements of the relationship (i.e., therapist and client abilities to engage in the tasks of therapy and to agree on the targets of therapy) in the context of an affective bond or positive attachment" (p. 86). The working alliance is formed as a result of the development of an emotional, therapeutic bond between counselor and client, a shared commitment to mutually agreed-upon goals and the articulation of specific tasks that are employed as a means to achieve these goals (Bordin, 1979; Horvath & Bedi, 2002).

A careful consideration of the elements found within a working alliance reveals a number of important implications about this unique relationship (Hatcher & Barends, 2006). First, it must be noted that counseling is not simply the process of providing a friendly ear, a warm shoulder to cry on, and certainly not an opportunity to merely chat. Counseling is *purposive* in that the counselor engages the client in a collaborative, goal-directed exchange. Thus, those activities in which the counselor and client engage to identify the nature of the problem, to understand the factors creating and or contributing to its existence, and the steps that need to be taken to resolve the issue and move to a more desired state are more than fact-finding activities. They are activities that have as their foundation the intent of creating, maintaining, and employing the interpersonal relationship—this working alliance as a way of facilitating the achievement of a desired outcome. Counseling is not what a counselor does *to* a client, but it is what a counselor and client do together collaboratively. This is the essence of the working alliance.

The existence of this working alliance cannot be assumed simply because the client and counselor experience their relationship as comfortable or "nice." Granted while it is important that both counselor and client feel comfortable and safe within the relationship, the reality is that counseling can at times be discomforting. It is not unusual for the counselor and client to unearth painful memories or address difficult issues, and these can result in moments of distress and discomfort. However, even in these moments, the purposive nature of the alliance can be seen if the counselor and client share an understanding of the value of these discoveries and a belief that discussing and addressing these issues move them closer to their desired goal(s). The existence of a working alliance is thus measured not just by the client's experience of connectedness (while that is important) but also by the collaborative and purposive nature of the relationship.

The *Why:* Understanding the Value of and Need for a Working Alliance

As noted previously, the creation and maintenance of a helping relationship is not merely a nice idea; rather, the development and maintenance of a helping relationship is a valuable contributor to the outcome of the helping process. The impact of a therapeutic relationship on the outcome of counseling has been examined extensively in the past few decades.

Research has consistently found a significant relationship between the working alliance in therapy or counseling and the quality of the helping process and outcome of that helping (Eames & Roth, 2000; Horvath & Greenberg, 1989, 1994; Horvath & Symonds, 1991; Mallinckrodt, 2000; Martin et al., 2000; Norcross, 2002; Zuroff & Blatt, 2006). Over 1,000 studies have demonstrated that a positive working alliance is one of the best predictors of counseling outcome (Orlinsky, Rønnestad, & Willutzki, 2004). In fact, the working alliance has been found to be one of the strongest predictors of positive outcome to counseling or therapy, regardless of the type of therapy used (Horvath, 2001; Horvath & Luborsky, 1993). Simply put, therapists and counselors who form stronger alliances with their clients generally demonstrate better therapeutic outcomes (Baldwin, Wampold, & Imel, 2007).

Clearly, this research supports the notion that the creation and maintenance of a helping relationship—a working alliance—is a valuable and needed element in the helping process and the achievement of the desired helping outcomes. Thus, it is safe to assume that regardless of the presenting concern or even the counselor's model or approach, the establishment and maintenance of a positive bond and a strong level of collaboration with clients is essential to the counseling outcome (Castonguay et al., 2006).

The *How:* Counselor Disposition and Skills Necessary for Creating and Maintaining a Working Alliance

Given the research demonstrating the value of the working alliance to the counseling process and outcome (e.g., Martin et al., 2000; Norcross, 2002; Zuroff & Blatt, 2006) it is incumbent on all counselors to understand and engage those factors that contribute to the creation and maintenance of a working alliance. The good news for those counselors-in-training is that the specific knowledge and skills needed to foster a working alliance can be learned, and their effective use improved with practice and supervision (Crits-Christoph, Connolly Gibbons, Narducci, Schamberger, & Gallop, 2005; Grawe, Caspar, & Ambühl, 1990).

In a review of 25 mostly small studies and single case analyses on the topic of therapist behaviors designed to foster the alliance, Ackerman and Hilsenroth (2003) concluded that when the therapist conveys a sense of being trustworthy, affirming, flexible, interested, alert, relaxed, confident, respectful, and is more experienced and communicates clearly, a more positive alliance is present. These authors and others (i.e., Ackerman & Hilsenroth, 2003; Hilsenroth, Peters, & Ackerman, 2004; Principe, Marci, Glick, & Ablon, 2006) found counselors who allow the client to initiate discussion of salient themes, facilitate client affect and experience, explore uncomfortable feelings, clarify sources of distress, as well as explore in-session process and affect between counselor and client also facilitate the development of the working alliance. In addition to these conditions, research has identified a number of counselor attitudes and dispositions, which once communicated to the client, facilitate the development of a working relationship.

Counselor Attitudes and Dispositions Supporting a Working Alliance

It is clear that counselors who convey *understanding, competence, warmth, respect,* and *nonjudgment* are able to develop effective working alliances (Bachelor, 1995; Mohl, Martinez, Ticknor, Huang, & Cordell, 1991; Principe et al., 2006; Sexton, Littauer, Sexton, & Tommeras, 2005; Tryon, 1990). Conversely, counselors who appear disengaged, or who provide general, superficial advice, or simply remain too silent or when sharing, share in manner devoid of emotional content, seem to reduce the strength of the counseling relationship (Sexton et al., 2005). This is probably not news to any person who upon sharing an issue of significant concern received a response such as "oh that's a shame; it will all work out." While the respondent's intention may have been noble, the response was anything but helpful or supportive. Under these conditions the desire to continue to disclose and work together will most likely diminish.

Starting with the early experience of Carl Rogers (1951,1957), the conditions of counselor genuineness, accurate empathic understanding, and unconditional positive regard have been upheld within the professions as keystones to the development and maintenance of a working alliance (see Ackerman & Hilsenroth, 2003). As such, these conditions are discussed in some detail as follows.

Genuineness. According to Rogers (1951), the first and foremost quality that the counselor must possess in order to facilitate change in a client is congruence or genuineness/realness. This means that counselors must be genuine and authentic in the counseling process and any incongruence between their words and behaviors will undermine the trust from their clients. The condition of congruence or genuineness and authenticity does not suggest that counselors must always disclose everything about themselves to their clients but convey their experiences and feelings truthfully whenever it is necessary and appropriate.

When a professional helper is genuine, owning her honest thoughts and feelings, true contact becomes possible between the helper and her client (Moursund & Kenny, 2002). Entering the counseling process as a real person without a front or façade, the counselor will be aware of his feelings and experiences, and will be able to appropriately share these in ways that increase his effectiveness (Smith, 1997, 2004).

While the concept of genuineness may be clear and relatively simple to understand, embodying true genuineness within our interactions with our clients is not always so simple, nor easy, especially when first starting out in the profession. It is not unusual to become concerned about doing it the right way, or being sure that we put our best image forward while we are interacting with a client, and thus we may find ourselves stepping into the role or playing to the image of counselor. Perhaps as part of your training you have had the opportunity to videotape yourself in interaction with a "volunteer" client. Upon watching the interaction, did you find yourself asking, "who was that person?" Perhaps as you engaged with this client, you found yourself putting on the role of counselor at the expense of being the real, authentic, and genuine you. Exercise 3.1 is provided to help you to more fully understand this concept (and experience) of genuineness.

Unconditional Positive Regard. The second condition that the counselor must retain and convey to the client is unconditional positive regard. This characteristic reflects the counselor's deep nonevaluative respect for the client's thoughts, feelings, wishes, and potential. The counselor who experiences unconditional positive regard for a client is truly able to look beyond the conditions of the client such as physical

Exercise 3.1

TO BE REAL OR UNREAL . . . THAT'S THE QUESTION

Directions: This exercise requires you to videotape or taperecord (video is preferable) an intake with a classmate or colleague who will volunteer to serve as a client. The goal is for you to increase your awareness of genuineness as it "looks" on you.

Part I: For the first part of this exercise, review the initial 10 or 15 minutes of the session with the sound turned off. Your task is to simply note your body language and respond to the following:

- Do you appear relaxed?
- Do you seem to be truly interested and attentive to the client?
- Do you notice any behavioral indications that you may be nervous and distracted?
- If you were to contrast your behavior in this video to what you imagine you look like having a meaningful, informal discussion with a friend, would there be significant differences in style? If so, what?
- When you observe your behavior, does it appear to be the "natural" you or the you that has put on the hat and role of the counselor?

Part II: For the remainder of the session, turn the sound back on. As you listen, the focus should be on contrasting what you are saying with what you may remember you were thinking or feeling at the moment. Reflect on the following:

- Can you identify moments when your words were neither a complete nor accurate reflection of your thoughts or your feelings at that particular moment?
- Is there evidence in your communication that you may be responding more to the internal message of "doing it right" and truly engaging with the client in that specific moment?
- Do the words selected, the tone employed, even the subtle inflections in your voice reflect that which is genuinely you and your style of communication?

Part III: Finally, for Part III, invite the client (friend volunteering) to view the videotape with you. Your task is:

- Have the client (friend) identify specific incidents of your interaction that seemed artificial—less than genuine—or simply not you.

appearance, social economic status, levels of demonstrated intelligence, or even the socially appropriateness of her behavior to see and value the person beneath these conditions. This unconditional positive regard means that there are no conditions on acceptance by the counselor. There is no "I will value you if you do this or that, or be this or that way."

Perhaps one way this condition can be made real is to ask you to imagine an encounter with a newborn baby. A newborn comes into this world without any of the trappings—the conditions—that we typically value. Newborns have no money, no formal education, and certainly do not occupy careers that are prestigious. They do not have designer clothes, expensive cars, or hillside houses. And often these newborns fail to match the glamour magazines' standards for beauty. They are absent of the conditions that often serve as the bases for positively valuing others and yet they elicit our unconditional love. They are valued—prized just as they are, as fellow human beings. This is the experience of unconditional positive regard.

In exhibiting unconditional positive regard, the counselor demonstrates genuine care and respect for the client as a person and trusts the client. This does not mean that the counselor must feel positively about all client actions. The focus is on the fact that the counselor accepts, without any overt or covert evaluation or judgment, the client with all his feelings, thoughts, and behaviors. For example, the client who gives clear evidence of acting in destructive ways towards his spouse will still be held in value and respected by the counselor as a person—a human being—who is clearly struggling with his life and is need of support. That does not mean that the counselor won't take steps to protect the spouse and thus demonstrate the belief that such actions are unacceptable, but it will be clear that it is the actions and not the person of the client that is unacceptable. In other words, the counselor respects the client and unconditionally accepts the client as who he is even when disapproving of his actions.

As indicated by Rogers (1957), "The greater the degree of caring, prizing, accepting, and valuing of the client in a non-possessive way, the greater the chance that therapy will be successful" (as cited in Corey, 2005, p. 173). And while research such as that by Farber and Lane (2002) reports that "the therapist's ability to provide positive regard seems to be significantly associated with therapeutic success . . ." (p. 191), our ability to actually exhibit such unconditional positive regard for our clients is not always an easy thing to do.

It is obvious that we are and have been bombarded by market and advertising experts who have tried to convince us that one becomes more valuable in the right clothes, driving the latest car, and smelling like a star in Hollywood. The messages are clear—being valued, being prized is a function of conditions. Sadly, these conditions often extend to things other than possessions—including body type, skin color, and cultural beliefs. Counselors are not immune to such media messaging and if we assimilate the message and the value implied, we will find it difficult to truly experience and convey unconditional positive regard for our clients. Exercise 3.2 provides a way to help you identify those factors that could challenge your ability to exhibit unconditional positive regard.

Exercise 3.2

CHALLENGES TO UNCONDITIONALLY PRIZING ANOTHER

Looking beyond a person's conditions of life—be they the possessions they have or their physical and cultural characteristics and traits—is not an easy thing to do.

Directions: For each of the following, identify the value you may typically assign to the characteristic and identify how that may affect your expectations of a client with that characteristic and your ability to feel and express unconditional positive regard.

Client Condition	Personally Held Value Regarding That Characteristic	Possible Challenge to Expression of Unconditional Positive Regard
Example: A client who is morbidly obese	People that are obese are over indulgent and show poor control.	Difficulty placing self in the client's shoes and valuing that they are struggling with life, feel like holding them to blame for their situation.
Alcohol addiction	_____ _____ _____	_____ _____ _____
Obstinate and defiant child	_____ _____ _____	_____ _____ _____

(Continued)

(Continued)

Client Condition	Personally Held Value Regarding That Characteristic	Possible Challenge to Expression of Unconditional Positive Regard
Abusive person	_____ _____ _____	_____ _____ _____
A resistant client who was mandated to come to counseling	_____ _____ _____	_____ _____ _____
A person who is self-mutilating	_____ _____ _____	_____ _____ _____
(other conditions that may arouse a reaction in you)	_____ _____	_____ _____
(other)	_____	_____

Empathy. Long considered a cornerstone of the therapeutic encounter, empathy is often described as an experiential attunement or resonance to the other, a direct and visceral understanding of the patient's emotional state and difficulties (Aragno, 2008; Goldman, 2006; Stueber, 2006). Empathic understanding refers to the counselor's ability to perceive the client's world precisely from the client's perspective and communicate such understanding to the client. For counselors experiencing empathy, it is as if they have exited their own personal perception of the moment and now perceive the world through the lived experience of the client.

Rogers (1951) described empathy as ". . . an accurate, empathic understanding of the client's world as seen from the inside . . ." (p. 348). It is the counselor's ability to temporarily suspend her own point of reference and take on the experienced reality and point of view of the client as if she was the client. The saying that may best describe the first part of this concept of empathy is the ability to *truly walk in another's shoes.*

Imagine the benefits to be accrued by a counselor who attempts to truly understand the client's story—to be able to step into that client's shoes, that perspective and experience the world, the story, from that perspective. Empathy allows a counselor to understand the full meaning of the words employed, the style of delivery, even that which is unspoken yet implied. Empathy allows a counselor to accurately understand the client and the client's story.

It is important here to distinguish *empathy* from sympathy. With sympathy, we take our experience and filter the story shared by another person through that experience thus relating how we would encounter the other person's situation from our life position and perspective. So, hearing that a friend is grieving the loss of a loved one, you may tap your own memory of the pain and anxiety that accompanied the loss of your own loved one and assume that your friend is experiencing something of the same. This is sympathy, a feeling for someone.

Achieving empathic understanding is not easy. It is not a simple game and it is not something that should be approached as a tactic. Opening oneself to the message of another in such a way as to fully comprehend the value and the meaning of that message is an awesome gift and should be respected. As Carkhuff and Berenson (1967) noted, the counselor who is able to be truly open and attending to the client's message and able to step into that client's lived reality will soon experience levels of feelings and depths of meaning that were not initially presented in the client's original communication. It is in sharing this depth of understanding that strengthens the bond of counselor and client.

Counselor Skills of Communicating Genuineness, Nonjudgment, and Empathic Understanding

In order for the counselor's genuineness, unconditional positive regard, and empathic understanding to be effective in creating the conditions for a working alliance, these attitudes—these dispositions—must be communicated to the client. It is with this in mind that counselors engage in the processes of *attending* to the client and then actively reflect their understanding of the messages that the client is attempting to convey. The counselor's ability to attend to and accurately understand the client's message can be facilitated by the counselor assuming an attending posture and employing reflections of content and feelings.

Attending Posture

Following their extensive literature review Hill and O'Brien (1999) concluded: ". . . smiling, a body orientation directly facing the client, a forward trunk lean, both horizontal and vertical arm movements and a median distance of about 55 inches between the helper and the client are all generally helpful nonverbal behaviors" (p. 99). Research suggests adopting this body posture not only prepares the counselor to receive the information about to be shared but conveys to the client that the counselor is fully attentive and ready to receive the client's disclosures and thus facilitates disclosure (see Daniels & Ivey, 2007 for review). One formulation of this facilitating body posture was offered by Egan (2009) and is represented with the acronym SOLER (face the client Square, adopt an Open posture, Lean toward the other, maintain good Eye contact, try to be relatively Relaxed when presenting all these behaviors).

The SOLER posture will help the counselor become more receptive of the client's message and be more accepted by the client. Sitting squarely in front of the client, while leaning slightly forward and maintaining comfortable and appropriate eye contact, not only engages all of the counselor's channels for information reception but also helps to narrow the band of potential interference.

As with most "rules" of counseling, a counselor's body position should not be assumed if it is either uncomfortable, unnatural, or fails to reflect the unique cultural and individual characteristics of the client. For example, while it is generally agreed that a counselor should sit directly in front of the client (i.e., squarely), such a directive may certainly be modified while working with a young child and play materials. Similarly, while a slight lean forward may nonverbally convey the message that the counselor is eager to hear what the client wishes to share, counselors need to be observant of the client's reaction to such forward leaning; when it is clear that this behavior is received as intrusive, perhaps even threatening, an appropriate adjustment should be made. Further, eye contact allows for the reception of many subtle nonverbal messages in some cultures, for example, in Hispanic, Asian, Middle Eastern, and Native American cultures eye contact may mean disrespectful or rude, and lack of eye contact may not mean that a person is not paying attention.

In addition to increasing one's ability to attend by way of employing a facilitative body posture, it is also important for counselors to engage in processes that maintain their focus on the client's disclosure. This maintenance of attention and focus and the increased assurance of accurately understanding the client's disclosures can be facilitated by the use of techniques of active listening and reflection of content and feeling.

Employing Reflection

Reflection, as used here, refers to the ability of the counselor to receive and process the content and feeling of the explicit and implied message sent by the client and then represent these messages, as received, to the client in order to check their accuracy. Counselors engaging in reflection will not only increase their understanding of a client's intended message, but will demonstrate that they are truly attentive and interested in understanding what it is the client wishes to convey. To be truly open and receptive to the client's messages and to be able to accurately reflect those messages requires the counselor to suspend judgment and accept the client perspective. The use of active listening and reflection will not only assist the counselor in gathering and accurately understanding that which is conveyed by the client, but will also encourage the client to disclose with greater depth. It is often through this movement toward greater depth of disclosure, and the reflections of those disclosures, that clients come to an awareness of issues and concerns which they had not previously recognized—issues that may be the real source of the current presenting complaint.

Reflection of Content. At a very basic level, reflection can take the form of the counselor's *paraphrasing* of the explicit content of the client's disclosure. The process of paraphrasing is not meant to be a test of memory wherein the counselor attempts to reflect each specific word or detail provided by the client. Rather, paraphrasing involves capturing the essence of what the client says, and then through counselor rephrasing, presenting that message back to the client for validation. When the counselor's paraphrase is on target, the client often recognizes the accuracy with a comment such as, "Yeah, that's it" or some other form of affirmation.

Too often, counselors-in-training attempt to "parrot" back the exact words of the client and in doing so often appear uncaring and nongenuine. The essence of reflection of content is that the counselor attempts to highlight the essence of the message, focusing on the significant persons involved, the actions occurring, and the outcome or consequences described.

The counselor employing reflection of content attempts to target the elements of the messages that have personal value to the client, rather than simply repeating all the words. Thus, a counselor who hears a client state, "I'm really worried that I am going to fail out of the program, having screwed up that assignment," would try to focus on the worry the client expresses rather than the assignment he apparently failed. As such, the reflection may be, "So the possibility of failing out of the program has you very worried?" rather than "So, you really screwed up the last assignment." When the counselor reflects the personal statements rather than impersonal ones, the client is more apt to stay at the personal level, exploring further aspects of his experience and thus improving his understanding of the situation. Case Illustration 3.1 provides examples of counselors reflecting different parts of the expressed message. The exercise also provides the counselors' goals for their specific reflection. As you read the examples of the reflections, consider how you as the client, upon hearing the reflection, may then respond. Would your response be in the direction the counselor desires?

It is helpful to remember that the goal of reflection such as that in Case Illustration 3.1 is to demonstrate understanding and respect for the client and the client's story. These reflections are meant to be an accurate reflection, in the counselor's own words, of the client's explicit message; they are *not* meant to be interpretations or alternative suggestions about what is truly meant. While this may sound easy, it is not always easy to resist interjecting some advice or one's own interpretation. Exercise 3.3 provides both an illustration of accurate reflection of content and the opportunity to practice this particular communicational skill.

Prior to engaging in the practice exercise, it is important to understand one point of caution. Often when learning how to employ reflection of content, counselors-in-training are taught to employ an opening phrase such as "What I hear you saying is . . ." Though we have also employed this convention (see Exercise 3.3), it is important to realize that such a formula, while beneficial for training, can be destructive to a genuine relationship with a client if used repetitively as if formulaic. The reflection of content by way of paraphrase needs to not only reflect the counselor's understanding of the client's message, but also do so using words that are genuine and natural to the counselor.

Reflecting Feelings. Communicating accurate understanding of the client's message should not be restricted to the objective details and content of that message. Counselors must also be attentive and responsive to the feelings that accompany the client's message. Listening to this emotional tone of the client's disclosures will allow the counselor to hear and understand the real import of the message being sent. Just as when listening to music, we find that the words convey the content of the song, whereas the melody carries the emotional tone of the music. It is also true for client disclosures.

The effective counselor will listen not just for words of emotion, such as *I am anxious, angry, sad,* and so forth, but for the subtle inflections, changes in pitch, and even the moments of hesitations and stammers as they may suggest feelings of sadness, fear, discouragement, or even joy and happiness. Carkhuff (1987) suggests that in order to identify what the client may be experiencing, counselors should ask themselves the *empathy question,* "How would I feel

CASE ILLUSTRATION 3.1

REFLECTION AS DIRECTION

The following exchanges provide examples of how a counselor has employed reflection as a means of highlighting a part of the client's disclosure that may be of importance to the client and worth pursuing in greater depth.

Janet (34 years old, recently divorced)

Janet: I know this is silly and I am wasting your time—time you could use with someone who really needs your help, but it just really threw me for a loop when I heard that he was dating someone new. I mean we have only been divorced for 6 months. I am not even interested in dating.

Counselor: Janet, I know you are saying this concern is silly—but it doesn't sound like you feel it is silly and that the news really had a pretty significant impact on you?

Counselor Reflection

I could have focused on the details of the ex's dating or even Janet's own statement regarding her interest in dating, but I felt that she was devaluing herself in declaring the issue was a waste of my time, so I wanted to pursue that issue of her value and importance of her current experience.

Robbie (11 years old, referred for failing)

Robbie: I don't really care. It's not a big deal. So I'm failing—who cares. Nobody cares about me so why should I care? Anyway history is stupid . . . I'll never need to know that stuff.

Counselor: Robbie, it sounds as if you feel that no one really cares about you?

Counselor Reflection

I think I heard Robbie's dismissal of history as a subject and his minimizing of his failing in that. These are all things we could pursue, but at the moment I thought the bigger issue which needed some further investigation was his message of having nobody really care about him.

Carlos (48 years old, recently suspended from work for coming to work drunk)

Carlos:	I don't get it. I've worked for the company almost 5 years, and haven't missed a day or been late or screwed up or anything else. I have never had an accident on route and I take care of my truck. I come to work one morning having had a beer— one lousy beer for breakfast—big deal and they suspend me until I get help. This is really unfair!
Counselor:	Carlos, so your view is that their suspending you for coming to work having had a beer for breakfast is unfair.

Counselor Reflection

While I could have focused on Carlos's successful work history or his sense of having experienced an injustice, I thought it was important to direct the discussion to the morning drinking and the reality tied to drinking and driving.

Exercise 3.3

REFLECTION OF CONTENT

Directions: For each of the following client disclosure you are to complete the following:

1. Identify the personal theme(s) or issue(s) being disclosed.

2. Rephrase this message using your own words, remembering it is the client's message you are attempting to reflect not interpret.

3. Write out your paraphrase.

It is helpful to share your response with a colleague or classmate and to ask how your reflection may have directed the next disclosure if he or she were the client.

Example

I damned near wet myself I was so nervous. I know I was prepared to give the presentation because I really know the stuff. I had great handouts and a PowerPoint. I practiced for days. I had it down pat but here I was standing there and I could feel my heart pounding, my mouth was dry, and I started to feel dizzy. I couldn't help think about what they were all thinking. I just know they are going to look at the loser; he is really a jerk.

Paraphrase: "So, Tom, if I understand what you are saying, this was a pretty anxious experience with your major concern being the possibility of being negatively evaluated by your audience—even the possibility that they may think that you are a loser?"

Client 1

So my mom is constantly on my case about this and that. I can't do a damn thing right. Nothing is good enough for her. I'm really sick and tired of being treated like a second-class citizen.

Paraphrase:_____

_____

_____

Client 2

What am I going to do? I'm failing every class. I don't have a job. I'm not sure how I am going to pay my rent and I sure as hell can't go back home. I mean really I'm 20 years old and I can't go back to mommy and daddy's boy. That would be such a loser move.

Paraphrase:_____

_____

_____

(Continued)

(Continued)

Client 3

She doesn't like me . . . she's always picking on me. The other kids in class can talk and goof around and they are never given punishment or sent to the principal. Why does she have to pick on me? What have I done? I can't stand it . . . nobody likes me.

Paraphrase:_____

_____

_____

Client 4

Yeah so okay—my wife is on my case, my boss thinks it's a good idea and even my parents, god bless them, are after me. Look everybody wants me to go to AA cause I drink a little bit. Hey I don't think it's a big deal—I know they do—but I've got it under control. Okay so I had my license suspended for DUI and my boss is threatening to suspend me cause I was found drinking on the job one time. One friggin' time!

Paraphrase:_____

_____

_____

if I were doing or experiencing these things?" Answering this question can help counselors better understand the client's feeling and even the intensity of that feeling. This information is what we wish to reflect to the helpee, as our *reflection of feelings.*

The ability of the counselor to reflect feelings, especially when those feelings could be labeled as negative, allow clients to feel completely heard and accepted with nonjudgment. This acceptance and understanding allow clients to feel supported in their struggle and may facilitate further explorations and disclosure around those feelings. If we return to the case illustrations previously presented we may be able to "hear" beyond the explicit content to the tune with which that content was delivered (see Case Illustration 3.2). Further, clearly such an exercise is artificial in the absence of actually hearing the client's tone, timber, inflection, and vocal quality, but with a little literary freedom and your imagination you may be able to discern the emotional quality of the message conveyed.

There is a significant caution to note when employing reflection of content and feeling. It is important to remember the purpose of this strategy. The purpose of

CASE ILLUSTRATION 3.2

HEARING THE WORDS AND MELODY

In Case Illustration 3.1, we saw how the counselor in each of the following case illustrations employed paraphrase of content to highlight parts of the client's message which were important to pursue. In the following illustration, we will see the same counselors including reflection of the feelings as a way of conveying their full understanding of the importance of the message being shared.

Janet (34 years old, recently divorced)

Janet:	I know this is silly and I am wasting your time—time you could use with someone who really needs your help, but it just really threw me for a loop when I heard that he was dating someone new. I mean we have only been divorced for 6 months. I am not even interested in dating.
Counselor:	Janet, I know you are saying this concern is silly, but it doesn't sound like you feel it is silly; in fact, listening to your voice as you say that it threw you for a loop suggests to me that this experience is and has been very upsetting.

Robbie (11 years old, referred for failing)

Robbie:	I don't really care. It's not a big deal. So I'm failing—who cares. Nobody cares about me so why should I care? Anyway history is stupid . . . I'll never need to know that stuff.
Counselor:	Robbie, I know you are saying that it's not a big deal and that you really don't care, yet the quiver in your voice suggests to me that you are really quite upset and worried about how things are going.

(Continued)

(Continued)

Carlos (48 years old, recently suspended from work for coming to work drunk)

Carlos: I don't get it. I've worked for the company almost 5 years. Haven't missed a day or been late or screwed up or anything else. I have never had an accident on route and I take care of my truck. I come to work one morning having had a beer—one lousy beer for breakfast—big deal and they suspend me until I get help. This is really unfair!

Counselor: Carlos, clearly you have had a good work record and while I know you are saying this is unfair, you sound as if you are somewhat embarrassed about the whole situation?

Exercise 3.4

ACCURATE REFLECTION OF FEELINGS

Directions: In Exercise 3.3, you provided paraphrases as reflections of the content of the client's disclosure, and you are now invited to revisit the client's message and attempt to accurately reflect the feelings conveyed. As noted in text, this is not an exercise in interpretation. Look for "feeling words," and given the constraint of printed material, identify phrases that most likely would have been delivered with emotional overlay. It would be helpful to share your responses with a colleague in order to check that you were not interrupting but merely reflecting.

Example

I damned near wet myself I was so nervous. I know I was prepared to give the presentation because I really know the stuff. I had great handouts and a PowerPoint. I practiced for days. I had it down pat but here I was standing there and I could feel my heart pounding, my mouth was dry, and I started to feel dizzy. I couldn't help think about what they were all thinking. I just know they are going look at the loser; he is really a jerk.

Reflection of feelings: "So, Tom it really seems that you were experiencing quite a bit of nervousness and anxiety at the time of your presentation."

Client 1

So my mom is constantly on my case about this and that. I can't do a damn thing right. Nothing is good enough for her. I'm really sick and tired of being treated like a second-class citizen.

Reflection of feelings: _____

_____

_____

Client 2

What am I going to do? I'm failing every class. I don't have a job. I'm not sure how I am going to pay my rent and I sure as hell can't go back home. I mean really I'm 20 years old and I can't go back to mommy and daddy's boy. That would be such a loser move.

Reflection of feelings: _____

_____

_____

Client 3

She doesn't like me...she's always picking on me. The other kids in class can talk and goof around and they are never given punishment or sent to the principal. Why does she have to pick on me? What have I done? I can't stand it . . . nobody likes me.

Reflection of feelings: _____

_____

_____

Client 4

Yeah so okay—my wife is on my case, my boss thinks it's a good idea and even my parents, god bless them, are after me. Look everybody wants me to go to AA cause I drink a little bit. Hey I don't think it's a big deal—I know they do—but I've got it under control. Okay so I had my license suspended for DUI and my boss is threatening to suspend me cause I was found drinking on the job one time. One friggin' time!

Reflection of feelings: _____

_____

_____

this and any of the communication techniques that are discussed is to increase the counselor's *understanding* of the client and the client's story and *to join with* the client in addressing the issues revealed. These are not tricks of counseling or things to *do* to the client. The value of reflection of content and feeling—as is true for each of the communications skills to be addressed in future chapters—is in its manifestation of a sincere, honest, accepting, nonjudgmental, and genuine desire of the counselor to be of help. Therefore, it is important to avoid each of the following pitfalls while employing reflection.

- *Stereotyped-Formulaic Responses.* Constantly repeating a phrase like "what I hear you saying is . . ." will eventually become a distraction to the client and may be seen as artificial and uncaring.
- *Parroting.* Simply echoing the last words spoken without evidence of understanding the meaning behind the words can be done mindlessly. If done in such a manner, the client can perceive it as nongenuine and uncaring.
- *Interpretations.* While there will be a time and place for ascribing meanings that go beyond that which was presented, in reflecting counselors need to demonstrate understanding the client's message and not share their interpretation of that message.
- *Pretending to Understand.* It is a reality that counselors can be distracted or lost even as they attempt to listen. Feigning understanding demonstrates not just a lack of attending but an uncaring, disrespectful, and dishonest approach to the client. It is better to simply admit that one was distracted and ask the client to repeat.
- *Extensive Reflection.* It is important to provide short, simple reflections highlighting the essential content and feelings of the client's disclosure. Providing long-winded, extensive reflections of every detail can prove distracting to the client and may break the rhythm and comfort of the client's disclosing.

Going Beyond the Explicit Message: Advanced Empathy

Truax and Carkhuff (1967) developed a scale that discriminated the various levels in which a counselor or therapist could exhibit empathy, as well as the other conditions of respect, genuineness, immediacy, concreteness, confrontation, and self-disclosure. In their empathy scale they identified five levels to which a counselor could exhibit empathy (see Table 3.2).

It would appear that what Truax and Carkhuff (1967) present at Level 3 is what has been presented here as accurate reflections of the explicit content and feeling of the client's message. However, if we look at Levels 4 and 5, we find the suggestion that the counselor—with increased empathy—can get in touch with implied

Table 3.2   Carkhuff's (1969) Discrimination Scale

Level 1

When the empathic response of the counselor does not attend to or detracts significantly from the affect or meaning expressed by the client, or does not attend to the affect or meaning, the rating is 1.0.

Level 2

Here the counselor responds to affect and meaning in such a way as to subtract noticeable affect from what the client expressed.

Level 3

A counselor responding here will reflect affect and meaning at a level that is interchangeable with the client's expression (verbal, nonverbal, or behavior).

Level 4

This is when the counselor's response to meaning and affect is noticeably deeper than the client expressed.

Level 5

This demonstrates a significantly deeper level of counselor response to the client's meaning and affect.

---

messages and thus reflects the feelings and content not specifically shared by the client. This level of reflections is what Egan (1994) characterized as *advanced empathy.*

As one becomes more deeply engaged with the client, it is not unusual to find meaning that goes well beyond that which is explicitly shared. Advanced empathy occurs when the counselor is able to move beyond the story being shared and truly step into the client's experience. With the perspective of each client as their own, counselors begin to understand the intentions, desires, or hidden meanings found behind the client's explicit message, even when these same intentions, desires, and meanings are unclear to the client.

For example, in the case of a person going through divorce, the client may express anger with his spouse, and the counselor acknowledges and reflects that anger. However, for the counselor who has connected more deeply and empathically with the client, the message of anger may be seen as a cover for the real underlying feelings of sadness and anxiety over the possibility of being alone. Sharing this deeper meaning may not only provide the client with insight, but will also reinforce the connection between client and counselor.

Again it must be emphasized that this type of advanced empathy is not a technique, tactic, or strategy to be manipulated by the counselor. The insights gained as a result of experiencing advanced empathy cannot be artificially created nor forced, but must be the result of the counselor's deep and personal experiencing of the client's story—from the perspective and lived experience of that client.

CHALLENGES TO THE DEVELOPMENT AND MAINTENANCE OF A COUNSELING RELATIONSHIP

As previously noted, the depiction of the counseling process in a textbook can be, and in many ways is, artificial. In order to highlight and teach the reader about the factors, or elements, involved in counseling authors typically define the elements and then provide ideal illustrations of their use within counseling. This is certainly true of the present chapter.

We have outlined the *what, why,* and *how* of creating a working alliance and hopefully have been able to depict the elements needed by way of our case illustrations and guided practice exercises. However, the formation of a counseling relationship and effective working alliance is not always so easy to achieve in real life. There are numerous challenges to the creation and maintenance of a working professional relationship, which counselors will need to navigate. What follows is a very brief depiction of some of those challenges—emanating from the client, from the counselor, and coming from the dynamic of their interaction.

Challenges Emanating From the Client

If you practice long enough, you are sure to experience clients whom you will perceive as stubborn, obstinate, uncooperative, obstructive, or simply resistant. Often these clients present as having a chip on their shoulder, filled with anger and rage, and protesting the forced nature of their appearance within your office, as might be the case with the court-mandated client or the school-referred adolescent.

But these are not the only forms of challenge and resistance that a counselor encounters. It is not unusual to find clients resisting the counselor's efforts to engage in a working alliance as a result of their fear of disclosure, their limited history with sharing with strangers (e.g., those from other cultural backgrounds), or even those who enter counseling wanting yet fearing intimacy.

Whatever the specifics, all professional counselors at one time or another encounter the difficult client—the client who tests the limits of what the counselor expects and what the counselor can do. And in each situation, these clients test the counselor's ability to be genuine, accepting, prizing, and empathic. Yet, it is these specific attitudes and values that these clients need to experience while in the presence of a counselor.

Kottler (1992) suggested that there are five distinct types of client resistance. And while it is beyond the scope of this text to discuss in detail Kottler's presentation, professional counselors need to understand the motivation behind each type's resistance so that strategies for resolution can be engaged. The types are described as follows.

Type 1. Resistance is present when clients do not understand what the counselor wants or expects. This can occur when clients are new to counseling and naive about the process or when they have challenges to their cognitive abilities. Clearly, under these circumstances, it is important for the counselor to provide education about the counseling process and provide the information necessary for acquiring informed consent.

Type 2. This resistance occurs when the clients do not comply with tasks asked of them because they lack the skills or knowledge needed to carry out the assignments. In this situation, it is not stubbornness that serves as the source of the resistance. With these clients, it is important that the counselor considers where they are along the continuum of change and collaboratively plan those steps necessary and possible for movement toward the desired goals.

Type 3. The third type of resistance is that reflecting client indifference and apathy. Some clients simply expect the world to change for them and fail to see the need nor the value of engaging in personal change strategies. It is important for the counselor to not only help the client develop positive expectations about their abilities to impact their lives, but also structure the goals in such a way that significant gains can be made with minimal personal cost to the client.

Type 4. Resistance at this level typically reflects the clients' intense anxiety about letting go of their current pattern (even though it is ineffective) and adopting a new yet unproven approach. Under this situation, the counselor needs to work on increasing the level of trust in the relationship and invite the client to actually process the anxiety about the changes being suggested.

Type 5. This type of resistance occurs because, at some level, the client achieves some form of payoff as a result of the current life condition. This might be the example of a person who, as a result of being depressed, is no longer expected to be successful at work or take responsibilities at home. These gains are not intentional and deliberate, but nonetheless work to maintain the current situation. Under these conditions, the counselor needs to elevate the client's awareness of these so-called payoffs and attempt to reduce the ability to achieve these by way of current behaviors while assisting the client to find other more productive ways of meeting these needs.

For all counselors, it is important to remember that these "difficult" clients are not intentionally trying to make the counselor's life miserable. The effective counselor will attempt to understand the client's frame of reference—to increase the experience of empathy—and in so doing become more aware of the bases for the client's resistance. With such an increased awareness, the counselor can create interventions unique to those specific client concerns and limitations.

Challenges Emanating From the Counselor

Resistance a counselor experiences may be a reflection of client issues, but it may also be a reflection of an issue, a style, or personal characteristic of the counselor. It is possible that a particular client can elicit a counselor's own unresolved, personal issues. This is the experience of countertransference, a specific form of loss of objectivity that can impair the counselor's clarity and effectiveness.

Under these conditions, it could be entirely reasonable and most likely appropriate for a client to resist the inappropriate behavior exhibited by the counselor. For example, consider the counselor who, after having experienced a long, drawn out and painful divorce, finds himself expressing aggressive confrontations and judgmental interpretations to a new client sharing her upset about her husband's filing for divorce. Under these conditions, it is not unreasonable to assume that the client will fully resist the counselor's "interventions," and having failed to establish a collaborative working alliance, will most likely terminate the relationship.

It is important for counselors to be aware of the motivations for their actions and insure their actions are motivated by the client's treatment needs and best interests and not by their own needs.

But countertransference is not the only condition under which a counselor may stimulate client resistance. It is also possible that our clients will appear more resistant and difficult when we, as counselors, are unhappy with some specific aspects of our life. Counselors under such stress can interpret a client's question or challenge as evidence of that client's disrespect and hostility—a personal attack—rather than simply an element to the unfolding relationship.

Also, the resistance we experience may actually be a reflection of a subtle power struggle between the client and the counselor, stimulated by the counselor's attempts to impose his worldview on clients with different and diverse backgrounds

(Mens-Verhulst, 1991). Under these situations, it is important for the counselor to gain training and supervision in the area of counseling diverse populations.

Challenges Emanating From the Counselor–Client Dynamics

While there can be many elements existing within the actual dynamic and relationship between a counselor and client—elements such as struggles over power and control, diversity of worldviews, and a clash of expectations—one area that has received a lot of attention within the latest literature is the issue of multiple relationships and the threats of boundary crossings and boundary violations.

The ethical counselor understands that she should make every effort to avoid dual relationships with clients that could impair her professional judgment or increase the risk of harm to clients. A *dual relationship* in counseling refers to any situation whereby multiple roles exist between a counselor and a client. Examples of dual relationships are when the client is also a student, friend, family member, employee, or business associate of the counselor. Under these conditions, counselors are susceptible to boundary violations and boundary crossing. As such, when multiple relationships cannot be avoided, it is important to acknowledge them and take steps to ensure that the counselor's professional judgment and behavior are not impaired.

Boundary violations refer to any deviation from professional practice that results in the exploitation of a client. *Boundary crossing* also involves a counselor's deviation from strict professional role, but most often does not occur with the intent of client exploitation. For example, a counselor who accepts a token gift from a client could be said to have crossed a professional boundary. However, it can be argued that engaging in such limited personal connections can be helpful interventions, or at the worst innocuous, depending on the context (Slattery, 2004). The professional challenge is to determine when circumstances justify a boundary crossing and to insure that the client understands the purpose and intent of such a crossing as being in service of the therapeutic goals.

Because the boundaries in counseling can be fragile, it is important for professional counselors to seek and employ consultation and supervision anytime they feel they are stepping out of their professional roles in their interactions with their client.

COUNSELING KEYSTONES

- Helping, when it takes form in counseling, is a shared process in which a counselor and a client work together in facilitating the change desired (ACA, 2005, sec. A.1.c).

- Unlike other social encounters where the relationship serves as a medium or context within which the "work" is done, the relationship in counseling is more than the mere context of work—it *is* an essential part of the work being done.
- The dialogue found within counseling is unique in that it is focused upon the concerns, wishes, wants, and experiences of just one member, the client. In this conversation, the client explores difficult situations, missed opportunities, uncertain feelings, or challenging choices with the counselor.
- Counselors need to be aware that the physical setting plays an important role in the creation of the expectations of privacy, confidentiality, and even emotional intimacy.
- In addition to creating the physical environment conducive to the formation and maintenance of this unique relationship, counselors need to establish the social conditions necessary to support the process in which they are about to engage.
- Counselors need to provide enough information about the nature of the relationship in which the client is soon to be engaged so that the client can provide informed consent.
- Counselors attempt to create a working alliance with the clients, characterized by an honest give-and-take of information and the client's willingness to risk and become somewhat vulnerable to share personal information with the counselor.
- The working alliance is facilitated by the counselor's manifestation of dispositions such as being genuine, unconditionally valuing of the client, and empathic.
- Empathy is nurtured and conveyed by way of the counselors physically attending to the client and actively listening to and reflecting the content and feelings of the client's messages.
- Often difficulty in establishing and or maintaining a working alliance reflects resistance coming as a result of client issues, counselor characteristics, and actions or the dynamic of counselor–client relationship.

ADDITIONAL RESOURCES

Readings

Bordin, E. S. (1979). The generalizability of the psychoanalytic concept of the working alliance. *Psychotherapy: Theory, Research, Practice, Training, 16,* 252–260.

Horvath, A. O., & Greenberg, L. S. (Eds.) (1994). *The working alliance: Theory and research.* New York: John Wiley & Sons.

Jensen, T. K., Haavind, H., Gulbrandsen, W., Mossige, S., Reichelt, S., & Tjersland, O. A. (2010). What constitutes a good working alliance in therapy with children that may have been sexually abused? *Qualitative Social Work, 9*(4), 461–478.

Krupnick, J. L., Sotsky, S. M., Elkin, I., Simmens, S., Moyer, J., Watkins, J., & Pilkonis, P. A. (2006). The role of the therapeutic alliance in psychotherapy and pharmacotherapy outcome: Findings in the National Institute of Mental Health Treatment of Depression Collaborative Research Program. *Focus, 4,* 269–277.

Rogers, C. (1957). The necessary and sufficient conditions of therapeutic personality change. *Journal of Consulting Psychology, 21,* 95–103.

Rogers, C. (1980). *A way of being.* Boston: Houghton Mifflin.

Web Resources

Counselling Skills Lecture 4 Paraphrasing
www.youtube.com/watch?v=_M67ioQ1K2Y&feature=results_video&playnext=1&list=PL8F93
FE9BD5FA497D

Reflecting Back and Paraphrasing
www.youtube.com/watch?v=xrbXMaiR_Ww&feature=related

REFERENCES

Ackerman, S. J., & Hilsenroth, M. J. (2003). A review of therapist characteristics and techniques positively impacting the therapeutic alliance. *Clinical Psychology Review, 23,* 1–33.

American Counseling Association. (2005*). ACA code of ethics.* Alexandria, VA: Author.

Aragno, A. (2008). The language of empathy: An analysis of its constitution, development, and role in psychoanalytic listening. *Journal of the American Psychoanalytic Association, 56,* 709–740.

Bachelor, A. (1995). Clients' perception of the therapeutic alliance: A qualitative analysis. *Journal of Counseling Psychology, 42,* 323–337.

Baldwin, S. A., Wampold, B. E., & Imel, Z. E. (2007). Untangling the alliance-outcome correlation: Exploring the relative importance of therapist and patient variability in the alliance. *Journal of Consulting and Clinical Psychology, 75*(6), 842–852.

Barich, A.W. (2002). Client expectations about counseling. In G. Tryon (Ed.), *Counseling based on process research: Applying what we know* (pp. 27–65). Boston: Allyn & Bacon.

Bordin, E. S. (1979). The generalizability of the psychoanalytic concept of the working alliance. *Psychotherapy: Theory, Research, Practice, Training, 16,* 252–260.

Brammer, L. M., & MacDonald, G. (1999). *The helping relationship: Process.* Needham Heights, MA: Allyn & Bacon.

Carkhuff, R. (1969). *Helping and human relations: A primer for lay and professional helpers* (Vol. II). New York: Holt, Rinehart and Winston.

Carkhuff, R. R. (1987). *The art of helping, VI.* Amherst, MA: Human Resource Development Press.

Carkhuff, R. R., & Berenson, B. G. (1967). *Beyond counseling and therapy.* New York: Holt, Rinehart and Winston.

Caatonguay, L. G., Constantino, M. J., & Grosse Holtforth, M. (2006). The working alliance: Where are we and where should we go? *Psychotherapy: Theory, Research, Practice, Training, 43*(3), 271–279.

Constantino, M. J., Castonguay, L. G., & Schut, A. J. (2002). The working alliance: A flagship for the "scientist-practitioner" model in psychotherapy. In G. S. Tryon (Ed.), *Counseling based on process research: Applying what we know* (pp. 81–131). Boston: Allyn & Bacon.

Corey, G. (2005). *Theory and practice of counseling & psychotherapy* (7th ed.). Belmont, CA: Brooks/Cole.

Crits-Christoph, P., Connolly Gibbons, M. B., Narducci, J., Schamberger, M., & Gallop, R. (2005). Interpersonal problems and the outcome of interpersonally oriented psychodynamic treatment of GAD. *Psychotherapy: Theory, Research, Practice, Training, 42,* 211–224.

Daniels, T., & Ivey, A. (2007). *Microcounseling: Making skills training work in a multicultural world* (3rd ed.). Springfield, IL: Charles C Thomas.

Eames, V., & Roth, A. (2000). Patient attachment orientation and the early working alliance—a study of patient and therapist reports of alliance quality and ruptures. *Psychotherapy Research, 10,* 421–434.

Egan, G. (1994). *The skilled helper: A problem-management approach to helping* (5th ed.). Belmont, CA: Brooks/Cole.

Egan, G. (2009). *The skilled helper: A problem-management and opportunity development approach to helping* (9th ed.). Belmont CA: Brooks/Cole.

Farber, A. A., & Lane, J. S. (2002). Positive regard. In J. C. Norcross (Ed.), *Psychotherapy relationships that work: Therapist contributions and responsiveness to patients* (pp. 175–194). New York: Oxford University Press.

Goldman, A. I. (2006). *Simulating minds: The philosophy, psychology, and neuroscience of mind reading.* New York: Oxford University Press.

Grawe, K., Caspar, F., & Ambühl, H. (1990). Differential psychotherapy research: Four types of therapy in comparison: Process comparison. *Zeitschrift fur Klinische Psychologie, 19,* 316–377.

Hatcher, R. L., & Barends, A. W. (2006). How a return to theory could help alliance research. *Psychotherapy: Theory, Research, Practice, Training, 43,* 292–299.

Heppner, P. P., & Dixon, D. N. (1981). A review of the interpersonal influence process in counseling. *Personnel & Guidance Journal, 59*(8), 542–550.

Hill, C. E., & O'Brien, K. M. (1999). *Helping skills: Facilitating exploration, insight, and action.* Washington, DC: American Psychological Association.

Hilsenroth, M., Peters, E., & Ackerman, S. (2004). The development of therapeutic alliance during psychological assessment: Patient and therapist perspectives across treatment. *Journal of Personality Assessment, 83,* 332–344

Horvath, A. O. (2001). The alliance. *Psychotherapy, 38,* 365–372.

Horvath, A. O., & Bedi, R. P. (2002). The alliance. In J. C. Norcross (Ed.), *Psychotherapy relationships that work: Therapists contributions and responsiveness to patients* (pp. 37–69). New York: Oxford University Press.

Horvath, A. O., & Greenberg, L. S. (1989). Development and validation of the Working Alliance Inventory. *Journal of Counseling Psychology, 36,* 223–233.

Horvath, A. O., & Greenberg, L. S. (1994). *The working alliance: Theory, research, and practice.* New York: Wiley.

Horvath, A. O., & Luborsky, L. (1993) The role of the therapeutic alliance in psychotherapy. *Journal of Consulting and Clinical Psychology, 64,* 561–573.

Horvath, A. O., & Symonds, B. D. (1991). Relation between working alliance and outcome in psychotherapy: A meta-analysis. *Journal of Counseling Psychology, 38,* 139–149.

Kottler, J. A. (1992). *Compassionate therapy: Working with difficult clients.* San Francisco: Jossey-Bass.

Mallinckrodt, B. (2000). Attachment, social competencies, social support and interpersonal process in psychotherapy. *Psychotherapy Research, 10,* 239–266.

Martin, D. J., Garske, J. P., & Davis, M. K. (2000). Relation of the therapeutic *alliance* with outcome and other variables: A meta-analytic review. *Journal of Consulting and Clinical Psychology, 68,* 438–450.

Mens-Verhulst, J. (1991). Perspectives of power in therapeutic relationships. *American Journal of Psychotherapy, 45*(2), 198–210.

Miwa, Y., & Hanyu, K. (2006). The effects of interior design on communication and impressions of a counselor in a counseling room. *Environment and Behavior, 38,* 4, 484–502.

Mohl, P. C., Martinez, D., Ticknor, C., Huang, M., & Cordell, L. (1991). Early dropouts from psychotherapy. *Journal of Nervous and Mental Disorders, 179,* 478–481.

Moursund, J., & Kenny, M. C. (2002). *The process of counseling and therapy* (4th ed.). Upper Saddle River, NJ: Prentice Hall.

Norcross, J. C. (Ed.). (2002). *Psychotherapy relationships that work: Therapist contributions and responsiveness to patients.* New York: Oxford University Press.

Norcross, J. C., & Wampold, B. E. (2011). Evidence-based therapy relationships: Research conclusions and clinical practices. *Psychotherapy, 48*(1), 98–102.

Orlinsky, D. E., Rønnestad, M. H., & Willutzki, U. (2004). Fifty years of psychotherapy process-outcome research: Continuity and change. In Michael J. Lambert (Ed.), *Bergin and Garfield's handbook of psychotherapy and behavior change.* New York: John Wiley & Sons.

Principe, J. M., Marci, C. D., Glick, D. M., & Ablon, J. S. (2006). The relationship among patient contemplation, early alliance, and continuation in psychotherapy. *Psychotherapy: Theory, Research, Practice, Training, 43,* 238–242.

Rogers, C. R. (1951). *Client-centered therapy.* Boston: Houghton Mifflin.

Rogers, C. R. (1957). The necessary and sufficient conditions of therapeutic personality change. *Journal of Consulting Psychology, 21,* 95–103.

Rothmeier, R. C., & Dixon, D. N. (1980). Trustworthiness and influence: A reexamination in an extended counseling analogue. *Journal of Counseling Psychology, 27*(4), 315–319.

Sexton, H., Littauer, H., Sexton, A., & Tommeras, E. (2005). Building the alliance: Early therapeutic process and the client-therapist connection. *Psychotherapy Research, 15,* 103–116.

Slattery, J. M. (2004). *Counseling diverse clients: Bringing context into therapy.* Pacific Grove, CA: Brooks/Cole.

Smith, M. K. (1997, 2004). Carl Rogers and informal education. *The encyclopaedia of informal education.* Available at www.infed.org/thinkers/et-rogers.htm.

Stueber, K. R. (2006). *Rediscovering empathy: Agency, folk psychology and the human sciences.* Cambridge, MA: MIT Press.

Teyber, E. (1997). *Interpersonal process in psychotherapy: A relational approach.* Pacific Grove, CA: Brooks/Cole.

Truax, C., & Carkhuff, R. (1967). *Toward effective counseling and psychotherapy: Training and practice* (Vol. I). Chicago: Aldine.

Tryon, G. S. (1990). Session depth and smoothness in relation to the concept of engagement in counseling. *Journal of Counseling Psychology, 37,* 248–263.

Zuroff, D. C., & Blatt, S. J. (2006). The therapeutic relationship in the brief treatment of depression: Contributions to clinical improvement and advanced adaptive capacities. *Journal of Consulting and Clinical Psychology, 74,* 130–140.

Chapter 4

Identifying What Is
Probing the Client's Issues

*I just don't know what to do; I'm not even sure what's wrong,
or, for that matter . . . who I have become.*

INTRODUCTION

As a counselor, you will soon come to appreciate that many of those who seek your help do so without a real clear understanding of what it is that troubles them, how this came to be, and most certainly what to do. In fact, it is not unusual to find clients who, while initially presenting a very specific concern, through the process of counseling, come to realize that the issue they presented was only a tip of a much bigger issue.

The effective counselor uses knowledge and skills which allow her to assist the client not only to tell his story but to delve the depths of that story and unveil the important issues which need to be addressed in counseling. The current chapter provides a look at the knowledge and skill needed to explore and probe client issues in order to identify as completely and clearly as possible the *what is* that the client desires to change.

Specifically, at the end of this chapter you will be able to do the following:

- Describe what is meant by each of the following: open-ended questions, closed-ended questions, encouragers, clarifications, therapeutic confrontation, summarization, informing, and interpretation.
- Distinguish between interpretation and simple paraphrasing or reflection.
- Explain what it means to move a client from outer talk, through middle, and toward inner talk.
- Develop a summarization for a simulated client.
- Explain the characteristics that typically distinguish therapeutic confrontation from the more secular form of confrontation.

THE OBVIOUS IS NOT ALWAYS SO OBVIOUS

Clients will vary greatly in terms of the degree to which they fully understand the nature and origin of their difficulty. Some may not only lack such insight, but actually deny that a problem exists. Perhaps it is the person who has been ordered by the court to come to counseling as a result of being found guilty of driving while under the influence. It would not be so unusual for such a client to proclaim that "I don't need to be here . . . I don't have a drinking problem!" Or, consider the experience of many school counselors who are presented with clients who have been sent to their office by a teacher. With many of these students, the problem rests not with them but with the teacher who sent them—"I don't know why I'm here. Mr. K just doesn't like me."

While it may be clear in the case of our DUI and reluctant student clients, the need for unearthing the reason for their referral as well as moving them to ownership of that issue will be central to the outcome of the counseling. What may not be as clear is that sometimes even those clients who appear to understand the nature of their problem, may through the process of counseling come to understand that what first appeared to be the issue, was not. In both circumstances, it is incumbent upon the counselor to help the client to move from superficial exchange to a deeper personal disclosure, from surface issues to those lying beneath.

Moving Toward Intimate Disclosure

While all communication may be revealing, not all communication reveals or discloses to the same degree. Within our typical day-to-day encounters we would rarely assume that we should engage in deep, personal disclosure with a person whom we just met. The same is true for clients entering counseling and a new relationship with the counselor. Clients will often engage in safe social bantering about the weather, traffic, or a recent sporting event before proceeding to sharing more personally and intimately (Blimling, 2010). Movement beyond these somewhat safe, public issues to the sharing of deeper personal, intimate, and closely valued experiences can be facilitated by the counselors embodying the facilitative characteristics of genuineness, attending, nonjudgment, and unconditional positive regard. These elements help the client experience this relationship as one that is safe and thus promotes deeper, personal disclosure.

One model that addresses this progression of disclosure from the relatively safe to the deeply personal was presented by Dusty Miller. Miller (1996) proposed three domains of communication: (1) outer circle talk, (2) middle circle talk, and (3) inner circle talk. According to Miller, the outer circle is where the opening or the surface exploratory conversation occurs between people who don't know each other well. In counseling, the outer circle talk occurs early in the conversation between the counselor and the client, and it is during the outer circle talk the counselor works hard to establish trust and build the therapeutic relationship with the client. It is also during this outer circle talk when the client attests to the counselor's trustworthiness, attractiveness, and expertness. The outer circle talk begins from the very first time the counselor greets the client and continues with the elucidation of the counselor–client roles, and the establishment of agreement on how to proceed in counseling (Murphy & Dillon, 2003). This type of communication is valuable in that it provides for an understanding of the basics of counseling and the depiction of public information about the client (e.g., demographics). This outer circle talk provides the client with an experience with the counselor that is safe, thus encouraging movement toward more personal communication.

While communication in the outer circle talk tends to focus on information sharing, the focus shifts to the client's feelings and conflicts when operating within the middle circle. During the middle circle talk the counselor may begin to help the client discover thoughts and feelings that the client has, to this point, not brought onto the surface and relationship issues and behavior patterns of which the client is unaware (Murphy & Dillon, 2003). At this level of talk the client sees the trust in the counseling relationship and feels safe and comfortable to disclose details about his or her suffering or concerning experiences. It is also at this level that the client's strengths, perceptions, expectations, values, worldviews, meanings, acculturation, needs, and wants are explored.

The inner circle talk directs attention to the issues and experiences that lay deep inside the client. In the inner circle talk, attention is turned to the client's "feelings and content about frightening, taboo, or shame-bound areas . . ." (Murphy & Dillon, 2003, p. 104). At this level, the counselor and client identify the client's unspoken concerns, desires, and even their feelings—including guilt—about these desires or concerns. The inner circle addresses areas of embarrassment, confusion, self-contradiction, and issues such as dormant rage including self-destruction, vulnerability, fears, and blind spots to the client's self-awareness.

Facilitating the client's engagement in the inner circle talk requires that counselors demonstrate understanding of, respect for, and valuing of the client. In order to conduct an effective conversation in the inner circle with the client, counselors must thoroughly understand themselves and the client, gain the trust from the client, and possess the skills of conducting the inner circle conversation. Case Illustration 4.1 is an example of how the counselor moves from the outer circle to the inner circle talk with her client.

As Murphy and Dillon (2003) pointed out that these three levels of talk do not present as discrete and neatly ordered; rather, they intertwine and intermingle in the flow of the conversation and spiral in the process of counseling. While it may be

CASE ILLUSTRATION 4.1

DIFFERENT LEVELS OF CIRCLE TALK

This is the first session between the counselor and her client. The dialogue provides an example of how discussion can move from rather public, safe information (outer circle) through to deeply personal and intimate sharing (inner circle). It is important to remember the goal of such a transition. Facilitating a client's intimate sharing is to be done for the benefit of the client and not for the benefit of the counselor's need. Counselors must be on guard not to pursue such inner circle talk for their own titillation or for its voyeuristic value.

Outer Circle Talk

Counselor: You indicate that you want to talk about your marital relationship. Perhaps you could give me some details about your marriage?

Robert: I married twice and my first marriage ended three years ago, and then a year later I remarried my current wife. Recently our marriage relationship has some ups and downs.

Counselor: You have married twice and the current marriage is pretty recent.

Robert: Correct.

Middle Circle Talk

Counselor: Can you elaborate on what you mean about the ups and downs in your current marital relationship?

Robert: My wife and I got along well when we took a vacation on a cruise recently; for example, we held hands, kissed each other a lot, and had good feelings about each other. But after we came home, we become less affectionate and issues with our adult children seem to get in the way . . . ah, and oh yea I was watching some gay pornography and got caught by my wife.

	She thinks I may be gay and wants me to get out of the house.
Counselor:	You are attracted to each other when you are away from home but the relationship tenses up at home, particularly when your adult children's issues get involved in your marriage life. Also, you were caught by your wife for watching gay porno. Because you did, she believes that you're gay and wants to separate with you.
Robert:	Yes. That is the situation.

Inner Circle Talk

Counselor:	It seems a lot has happened within the past few weeks—going from feeling close and sharing affection while away and then returning to the experience of emotional distance, and now the tension regarding your reviewing gay porn.
Robert:	Yeah. Absolutely. I felt happy and in love when we were on the cruise. During that time I wanted to be with her. However, when I was caught watching the gay porno, I began to feel horrible, really guilty because it seems that I'm hiding something from my wife. She yelled at me using the F-word and does not trust whatever I say. I'm not gay—really—I was just curious. Now she has told all people we know that I'm gay. I feel embarrassed, ashamed, and deeply hurt. I'm lost and don't know what to do.

assumed that typically counselors engage the client in outer circle talk during initial periods of contact, it is clear that moving the client to middle and inner circles is the goal. The counselor's decision to invite the client to the inner circle conversation will be based on judgment about the following: the level of trust that has been established, the psychological readiness of the client, and even the psychological readiness of the counselor. This last point, while perhaps unexpected, is important.

It is not unusual to find beginning counselors, or those in training, to stay with their clients at the outer circle and middle circle talk. Keeping the conversation at cultural or sociological levels can be "safe" for the counselor as well as the client. The counseling process is an awesome process and counseling is an equally awesome responsibility. Having clients share private aspects of their lives, aspects that may be difficult for them to reexperience and share, can feel overwhelming and anxiety provoking to the counselor in whom the client has placed such trust and hope. For counselors who are unprepared and thus unable to handle the intensity of counseling, their strategy for coping may be to keep the discussion and the exchange on a safe—and somewhat impersonal—level. Doing such, while serving the needs of the counselor, is a violation of the responsibility of the counselor—to help the client.

Exception to "Normal" Progression of Disclosure

While the previous model may be useful as a description of the normal progression of personal disclosure, there are times when normal progression is not to be expected or followed. Sigmund Freud, the father of psychoanalysis, is reported to have said that sometimes a cigar is just a cigar. What was meant by this statement is that there are times when a client presents an issue which is simple, clear-cut, and without any hidden deeper, darker, more serious meaning. In these situations, the counseling exchange can successfully take place at the outer and middle circles. This may be the case with a client who comes to counseling in hopes of gaining assistance in making a career choice, learning more effective decision-making skills, or even modifying a behavior, such as smoking, which the client would like to change. Under these conditions, it is just as important for the counselor to demonstrate respect for the client by maintaining the conversation only at the depth required to facilitate the client's goal achievement. Probing the depth of a client, when done simply out of the voyeuristic desires of the counselor and without benefit to the client, is unethical. As counselors, we are to remember that what we do and how we do it is for the benefit of the client and not our own personal interests or needs.

Another situation in which the counselor may find that maintaining discussion at the outer and middle levels of conversation is what is needed would be when a client comes to counseling in severe crisis as might be the case of a client contemplating suicide or homicide, or having experienced an extreme tragedy or unexpected loss of a loved one. Under these conditions, the effective counselor targets the dialogue on the specific feelings and thoughts the client has around these very intimate and personal experiences. In these situations, it would not be unusual for the counselor to actually begin the conversation at the inner circle without the typical progression. A third situation in which the theoretical progression of outer, middle, and inner conversation may be disrupted is when working with multicultural clients. Many cultures, for example Native Americans, can be very private and as such very sensitive to such depth of disclosure to one outside of their culture (Pedersen, 1976). Pushing or even prematurely inviting such disclosure can negatively affect the counseling relationship. The final situation in which progression to a depth of disclosure may be difficult and perhaps unnecessary is when working with very young children or those with intellectual challenges. Attempting to probe the inner circle may be too demanding and frustrating for these clients and as such, counselors must consider the appropriateness of doing so.

SKILLS USED IN IDENTIFYING THE *WHAT IS*

While it may seem obvious that in order to identify the *what is,* counselors need to simply ask clients to share their story. While this is certainly true, it is not just "a story" that the counselor wants to hear. The counselor needs to understand the meaning of that story and discern the information that will prove useful in developing and implementing a helping strategy. As such, the effective counselor employs communication skills to facilitate the client's disclosure of relevant and meaningful elements of the story in a way that both the counselor and client understand, and through which both gain insight into the nature of the problem. The skills employed in the process include: questioning, encouraging, clarifying, challenging, summarizing, and informing.

Questioning

The counselor's use of questioning within a session can be a valuable tool for gathering needed information about the client, the client's story, and what needs to be considered in the formulation and implementation of a helping plan. However, when employing questions within a helping session, counselors need to be aware of the *how* and the *why* of questioning.

The How of Questioning

Questions can be presented in one of two forms—open-ended and closed-ended. *Open-ended questions* are questions that invite the client to give direction to the answer and provide somewhat of an elaborate explanation. These open-ended questions typically begin with *what* (e.g., What's changed since we last talked?); *how* (e.g., How do you see this happening?); *who* (e.g., Who else is involved in this decision?); *when* (e.g., When was the last time you experienced . . . ?); or *where* (e.g., Where do you see this going?). However, open-ended questions can be framed in ways that invite elaboration (e.g., Could you tell me more?) or clarification (e.g., Can you help me understand that a little better?).

The benefit of such open-ended questions is in the fact that they provide little direction or structure to the answer sought and, as such, allow clients to give form and direction to the response as they see fit. The use of open-ended questions is particularly useful early in the relationship when the counselor may really seek no specific direction to take, but is rather wanting to gather as much data as possible. Further, the use of open-ended questions allows the counselor to be economical in gathering information. One open-ended question such as, "What is it that you hope would be the result of our meeting today?" invites the disclosure of a wide spectrum of information including the clients feelings (e.g., I would like to be less stressed), concerns (e.g., I'm not sure—I am really confused about what I should do in my relationship), or even specific goals (e.g., I would like help with weight reduction). One can imagine the energy expended plus the negative impact on the client should the counselor have attempted to guess what it is that brought the client to counseling and then proceeded to ask a series of yes-no structured questions such as the following: Do you want help with stress? Do you want help with relationship issues? Do you want help with weight loss? Clearly, if the counselor "guessed" correctly the first time, that would be wonderful, but the chances of that, given the limited amount of information gathered at an early point in the process, is slim and the result would be a client who may feel as if he is being cross-examined or interrogated.

While the benefit of an open-ended question is that it allows the client to shape the direction of the response, this can also be a drawback when the counselor attempts to drill down to a specific piece of information or attempts to find a path between a *this* or a *that*. In these situations, a counselor may employ a closed-ended question.

Closed-ended questions are structured in a way to typically require a simple one-word answer, for example, yes or no (e.g., Do you feel stressed?) or selection from multiple choices (e.g., Which are you feeling—anger, frustration, sadness . . . all of these?). Closed-ended questions are useful when attempting to narrow down the information or focus of the exchange. However, when presented in a rapid fire or barrage, closed-ended questions can be intimidating to a client and negatively impact the dynamic. Thus, the issue of closed-ended or open-ended ultimately needs to be decided upon two issues: (1) What is the purpose of the question and the results sought by the counselor? and (2) How effective was the question?

Whether one employs an open-ended or closed-ended form of questioning, it is important to keep the questions clear, specific, and simple (i.e., not compounded). Too often, counselors-in-training will pose compounded or multiple questions at the same time. For example, the counselor may ask the client, "Are you sad? Is that because you have ended your relationship or because of your job situation?" The combination of multiple questions into a single inquiry may result in the following: (1) the client may feel frustrated with which question the counselor wants answered, (2) the counselor may not get the answer sought, and (3) the client may pick the last one or the one that is easy to answer. Case Illustration 4.2 demonstrates the skill of questioning as a means of inviting client story disclosure.

CASE ILLUSTRATION 4.2

THE SKILLFUL USE OF QUESTIONING

The following demonstrates one counselor's skillful use of both open- and closed-ended questions to help the client share his story.

Counselor:	Now Ben, perhaps you could tell me what brought you here today?
Ben:	Well, this is my first year at college and I'm having trouble focusing on my studies lately cause there is some problems between my girlfriend and me.
Counselor:	There are problems in your relationship that seem to be distracting you from studies—could you tell me more about that?
Ben:	My girlfriend and I have been dating since high school. This year we both got into college. Unfortunately we were not able to go to the same school. After a semester she seems to contact me less frequently than before. When I call her, she oftentimes rushes the conversation saying that she had some sort of event or something she had to do. For the first couple of times I was okay, but . . . (pauses)
Counselor:	(eyes remain on the client's face while leaning her body forward) First couple of times . . . but what happened then?
Ben:	I said those were excuses but she said they were not. I argued with her over the phone. She hung up on me.
Counselor:	Hung up . . . how did you feel then?

(Continued)

(Continued)

Ben:	I was pissed off.
Counselor:	Did you share this feeling with her?
Ben:	No.
Counselor:	So, clearly there is tension—perhaps a rip in your relationship—with you feeling angry, and I sense a little hurt and not really understanding what is going on with your girlfriend. Could you tell me what you are thinking about this situation?

The Why of Questioning

While understanding the impact of various forms of questioning is important, what is more essential is for the counselor to understand the reason behind a question. Previously, we highlighted the fact that counseling is *an intentional act.* This is true of a counselor's employment of questioning. The goal here is not a simple free tour through the various experiences and conditions of our client's life. Counselors should not use questions for their own simple curiosity. The intention of all counselor behavior is fundamentally grounded in a desire to be of help. Thus, when asking questions—open or closed—the counselor should have an awareness of the data sought and the value of those data to the helping process.

This ability to connect the *what* of a counselor's questions to the direction the counselor hopes these data will take the counseling is often lacking among counselors-in-training. Too often, counselors-in-training get lost in doing it correctly, that is, employing the proper form (e.g., open-ended) of questioning as opposed to focusing on what it is that they are seeking and how they will use the data acquired. For example, consider the situation in which the counselor asks the client the question, "How do you feel?" and the client replies, "I feel angry." Okay, but now what? If the counselor's question was not embedded in a hypothesis about the intended direction of the relationship, the data received (i.e., I feel angry) may simply be discarded and the counselor may jump on to a new topic and ask another question.

Without an expectation of the type of response one may receive when asking a question and how those data might be used, the counselor may fail to follow up when a question asked was really not answered. Consider a situation in which a counselor seeks to know how a client feels about a situation and asks, "How did you feel when she said that?" If the counselor is truly attempting to identify the emotional response experienced by the client, then the client's response, "I thought she was rude" would have failed to provide the data sought. Under this condition, the counselor would most likely rephrase the question in hopes of identifying the feelings, or gathering evidence of the client's lack of awareness of feeling or unwillingness to share feelings. In either case, the follow-up question would simply be part of a larger plan for data collection. Without such a plan, without an understanding of the purpose for posing a question, a counselor's questioning may simply result in a mass of disconnected pieces of information.

Encouraging

Quite often, a counselor may feel that the client is sharing important data and may wish for the client to continue along that line of disclosure. Questions to follow up on what the client shared can be one useful tool to facilitate that continued disclosure. Another technique often used is that of verbal and nonverbal encouragement.

Encouraging, as used here, is a nonverbal and verbal skill that counselors frequently use in the counseling process. It consists of elements such as positive facial expressions including eye contact of interest, head nods, and leaning-forward body posture that encourage clients' self-disclosures or storytelling. When employed in verbal form, encouraging often appears as a simple restatement or repetition of key words from what the client says. For example, consider the situation in which the client discloses, "This job is so frustrating." The counselor could encourage the client to expand on the disclosure by repeating "this job?" or perhaps restating "frustrating?" The subtle tone of inquiry with the emphasis on a particular disclosure encourages the client to expand. As with questioning, the use of *encouragers* should reflect the counselor's intent and overall data-gathering plan. If the counselor is curious about job details then she may employ the first reflection of "this job?" However, if the counselor is more interested in the client's emotional reactions, the target of the encouragement may be on "frustrating?"

Other forms of verbal encouragement include: *Mm hmm, I see, Go on, Tell me more, Keep going,* and *All right.*

Encouraging is an effective skill that can be used to highlight one of the many elements in what the client says such as thought, feelings, behavior, or point of view. By using encouraging, the counselor simultaneously gives the client confidence to talk more, shows the client that he or she is listening, leads the client in a certain direction which the counselor believes is therapeutic, and continues to build upon a working alliance by demonstrating attending behavior. Case Illustration 4.3 is a sample on how the counselor uses encouraging skill to facilitate the client's self-disclosure.

CASE ILLUSTRATION 4.3

ENCOURAGING

The client talks to the counselor about his past weekend experience with his wife at home. The relationship is strained and he is unsure what to do. The counselor employs minimal encouragers to assist the client in sharing what is experienced as a difficult story.

Reynaldo: I've done what I could. I understand she wants to save money. I called nine contractors, nine contractors, to do the patio. I think that is enough. But she came over asking what I was doing, whether I made phone calls. I told her I did and called nine. She asked what I should do then. It's her tone and attitude that pissed me off.

Counselor: Her tone of voice and her attitude made you angry.

Reynaldo: I'm angry but I couldn't say anything to her. I know I could blow it off. I don't wanna get into it with her, she's pregnant . . . (pauses)

Counselor: Uh, huh . . . angry.

Reynaldo: Well I don't want to be upset but damn she acts just like my boss at work; it's really upsetting . . . (takes long pause)

Counselor: Upsetting?

Reynaldo: I mean, he treats me like I'm always screwing up . . . he never acknowledges the good stuff I do . . . and now she's doing the same thing.

Counselor: So, you feel upset . . . angry?

Reynaldo: Yeah, well . . . I feel I'm . . . (pauses)

Counselor: (waits in silence, but maintains attending body posture and nods slightly)

Reynaldo: I guess. I'm feeling a little sorry for myself . . . you know, unappreciated.

Counselor Reflection

I chose to focus on the client's feelings because I see focusing on client's feelings at this point can be more therapeutic than exploring client's perception of how others treat him. There are a couple of other elements that could be emphasized. One element is the lack of acknowledgment from his wife, the second element could be the client's control of his anger because his wife is pregnant, and the third one can be the lack of acknowledgment from his boss at work. But I feel it is important to explore the inner experiences of the client—that is why I used encouragers around his disclosures of feelings.

Clarifying

Though we human beings are by nature communicative, we are not always clear in our communications. Most people have encountered situations where things were said or words were used that simply were too vague or unclear as to convey the message intended. Some clients employ phrases that are vague (e.g., you know); too generalized (e.g., everybody); or even unique to a culture or a subgroup (e.g., trippin'). Words or phrases that are unclear to the counselor are of little help in the counselor's desire to understand and, as such, must be clarified. For some counselors-in-training, the thought of revealing their lack of understanding can be anxiety provoking. They may feel that exhibiting this lack of understanding could be insulting to the client or suggest they are "not cool" or "not attentive." It is important to continue to remind ourselves that our purpose, or our intention, is to understand our clients' stories in all of their depth and breadth so that we can help our clients achieve their desired goals. Our focus must remain on each client and not on our own needs to appear cool or feign understanding. Thus, whenever a counselor is unclear about the client's disclosure, it is essential to seek clarification.

Clarifications are used to make sure that the counselor understands clients accurately, to clear up vague and confusing messages, to encourage clients to elaborate, to assist clients to better understand themselves, and to help clients learn how to express themselves clearly and precisely and develop a more effective communication style. Counselors can seek clarification by asking clients to give an example of what they are saying, asking if they can use other words to describe the disclosure, or even responding with what the counselor "heard" and asking if that is accurate. But regardless of the strategy, it is helpful for counselors to first reiterate their desire to understand and then state their point of confusion.

Challenging

In keeping with the theme of increasing counselor understanding of a client's disclosure, there is another skill that is often needed during points of counselor confusion. That is the skill of *therapeutic confrontation.*

If you come from a background or culture in which the concept of confrontation has been equated with a hostile, sometimes rude, aggressive act, then the thought of using confrontation within a helping relationship may seem a bit strange, even inappropriate. Too often, confrontation implies the use of judgment, or strong, often violent words and actions. As used here and within the helping relationship, therapeutic confrontation is an *invitation* from the counselor to the client—an invitation seeking the client's assistance in resolving the counselor's confusion. Yes, a therapeutic confrontation can be challenging to the client in that it invites the client to stop and reflect on what is being conveyed so that the client can do so in a clear, consistent manner.

But while challenging for the client, the focus of a therapeutic confrontation is actually on the counselor and not the client. It is the counselor seeking clarification. This is an important point in that it highlights the purpose of therapeutic confrontation as that of gaining clarification and not blaming, accusing, or judging the client. This is certainly a contrast to the more typical and secular view of confrontation, which generally is one person's attack on another. Thus, rather than using *you* statements, which entail judgmental language, a therapeutic confrontation is one framed from the perspective of the counselor using *I* language and describing the point of personal confusion rather than blaming the client for being confusing. For example, consider the two exchanges that follow. While both exchanges are around a time issue, the first is less than *therapeutic* or *inviting.*

> Counselor 1:   (looking at watch) Where the hell have you been. I've been standing here for 20 minutes. What's up with you?
>
> Counselor 2:   Hi Ray. I hope everything is okay—I was concerned. I thought we decided to meet at 12 and it is 12:20. Did something happen?

While both comments come from a point of confusion about the time of a meeting, the first would most likely elicit a defensive or even counter-attacking response, which would fail to clarify what was going on. Counselor 2 employed *I* language, was descriptive about the time, and simply invited Ray to elaborate on what was happening. If Counselor 1 presented this descriptive, nonjudgmental point of personal confusion with a tone and nonverbal behavior to match, a meaningful informative exchange would most likely result.

There are times when counselors are confused by what appears to them as some inconsistency in the client's story. This may occur when the counselor experiences:

- An inconsistency between what the client says and how the client behaves, as might be the case when people say they are angry, yet smile.
- A discrepancy between two pieces of information shared by the client, as would be the case of a client who at one point speaks of how she loves her job and at another talks about how she can't wait to leave the job.
- A gap between what the counselor knows to be true, a fact, such as knowing that a client was arrested for a DUI, and hearing the client's presentation of just having "a little to drink."

If the counselor is to truly understand the client's story, the counselor will need some further information to help him resolve what he experiences as inconsistencies. But to acquire the needed information and gain that resolution, the counselor will need to present the therapeutic confrontation in a form that the client can embrace and provide the desired response. This is certainly not going to be the case if the client feels judged or attacked or in any way placed on the defensive. It is helpful for counselors to consider each of the following four guidelines for the presentation of therapeutic confrontation.

1. Describe, in nonevaluative, nonjudgmental terms, the points of confusion or points of apparent (to the counselor) inconsistency.

2. Use *I* language, because it is the counselor and not necessarily the client who is confused.

3. Be mindful of the client's current state—are they in a position physically or emotionally where they can accept your invitation to discuss this or is there something that would block that ability? For example, they are in crisis or clearly overwhelmed.

4. Remember the goal is to clarify; there is no intent to fault find or prove one position over another.

Exercise 4.1 provides both an example of a therapeutic confrontation and the opportunity to practice the formulation of therapeutic confrontations.

Summarizing

As counselors engage in the use of well-directed questions and methods of encouragement, they may find that the data presented is becoming somewhat overwhelming in simple quantity. Fortunately, counselors are not called to record and remember all the data shared. Rather, counselors listen for the significant points of

Exercise 4.1

THERAPEUTIC CONFRONTATION AS A HELPFUL SKILL

As noted within the text, therapeutic confrontation is helpful anytime a counselor feels that the client provides inconsistent or confusing messages. As used within the text, a helping or therapeutic confrontation is presented as an invitation—one in which the counselor using descriptive, nonjudgmental, tentative language asks the client to help clear up the counselor's confusion about what is seen as some inconsistency.

Directions: The following exercise provides data that seems to suggest some inconsistency in the client disclosure. Using the example as your guide, develop a therapeutic confrontation.

Client Disclosure	Therapeutic Confrontation
Example: The client states, "I can't do anything right; I am always screwing things up." The facts known to the therapist are that the client has recently received a promotion at work.	Tom, I can hear how frustrated you feel but I'm a little confused when you state you can't do anything right, especially in light of what you told me about your recent promotion at work?
Client denies that he is angry at the therapist's questions but does so while standing up and raising his voice.	_____ _____ _____
The client expressed a desire to really work with the counselor on improving her assertiveness skills but has "forgotten" to do her homework over the past three sessions.	_____ _____ _____ _____ _____
The client comes to the office door and knocks, interrupting the session in process. The client says, "I'm sorry that I am an hour late but it is important that we speak."	_____ _____ _____ _____

information, perhaps the recurrent themes or common threads. These are the data that provide the insight into what is going on with each client and what needs to be done. As counselors listen to the unfolding story, they attempt to pull together several ideas, experiences, or feelings that have been shared. Counselors then attempt to present these in succinct, concrete summary statements to their clients in order to test for accuracy of understanding. This presentation of the data in this coherent format is achieved by employing the summarization skill.

Summarization in counseling is an extension of paraphrasing and reflecting that involves tying together and rephrasing two or more different parts of messages (Ivey & Ivey, 1999). Summarizations take into consideration not only the content of what the client says, but also the client's feelings and the manner in which the message was delivered (Brammer & MacDonald, 2003). Summarization is a valuable tool. Its timely use shows the client that the counselor is fully attentive and assists both the counselor and client to focus on the essential points of disclosure. The counselor may use this skill to review the essence of what has occurred in counseling up to any one point within a session or across sessions.

Summarization is also useful as a tool to refocus the client who has scattered thoughts or has ventured off on an unrelated and perhaps irrelevant tangent. For example, assume that the client has been talking about her anxiety about no longer being engaged and fearing she will never meet another person when she becomes sidetracked and talks about all the wedding plans she was making, going into great elaboration about each and every detail. The counselor in this case while wanting to demonstrate that he is listening and truly caring for the client, would like to refocus the discussion on the client's belief that she will always be alone. To do this, he must first draw the wedding plans discussion to a closure in a way that is sensitive and caring. The counselor, illustrated as follows, uses a summarization to accomplish this goal.

Counselor: Wow, Ellen, it is clear that you put a lot of time
and energy into thinking about the wedding.
I mean you had the date, did all the arranging with
the caterer, scheduled the hall, and even the band.
That was a lot of work, I'm sure. I'm curious,
however, about your suggestion that since this
one relationship did not work out, that you will be
alone for the rest of your life. Please tell me more
about this belief that you will be alone for the rest
of your life.

The use of the summary in this illustration provides a sense of closure to the wedding talk, placing, if you will, a "period" to the extensive discussion of wedding plans without disrespecting the client or the client's story. The summary invited the client to feel closure to this aspect of her disclosure and thus be ready to move on— movement which in this case was prompted by the counselor's request for more information about her belief of being alone.

The effective counselor does not seek to restrict the nature of the client's disclosure but shapes and guides the discussion so that it leads to a full understanding of the client's issues and what may be done to assist that client. This counselor control over the direction of the session or sessions is important.

Remember what the counselor does should be intentional, with the intention to facilitate helping. Thus, if the client engages in irrelevant speech or unrelated disclosures, it is important for the counselor to gently guide the client back to focus on what will ultimately prove helpful. This may be especially true for clients who are very chatty and tend to talk extensively. This can be challenging especially for the beginning counselor. Employing summarizations throughout the session helps maintain focus for both client and counselor. Case Illustration 4.4 shows how the counselor uses summarization with her client during the first session. Exercise 4.2 offers an opportunity to practice formulating summaries.

Informing

While it is clear that an effective helper is not merely an advice giver and in fact imposing advice on a client could be detrimental to a helping process, the sharing of information is at times both required and helpful. We have previously discussed the need to provide clients with enough information about the process of counseling so that they can give informed consent. This is one of those times when informing a client is seen as an ethical mandate (see Case Illustration 4.5). But, *informing,* or simply providing the client with information, can prove effective at other times in the helping process as well. The counselor working with test results may certainly find it helpful to share, explain, and present these results to the client. Or, a counselor who employs a specific approach, for example, a cognitive model of counseling, may find that informing the client on the basic premises or assumptions of the model may help the client more eagerly embrace and engage with the model.

Clearly the counselor has information and expertise that may not only assist the client with a given issue or problem, but may also be helpful in promoting client growth.

CASE ILLUSTRATION 4.4

SUMMARIZATION SKILL

The following is the closing dialogue between the counselor, Dr. Wood, and the client. This was the first session and Dr. Wood is attempting to use a summary to pull together the salient information shared during the session.

Counselor:	Cindy, I appreciate your willingness to share your story with me today. As we wind down the session, I wonder if you could share how you feel?
Cindy:	I feel a little bit better . . . thanks.
Counselor:	Feel better?
Cindy:	I feel the session was very informative, and while I'm still feeling anxious, I believe you understand and will be able to help and therefore I'm a lot less anxious than when I first walked in. I mean I know this will take some time . . . but I'm really hopeful.
Counselor:	I'm glad to hear that . . . I am hopeful as well. In the minute or so we have left I'd like to share some of what I heard today in order to be sure I didn't miss anything. After sharing information about my practice and the issues of confidentiality you provided a pretty extensive description of your anxiety as it occurs in numerous situations at work, in social situations, and now with your interactions with your daughter and son-in-law. It seemed that with the information I provided you about the nature of anxiety and the role that thinking and behaving play in the experience of anxiety, you seemed as if it made sense and you even shared some experiences that demonstrated what I was discussing. I appreciate your understanding that while we can get through this, it will take work on your part and a number of sessions. And, I believe

(Continued)

(Continued)

	that we agreed, at least at this point, that it could take 12 or more sessions but that we would set up the goal and evaluate this on an ongoing basis. I'm wondering if there is anything else that I may have missed.
Cindy:	Just that I have homework to do!
Counselor:	Oh right . . . thanks for reminding me! You are going to keep the thinking and feeling journal we discussed—is that correct?
Cindy:	Yep . . . I understand that and I really think that will help.

Counselor Reflection

I often do a summary at the end of each individual session, the first session in particular. Sometimes I may even provide a summary of the last session as a prelude to the new session. I do this often when I have given the client homework in order to set the stage for follow-through. In general, I use summary to achieve a few goals in counseling: (1) to communicate to clients that I'm listening and giving them my full attention, (2) to let clients know that I not only listen to but also remember and ponder what they tell me, (3) to help clients organize their thinking and learn how to communicate with others, (4) to make a transition to a new topic, and (5) to emphasize what, if anything, the client has made a commitment to do.

Exercise 4.2

SUMMARIZATION

Directions: The following provides a look at one client's disclosure regarding his concerns around his relationship. The client loves his girlfriend and wants things to work out. Your task is to look for themes, key points, key feelings, or behaviors and provide a brief summary of these elements as if you were responding to the client. It may be helpful to share your summary with a colleague, peer, or teacher for feedback.

Counselor:	You indicate that you have some concerns regarding your girlfriend. Can you tell me more about it?
Client:	Well, it just seems like she really doesn't care about me much anymore. Like, we'll talk but when I say things she doesn't seem to care. It showed a lot last night because we were suppose to go to a show and I wasn't allowed to go. She didn't really seem to care that I wasn't going. She was just like . . . fine, no problem. And then she went and I just ended up hanging out with my friends. She used to get upset when she wouldn't see me because we don't see each other a lot anyways because of school. It just doesn't seem like she cares anymore. So, it hurts.
	Last week she had a rough week, and uh, a lot of things were stressing her out. She was really depressed and after last week things seemed to go down for us because when she is upset about things she doesn't talk to anybody about it. No matter how much I try to be there for her. I'll call her and get her to talk but she won't say anything. The other thing is she's lying to me. Like the other night, she actually snuck out of her house to hang out with a 20-year-old guy . . . I mean she's only fifteen. I mean it's weird she snuck out at 12 o'clock at night to hang out with him at his house. I don't like that and she told me she wasn't going to go but ended up going.

Identifying Themes or Salient Elements

As you review the previous client disclosure identify three pivotal elements to the disclosure and jot those down.

Integrating Elements

Now draft a summary statement, which integrates the identified pivotal elements into a coherent statement.

CASE ILLUSTRATION 4.5

INFORMING TO ALLOW FOR INFORMED CONSENT

The following illustrates one counselor's skillful use of informing to allow for client informed consent.

Counselor:	Before we begin, I would like to provide you with some general information about my approach to counseling and what typically occurs in my sessions. I would like to make sure that you have enough information about what we may do together in order for you to provide informed consent. I know you read all the information provided in the "Understanding My Practice" pamphlet, but I wonder if you have any questions?
Ben:	Not really. Everything seems clear.
Counselor:	You understand the limits to confidentiality?
Ben:	Sort of, don't tell what a person tells you to others.
Counselor:	Yep, you're right. You have the right to the confidentiality. I cannot and will not tell anyone else what you tell me, not even the fact that you're in counseling with me without your prior written permission.
Ben:	Oh, that's good.
Counselor:	However, there are a few exceptions to this confidentiality rule.
Ben:	There are? What are they?
Counselor:	First, if I have good reason to believe that you will harm another individual, I must make an effort to inform that person and warn him or her of your intention. I must contact the police to protect that person as well. The second one is that if

I believe that you are in imminent danger of harming yourself I must breach the confidentiality by calling the hospital or police to protect you. Clearly your life is too important not to take the steps necessary to protect. Another condition in which I may have to break confidentiality is if I have good reason to believe that you're abusing a child or a vulnerable adult or if you give me information about someone else doing this. In this situation, I must report it to the Child Protective Services or the Adult Protective Services. Also, if you tell me another health provider is having sexual contact with a patient or you, or a behaviorally or mentally impaired person, I must report this to his or her licensing board. However, your information with me in counseling is still confidential under this situation. Last, if you're involved in legal proceedings and the court orders me to give your information, I have to do so. I know this is a lot to understand—is it clear? Do you have any questions?

Ben: No. I understand. I don't think any of these issues will be a problem but thank you for clarifying these things.

Counselor Reflection

I always address the issue of confidentiality at the beginning of therapy and throughout the counseling process, even after the client signs the informed consent form. I discuss confidentiality with all clients no matter if they have been to counseling before or not. I strongly believe that a safe and comfortable environment is created for the clients if this issue is addressed at the beginning and whenever necessary and appropriate. When clients hear about the confidentiality and not just read it on paper, they feel safe to disclose themselves and do not have to worry about whether the information they provide in session would be used in ways other than serving themselves.

Interpreting

Up to this point, the skills presented have had as their major purpose the facilitation of clients' ability share their story. But, as should be obvious, it is not the storytelling alone that is of value to the counselor. The counselor, by way of these specific skills, attempts to understand the client's story and to be able to discern those elements that will prove essential to the helping process. As the counselor begins to make meaning from the client's disclosures, the counselor may begin to have a different perspective or slant on what is being shared from what the client offers. In this case, a counselor may employ the skills of *interpretation,* or reframing, as a way of inviting the client to a new perspective or insight.

Unlike paraphrasing in which the counselor attempts to accurately present the explicit message the client sent, interpretation moves beyond such reflection on the explicit message. With interpretation, the counselor draws on all the data the client provides, as well as the counselor's expertise in the theory of human behavior and even personal experience and intuition, to suggest an alternative meaning of that which has been presented. Interpretation provides a spin or a reframe on the data presented and invites the client to consider this alternative perspective.

It is important for counselors to understand that their interpretations—no matter how well thought out and developed—can be wrong. Providing the client with an interpretation is just a way to invite the client to consider a different perspective. It is not the "right" answer, nor is it one the client must embrace.

When presenting an interpretation, it helps to first reflect the explicit messages or data upon which the interpretation is based, and then present the interpretation not as factual truth, but as a hypothesis to be tested. Thus, a counselor may preface the interpretation with phrases such as "Correct me if I'm wrong . . . ," "I wonder if . . . ," "It seems to me that . . . ," "As I'm listening to your story, you seem to be saying . . . ," or "As you are speaking, a picture appears to emerge . . ."

Case Illustration 4.6 demonstrates how the counselor connects the elements in the client's statements as part of providing an interpretation and reframing of these data in order to move the client to a more productive way of dealing with her life circumstances.

One of the benefits of an effective interpretation is that it may increase the clients' awareness and insight about the multiple issues or dimensions to their story. Often clients become so focused on a singular issue that they fail to see the larger picture. An effective interpretation, as illustrated in Case Illustration 4.7, can help the clients broaden their view of the events, problematic situations, thoughts, feelings, and behaviors, and create a new perspective of these experiences.

CASE ILLUSTRATION 4.6

CRYING IS ALL I CAN DO

Kelly is a 35-year-old middle school teacher and comes to counseling for her issues of low self-esteem. Another goal she has for counseling is to gain control over her crying, a response she frequently employs when she has a conflict with others.

Counselor:	Kelly, you are saying that people call you a crybaby. Can you tell me more about that?
Kelly:	Sure. I do cry a lot, even now at my mid-30s. People call me a crybaby because whenever there is some kind of conflict, I cry. I hate it.
Counselor:	Hmm . . . . you cry when encountering conflict?
Kelly:	Yeah . . . and I remember when I was little I cried whenever I wanted something from my parents. The reason was that they did not give what I wanted and even didn't hear what I wanted. Whenever I got into an argument with my brother, I cried.
Counselor:	You cried to get them to attend to you?
Kelly:	Kinda . . . I mean after I cried, my parents would come to help me when my brother was teasing me or being mean and he would stop being mean to me.
Counselor:	Oh, so it was somewhat effective in getting the help you wanted.
Kelly:	I guess.
Counselor:	How about now?
Kelly:	I cry when I argue with my husband and even cry when my kids don't listen. I cry at my workplace as well. For example, I came out with a project and I thought it was very creative but no one supported me. I took my project to my boss and told him what I was

(*Continued*)

(Continued)

> trying to achieve. I didn't know why I was crying just after I began explaining to him my project. Anyway he finally agreed to give me a chance. You know what, it ended up very successful.

Counselor: Let me be sure I understand. You seem to be saying that you cried when your parents did not give you what you wanted, when you had a conflict with your brother, and now cry when you have a disagreement with your husband, or when your children don't listen, and when your project at work was not well taken.

Kelly: Yeah . . . that's right.

Counselor: It seems to me there is a repeated pattern with your crying. I could be wrong but it seems that your crying is something that has actually worked in the past. I mean it has gotten the attention from your parents or children and even helped with your work project. It seems that you may be using crying as a method or strategy to get what you want? One which at some level has been successful?

Kelly: (pauses) That sounds really immature . . . but . . . it makes sense. I've never thought of it that way and I don't think I'm consciously or deliberately choosing to cry . . . but . . . I think you may be right, but I'm not sure where to go?

Counselor Reflection

It's obvious that the client's crying behavior has been a pattern her entire life. Since it seemed to work in the past it looks as if this behavior has become one of her coping mechanisms when encountering conflicts. I know suggesting this to the client could be received as judgmental and may elicit some defensiveness; that is why when I present an interpretation I usually preface my comment with a summary of the data the client has presented. It seemed to work in this situation. Her apparent acceptance of the interpretation, along with the query as to where to go, will allow us to pursue more effective conflict resolving strategies.

CASE ILLUSTRATION 4.7

I NEVER CRY

Eric is a 37-year-old Caucasian American man who is a middle school teacher. He comes to counseling for help because his wife cheated on him and he has decided to divorce her.

Eric:	Really I am very, very sad about my divorce, but I just don't seem to be able to express it . . . I can't cry. You know, I still love her but I can't believe what she did to me.
Counselor:	I am not sure what you mean when you say that you are very sad but you can't cry?
Eric:	I have never cried in my life.
Counselor:	Never?
Eric:	Well, as long as I can remember. I remember when I was little others in the family always remarked that I was brave. Like when my grandpa died. I was very close to him . . . but I went to the wake and the funeral, everyone was crying but not me. That was 20 years ago, and I still feel sad when I think about my grandpa but I kind of feel he is still with me.
Counselor:	So, you're saying there are times when you feel very sad and even then you can't cry, like when your grandpa died. How do you make sense of this? What does that suggest to you?
Eric:	I don't know, I've never thought about it.
Counselor:	Well I'm wondering. There seems to be a number of pieces to this experience of not being able to cry . . . or as you stated, "I can't cry."
Eric:	Pieces? Not sure what you mean?

(Continued)

(Continued)

Counselor:	Well, when you shared your memory of being called brave, I began to wonder if while being called brave could be viewed as a compliment, it could also be a directive, with the subtle or implied message being brave boys don't cry?
Eric:	Wow. I know that in my family men didn't cry . . . that was wimpy.
Counselor:	Okay, but I am also wondering if somehow not crying is a way of not accepting a painful event. Like when you said you haven't cried about your grandpa's passing and you really feel as if he is with you . . . as if it is hard for you to believe he is dead.
Eric:	That's weird cause when I was a kid I used to think as long as I didn't cry, nothing bad would happen. I know that is weird but I did.
Counselor:	So again I wonder if you are applying that same thinking to your current situation, that is, as long as you don't cry about the marriage, you don't have to accept what actually happened and that you will be divorcing?
Eric:	I've never thought of that. It makes a lot of sense.

Counselor Reflection

The client appears to have both an enculturated prohibition against crying as a male, and maybe even some magical thinking regarding the power of not crying as a way to prevent painful events. The interpretations were offered as a way of inviting the client to not only consider this perspective but to begin to move inward to greater depth of understanding of the impact of these recent events as well as his general style of coping with loss.

MOVING FROM THE FACTS OF THE STORY TO THE MEANING

The skills presented within this chapter, when counselors effectively employ them, will result in clients' disclosure of their story. But the utility of this disclosure rests on one more factor, and that is the ability of the counselor to understand the *meaning* of this story as viewed from the perspective of the counselor. Losing a job may be a factual depiction of a client's life condition; however, a client who has tied his personal worth as a human being to his job will not be only impacted by the financial impact of losing this job but will also feel that his worth or his value as a person is zero. With this perspective, the client will have diminished self-esteem so much so that he fails to have the desire to seek new employment. This could be contrasted to the client who sees the loss of her job as strictly a financial concern and engages immediately in seeking new sources of finances; or the client who sees the loss as a blessing, believing that he is now free to pursue his dream job.

Focusing the Client Inward

Clearly the story the counselor elicits is useful in that it helps the counselor and the client assemble the facts of the client's experience. But to more fully understand the client's lived experience, counselors need not only to acknowledge their clients' complaints as valid and legitimate concerns, but also help clients turn inward and focus on their own thoughts, feelings, and reactions to the problematic conditions (Teyber, 2006). Case Illustration 4.8 is a sample of how the counselor validates the client's complaints while at the same time inviting the client to turn inward in order to become aware of the thoughts and feelings tied to this experience.

In reviewing Case Illustration 4.8, one can see that the counselor did not merely invite the client to encounter the feelings and thoughts tied to the experience, but actually probed these as evidence of the way this client gives unique meaning to these conditions of life.

Probing for Meaning

With an awareness of the issues, events, and experiences presented by the client, the counselor moves deeper in order to understand the meaning these have for the client. This is not an easy process because, quite often, the client may not have really considered the special meaning she gives to this life experience. The meaning making reflects the thoughts, beliefs, and assumptions the client has embraced over the course of her development—elements which will tint the emotional impact of any one life event. This was illustrated with the simple examples of clients losing their jobs. Have the different clients learned to see a job as the reflection of their personal worth or merely an activity that allows them to meet other needs or give form to special interest? It is in exploring this personal meaning that both the client and the counselor begin to have a more complete picture of the client and the issues being presented.

Probing for meaning often involves the use of open-ended questions. Counselors probing for meaning most likely employ the word *mean* or *meaning* in their question. The counselor upon hearing about some experience that appears significant to

CASE ILLUSTRATION 4.8

HELPING CLIENT FOCUS INWARD

An elementary teacher complains in counseling that everyone takes advantage of her.

Jennifer: I'm the youngest teacher at school. All the other teachers are much older than me. Oftentimes the women will say things like I'm just like their daughter. It's true that one of my friend's mom works with me. But they all treat me like a kid and take everything I say or do lightly. Some of them ask me to do things for them, like they are my mom or something. For example, last week two classes, mine and Mrs. Wood's, were outside. Within 10 minutes of being outside, Mrs. Wood turns to me and says, "Jennifer, can you take care of my kids? I'm going inside." What could I say? I took care of her kids. Yesterday another teacher called me telling me that she's sick and asking me to stop at the pharmacy on my way home to get some medication for her. I was busy with my children at home but I could not say no to her because she is sick. Afterwards I started wondering why she asked me and not her own daughter—I mean she just lives a couple of doors down from her mom.

Counselor: Jennifer, if I understand what you are sharing, you seem to feel that the other teachers at school take advantage of you and this is because you are so much younger than they?

Jennifer: That's right . . . they do.

Counselor: And how do you respond when they do these things?

Jennifer: I usually do what they ask.

> Counselor: So they place what you feel are unreasonable demands on you, but then you respond by doing what they ask? I wonder if your response of complying is contributing to their behaviors?

Counselor Reflection

The client complains about her colleagues who are older and take advantage of her. Her focus is pretty much on others who have given her difficult times, but she does not discuss anything about herself, her role in what has happened, and the impact of her experiences on her life. Moreover, she has not become aware that her nonassertive behavior may also play a role in what has happened. Helping her achieve an inward focus and eventually become assertive is my major task.

the client may respond by asking a question such as "What does this mean to you?" or "What meaning do you see in what you experienced?" However, understanding meaning can also be gained by use of questions—even when lacking the word *mean* or *meaning,* for example, "Why is this so significant (or important) for you?" "How do you understand (or see) yourself based on what had happened?" or "How do you make sense of this experience?"

The reflection of meaning helps to move clients' focus from the external conditions of their life inward to their unique thoughts and feelings in response to these external conditions. With these data, both clients and counselors have a more complete understanding of the *what is* as identified by the conditions external to each client—and the clients' unique internal response to these conditions emanating from their meaning making.

Challenges to Probing for Meaning

Probing for meaning may be difficult when working with children or those clients who may be intellectually challenged. To be able to stop and psychologically turn inward to assess the specific meaning one attributes to some life experience requires a level of abstract thinking which may be limited in these two populations. Under these conditions, the counselor needs to provide prompts or concrete examples to assist the client to get in touch with the internal experience. This is illustrated in the following exchange between a counselor and Joshua, a 9-year-old boy who just lost his grandpa a few days before. The boy had lived with his grandpa since he was born.

Counselor:	How did you feel when you heard that your grandpa passed away?
Joshua:	I felt sad.
Counselor:	I understand that you feel sad, very sad, having lived with your grandpa since you were born. I'm wondering, besides feeling sad, has anything else changed as a result of your grandpa dying?
Joshua:	I don't know. I just miss him.
Counselor:	Miss him? How does that feel . . . to miss him?
Joshua:	I feel there is a hole somewhere in my mind . . . like there is something missing . . . like it's all different.
Counselor:	All different?
Joshua:	Yeah like I can't see him anymore (crying) . . .
Counselor:	I guess that is true; you really can't see him anymore, but I know sometimes people still "see" their loved ones in dreams or in their memories. What memories do you have of your grandpa?
Joshua:	I have lots and (smiling) I do see him sometimes in my dreams or when I'm just thinking about him.
Counselor:	You were smiling when you said you have memories of your grandpa and sometimes see him. What were you feeling when you said that?
Joshua:	I was happy cause I remember I sometimes see him with God and grannie in heaven.
Counselor:	Oh, so when you think about your grandpa being in heaven with your grandmother and God it makes you feel happy. What is it that makes you happy when you think that?
Joshua:	I know he's happy and that makes me feel better.

Counselor:	So when you think about your grandpa that way you don't feel as sad, and you even feel happy for him?
Joshua:	I guess, and I know someday that I'll see him and grannie too.

FROM WHAT IS TO WHAT IS DESIRED

The skills described in this chapter, when counselors effectively employ them, will help clients move from social talk to personal, intimate disclosure and, in the process, begin to increase their awareness of all of the issues impacting their current lived experience. Further, with the tactful use of questions, therapeutic confrontations, probes for meaning, and interpretation, counselors can redirect their clients' focus from the external conditions of their lives, to the unique meaning and personal impact these conditions have had and are having. With the skills effectively employed both counselors and clients will have a more complete understanding of the *what is,* but now the attention of the counseling process turns to the *what is desired,* the topic for the next chapter.

COUNSELING KEYSTONES

- Effective counselors use knowledge and skills which allow them to assist their clients in not only telling their stories, but also delving the depths of those stories and unveiling the important issues which need to be addressed in counseling.
- The ability to engage the client around safe topics (cultural and sociological communication) while demonstrating the facilitative characteristics of genuineness, attending, nonjudgment, and unconditional positive regard establishes that this relationship is safe and thus promotes deeper, personal disclosure.
- Open-ended questions can be framed in ways that invite elaboration, thus allowing the client to give form and direction to the response.
- Closed-ended questions are structured in a way to typically require a simple one-word answer, for example, yes or no or selection from multiple choices. Closed-ended questions are useful when attempting to narrow down the information or focus of the exchange.

- Clarifications are used to make sure that the counselor understands clients accurately, to clear up vague and confusing messages, to encourage clients to elaborate; to assist clients in better to understanding themselves, and to help clients learn how to express themselves clearly and precisely and develop a more effective communication style.

- Summarizations are extensions of paraphrasing and reflecting that involve tying together and rephrasing two or more different parts of messages. Counselors may use this skill to review the essence of what has occurred in counseling up to any one point within a session or across sessions. Summarizations are also useful as a tool to refocus clients who have scattered thoughts or who have ventured off on an unrelated and perhaps irrelevant tangent.

- Interpretation is the counselor's response to move beyond reflection on the explicit message and, drawing on all the data provided by the client, as well as the counselor's expertise in the theory of human behavior and even personal experience and intuition, suggest an alternative meaning or message implied of that which has been presented.

- Probing Meaning is the counselor's attempt to turn clients inward and focus on their own thoughts and feelings in light of problematic conditions they have identified.

ADDITIONAL RESOURCES

Readings

Evan, D. R., Hearn, M. T., Uhlemann, M. R., & Ivey, A. E. (2004). *Essential Interviewing: A programmed approach to effective communication.* Belmont, CA: Brooks/Cole.

Heppner, P. P., & Dixon, D. N. (1981). A review of the interpersonal influence process in counseling. *The Personnel and Guidance Journal, 59*(8), 542–550.

McClintock, E. (1999). *Room for change.* Needham Heights, MA: Allyn & Bacon.

Strong, S., Yoder, B., & Corcoran, J. (1995). Counseling: A social process for encouraging personal powers. *The Counseling Psychologist, 23,* 374–384.

Web Resources

Psychojargon: Unconditional Positive Regard
    www.youtube.com/watch?v=9gbziXBIppQ

The Great Carl Rogers—Person Centered Therapy
    www.youtube.com/watch?v=DjTpEL8acfo

Counseling Roleplay—Asking Only Open Questions
    www.youtube.com/watch?v=Lif4saka70g

Counseling Skills Lecture 5 Summarising and Questions
    www.youtube.com/watch?v=zoMnSHBq77I

REFERENCES

Blimling, G. S. (2010). *The resident assistant: Applications and strategies for working with college students in residence halls* (7th ed.). Dubuque, IA: Kendall/Hunt.

Brammer, L. M., & MacDonald, G. (2003). *The helping relationship: Process and skills* (8th ed.). Needham Heights, MA: Allyn & Bacon.

Ivey, A. E., & Ivey, M. B. (1999). *Intentional interviewing & counseling: Facilitating client development in a multicultural society* (4th ed.). Pacific Grove, CA: Brooks/Cole.

Miller, D. (1996). Challenging self-harm through transformation of the trauma story. *Journal of Sexual Addiction and Compulsivity, 3,* 213–227.

Murphy, B. C., & Dillon, C. (2003). *Interviewing in action: Relationship process and change* (2nd ed.). Belmont, CA: Brooks/Cole.

Pedersen, P. (1976). The field of intercultural counseling. In P. Pedersen, W. J. Lonners, & J. G. Draguns (Eds.), *Counseling across cultures* (pp. 17–41). Honolulu: University Press of Hawaii.

Teyber, E. (2006). *Interpersonal process in therapy: An integrative model* (5th ed.). Pacific Grove, CA. Brooks/Cole.

Chapter 5

Goal Setting
Identifying What Is Desired

If you don't know where you are going, you'll end up someplace else.

—Yogi Berra

INTRODUCTION

The opening quote was uttered by Yogi Berra, the New York Yankees baseball team's hall of fame catcher. While humorous, it is a sad reflection of the experience of many clients seeking a counselor's assistance. Our clients are most likely quite clear about their displeasure of being where they are but may be unclear about where they would rather be in terms of their life experience. Helping a client move from the identification of the *what is* to an articulation of *what is desired* is the focus of *goal setting,* a process that requires both special knowledge and skill on the part of the counselor.

This chapter explores how the counselor helps the client envision a state of what is desired, and articulate that vision as clear, concrete, and achievable goals. Specifically, after reading this chapter you will be able to do the following:

- Describe the value and need for the clear articulation of goals.
- Explain the characteristics of a goal which contributes to the goal's utility and therapeutic value using the acronym SMARTGOALS as a guide.
- Describe the factors that should be considered in setting priorities for addressing multiple goals.
- Identify challenges to the creation of therapeutic goals.

WHY GOALS?

The term *goal* typically refers to an object or end of some sequence of events or experiences. In counseling, a client's goal actually signals two things. At one level, achieving the goal signals that the client has been moving away from the *what is*—the state of a problem, concern, or unpleasant experience. Second, achieving a goal is the announcement that the client is now starting a new phase of his lived experience, starting from the point of being in his desired state. Goal achievement clearly signals the ridding of an unhealthy behavior and developing a healthy one, ending a negative thinking style and cultivating a positive one, and ending the feelings of hopelessness and instilling the feelings of hope. But what value, if any, does goal setting have for the helping process?

Extensive research has demonstrated that goal setting is necessary and effective in the problem solving or task completion processes (e.g., Locke & Latham, 1990, 2002; Seijts & Latham, 2001; Seijts, Latham, Tasa, & Latham, 2004). The simple truth is that engaging in helping without a sense of direction and purpose is like navigating without a compass. It is difficult to act without a clear picture of where one is going or intends to go. A goal can help a person become the person she wants to be, stretch the person's comfort zone, boost the person's confidence, give the person a life purpose, encourage the person to trust her decisions, make the person more self-reliant, help the person turn the impossible into the possible, prove that the person can make a difference, improve the person's outlook on life, and lead the client to feelings of satisfaction (Bachel, 2001). As such, goal setting is simply a practical and essential element of the counseling process. Goals are valuable to the helping process in that they serve in various capacities, described in the following sections.

Mapping Direction and Progress. Knowing the *what is* provides the counselor and client with a starting point but success can only be measured by efficient progress toward an end point—the *what is wished for* or goal. Establishing goals allows the counselor to establish milestones to monitor both the direction and progress of the helping process.

Increasing Client Hope and Motivation. While goals are rooted in the future, their articulation tends to change the client's current condition (Presbury, Echterling, & McKee, 2002). With clear, concrete, and achievable goals, a client's focus, sense of purpose, and experience of hope in the future will serve to motivate the client to change the present situations. Goals can provide the client with a vision and direction in terms of where he or she can go and what can be gained from counseling. This vision or direction gives the client hope or a dream, and energizes the client to make this dream come true. Moreover, goals not only provide the client with a direction in counseling, but also offer the client the direction in his or her actual life, which further helps the client see a way out of the current situation. When the client knows what to do, where to go, and what can be gained, the client is able to focus and mobilize himself or herself for action.

Contributing to Sense of Client Autonomy. Clients often enter counseling feeling discouraged, having experienced difficulty for some time and the inability to resolve their current concerns. There is evidence that goal attainment results in enhanced well-being because it promotes need-satisfying experiences related to feeling autonomous (Sheldon & Elliot, 1999). Working with the counselor to identify and specify goals that address the clients' interests and values promote not just a feeling of hope but also empowerment and autonomy. Through goal setting, the counselor encourages clients to face their anxieties; helps clients enhance their sense of mastery and self-efficacy, overcome demoralization, gain hope, achieve insights; and teaches clients to accept their realities (Kleinke, 1994).

Providing Structure. The establishment of goals provides some initial structuring to a client who may have entered counseling without any true sense of what to do or where to go. This is true for the counselor as well. Knowing where the client is, and where the client hopes to go (i.e., goals) provides the structure for the counselor to begin to conceptualize strategies and plans for goal achievement.

Serving as Prescriptive. The ACA (2005) *Code of Ethics* states, "Counselors terminate a counseling relationship when it becomes reasonably apparent that the client no longer needs assistance, is not likely to benefit, or is being harmed by continued counseling" (sec. A.11.c). The counseling relationship should not be open-ended or foster client dependence. Having clearly articulated goals allows both the counselor and the client to know when the particulars of a counseling contract have been met and thus termination is in order. Similarly, having clearly identified goals allows both the counselor and client to understand when progress is lacking and that perhaps referral is in order. This is in line with the ACA (2005) *Code of Ethics* addressing the counselor's inability to assist clients, which states: "If counselors determine an inability to be of professional assistance to clients, they avoid entering or continuing counseling relationships. Counselors are knowledgeable about culturally and clinically appropriate referral resources and suggest these alternatives" (A.11.b).

GOALS: CLEAR, CONCRETE, AND ACHIEVABLE

Goals that are impersonal, vague in presentation, overly generalized, or simply unrealistic will not only prove valueless but may actually increase the client's sense of frustration, hopelessness, and poor self-esteem and thus prove destructive to the helping process. Therefore the articulation of goals is only useful to the helping process when counseling goals reflect a number of specific characteristics.

Goal-setting theory asserts that effective goals have the characteristics of *specificity, measurability, attainability, result,* and *time* (Locke & Latham, 2002). In addition, as presented here, effective goals are *gainful, optimistic, appropriate, legitimate,* and *simple.* These characteristics of effective goals are represented by the acronym *SMARTGOALS,* and are more fully presented in the following sections.

Specificity

Specific goals have been found to produce higher levels of performance and success than ambiguous goals (Locke, 1968). Ambiguity in goal articulation or goals that are vague can result in general confusion and fail to provide the needed direction. Consider the situation in which the client presents the following goals.

> *I would like to be happy.*
> *I like having peace in my life.*
> *I want to feel better.*
> *I want to do better in my relationship with my partner.*

What exactly would these states look like? How will we, others, and even the clients know when they have achieved these goals, these desired states? For goals to be of use in forming our plans of helping, they need to be described in terms that are specific, concrete, and action oriented. It is the role of the counselor to assist the client to reformulate goals so that they exhibit this characteristic of specificity.

The following are examples of goals that are specific, concrete, and action oriented.

> *I will apply for a graduate program in psychology and get a master's degree within two years.*
> *I will take care of my health by exercising 1 hour a day and eating more fruits and vegetables from now on.*
> *I will volunteer to distribute food once a month in my church.*

Exercise 5.1 invites you to practice making goals specific.

Measurability

Framing our goals in ways that allow them to be measured not only contributes to the specificity, previously discussed, but also allows both the counselor and the client to measure the progress made along the continuum of what is to what is desired.

Some goals lend themselves to being measured in that they are easily quantified. This is true with goals such as losing 10 pounds, improving a math grade by one

Exercise 5.1

GOAL SPECIFICATION

Directions: Each of the following represents a goal expressed by a client in counseling. The goals are somewhat vague and ill-defined, so your task is to make each of the following more specific. Compare your work with a learning partner to see if your partner has a better understanding of the goal following your transformation.

- I will develop interests that are similar to those of my partner.
- I will do better in my relationship with my boyfriend.
- I will develop trust and show respect for my husband.
- I want to feel positive and optimistic.
- I will work on my unwanted behaviors.
- I will interact with my colleagues wisely.

full letter grade, calling a spouse once a day, or having a maximum of one drink a day. Sometimes, however, our clients have goals that reflect internal states, such as feeling less anxious, being stress-free, or increasing self-esteem. These goals don't easily lend themselves to observation and direct measurement. However, one strategy counselors often use to help clients measure progress and achievement of goals such as these is the creation of a subjective goal scale.

The client and counselor develop a subjective goal scale through simply drawing a horizontal line and labeling the left end of that line with a description of what is, and at the right end of the line with a description of what is desired. The counselor can assign a 1 to the current state of what is, and then mark the line in equal units of one space each, ending at the desired state which is identified as a 10. Using this subjective scale, clients can report on their personal experience of stress, anxiety, or self-esteem levels along the continuum at various points along the helping process.

The counselor should also help the client identify or set up criteria of successful completion of goals. For example, a client may state a goal as a desire to overcome her depression. With this as a general target, specific criteria such as the absence of symptoms of depression—which may include depressed mood; markedly diminished interest in all or almost all activities; diminished ability to concentrate; recurrent thoughts of death, insomnia, or hypersomnia nearly every day; fatigue or loss of energy; or feelings of worthless—may be set and serve as the measuring stick for successful goal attainment. The successful completion of the client's goal occurs when all these symptoms disappear.

Attainability

Attainability is another important characteristic of effective goals. To be effective, goals need to be realistically attainable or achievable given the client's resources, capabilities, and current circumstances. While a client may wish to complete his college education in 3 years, this may be unreasonable and unattainable if financial resources are limited or the client's family demands are such as to interfere with his studies.

Goals need to be reasonably challenging and require clients to stretch themselves while at the same time be achievable. When goals are too challenging or unrealistic, clients not only experience frustration, but may also assume progress is hopeless. Similarly, if goals lack challenge, clients might lose interest in the process of goal implementation.

Result

When specifying goals, it is important for the client to consider the impact of achieving this or that specific goal. It is also important to consider the result of attaining the specified goal, insuring that it is associated with positive and valuable impacts on the client (Fried & Slowik, 2004).

Helping clients see the impact of their goal achievement as it affects their lives, as well as possibly the lives of others, sets the stage for committing to achieve these goals and serves as a major motivator for engaging in those activities necessary for goal achievement. For example, a client who achieves the long desired sobriety may also realize that in addition to remaining sober his performance at work has improved as have his relationships with his spouse and his children. Be aware of the multiple layers of impact that achieving sobriety has, as it helps to maintain the client's motivation and goal directedness.

Time

Goals that are time-bound, that is, having a clearly identified target date and time, increase motivation for goal achievement (Fried & Slowik, 2004). The time lines not only serve as a motivator but also provide both the client and counselor the means for gauging progress and adjusting strategies if need be.

In setting a time line for goal achievement, it may be obvious that sufficient time be allowed, however what may not be as obvious is that it is important not to provide too much time. Setting an unnecessary lengthy time horizon for goal achievement may invite the client to slow efforts and even result in a loss of motivation with goal attainment taking too long. Needless to say, the time line established needs to be reasonable and flexible, thus allowing for adjustment as progress occurs. The idea is for the time line to serve as a support for goal achievement and not an added stress or hindrance. As research suggests, deadlines with insufficient time tend to lead to less effective performance (Locke, 1996).

Gain

In setting goals, it is helpful for counselors to assist their clients to highlight or articulate the benefits, or gains, they will experience in achieving the goal. Specifying the benefits to be accrued by achieving the goal helps clients maintain motivation and hope. Egan (2010) has suggested a number of questions that may help a client identify the gains to be accrued by way of goal achievement and these include:

> *Why should I pursue this goal?*
> *Is it worth it?*
> *Is this where I want to invest my limited resources of time, money, and energy?*
> *What competes for my attention?*
> *What are the incentives for pursuing this agenda?*

The more the value of the goal can be identified, the more likely the client will make and maintain a commitment to engaging in those activities necessary for goal attainment. Case Illustration 5.1 demonstrates how the counselor helps the client see his potential gain from his goal of stopping smoking.

CASE ILLUSTRATION 5.1

THE BENEFITS OF SMOKING CESSATION

Jim is a 55-year-old male who has been married for 27 years with two children; one is a 22-year-old girl and the other is a 19-year-old boy. Jim started smoking when he was a teenager and became a heavy smoker after he got married. Whenever his family complains about his smoking problem, Jim says that he can't help himself. Recently Jim had a physical exam and the doctor told him that his smoking has caused some damage to his blood vessels. The result of his physical exam does scare Jim, so he has decided to seek counseling for help.

Counselor: So Jim, if I understand what you are sharing, your recent doctor's visit has motivated you to stop smoking.

(Continued)

(Continued)

Jim:	That is correct. But I feel it is going to be difficult. I have smoked since I was a teenager and smoking is already part of my life.
Counselor:	Yes, your body has been craving it and it will be very challenging for you to stop.
Jim:	Yeah (sounding less deflated).
Counselor:	I'm wondering … what do you see are the possible gains for quitting?
Jim:	It might help; my blood vessels become worse if I don't stop.
Counselor:	So stopping may have health benefits. Okay, what other benefits can you get?
Jim:	I don't know. Maybe my clothes won't be stinking.
Counselor:	That's good. What else?
Jim:	That's it.
Counselor:	(sitting in silence as Jim reflects)
Jim:	Oh, my wife and my children would stop complaining.
Counselor:	Stop complaining?
Jim:	Yeah, they are really concerned I'm killing myself with smoking and they get really upset.
Counselor:	Oh, so a benefit is not just that they would stop complaining, but actually may stop worrying so much about losing you?
Jim:	Yeah, I know; they really love me.
Counselor:	It sounds like they do. And these are all real payoffs for stopping, but as I listen to your story it seems to me there are a number of other gains for you by quitting. You have smoked for almost 40 years and your wife and children are all

secondhand smokers. If you stop smoking, none of them would suffer from secondhand smoking. Moreover, you smoke about two packs a day and spend quite a bit on buying cigarettes. Once you stop smoking, you would save a lot of money and you could spend it on something else. In addition to eliminating your behavior of smoking, you would set up a good role model for your children and gain respect from them.

Jim: Wow, I never thought about those benefits.

Counselor's Reflection

The goal to eliminate the client's behavior of smoking has potential gain or enriched result. The counselor needs to help the client see this potential gain—not only will the client experience immediate health benefits but also financial benefits, and benefits of eliminating the harm of secondhand smoking to his loved ones, reducing their anxiety about the possibility of smoking killing him, and serving as a strong role model for his children. I felt that pointing out these added benefits would help motivate him to take on this difficult task and commit to his goal of stopping smoking.

Optimism

Often people present negative goals, that is, things they would like to stop, or no longer do or experience. It is helpful for counselors to assist these clients to reframe their goal to a positive goal—something that the client would like to do, acquire, or experience. While it may be a subtle thing, reframing the goal as something to be worked toward helps to increase the client's sense of hope and optimism. When goals are optimistic or positive, they themselves are an incentive, which will make the client feel energized, excited, and motivated to make effort for achievement. One way to assist clients with reframing negative goals to positive goals is to ask them what they would do, have, or experience if they stopped doing, having, or experiencing the current situation. For example, one client stated she would like to stop eating so many sweets. While this is certainly a worthwhile goal, her response to the counselor's question, "What would be happening instead of eating sweets?" would help her to identify a desire to eat more fruits and vegetables at each meal, and maintain a balanced blood sugar level. This reframe directed her in terms of what to do, rather than attempting to stop doing. Such a reframe proved much more motivational.

So, here the idea of stop, start, and continue can be used to help the client manage her changing of behaviors. That is to say, we can't simply *stop* a behavior, but that we have to *start* a new (more healthy) behavior, and then we *continue* the positive behaviors that are already in place. This brings out the strengths that the client already has and acknowledges that unhealthy behaviors must be replaced by other behaviors for success to occur. Exercise 5.2 invites you to practice identifying negatively and positively framed goals, and then convert negatively phrased goals into positive ones.

Exercise 5.2

POSITIVE VERSUS NEGATIVE GOALS

Directions: Mark which of the following goal statements in Group 1 are positively and which are negatively phrased goals. Next, review the statements in Group 2. These are all negatively phrased goals. Your task is to then change all negative statements into a positive format.

Group 1

- I will stop wasting my time.
- I will plan my time carefully.
- I will stop thinking negatively.
- I will get rid of my behavior of procrastination.
- I will complete my projects in a timely manner.
- I will stop complaining about things that don't go my way.

Group 2

- I want to avoid getting fired.
- I will stop arguing with my partner.
- I will eliminate my habit of interrupting others during the conversation.
- I will stop wasting money on things I don't need.
- I won't fight with my brother.

Appropriateness

Appropriateness may be viewed as an extension of our desire to establish realistic goals. In identifying goals, it is important to develop those which are appropriate, given the client's current condition and situation. Goals need to be appropriate and not only align with the client's developmental level; mental stability; and adaptive social, behavioral, and communicational skills. They also need to align with values, beliefs, and cultural experience. Case Illustration 5.2 provides an example of one counselor assisting a client in setting appropriate goals.

CASE ILLUSTRATION 5.2

SETTING APPROPRIATE GOALS

José is a 16-year-old Latino American. He is currently attending a public high school and his academic performance has been problematic. His parents immigrated to the United States when José was 7 years old. Unfortunately, José's father died in a car accident 2 years later. José's mother has been raising José by herself and she holds a minimum wage job in a local restaurant. Due to his physical disability, José has also been on welfare. José is referred by his mother to counseling after he failed two of his classes and can't make friends at school and in the community. For these reasons, José has very low self-esteem and is mildly depressed. This is José's second counseling session.

Counselor:	José, we have talked about your concerns regarding your schoolwork and your situation with people at school and the community. If I understood what you have shared, it seems like you want to change things at school?
José:	Yes, I want to get better grades and have people to play with.
Counselor:	That is good, better grades and playing with others. I wonder if we could set up some specific goals around this?
José:	Sure. What goals?

(Continued)

(Continued)

Counselor:	Let's first set goals for your schoolwork, better grades as you stated. According to your teachers, you are currently failing both English and social studies. Is that correct?
José:	Yeah, I've screwed up the midterms.
Counselor:	Okay, so maybe you could start by saying that your first goal would be improving your English and social studies grades to passing by the end of this semester.
José:	Sure. But that means I'm going to need to read the books and stuff.
Counselor:	Yes, it would seem that in order to pass, you will have to read the materials and write out any assignments.
José:	I did not put much effort into English and social studies because I don't know how to study them. Like I'm really not good at reading a lot. I mean I find it really hard to read all those pages that are assigned.
Counselor:	Okay, how about this. Before we set a real specific goal, let's see how long it takes you to read just two pages of this article as fast as you can. Would you try that?
José:	Okay, sure, I can do that.
Counselor:	Wait for a second. I'll time and then you start (looks at the clock). Start.
José:	(begins reading)
Counselor:	Good. You actually read that pretty quickly.
José:	Yeah, I guess I can do it. It seems hard to do it for a long time.
Counselor:	That's understandable since you are not used to staying focused on your schoolwork for extended

periods of time. So how about this? Maybe our first goal would be to improve your social studies grade by spending 30 minutes each night reading your textbook and taking notes. What do you think?

José: I can do that.

Counselor: Well, let's try it as a little experiment and I'll check in with you in a couple of days to see how it is going.

Counselor Reflection

By assessing José's reading speed I would get to know how many hours he would need to finish the chapters before he retakes the exam. His reading speed appears typical for children in his grade but he's apprehensive about being able to persist. That is understandable since he has spent the last few months doing little to no reading at home. So ruling out reading speed as a problem, I thought we would set the goal to increase the time on task starting with 30 minutes. If José showed that he had a reading problem I would have changed the goals.

Legitimate

In addition to answering questions such as "Are the goals possible and realistic for the client?" and "Are the goals practical and relevant given the client's personal, social, academic, or vocational needs?" the counselor must also answer the question "Are the goals legitimate, reasonable, acceptable, justifiable, or valid?" As counselors, we are called to a profession that assists individuals with not only moving from conditions of pain and dysfunction but also growing in their ability to address life's conditions as well as maximizing their personal potential. Both of these aspirations assume that the goals we address with our clients are goals that legitimately will, once achieved, result in their increase of health and well-being. Clients whose goals, if achieved, will ultimately inhibit their development and healthy functioning, or may inappropriately impact others within the clients' lives, will need to be confronted and assisted to rework the goals so that they are more healthy and health-filled for the clients.

For example, consider a counselor who is presented by clients with the following conditions: a husband who seeks help from counseling to stop his wife from visiting her parents on weekends, a gay person who comes to counseling looking for help to change her partner's bisexual behavior, or a white female college student who wants the counselor to help her move her black roommate out of her room. A counselor in each of these situations needs to help the client see that these are not goals in the client's best interest. Each of these clients seeks to achieve goals that truly will not lead to personal growth and development and may inappropriately impact another person. In these situations, the counselor needs to help the clients focus within and explore their issues in order to identify goals that will result in growth and increased well-being, without the inappropriate expense or negative impact on others.

Simplicity

Framing goals to reflect each of the previous characteristics helps maintain a client's motivation and sense of hope about reasonably achieving the goals, and provides both the counselor and client with targets for assessing achievement of that goal. Sometimes, even when the goal is developed to include each of the previous elements, the very magnitude of the goal can result in the client feeling overwhelmed and unable to be successful.

Complex and intricate goals need to be simplified so that they are presented in "do-able" chunks. There is a little story about a boy, an eighth grader, who waited until the last minute to complete a semester project on the classification of the birds of prey. The boy sat at his desk feeling totally overwhelmed and unable to start the project, which to him, felt so massive and un-do-able. The grandfather, seeing the child struggling, approached the child and asked: "Would you like to know a secret on how to do this?" The young boy, feeling like he had just been rescued, responded: "Absolutely!" The grandfather, with a gentle hand on the boys back, smiled and said . . . "bird by bird."

While the story is less than eloquent, it drives home the idea that sometimes big goals, as in this case to complete a semester project, need to be broken down into a series of smaller goals (i.e., one bird at a time). Helping a client to simplify large and complicated goals is essential to all helping relationships, but is particularly important when working with young clients or those with limited physical, emotional, and intellectual resources. Chapter 6 discusses one strategy, *goal scaling*, which may prove effective in assisting a client in the process of simplifying goals. The use of goal scaling cannot only assist the client in simplifying goals, but also help maintain the client's sense of hope and optimism while taking small steps through to the end point of goal achievement.

Before moving on, Exercise 5.3 invites you to apply SMARTGOALS to your own life.

Exercise 5.3

SETTING SMARTGOALS

Directions: The following is intended to help you apply the characteristics of effective goals to one area of your life.

> Step 1: Identify one area of your life in which you would like to see some change and write it down on a piece of paper starting with "I would like to …"

> Step 2: Using your goal description (Step 1), revise the statement as written so that it meets the following criteria:

Specific_____

Measurable_____

Attainable_____

Result oriented_____

Timed_____

Gainful_____

Optimistic_____

Appropriate_____

Legitimate_____

Simple _____

> Step 3: Rewrite your goal so that it reflects the characteristics of SMARTGOALS and invite a colleague or learning partner to critique your goal as effective and inclusive of the elements of SMARTGOALS.

CHANGE MODEL AND GOAL SETTING

While we hope all clients come to counseling with a clear awareness of what needs to change, as well as have the skills and the motivation to make the changes required, this is not always the case. Not everyone in counseling is ready to change or has a goal for change. There are clients who are forced to counseling; for example, many children are brought or sent to counseling by either their parents or guardians or school officials; some clients are ordered to counseling by the court; also a person may be sent to counseling by his or her spouse. For these clients, the goal may be increasing their awareness and ownership of the need to change. There are other clients who come to counseling being aware that they need to change, that they need to do something differently, but may lack the motivation to do so. For these clients, a goal—at least an immediate goal—may be to help them see the benefits of change over the costs of their present condition.

Thus, when a counselor engages in goal setting, it may include more than the achievement of a client's desired state of being. As noted previously, for some clients, preliminary goals of increasing awareness of the need for change, creating the belief in the value of change, and even developing the preliminary skills necessary for change may all serve as legitimate goals for counseling.

As noted earlier (see Chapter 2), Prochaska, DiClemente, and Norcross (1992), in their transtheoretical model of change, highlight the fact that clients often enter the process of change at different places along a continuum of change. It is important for a counselor to be able to assess a client's position on this continuum of change ranging from precontemplation, contemplation, preparation, and action to maintenance, in order to set reasonable goals and develop meaningful, effective interventions.

SPECIAL CHALLENGES AND CONSIDERATIONS

While goal setting is a valuable element found within the helping process, it does often come with a number of special challenges and considerations. Goal setting may appear to be simple and natural but counselors will often find that clients are inhibited in their ability to establish goals and set priorities by a number of factors, each of which is explored below.

Client's Constricted Views

Often when clients are asked to articulate a goal for counseling, they find that their concerns over the resources they have, the apparent level of work a goal will take, or simply their history of failure inhibit their ability to generate goals. It is as if they begin to think of a goal and then something within their brains stops them with thoughts of "you can't do that," or "you don't have the resources," and so forth.

Berg and Miller (1992) have offered one creative approach to this dilemma in the form of the miracle question. The miracle question is a future-oriented question that invites clients to envision a future time when their world would be exactly as they wished it to be. The benefit of the "miracle" format is that it invites clients to think out of the box, expanding their vision of what is desired without concerns for practical constraints or even the reality of their current circumstances.

The focus of the question is deliberately vague and open so as to allow clients the freedom to respond in any way that would be important to them. For example,

> Suppose that while you are sleeping tonight and the entire house is quiet, a miracle happens. The miracle is that the problem that brought you here is solved. However, because you are sleeping, you don't know that the miracle has happened. So when you wake up tomorrow morning, what will be different that will tell you that a miracle has happened and the problem that brought you here is solved? (de Shazer, 1985, p. 5).

The openness of the question allows clients to respond with an emphasis on a changed self (e.g., I would assert myself; I would be able to meet my work deadlines) or a changed context (e.g., I would be more accepted at work; I would be in a meaningful relationship). While the question is not supposed to invite magical thinking, it is structured to allow expansive dreaming, which in turn may be an excellent starting place for the formulation of meaningful and useful goals.

Client's Confusing Strategy With Goals

Clients often confuse strategies for goals and in so doing restrict the avenues available for goal achievement. Consider the situation in which a counselor asks his young client: "So what would you like to see happen as a result of this counseling?" to which the client responds: "I would like to have a girlfriend." It is very possible that developing a meaningful relationship and "having" a girlfriend may be the client's goal. As such, it would appear that focusing on the development of his social skills, increasing his social contacts, and finding opportunities to have him engage in meaningful activities with girls of the same age and interest may be some of the steps taken to achieve this goal. However, what if his "goal," that is, to have a girl friend, is actually a strategy to achieve some other, unspoken goal? Assume that the counselor in this scenario pushes his client a little by stating: "Let's assume that you had a girlfriend; how would that work for you?" The question posed was intended to have the client consider if having a girlfriend was a terminal goal or merely a step to some other outcome the client sought. Perhaps the client believed that a girlfriend would be the pathway to being seen as cool by his male friends, resolving his concerns about his own sexual orientation, or allowing him to participate in activities—such as dancing—that he assumed required a partner. In this situation, helping the client move beyond his initial goal to the underlying desires would also open up the various avenues which may be available to reach this goal, with finding a girlfriend being but one possibility.

Not Knowing Where to Start

Clients may present with numerous problems and concerns. The counselor presented with multiple issues thus may not be sure where to begin. Egan (2010) suggested that the counselor should begin with the problem that may cause the client the most pain. When pain, either psychological or physical, is not the defining experience, a counselor may consider starting with the issue on which the client chooses to work.

This may appear obvious but it is an important point to highlight. It is not unusual for a counselor to identify an issue which she feels is important even pivotal to the whole case. While the counselor may be accurate in her estimation if the client has no or limited interest in working on that point at the moment, it will prove ineffective to continue to push for it as a starting point. Rather, it would be more helpful to continue to work on the strength of the helping relationship while exploring the reasons the counselor feels this or that is an important issue to investigate while inviting the client to share his perspective. One final element to consider when identifying a place to start is selecting a goal that the client not only has a reasonable chance of achieving, but is also a goal that has the biggest impact for the least amount of costs (psychological, social, physical) to the client. Cost-effective goal attainment would do much to strengthen the helping relationship and allow for the client and counselor to pursue more difficult areas.

MOVING ON TO STRATEGIES

In the early chapters, we made an effort to highlight the swirling nature of the helping process, a process that does not lend itself to neat, sequential steps and stages. As we reflect on the helping process—a process involving the development of a meaningful, trusting, and caring relationship in which counselors help clients move from enmeshment in their problems or concerns to the articulation of smart goals—it should become quite obvious that "real helping" has occurred. The establishment of the relationship, the exploration of the client's issues and the formulation of meaningful goals, were not steps in the preparation of helping, they were helping. Now, with SMARTGOALS in place, we turn our attention to the development, implementation, and maintenance of strategies that will support clients as they move from what is to what is desired.

COUNSELING KEYSTONES

- Establishing goals allows the counselor to establish milestones to monitor both the direction and progress of the helping process.
- With clear, concrete, and achievable goals, a client's focus, sense of purpose, and experience of hope in the future serve to motivate the client to change present situations.
- Through goal setting, the counselor encourages clients to face their anxieties; helps clients enhance their sense of mastery and self-efficacy, overcome demoralization, gain hope, achieve insights; and teaches clients to accept their realities (Kleinke, 1994).
- Knowing where the client is, and where the client hopes to go (i.e., goals) provides the structure for the counselor to begin to conceptualize strategies and plans for goal achievement.
- Having clearly articulated goals allows both the counselor and the client to know when the particulars of a counseling contract have been met and thus termination is in order.
- Effective goals are characterized by the elements included in the acronym SMARTGOALS (specificity, measurability, attainability, result, time, gainful, optimistic, appropriate, legitimate, and simple).
- When setting goals, the counselor needs to help clients expand their focus, and not confuse strategies with goals, and address those goals that will provide the most immediate relief with the least cost to the client.

ADDITIONAL RESOURCES

Readings

Blair, G. R. (2002) *Goal setting 101: An essay, step-by-step guide for setting and achieving a goal.* Syracuse, NY: Goalsguy Learning Systems.

Christiansen, R. (2012). *Zig zag principle: The goal setting strategy that will revolutionize your business and life.* New York: McGraw-Hill.

Ellis, K. (1998). *Goal setting for people who hate setting goals.* New York: Three Rivers Press.

Lopper, J. (2007). *Personal development: 40 best articles on cheering up, positive attitude, goal setting, and much, much more.* United States: Author.

Smith, D. K. (1999). *Make success measurable! A mindbook-workbook for setting goals and taking action.* New York: John Wiley & Sons.

Web Resources

Jim Rohn Setting Goals Part 1
　　www.youtube.com/watch?v=YuObJcgfSQA

Jim Rohn Setting Goals Part 2
www.youtube.com/watch?v=kmM_XkxuCxY&NR=1

REFERENCES

American Counseling Association. (2005). *ACA code of ethics.* Alexandria, VA: Author.

Bachel, B. K. (2001). *What do you really want? How to set a goal and go for it! A guide for teens.* Minneapolis, MN: Free Spirit Publishing.

Berg, I. K., & Miller, S. D. (1992). *Working with the problem drinker: A solution-focused approach.* New York: W. W. Norton.

de Shazer, S. (1985). *Keys to solution in brief therapy.* New York: Norton.

Egan, G. (2010). *The skilled helper: A problem management and opportunity development approach to counseling.* Belmont, CA: Brooks/Cole.

Fried, Y., & Slowik, L. H. (2004). Enriching goal-setting theory with time: An integrated approach. *Academy of Management Review, 29*(3), 404–422.

Kleinke, C. L. (1994). *Common principles of psychotherapy.* Belmont, CA: Brooks/Cole.

Locke, E. A. (1968). Toward a theory of task motivation and incentives. *Organizational Behavior: Human Performance, 3,* 157–189.

Locke, E. A. (1996). Motivation through conscious goal-setting. *Applied and Preventive Psychology, 5,* 117–124.

Locke, E. A., & Latham, G. P. (1990). *A theory of goal-setting and task performance.* Englewood Cliffs, NJ: Prentice Hall.

Locke, E. A., & Latham, G. P. (2002). Building a practically useful theory of goal setting and task motivation: A 35-year odyssey. *American Psychologist, 57,* 705–717.

Paul, G. L., & Shannon, D. T. (1966). Treatment of anxiety through systematic desensitization in therapy groups. *Journal of Abnormal Psychology, 71,*124–135.

Presbury, J. H., Echterling, L. G., & McKee, J. E. (2002). *Ideas and tools for brief counseling.* Upper Saddle River, NJ: Merrill Prentice Hall.

Prochaska, J. O., DiClemente, C., & Norcross, J. (1992). In search of how people change: Applications to addictive behaviors. *American Psychologist, 47,* 1102–1114.

Seijts, G. H., & Latham, G. P. (2001). The effect of learning, outcome, and proximal goals on a moderately complex task. *Journal of Organizational Behavior, 22,* 291–307.

Seijts, G. H., Latham, G. P., Tasa, K., & Latham, B. W. (2004). Goal setting and goal orientation: An integration of two different yet related literatures. *Academy of Management Journal, 47,* 227–239.

Sheldon, K. M., & Elliot, A. J. (1999). Goal striving, need satisfaction, and longitudinal well-being: The self-concordance model. *Journal of Personality and Social Psychology, 76,* 482–497.

Chapter 6

Moving From What Is to What Is Desired

I know I can do this!

INTRODUCTION

In order for counseling to be truly a helping process, the counselor must help the client to successfully *do this,* where the *this* is a plan that will prove effective in moving the client to the desired state.

Counseling is a helping process. It is a process that assists one individual to move from an undesirable life condition to one that is more desirable. The previous chapters presented the knowledge and skills required of a counselor to assist clients in sharing their story, identified the elements causing difficulty, and articulated the preferred state of functioning by way of goal setting. With these data in place, the counselor and the client can now move to the identification of the specific steps or strategies to be employed to facilitate this movement from what is to what is desired.

This chapter introduces the elements that go into this process of plan formulation and implementation. Specifically, after reading this chapter you will be able to do the following:

- Understand that path finding, or strategizing and intervening, is a process that happens throughout the counseling process and is not restricted to one element later in the counseling.
- Understand that intervention plans can be created from the analyses of a client's previous successes, the existing research supporting theories of counseling, and even by way of a generic problem-solving model.
- Apply the processes of brainstorming and cost-benefit analyses to the selection of a strategy for goal attainment.

- Value the ethical need to be competent in strategies selected to implement.
- List possible challenges one may encounter during the development, implementation, and maintenance of treatment strategies.

INTERVENTION PLANNING: NOT STATIC, NOR A ONE-TIME EVENT

With the counselors and the client gaining clarity about the *what is* in terms of presenting concerns and client's resources and the *what is hoped for,* that is, the goals and outcomes for the counseling, they will increase their attention to the consideration of the strategies and techniques needed to move the client toward the desired outcome. This process of attending to strategies of change is not a one-shot operation, nor is it a fixed stage to be employed at the end of some time together. As noted throughout the previous chapters, counseling, as an intentional process, is one in which the counselor has selected and employed a variety of interventions all geared to moving the client toward some outcome. From intake to termination, clinicians must gather and analyze case information, formulate hypotheses, and implement treatment decisions (Makover, 1996; Tillett, 1996). Whether the intervention is a simple greeting aimed at relaxing the client or the use of a probe or a well-timed challenge to assist the client in gaining clarity, intervention has been occurring all along the counseling process. Having said that, we anticipate there will be a time or times when the client and the counselor turn attention to the identification and implementation of steps which will be employed in hopes of moving the client to some ultimate outcome.

THE USE OF THEORY AND RESEARCH AS GUIDES TO INTERVENTION PLANNING

James Prochaska (1995) noted that change is a process in which clients engage in covert and overt activities that alter their affect, thinking, behaviors, and relationships as related to a particular problem or pattern of living. In their attempt to identify and select specific activities that will affect such change in their clients, counselors often turn to their theoretical model or the professional research highlighting effective interventions. The theories of counseling, along with the research supporting their utility and validity, serve as the core of counseling as a discipline and a profession.

Theories: Framework for Making Meaning

As every neophyte counselor soon comes to appreciate, facilitating the sharing of the client's story often results in an overabundance of information. There are things said and unique tones and styles in saying them: The client's body signals, responses to counselor questioning, and even selected periods of silence may be essential in understanding the full meaning of the story that is unfolding. But as each of these pieces of information may be relevant and essential to the helping process, it is equally possible that they are irrelevant and potential distractions. The theory or theories a counselor employs serve as a framework within which the details of the client's story are processed. Counseling theory thus provides a guide for discerning what is important from that which is not. Theories serve as an organizing mechanism so that the counselor can not only make sense of the story being shared, but also know how best to respond to the data in order to help the client move from what is to what is desired.

Theories: All Equally Valuable and Useful?

An exercise sometimes assigned in a counseling course is for students to articulate their theory of counseling. While such an exercise invites a meaningful dialogue around the assumptions each student may bring to a helping encounter, it may be less productive if we are to assume that all such theories generated by those in the early stage of their professional development are of equal value and utility. The same can be asked of the more than 500 theories or approaches to counseling found within the literature (Kazdin, 2008). Are all 500 equally "good,"—of equal value and utility?

The tradition in science is to assess a theory against a set of standards or preferred qualities that collectively provide a measure of a theory's worth (Maddi, 1996). These include the following:

- *Precision.* A "good" theory employs constructs and concepts that are clear and precise, and their relationships are similarly specified.
- *Testability.* A good theory generates predictions that in turn are testable.
- *Parsimony.* A good theory provides the simplest explanation, assuming the other qualities are present.
- *Stimulation.* A good theory provokes research to test, to validate, to confirm, or to disconfirm.
- *Practicality.* A good theory is practical—that is, applicable—and within counseling, provides the useful framework from which to gather essential information, make meaning, and make effective practice decisions.

Theories of Counseling: A Rich History

Historically, with little understanding of psychopathology, individuals who presented with difficulties navigating life challenges would either be ignored and avoided as if possessed, or confined to institutions for warehousing. The history of counseling and therapy probably could find its origin in the early work of Sigmund Freud (1949) and those of the Vienna circle. These creative individuals moved emotional problems from the realm of the demonic to a natural illness rooted in some form of psychic conflict. It was with these early postulations of mental functioning and dysfunctioning that the treatment and the foundation for our profession as helpers found footing.

Since those days of the late 19th century, many others have stepped in to provide templates or models for understanding the human psyche and behavioral function and dysfunction. These theorists, some of whom are highlighted later in this chapter, articulated organizational frameworks to guide helpers in their attending to, processing of, and making meaning of each client's story.

In the 21st century, we find the theories employed across the profession of counseling to be the outcome of a rich history and evolutionary past. For example, the mid-1950s saw the influx of theories emanating from the labs and clinical experiences of J. D. Watson (1919), B. F. Skinner (1974), Joseph Wolpe (1990), and later the work of Albert Ellis, Aaron Beck (1976), and Donald Meichenbaum (1977). These individuals moved our thinking away from the psycho-historical emphasis and psychic conflict models of Freud and his followers to consider the influence of environment in shaping our behavior and our thinking. Their work has resulted in a variety of cognitive and behavioral theories, which emphasize the influence of thoughts and actions on emotions. Some have called the infusion of behavioral theory into counseling as the second force, with Freud and the psycho-dynamic models being the first force. A third force, one emphasizing the importance of emotions and sensations and the belief that individuals can and desire to take control of their lives in search of meaning and fulfillment, emerged in the 1960s with the initial work of Carl Rogers (1961) and his presentation of a humanistic, person-centered theory.

These three forces, along with our increasing awareness of alternative perspectives including those that highlight spiritual and religious experiences, the influence of gender and cultures, as well as those that offer insight from non-Western perspectives, continue to stimulate the development and use of theories to guide practice.

Contemporary Theories

There are simply too many theories for a book such as this to adequately cover. However, as a way of introducing the reader to the expanse of current theory, we have employed the organizational schema presented by Linda Seligman and Lourie Reichenberg (2010). For those seeking additional information, a list of additional resources are provided at the end of this chapter. Seligman and Reichenberg presented four categories in which one could list specific contemporary theories. These categories, along with their description, representative theories, and reference are listed in Table 6.1.

Table 6.1   Categorization of Contemporary Counseling Theory

Category	*Representative Theory or Theories*	*For Further Information*
Background These theories emphasized the client's history, placing importance on past experiences as formative to present concerns. The focus of helping is typically on helping the client resolve problems or issues carried from the past.	Classic psychoanalysis (Freud); individual psychology (Adler); object relations theory (St. Clair)	www.apsa.org Website of the American Psychoanalytical Association
Emotions While all theories will allow for the importance of emotions and feelings, the theories classed under this category give special attention to emotions and sensations and focus on the *experiential*—the way we experience ourselves and our world.	Person centered theory (Rogers); gestalt theory (Perls); feminist theory (Gilbert & Rader)	www.iceeft.com The Centre for Emotionally Focused Therapy
Thoughts Theories grouped within this category all share an emphasis on the role that our thoughts, our cognitions—our meaning making—plays in both causing and ameliorating our distress. The theorists within this category believe that it is our thoughts which lead to emotions and behaviors and thus it is through becoming aware of thoughts which are irrational or dysfunctional and changing these thoughts that a resultant change in feelings and action will occur.	Rational emotive theory (Ellis); cognitive theory (Beck)	www .beckinstitute .org/ Website of the Beck Institute for Cognitive Therapy and Research

(Continued)

Table 6.1 Continued

Category	Representative Theory or Theories	For Further Information
Actions Used here, action refers to overt, observable and thus measurable behavior. While our behaviors, our actions, are intertwined with our feelings and thoughts, theorists who employ action-focused theories target the modification of dysfunctional behaviors as the means through which to facilitate a client's growth.	Behavior theory, cognitive-behavior theory, reality theory, solution focus brief theory (see the work of theorists such as Albert Bandura, Joseph Wolpe, Arnold Lazarus, William Glasser, & Steve DeShazer).	www.nacbt.org Website of the National Association of Cognitive-Behavioral Therapists

A MODEL OF CHANGE AND GOAL ACHIEVEMENT

In addition to the use of intervention strategies derived from specific theories of counseling, counselors often engage general principles of problem solving in order to assist their clients. These principles are presented in the following sections as elements of a generic model of change and goal achievement. These include: the use of a creative process to identify pathways to the client's goals; the assessment of the cost and benefit of the various pathways, the selection and employment of a strategy, and the monitoring of progress toward the goal.

Identifying Pathways to Client Goals

Even when clients have clarity about their goals, they may feel frustrated, even hopeless because previous attempts have proved unsuccessful. One of the tasks of the counselor is to reenergize clients and help them feel hopeful about the possibility of achieving their goals. Employing strategies that highlight clients' competence (i.e., working with exceptions) and engage their creativity (i.e., brainstorming) can not only result in the identification of strategies that may prove effective in facilitating the desired change, but also serve to stimulate the sense of hope needed to energize clients in their own helping process.

Working With Exceptions

While a client may enter counseling feeling defeated, and believing herself to be a failure, the truth or facts of life are that while she may have hit a roadblock in her life, she has experienced numerous times and situations when she successfully navigated life challenges. The identification of these past successes not only affirms the client's competence but will be able to help the client identify the techniques or strategies that she has employed in the past to be successful. If the *exceptions* can be reviewed and analyzed, they can provide the materials for the creation of a solution to the presenting concern.

Valuing the wealth of resources that each client brings to the situation, the counselor helps the client understand how solutions have occurred in the past (exceptions) and how the elements that contributed to that success can be called up and reshaped for application to the present issue. Consider a student who was referred to the school counselor because he lashes out at other students who verbally tease him at lunch. The counselor working with that client was able to identify the *self-talk* strategies the client employed as a star football player when experiencing an opponent's "trash" talking. The student explained that he understood that the opponent was attempting to get him angry so that he would do something that elicited a penalty for his team, or even get him removed from the game. With this awareness of why the opponent was taunting him, the client was able to dismiss the comments as meaningless, just part of the game, and something to ignore. Further, he knew that he needed to focus on the game and not the comment. The counselor working with this exception helped the student see the teasing as the other student's attempt to get him in trouble, and as a result, encouraged him to treat it like the game and dismiss the teasing at lunch; this turned the client's focus away from the comment and refocused on his friends and their discussion occurring at his lunch table. In this case, the counselor simply helped the client tap his own successful problem-solving strategy and competency, and helped him reshape them for application in the current situation.

When using exceptions as a strategy for identifying interventions, it is important for the counselor and the client to investigate the details of the exception, including the where, what, when, and how of the exception (O'Connell, 1998). The counselor, in working with exceptions, will encourage the client to describe these exceptions and to identify what different circumstances exist in that case or what the client did differently. Thus, it is not sufficient to simply say, "Well, do that again." The counselor and the client need to understand all of the factors—all of the elements that went into doing it the first time. Questions that need to be answered include: What were the client's motivations and feelings? What was the client thinking? How did the client act? What support did the client experience?

What external conditions existed that made the exception possible? These are just a few of the questions to explore in hopes of identifying the specific elements that went into the successful employment of the strategies resulting in resolution of the previous situation.

Case Illustration 6.1 provides an example of how the counselor helps the client look for exceptions.

CASE ILLUSTRATION 6.1

SEEKING EXCEPTIONS: SOCIAL PHOBIA

Andrew is a 44-year-old Caucasian American male. He comes to counseling with severe social phobia.

Counselor:	You indicated that you are anxious in various social situations.
Andrew:	That is correct.
Counselor:	Can you be a little bit more specific about it?
Andrew:	I'm anxious all the time, every situation in my whole life. I'm even anxious while I'm with my daughter and my son-in-law, even when I am with my wife. You can tell that I'm anxious now, look at my hands, trembling and sweating. This has bothered me ever since I could remember. I really don't know what I should do about it.
Counselor:	Can you think of an occasion or a situation when you are interacting with someone, maybe your wife, and you don't feel anxious or feel less anxious?
Andrew:	(pauses) No. I don't think so. I'm always anxious . . . off the charts.
Counselor:	So even at times when, for example, you are saying goodnight to your wife, you experience maximal anxiety?

Andrew:	(smiling) No, of course not . . . we're just going to bed.
Counselor:	Okay, that is true, but you are going to bed "together"?
Andrew:	(smiling) Well, if that is the kind of thing you mean . . . then when we make love, I'm not anxious.
Counselor:	Wow. So when you go to sleep or when you make love with your wife you don't experience this anxiety?
Andrew:	Yes. It is not an issue.
Counselor:	Well, you say it's not an issue, but I think that is pretty interesting. I mean these are times when you are interacting, very intimately, with your wife and yet you are not anxious. I wonder what is different about those times?

Counselor Reflection

The client has been anxious for many years. His anxiety has been so overwhelming that he has been anxious about his anxiety. It is normal that he may not be able to think of an occasion when he does not have anxiety. His sharing of his ability to share intimate moments with his wife and remain nonanxious provided a great opportunity to investigate his focus—his self-talk—during these times, which allowed him to stay in the moment rather than generate anxious thoughts. As we investigated the elements that went into making this a nonanxious event, we were able to develop specific strategies that he could take from this experience and apply in an upcoming presentation that he needed to do at work.

Brainstorming Creative Options

Another strategy to use when attempting to identify pathways toward a goal is brainstorming. A value to brainstorming is that it is nonjudgmental and the client, with the counselor's facilitation, can be stimulated to create as many ideas as possible with the result being the identification of pathways not previously considered. The goal of brainstorming is the generation of a maximum quantity of ideas (with quality being assessed later). Three simple guidelines should be considered:

1. *Target quantity not quality.* As suggested in the first rule, the goal is to develop as many ideas as possible.

2. *Suspend judgment.* Because the goal of brainstorming is to foster creativity, and generate a quantity of ideas, the client and counselor need to suspend judgment about the value or even the practicality of any idea generated. Later within the process or selecting a pathway, the pros and cons of each idea will be assessed. During brainstorming, the rule should be "the crazier the better" in that sometimes the most creative ideas provide a starting point for the crafting of a very practical, creative, and do-able intervention.

3. *Build on previous ideas.* It is useful to combine ideas previously offered, or attempt to expand on ideas previously noted. When generating an idea, the client should be encouraged to build off of that idea and generate as many permutations as possible.

Case Illustration 6.2 provides an example of the use of brainstorming with a client attempting to identify strategies to help him control his anger.

CASE ILLUSTRATION 6.2

HELPING A CLIENT LEARN HOW TO BRAINSTORM

Jacob is a 17-year-old Asian-American high school junior, who is referred to counseling by his teacher for anger management. Jacob often gets angry with numerous things, some as little as waiting before the red traffic light. He frequently blows up and yells until he is hoarse. Even worse is that a couple of times he has gotten into physical fights with others. However, he has a lot of regrets later for what he does or says. Jacob's goal in counseling is to control his anger and he and the counselor now engage in strategizing around how this may be accomplished.

Counselor:	So . . . your goal is to control your anger.
Jacob:	Yeah.
Counselor:	Do you have any ideas how you can achieve the goal?
Jacob:	No, not really.

Counselor:	Maybe it would be helpful if we simply tried to generate as many ideas about how a person could control his or her anger as we can . . . you know, brainstorm?
Jacob:	We use brainstorming in creative writing class.
Counselor:	That's great. So you know that we are not going to judge if it is a good or bad idea or if it seems silly or too difficult. Let's just get as many ideas as we can out on the table and then we can come back to consider each.
Jacob:	Like what kind of things? I mean the things I do are yelling and getting into physical fights with others.
Counselor:	That's a start . . . let's put those down, but how about other ways people may deal with angry feelings?
Jacob:	I don't know . . . .
Counselor:	Well you have one here, getting into fights . . . that's pretty physical. I wonder if there are other things people do—you know, physical things—that help them deal with angry feelings?
Jacob:	You mean sports?
Counselor:	Hey . . . it's an idea . . . let's put it down.
Jacob:	Something like running or soccer?
Counselor:	Here I'll put those down.
Jacob:	That's about it . . . .
Counselor:	Well, we are getting there but I'm wondering if we really allow ourselves to think out of the box, what kind of physical activities or maybe even mental things or social things we could do to reduce feelings of anxiety?
Jacob:	Well, I yell when I'm mad . . . maybe just making loud noises, or blowing out lots of air . . . something like that.

(*Continued*)

)

ᴐunselor:	Now you are on a roll.
acob:	Socially, I guess I could try to call my friends or maybe just text them that I'm pissed off . . . sorry.
Counselor:	Got them . . . we are getting quite a list . . . hmm, how about anything you could do mentally . . . or with your thinking . . . .
Jacob:	Well, I know when I'm playing b-ball I try to focus and take some breaths before shooting foul shots— that calms me . . . maybe something like that?

Counselor Reflection

Jacob, like many clients, approaches the task with very narrow focus and needs a little encouragement to think out of the box. As I guided him, he became increasingly more energized by the process and more creative. We developed a number of very useful strategies and he felt as if he was the problem solver in this situation. This contributed to his ownership of the strategies we selected.

Exercise 6.2

GETTING A LITTLE HELP FROM A FRIEND

Directions: Your task is to invite two friends to participate in a process designed to help you develop strategies that will facilitate your attainment of some personal goal. As such, you are to identify a specific, concrete, observable, and measurable goal of personal improvement. Perhaps it is that you want to improve your grades, find a new job, quit smoking, or start exercising. The first step is to identify the goal and specify it in concrete terms. The next step is to explain to your friends the rules and goals of brainstorming. Remember to highlight the focus is on quantity of ideas, without judgment or criticism. Also, invite your friends to build on each other's ideas and to think out of the box.

The specific task is to generate as many strategies that could be used to achieve your goal. You have 10 minutes to generate ideas. If you end before 10 minutes, review the strategies presented, and push for more. List goal and strategy idea in the space below.

GOAL

_____

Strategies (use additional paper as needed)

As suggested by Case Illustration 6.2, clients often need encouragement to think out of the box in order to generate ideas not previously considered. It is important the counselor not only encourages such divergent thinking, but may also need to model the type of expansive thinking desire. Exercise 6.2 provides an opportunity to engage in divergent thinking by using brainstorming.

Assessing Possible Pathways

With the mandate to be nonjudgmental or nonevaluative during the brainstorming stage, the client and counselor may generate a number of strategies that prove more or less effective in helping the client reach her goal. Not all of the pathways or strategies identified are of equal value. Each has more or less potential for helping the client achieve her goal and each will require some expenditure of client resources (e.g., time, energy, etc.). As such, the counselor and client will engage in a process of assessing both the potential for benefit and positive outcome of each strategy, and weigh that against the incurred cost. With this evaluation in place, the client will be ready to select and implement a specific approach to goal attainment.

General Criteria for Judging Pathway Viability

In addressing each of the proposed strategies, the client should consider some very practical issues as well as take a more structured look at the costs and benefits of each. Before beginning a detailed analysis of the comparative cost and benefits of the generated strategies or pathways, the counselor and client should review each to insure that they meet the following criteria:

- They appear to offer a high degree of likelihood that the end goal will be achieved.
- The client understands and embraces the strategy as something do-able with which success is attainable.
- The knowledge, skills, and general resources needed to implement the strategy are available to the client.

This last point, while perhaps appearing obvious, is pivotal to the successful selection and implementation of an intervention strategy.

Available Resources

Resources are one of the key factors in the development and implementation of any problem-solving strategy. Client resources can be sorted into two categories: internal and external resources. Internal resources include things such as a client's knowledge and skills, as well as level of cooperativeness, motivation, energy level, sense of responsibilities, intellectual and physical capabilities, and so on. External resources can be identified as client's support systems including family members, community, school, churches, workplace, friends, and access to facilities and finances. Each of these has the potential for supporting clients in their effort toward problem resolution and needs to be creatively considered in the development of change strategies.

Taking advantage of resources that are under the client's control and reachable with reasonable effort is essential in the goal achievement process. For example, the counselor needs to help the client indentify the individuals who can help him to achieve his goals, or who can serve as role models or exemplars. In addition, counselors can help the client identify groups, organizations, programs, and events that will lend support to his change efforts (Egan, 2010).

Clearly strategies that are beyond the client's internal or external resources will prove ineffective, regardless of their theoretical soundness. One special internal resource that careful planning and implementation of an intervention plan can foster is client confidence. Client's confidence is the minimum requirement for client action toward goal achievement. Most clients have come to counseling having exhausted all their own efforts to resolve the difficulty they face and thus may come to counseling feeling defeated and even hopeless. Assisting a client to gain confidence can be facilitated through the creation of change strategies, which can be implemented in small steps—steps organized to maximize the probability of success. With each experience of successful implementation, a client's personal confidence as well as hopeful expectations will increase. A barrier to the client's confidence could be her fear of failure. Again, planning that attempts to insure the greatest possibility of success, while at the same time minimizing the impact of failure, assists in reducing this fear and the roadblock it may present. Case Illustration 6.3 demonstrates one counselor's attempt to assist the client's sense of confidence.

Once the strategies have been reviewed against these general criteria, those that fail to either logically lead to the outcome desired or those for which the client fails to take ownership or fails to possess the resource needed should be eliminated from consideration. For those remaining, the counselor and client may want to engage in a more focused analysis of possible costs and benefits as a way of helping the client choose the strategy or strategies to implement.

Detailing Costs and Benefits for Each Plausible Pathway

The list of possible intervention strategies can now narrow down to those which offer the biggest possibility of success at the least cost to the client and others in the client's life. The counselor and client can begin to narrow the list of pathways down to the most desirable by analyzing the expected benefits and costs to be incurred as a result of employing each of the strategies.

Costs and benefits can be grouped as physical, social, and psychological. Thus, a client who goes cold turkey in stopping smoking may experience the initial costs of physical discomfort (i.e., cravings), psychological stress, and social exclusion (i.e., not going out at break time to share a cigarette with friends). At the same time, this client may experience a personal sense of accomplishment (psychological

CASE ILLUSTRATION 6.3

BUILDING CLIENT CONFIDENCE IN SESSION

Tracey is a 28-year-old White female and a nontraditional college junior. She is also a single mother who has a 7-year-old daughter with physical disability. Tracey has a couple of part-time jobs to pay her college tuition and her and her daughter's living expenses. Tracey came to counseling as a result of having been raped and manifesting the symptoms of post-traumatic stress disorder (PTSD). The therapist attempted to provide Tracey with a set of strategies aimed at increasing her state of relaxation. However, as part of the strategy, Tracey was asked to close her eyes. This simple directive appeared too much for Tracey and clearly elicited heightened anxiety and resistance. From Tracey's perspective, closing her eyes in the presence of the therapist was too dangerous, making her too vulnerable and she simply believed it would be impossible and thus an ineffective strategy.

During the second session, Tracey formally sets her therapy goals and indicates what she wants to pursue. However, when the counselor intends to explore her emotional experience of being raped, Tracey keeps changing the topic. After the counselor brings her to the topic, Tracey openly tells the counselor that she doesn't want to go there because it is too painful and she is afraid that she would collapse if she starts talking about those heartrending experiences.

Counselor:	Thank you for letting me know your concerns about exploring your feelings that are connected with your past painful experiences.
Tracey:	I don't feel comfortable to go there now. It could be too much for me. But I can work on the stress that I have now.
Counselor:	What would you like to do?
Tracey:	I don't know. Some kind of relaxation exercise?
Counselor:	Okay. Let's do some mental relaxation exercise. I'll read some script for you while you're relaxing. Would you like to give it a try?
Tracey:	Sure. But I never did anything like that before.

Counselor:	Can you sit a little bit further to the edge of the chair, and relax your shoulders?
Tracey:	(follows the counselor's instruction and prepares for the exercise)
Counselor:	Now close your eyes.
Tracey:	No, I can't do that.
Counselor:	Do you mean you can't close your eyes?
Tracey:	No, I can't. I never close my eyes in front of anyone including my parents.
Counselor:	I think I understand. You feel vulnerable when you close your eyes and can't see what others around you are doing?
Tracey:	(looking down) Yes, it probably sounds silly but I can't help it.
Counselor:	No, actually the way you say it and the way you look when you say it suggests to me that it is not at all silly, but in some ways really frustrating to you?
Tracey:	I just wish I could relax like normal people.
Counselor:	(pauses a little bit and thinks about concept shifting) I have an idea. Can you blink?
Tracey:	Yeah, I can blink.
Counselor:	That's good. I'm thinking blinking, even though it is very quick, is in a way closing your eyes. So I'm wondering if we could try something?
Tracey:	I guess.
Counselor:	Great. I am going to count and I want you to try to blink on my count. For example, I count one, you blink once; I count two, you blink another time, so on and so forth. When you hear me say the number, you open your eyes. Do you understand what I'm trying to do?

(Continued)

(Continued)

Tracey:	I think so. You want me to blink, which in a way is closing my eyes, but just a little.
Counselor:	You're correct. Would you be willing to give a try?
Tracey:	Okay. I'm willing to give a try.
Counselor:	One, two, three, four, five.
Tracey:	(follows the counselor's instructions and blinks as the counselor counts)
Counselor:	That's very good. Let's do it again.
Tracey:	Okay (looking at the counselor and prepares to do it again).
Counselor:	(purposely slowing the speed of counting) One . . . two . . . three . . . four . . . five . . .
Tracey:	(waits for number six while her eyes are closed).
Counselor:	All right. Now open your eyes. You have closed your eyes just now.
Tracey:	Have I?
Counselor:	Yes, you have.
Tracey:	(becoming excited) I can close my eyes? I can close my eyes.

Counselor Reflection

The client was raped multiple times in her life and has completely lost trust in others. That lack of trust and sense of vulnerability was making her resist the simple directive to close her eyes. It was my feeling that gaining her trust—while at the same time helping her to experience success as a way of improving her confidence—was essential. It was clear that even the simple successful experience of closing her eyes boosted her sense of confidence and she became excited. It was my belief that this achievement would bring her courage and confidence, which would motivate her to take bigger steps to achieve her ultimate goal of recovery. This was not meant to be a game or a trick; that's why I wanted her to understand that blinking was in fact closing her eyes, just for very brief periods. She clearly understood and was willing to try it.

benefit), ease of breathing (physical benefit), and affirmation from loved ones (social benefit). Prior to selecting and implementing such a cold-turkey strategy, the client should compare the cost-benefit ratio of this approach as compared to another approach, such as a slow withdrawal method. Further, when identifying costs and benefits, as a way of maximizing the benefit to cost ratio of the strategy selected, the counselor and client can attempt to identify ways in which some of the costs could be reduced and some of the benefits increased for each of the strategies. Exercise 6.3 invites you to engage in a cost-benefit analysis.

Exercise 6.3

REVIEWING PATHWAYS

Directions: Select two of the strategies identified in Exercise 6.1. Using the table below, assess the costs and benefits of each strategy. Does one appear to provide the biggest payoff for the least cost? Do you have the resources to implement that strategy?

Strategy	Cost *Include physical, financial, psychological, and social costs.*	Payoff *Include physical, financial, psychological, and social*
1	_____	_____
	_____	_____
	_____	_____
2	_____	_____
	_____	_____
	_____	_____

Implementing a Plan

Change is difficult, even when the strategy selected is well thought out and embraced by all involved. Our interventions, while well thought, are not perfect. When implementing a program, clients will often encounter the unexpected and, as such, need to have the freedom to revisit the plan and make adjustments as needed. One way to instill this attitude of "pilot testing" the intervention plan is to help the client introduce the intervention in small steps—steps designed to increase the possibility of early success. One process often employed for such structuring of the implementation is that of goal scaling (e.g., Berg & Miller, 1992; O'Connell, 1998)

Goal Scaling

Goal scaling is a process through which the counselor and client identify a terminal goal, describing it in full detail, and then identify where the client is in relationship to that goal. The counselor and client could, for example, draw a line with spaces designated as 0 through 10, where 10 represents the final goal. Clients could be asked not only to describe what the 10 would look like but also to place themselves on the continuum in relationship to that goal. Having a starting place and an end point in sight, the counselor and client then attempt to describe what the next step (from the current position) would look like and use that as the initial target for intervention. For example, let's assume a client wishes to quit smoking. She notes that she has "cut back" but still smokes about five cigarettes a day. When asked to place herself on the scale of 0 through 10, she notes that she is at about a 5, having once smoked a pack a day. With the help of the counselor, she is then able to identify how a 6 would look like, stating that she would smoke only one cigarette (rather than two) during her work break, and only one (rather than two) after dinner. Pilot testing the intervention on such a graded goal will increase the possibility of initial success, or in the case of failure, provide valuable information that can guide client and counselor's adjustment of the treatment plan.

The use of this scaling process can be very empowering in that it helps make goals concrete and achievable, and it empowers the client to take responsibility for the change and the evaluation of individual progress. The scaling process also provides a structure for considering sequential steps that will bring the client closer to the ultimate goal.

Maintaining Motivation and Commitment

As noted, intervention plans do not always operate smoothly, nor are our desired outcomes always readily achieved. Setbacks are to be expected and client disappointment and frustration are not unusual. When implementing a program of change, the counselor needs to support the client in ways that maintain motivation and commitment to change. The steps that a counselor can take along these lines can be represented by the acronym ACCOUNTABLE, explained as follows:

> A—Approach the client's action plan.
> C—Commit to achieve the goals.
> C—Calculate what the client is able to do.
> O—Offer the client ongoing support, encouragement, and objective feedback.
> U—Underline the urgency and importance of the established goals.
> N—Nurture the client's autonomy and development of creative problem-solving abilities.
> T—Tailor the interventions to the uniqueness of the client and the client's life conditions.
> A—Agree upon the plan being implemented.
> B—Be specific in terms of the terminal goal.
> L—Link client efforts and outcomes, and the long-term benefits of goal achievement.
> E—Evaluate as a process that is not restricted to the final goal achievement.

Approach. It is important to set a positive expectation by approaching the clients' action plans with clear expectations of success.

Commit. After goals and expectations are set, clients need to commit to achieving them. It is not unusual to find clients who understand what needs to be done but for reasons unidentified are really not committed to engaging in the actions required to facilitate change. The drunk driver, for example, mandated to counseling as part of his DUI may truly understand the downside to his drinking and even help provide input into the development of an intervention process. However, without real ownership of both the problem and the benefit of the intervention, it is unlikely that this client will actually implement the intervention strategy.

In their basic coaching model, Ivey, Ivey, and Zalaquett (2010) proposed some powerful questions for clients to make commitment to their action. These questions are:

Are you ready and committed?

How committed are you to change and action?

On a scale of 1 to 10, how committed are you to actually doing this?

Will you do it tomorrow?

Can we write a contract for action?

Let's select something small enough that you actually want to and feel confident that you will do it. (p. 112)

These questions, as the authors indicated, will examine the clients' level of motivation—commitment—for actually reaching their goals.

Calculate. Successful implementation of a plan, along with evidence of progress, serve as major motivators to the maintenance of the intervention plan. Helping clients objectively define or calculate what they will be able to do, when they will be able to do it, and what small change could be identified as evidence of progress helps set the structure to guide clients' investment in the intervention plan. The calculation and comparison of the ongoing results to the clients' goals will help them see the gaps that require further effort.

Offer. Remembering that change is difficult, it is important for the counselor to offer clients ongoing support, encouragement, and objective feedback. According to Fishbach and Finkelstein (2012), feedback can possibly increase people's motivation by raising attainment expectancies and perception that the goals are valuable and attainable.

Underline. Underlining the urgency and importance of the established goals repeatedly is also crucial in the process of goal achievement. Goal achievement involves more than clients' commitment, tasks calculation, and feedback. Clients further need to remember why they are doing what they are doing and how they will benefit once the goals are achieved.

Nurture. While the focus is on a specific problem or goal, the counselor is also committed to the prevention of problems and the development of the whole client. Nurturing clients' autonomy and development of creative problem solving abilities is also a role for the counselor.

Tailor. Throughout the previous chapters we have emphasized the fact that counseling is *not* a formulaic, cookie-cutter process. The counselor must help clients *tailor* the interventions to the uniqueness of each client and their individual life conditions. Further, as interventions are implemented, unexpected events or unforeseen circumstances will require that the intervention be adjusted or further tailored to meet these conditions. Case Illustration 6.4 is one example of how the counselor helps the client tailor strategies on how to work on his goal to overcome his social anxiety.

CASE ILLUSTRATION 6.4

HELPING A CLIENT TAILOR STRATEGIES

Dave is a 42-year-old White male who has had problems of social anxiety for quite a few years. Dave is polite, friendly, cooperative, and motivated to change. At this point, Dave has become clear about his issue and agreed upon the goals that have been set for him.

Dave: Well, I know there is a church in my neighborhood that has a community breadbasket where they give meals out on Friday night, and I know there is a basketball league that meets at the church and they even have singles dances. Oh yeah, and I know there is a group of people who meet at the YMCA to play racquetball.

Counselor: Wow, they sound like some really good resources. What do you think about engaging in something like those?

Dave: I don't know. They all seem to be a little overwhelming.

Counselor: Well okay, but in thinking about them, are there any that seem less overwhelming or any one where you think you may be a little less anxious?

Dave: Maybe doing the church breadbasket.

Counselor: Well, that's super, would you be interested in trying that out?

The session continued with the counselor and client discussing the pros and cons of engaging in the breadbasket program and possible points of difficulty, and a plan was established. The client committed to participating.

(The following session)

Counselor: Well, how did it go?

Dave: (hesitates) I didn't do it . . . . I couldn't go.

(Continued)

(Continued)

Counselor:	That's okay. You know, if we look at what was going on it could really help us.
Dave:	Help? How?
Counselor:	Well, you and I gave our best shot thinking about what the challenges would be but we were doing our best guess. Now we have some real life experience—good data—that we can use to shape a new plan.
Dave:	So it wasn't a total waste?
Counselor:	Waste…absolutely not. This is tough stuff and you gave it your best shot so let's figure out what we can learn . . . .

Counselor Reflection

The client was initially committed to the plan of going to the breadbasket and we did what I thought was a good job anticipating possible problems. While the client presented as somewhat down about "failing" at his assignment, reframing the experience as one that would provide us good information to reshape our intervention helped to reengage him in the process and actually led to some creative adjustments to our original plan.

Agree. In order to have an intervention plan successfully put into action, the counselor needs to help clients fully understand what is involved in such a plan of change. In addition to understanding the plan, it is essential that clients agree to engage in the implementation of that plan. It is not unusual to experience clients who simply comply with a counselor's suggestions without a full and clear understanding of what it is they are committing to. To maintain clients' commitment and agreement, it is essential for the counselor to check throughout the course of plan implementation that clients understand the procedures to be used, the potential positive and negative impacts of these procedures, and the resources to be employed.

Be specific. As clients engage with the treatment plan and conditions change, the client and counselor need to revisit the expected outcomes, making adjustments as needed as always, being specific in terms of the terminal goal. While goal specification previously occurred, the counselor wants to help clients revisit those goals and progress toward them. As a result, clients will understand the connection between where they were, what they are doing, and where they are going.

Link. The work of counseling and intervention implementation needs to be counterbalanced by a clear awareness of the benefits to be accrued. Linking client efforts and outcomes, and the long-term benefits of goal achievement is necessary to the maintenance of a successful intervention plan.

When clients see the link between the goals and how the goals benefit them personally, they are most likely to make the effort to take action and be willing to hold themselves accountable for the results.

Evaluate. Evaluating is a process that is not restricted to the final goal achievement. It is also important for the client and counselor to monitor progress. The counselor must engage clients in the process of ongoing evaluation of not only the implementation of the intervention, but also the value of the working alliance. When the results are positive, the counselor may use them to inspire clients for further progress. When the results are negative, the counselor may work with clients to indentify and remove the barriers to client success. Strategies may be developed to overcome the identified barriers and goal modification may be made accordingly. Strategies a counselor can employ to evaluate progress and outcome are presented in Chapter 7.

CHALLENGES TO PROGRESS

In his poem "To a Mouse," Robert Burns (1785) stated that the best laid schemes of mice and men often go awry. This is certainly true for the best of a counselor's plans. While a counselor may ground her intervention plans in good theory, solid research, and a strong working alliance with the client, she may still experience challenges to progress. The following is but a brief sampling of the types of challenges that may be encountered within the counseling dynamic.

Client Resistance

It is not unusual for a counselor to encounter a client who exhibits reluctance or resistance to the plans developed. From a psychoanalytic point of view, "resistance refers to any idea, attitude, feeling, or action (conscious or unconscious) that fosters the status quo and gets in the way of change" (Corey, 2005, p. 72). The fact that a client exhibits resistance does not automatically signal something is wrong with the client. Resistance can also signal a legitimate hesitancy on the part of the client to proceed with a plan that is either too difficult to implement or one with which the client's perspective will not work.

A client's resistance may reflect a number of issues and concerns experienced by the client. Consider the client who is mandated to counseling by the courts, his company, teacher, or manager. This client may be resisting as a reaction to this coercion (Egan, 2010). The client's resistance under these conditions may simply be a form of asserting his own power and autonomy. While the resistance may be frustrating for the counselor, the client's right to autonomy and self-determination needs to be recognized and accepted, and the plans which are developed need to reflect the input of that client.

Clients With Special Needs

Most of the classic theories and techniques taught to those in counselor training were developed from a perspective of a male, who exhibits Western and capitalist values and worldviews. Moreover, the majority of the counseling textbooks employ as illustrations clients who speak standard English, exhibit logical thinking, and share similar values and worldviews with the counselor. Further, these illustrative cases most often involve individuals of average IQ and who respond well to questions posed by the counselor, understand the counselor's intention, and are willing to follow the prescription offered. Clearly, counselors' lived experiences do not reflect this profile as representative of all of those whom they serve.

Yet, given this "template," it is clear that clients who are under age 5, intellectually challenged, language incapable, English deficient, or from a culture different from that of the counselor present as a challenge to those counselors who lack training and experience with these unique populations. It is essential then that counselors seek training in applying intervention strategies with diverse populations and, if confronted with clients whose needs exceed the training and competency of the counselor, employ referral as the intervention of choice.

Clients Exhibiting Reactance

Reactance is a term applied to an individual's emotional reaction when experiencing a loss of personal control and pressure to accept a particular view or attitude. Counselors who present autocratically and inflexibly in pushing their point of view can elicit resistance, in the form of reactance, from the client. The client may simply adopt a view or attitude that is contrary to that of the counselor as a way of establishing a sense of freedom and autonomy.

For counselors encountering challenges such as those described, it is essential to first recognize the nature of the challenge and accept, even value, the challenge as providing essential information about the client and the counseling process. It is important that the counselor not simply view the client as stubborn and thus discount the basis upon which progress may have stalled. The counselor should instead view such challenges to progress as reflecting important information about the client and the helping relationship. This information, once understood, will allow for adjustments to be made and progress continued.

COUNSELING KEYSTONES

- This process of attending to strategies of change is not a one-shot operation for the client and counselor, nor is it a fixed element to be employed at the end of some time together.
- Change is a process in which clients engage in covert and overt activities that alter their affect, thinking, behaviors, and relationships as related to a particular problem or pattern of living.
- In developing intervention strategies, counselors employ counseling theory and research.
- In recent years, a shift has occurred toward the promotion of specific approaches for specific problems based on empirical support for those treatments.
- Strategies for change can be developed by analyzing clients' previous successes, and crafting the elements of those successes into a prescription for the current situation.
- A generic approach to the development of intervention strategies involves the use of brainstorming techniques, cost-benefit analysis of various options, and selection of those strategies that offer the greatest possibility of success with least cost.
- Goal scaling is a technique that helps clients set small achievable goals on their way to the ultimate outcome.
- Regardless of theoretical or empirical support for an intervention, plans selected must be those for which the counselor is competent to employ.
- Counselors often encounter challenges along the way during their counseling—challenges reflecting the uniqueness of their client or an artifact of their own style. In these cases, counselors do well to see these challenges as offering valuable information, which, once understood, can facilitate continued progress.

ADDITIONAL RESOURCES

Clegg, B., & Birch, P. (2007). *Instant creativity: Simple techniques to ignite innovation & problem solving.* London: Kogan Page Limited.

Fawcett, M. L., & Evans, K. M. (2012). *Experiential approach for developing multicultural counseling competence.* Thousand Oaks, CA: Sage.

Kendjelic, E. M., & Eells, T. D. (2007). Generic psychotherapy case formulation training improves formulation quality. *Psychotherapy: Theory, Research, Practice, Training, 44*(1), 66–77.

Kiresuk, T. J., Smith, A., & Cardillo, J. E. (1994). (Eds.). *Goal attainment scaling: Applications, theory, and measurement.* Hillsdale, NJ: Lawrence Erlbaum.

O'Connor, K. J., & Ammen, S. (1997). *Play therapy treatment planning and interventions: The ecosystemic model and workbook.* Cleveland, OH: Academic Press.

Schmidt, J. J. (2010). *The elementary / middle school counselor's survival guide* (J-B Ed: Survival Guides). New York: John Wiley & Sons.

Seligman, L., & Reichenberg, L. W. (2010). *Theories of counseling and psychotherapy: System, strategies and skills* (3rd ed). Upper Saddle River, NJ: Pearson Education.

REFERENCES

Beck, A. T. (1976). *Cognitive therapy and emotional disorders.* New York: International Universities Press.

Berg, I. K., & Miller, S. D. (1992). *Working with the problem drinker: A solution-focused approach.* New York: W. W. Norton.

Corey, G. (2005). *Theory and practice of counseling and psychotherapy* (7th ed.). Belmont, CA: Brooks/Cole.

Egan, G. (2010). The skilled helper: *A problem management and opportunity development approach to helping.* Belmont, CA: Brooks/Cole.

Fishbach, A., & Finkelstein, S. R. (2012). How feedback influences persistence, disengagement, and change in goal pursuit. In A. Fishbach & S. R. Finkelstein (Eds.), *Goal-directed behavior* (pp. 203–230). New York: Psychology Press.

Freud, S. (1949). *An outline of psychoanalysis.* New York: W. W. Norton.

Ivey, A. E., Ivey, M., & Zalaquett, C. P. (2010). *Intentional interviewing & counseling.* Belmont, CA: Brooks/Cole.

Kazdin, A. E. (2008). Evidence-based treatment and practice: New opportunities to bridge clinical research and practice, enhance the knowledge base and improve patient care. *American Psychologist, 63,* 146–150.

Maddi, S. R. (1996). *Personality theories: A comparative analysis* (6th ed.). Pacific Grove, CA: Brooks/Cole.

Makover, R. B. (1996). *Treatment planning for psychotherapists.* Washington, DC: American Psychiatric Association.

Meichenbaum, D. (1977). *Cognitive Behavior modification: An integrative approach.* New York: Plenum Press.

O'Connell, B. (1998). *Solution-focused therapy.* Thousand Oaks, CA: Sage.

Prochaska, J. O. (1995). An eclectic and integrative approach: Transtheoretical therapy. In A. S. Gurman & S. B. Messer (Eds.), *Essential psychotherapies: Theory and practice* (pp. 403–440). New York: Guilford Press.

Rogers, C. (1961). *On becoming a person.* Boston: Houghton Mifflin.

Seligman, L., & Reichenberg, L. W. (2010). *Theories of counseling and psychotherapy: System, strategies and skills* (3rd ed.). Upper Saddle River, NJ: Pearson Education.

Skinner, B. F. (1974). *Beyond freedom and dignity.* New York: Knopf.

Tillett, R. (1996). Psychotherapy assessment and treatment selection. *British Journal of Psychiatry, 168*(1), 10–15.

Watson, J. B. (1919). *Psychology, from the standpoint of a behaviorist.* Philadelphia: J. B. Lippincott.

Wolpe, J. (1990). *The practice of behavior therapy* (4th ed.). Elmsford, NY: Pergamon Press.

Chapter 7

Practice Accountability

An Ethical Mandate and a Practice Necessity

Is this working?

INTRODUCTION

Before we begin the chapter, we would like you to take a moment to reflect on how you may go about answering the question of "is it working?" as applied to your work with a client. Exercise 7.1 invites you to consider some criteria or measures you may employ to answer this question. Your responses to this exercise will not only help you begin to consider the issue of practice accountability, but may also help make the discussion to follow more meaningful for your own professional development.

Some counselors fail to see the need and value of assessing the effectiveness of their counseling while others often assume that as long as the client felt good about the sessions that a positive outcome most certainly had been achieved (Ridley, Li, & Hill, 1998). For these counselors, criteria of success are often items, such as those found in Exercise 7.1, that reflect a client's level of comfort or even enjoyment with the encounter.

Though there may be an intuitive appeal to using client satisfaction as a measure of effectiveness, research has demonstrated that such satisfaction does *not* translate directly into "treatment efficacy" (Pekarik & Guidry, 1999). It is important to remember that counseling, as noted throughout this text, is an intentional process with the generic goal being the facilitation of positive change for the client. Treatment efficacy goes beyond feeling good to include the demonstration of such desired change.

Clearly, not everything a counselor does is helpful in promoting such change. In fact, it is even possible that beyond failing to be effective, one's counseling may result in negative outcomes for clients, with them leaving treatment worse off than when they entered

Exercise 7.1

IS THIS WORKING?

Directions: Review each of the following, and identify those which you would employ as an indication that your work with any particular client was "working."

Criteria or Indicator of Effectiveness	*(Check if you would use.)*
The client states that he/she enjoyed the session.	_____
The client and counselor both feel good about the session.	_____
The client and counselor appear to be comfortable with each other.	_____
The counselor exhibits core conditions of genuineness, empathy, and unconditional positive regard.	_____
The client is willing and interested in scheduling future appointments.	_____
The client is freely disclosing.	_____
The client expresses satisfaction with the counseling.	_____
The client refers other clients for service.	_____
The client, following a session, announces that this has worked and there is no need to continue.	_____

(Lambert & Ogles, 2004; Mohr, 1995). Given this research, it can be argued that counselors cannot simply assume that this or that strategy is working, regardless of the literature supporting its "proven effectiveness" nor can they simply employ soft standards such as "it felt like a good session" as measures of effectiveness; rather, counselors must develop and employ valid and reliable processes to monitor the effectiveness and outcome of their work. Such monitoring not only serves as a means of accountability, but provides data essential to the counselor's professional development and the increased effectiveness of the service provided to clients.

Before we proceed further, completing Exercise 7.2 may help set the stage for what is to follow.

The purpose of both Exercise 7.1 and 7.2 is not to demean these indicators of the process and outcome of a counseling relationship, but instead to highlight the inadequacy of these measures as valid and reliable measures of effectiveness. The current chapter addresses both the need and value of practice assessments and introduces a number of strategies that counselors can employ to demonstrate effectiveness. Specifically, after reading the chapter, you will be able to do the following:

- Explain the ethical and practical impetus for practice assessment.
- Describe the psychometric considerations in selecting and employing standardized outcome measures.
- Differentiate between final outcome (summative) and progress assessments (formative).
- Describe the challenges that confront counselors as they attempt to answer the question, "Is this working?"

Exercise 7.2

MISLEADING INDICATORS

Each of the indicators listed in Exercise 7.1 may support the effectiveness of one's counseling and may be an indication of something other than progress. For example, a client who is free with disclosures may indicate the presence of the conditions necessary for the development of a working relationship, but this characteristic could also indicate that the focus of the discussion is on topics of low therapeutic value and thus nonchallenging and nontherapeutic.

For this exercise, it is suggested that you review each of the criteria listed in Exercise 7.1 with a learning partner and identify explanations for the appearance of such criteria that would be either nontherapeutic in nature (as might be the case with disclosure around nontherapeutic issues), or even damaging to the therapeutic process (as might be the situation when the comfort being experienced is a result of inappropriate behavior, such as hugs, physical contact, on the part of the counselor—that is, when the comfort level is a function of inappropriate boundary violations).

(Continued)

(Continued)

Directions: Review each of the presenting concerns presented below and identify strategies you would employ to measure desired outcomes by completing each of the blocks within the table.

Client and Presenting Concern	What changes are desired (stated or implied)?	Reframe / rephrase the desired changes so that they are measurable.	How would the desired changes be measured?
Example: Client is a 52-year-old male who came self-referred to the counselor noting that he has been "feeling down, losing weight, unmotivated to do anything . . ."	Have more energy physically and emotionally, maintain healthy weight, and engage in life tasks.	1. Client will be more optimistic and enthusiastic about his day. 2. Client will maintain current weight. 3. Client will return to work. 4. Client will engage in typical household chores.	1. The client will chart his daily moods along a scale where 1 = the most down he has ever felt and 10 = the most energized and optimistic he can remember ever being. 2. The client will record his weight on a daily basis. 3. Client will maintain an activity log demonstrating time and activity at work, chores completed, and recreational/entertaining activities in which he engages daily.
Client is a 16-year-old male, new to the school, who is socially withdrawn in school, sitting by himself at lunch and avoiding all extracurricular activities.			
Client is a 21-year-old college senior approaching graduation (in 2 months), presenting with general anxiety and concerns about her future post graduation.			
Client is a 38-year-old woman unhappy in her marriage.			

THE PRACTICAL AND ETHICAL IMPETUS TO PRACTICE ASSESSMENT

Though some may feel that accountability has become a catchword in today's sociopolitical climate, the truth is that counselors in all settings have experienced increased pressure to demonstrate the effectiveness of their services (see American School Counselor Association [ASCA], 2005; Lambert, Bergin, & Garfield, 2004; Reed & Eisman, 2006). Since the 1960s, local, state, and federal government spending has been more closely scrutinized and the effectiveness of social programs and initiatives, including counseling, have been more carefully questioned (Houser, 1998). Counselors are now finding the need to be accountable to a variety of stakeholders.

While current impetus for increased accountability may have started as counselors' response to stakeholders, it is now recognized as a process that reflects our professional ethical mandate and holds the promise of improving our professional practices.

Responding to Stakeholders

All mental health professionals, including counselors, are increasingly finding themselves in a position of needing to demonstrate client progress and treatment effectiveness to stakeholders such as school boards, institutional administrators, and third-party payers (Astramovich & Coke, 2007). This is true for not only the counselors who work within publicly funded settings such as schools, but also those who work in fee for service practices.

School Counselors

Historically, school counselors may have pointed to a simple listing of activities and services they offered or perhaps an actuarial reporting of the specific time they spent on each of their assigned tasks as a measure of accountability (Gysbers & Henderson, 2000). In our current sociopolitical climate, these earlier measures are simply inadequate. It is no longer sufficient to simply describe what one does. It is essential that counselors demonstrate the effects of what they do, along with the cost-benefit of what they did in light of alternatives. When it comes to school counselors, legislators, school boards, administrators, and faculty want to see evidence that the work of school counselors is an effective use of financial resources to improve student achievement (Adelman, 2002; Borders, 2002; Herr, 2002; House & Hayes, 2002; Lusky & Hayes, 2001).

In response to these pressures and as an extension of the school reform movement and standards-based education reforms (e.g., No Child Left Behind [NCLB] Act of 2001; U.S. Department of Education, 2001), school counselors are taking steps to demonstrate the value and effectiveness of their services (Albrecht & Joles, 2003; Dahir & Stone, 2003; Finn, 2002; Gandal & Vranek, 2001; Myrick, 2003). Even the American School Counselor Association (ASCA) has responded to the call for accountability by developing a new framework, which includes an emphasis on accountability in school counseling (ASCA, 2005).

The accountability component of the American School Counselor Association (2005) National Model® helps school counselors move from a "counting tasks" system of accountability to aligning the school counseling program with standards-based reform. This process enables school counselors to demonstrate how they are accountable for results and contribute to student achievement.

Given the various sources calling for accountability and outcomes-focused initiatives in our schools, it is clear that role and function of school counselors in the future will include the systematic evaluation of the impact of the services they provide (Trevisan, 2001).

Counselors as Mental Health Practitioners

As is true for counselors working in schools or other publicly funded agencies, those counselors working within a fee for service environment are also experiencing increased pressure to demonstrate the effectiveness of their services. For those in private practice working with managed care providers, the need to provide client information, session details, and evidence of progress as a means of justifying current treatment and the need for future sessions has been widely identified and lamented as negatively impacting practice (Danziger & Welfel, 2001). To secure managed care contracts and receive third-party reimbursements, mental health counselors are increasingly required to keep detailed records about specific interventions and outcomes of counseling sessions (Granello & Hill, 2003; Krousel-Wood, 2000; Sexton, 1996). Their task is to demonstrate not only the achievement of desired outcomes, but also the achievement of these goals by way of the most cost and time efficient manner possible.

Professional Identity

While much of the discussion around the issue of accountability targets justifying what we do in terms of cost and benefit to our stakeholders, embracing the need and value of accountability offers benefits to our profession. The collection of data demonstrating the impact of our services not only provides justification for these programs, services, and interventions but serves as a base from which a unique professional identity is articulated and demonstrate the value of our profession within the larger context of helping is demonstrated (Weinrach, Thomas, & Chan, 2001). More specifically, Lambert and Cattani-Thompson (1996) argued that measures of effectiveness are essential if counselors are to regard themselves as professionals who warrant reimbursement, licensure, or credentialing.

Without this evidence of unique value and effectiveness of our services, counselors may be relegated to an adjunctive or quasi-professional status among mental health providers.

Ethical Response

The requirement of accountability is simply not only a response to external pressures by third-party payers and institutional boards, but also a reflection of our professional standards of practice. The ACA (2005) *Code of Ethics,* for example, specifies that counselors should continually monitor their effectiveness as professionals and seek supervision to evaluate their efficacy as counselors (see sec. C.2.d). The American School Counselor Association (2004) *Ethical Standards* states that counselors should assess the effectiveness of their program in having an impact on students' academic, career, and personal/social development through accountability measures especially examining efforts to close achievement, opportunity, and attainment gaps (ASCA, 2004, sec. A.9.g). Further, the ASCA (2005) National Model® places accountability in the top quadrant of the framework and challenges school counselors to answer the question, "How are students different as a result of the school counseling program?" (p. 59).

Gathering data that reflects the effectiveness of our interventions clearly is not only good for the client, required by outside payers, but essential to the ongoing development of the counselor and the counseling profession.

ASSESSING THE PROGRESS AND OUTCOME OF COUNSELING

We opened this chapter with a simple question: "Is this working?" with the *this* being counseling. It is a question posed by multiple stakeholders—clients, employers, and funders seeking accountability—but when posed to counselors of their own work, it is also a question that can provide data for ongoing growth both for the counselor and the counseling profession.

To answer the question, counselors need to engage in both formative and summative evaluations of their counseling. These processes not only allow counselors to demonstrate the final outcome of their counseling efforts (summative evaluation), but also do so in a way which helps them monitor progress toward the desired goal and improve upon the strategies being employed to get there (formative evaluation).

Formative Assessment

While it is certainly important to collect data that supports the effectiveness of one's counseling and the ultimate outcome of such a helping relationship, assessment—the collection of data reflecting where we are in light of where we have been—can also be formative in nature. In terms of counseling, *formative assessment,* also called process evaluation, provides information about how well a program is being implemented, and monitors what services are being provided by whom, for whom, when, and at what cost (Gladding, 2011). Formative assessment helps counselors identify progress made or the lack thereof, and make adjustments in their approach to any one client at any one time along the way.

As previously noted, counseling is not a step-by-step, static, sequence of events, cleanly and predictably leading to a desired outcome. Counseling is a very personal and dynamic process reflecting the uniqueness of those engaged. As such, the best laid plans of counselor and client will often be presented with unexpected roadblocks and detours, which call upon the counselor's ability to make the needed and effective modifications. It is important for counselors to gather and analyze case information from initial intake to termination in order to reformulate hypotheses and adjust treatment decisions (Makover, 1996; Mordock, 1994; O'Donohue, Fisher, Plaud, & Curtis, 1990; Tillett, 1996). This is the process of formative assessment.

For counselors to be effective, they need to be aware of client data as it depicts client functioning at any one point in the counseling process and then compare the data to that which was expected. The differences between the *what is* and the *what was expected* provide the counselor with evidence of the effectiveness of the current path of counseling or demonstrate the need for an adjustment. Consider the data collected and the adjustments made by the counselor in Case Illustration 7.1.

It is clear that the counselor in Case Illustration 7.1 had hoped to engage the client in data collection in order to develop a behavioral program reducing slow and fast triggers to excessive drinking and the development of an alternative response to social drinking. The client's minimization of her current situation necessitated a change in the current treatment plan. The focus shifted from preventive strategies to increasing the client's ownership of both the problem and value of counseling. The expectation was that once the client took ownership of the problem, a refocusing onto the conditions supporting problematic drinking and the development of an alternative response could be possible. Such an adjustment in treatment focus and approach may not have been possible if it were not for the counselor's clear articulation of intended session goals, and reflection on data pointing to the degree to which these goals had been met. This is an illustration of the benefit of formative evaluation, even when it is done using informal and anecdotal data.

CASE ILLUSTRATION 7.1

A FORMATIVE ASSESSMENT OF AN INITIAL SESSION

Olivia, a 23-year-old computer programmer, was mandated to come to counseling by the courts following her recent DUI. In telephone intake, Olivia noted that "this is really unnecessary since I am not a drinker and this was a very weird set of conditions that led to my arrest." She understood that she "had" to attend a minimum of five sessions to get these "over" as soon as possible.

In preparation for the initial session, the counselor set the following as tentative goals:

1. Achieve informed consent from the client highlighting the mandated need to provide the courts with a report of attendance and clinical judgment of progress.

2. Clarify the initial reason for referral, including details of the conditions surrounding the arrest.

3. Acquire a client and family history with focus on drug and alcohol (D & A) use.

4. Assess client's level of alcohol use/abuse and potential dependency/addiction.

5. Increase the client's awareness of the nature of the "problem" and the value of counseling.

In order to achieve these goals, the counselor intended to employ effective communication and relationship skills, engage in a structured review of family history, employ the Michigan Alcoholism Screening Test (MAST), and use confrontation as a means of raising client awareness and ownership of the nature and seriousness of the problem. Following the initial intake, the counselor reflected on the session as a way of engaging in formative evaluation in order to adjust (if needed) the goals and approach for upcoming sessions.

The following represents both the outcomes and decisions derived from this reflective assessment.

(Continued)

(Continued)

Goal	Status	Plan
Achieve informed consent from the client.	Achieved.	Follow up to see if the client has any questions after reading the "Welcome to My Practice" packet.
Clarify the initial reason for referral.	In process. Client was evasive stating she was "unsure exactly" what she was charged with and what her blood alcohol level was at the time of arrest.	Client signed release of information form so that the arrest report could be acquired. The client will be presented a copy of the report and the data will be discussed in session.
Have client articulate specific, concrete goals she hopes to achieve through engagement with the counselor.	Follow up. Provided the client with miracle question and asked her to reflect on it to be discussed in upcoming session.	Review her response to the miracle question.
Acquire a client and family history with focus on D & A use.	Client presented a history of recreational use of alcohol, no drug involvement, and no family history of abuse, depression, or family members treated professionally for D & A or related issues.	Engage the client in a functional behavioral analysis of her own drinking behavior with the hopes of identifying triggers or conditions which result in excessive use.
Employ the MAST.	Data failed to support the presence of alcohol dependence.	Refocus counseling goals on the clarification of the poor decision making (driving following drinking) and strategizing ways to identify at-risk conditions.
Increase client's awareness of nature of the problem and value of the counseling.	Client employed minimization to dismiss the arrest and the need and or value of counseling beyond meeting the court mandate.	Attempt to employ a solution-focused approach (to deemphasize the suggestion of pathology, which the client seems to be defending) and engage the client with the miracle question and the identification of exceptions.

Some have suggested that such formative evaluations should be more structured and standardized as a system of quality assurance (QA) (see Barkham et al., 2001; Lambert, Hansen, & Finch, 2001). These quality assurance systems allow counselors to systematically and continuously monitor their client progress session by session and even compare this progress to expected levels of treatment progress. An important feature of a QA system is its ability to identify when treatment is not working (Shimokawa, Lambert, & Smart, 2010). This information is essential for counselors to adjust treatment methods or when needed to make appropriate referral.

There are a number of specific instruments (scales) and approaches that can facilitate formative assessment of the counseling process; two such measures are the Session Evaluation Scale and the Goal Attainment Scale.

Session Evaluation Scale (SES). The Session Evaluation Scale (SES; Hill & Kellems, 2002) is one instrument that can be used to capture counselors' and clients' perceptions of session quality. The SES contains four items (e.g., I did not feel satisfied with what I got out of this session; I thought that this session was helpful.).

In using the scale, counselors have the clients rate each statement along a 5-point scale ranging from 1 (strongly disagree) to 5 (strongly agree). After reverse scoring the two negatively worded items, item responses are totaled and divided by four, producing a 1 through 5 scale, with higher scores reflecting perceptions of higher session quality.

Goal Attainment Scale (GAS). The Goal Attainment Scale (GAS; Kiresuk, Smith, & Cardillo, 1994) is a measure that targets client change, rather than perception, and has been demonstrated to be effective for assessing even small changes with clients (King, McDougall, Palisano, Gritzan, & Tucker, 1999). This sensitivity to even small change makes the GAS a useful tool for formative assessment, noting progress across sessions.

The GAS process captures functional and meaningful aspects of a person's progress that are challenging to assess using available standardized measures. The GAS procedure involves (1) defining a unique set of goals for each client, (2) specifying a range of possible outcomes for each goal, and (3) using the scale to evaluate the client's functional change after a specified intervention period (King et al., 1999). In general, a 5-point scale (−2 to +2) is used for scaling goals. Kiresuk and colleagues (1994) specified that 0 (zero) is used as the predicted expected level of performance, with −1 indicating somewhat less than expected performance.

Case Illustration 7.2 provides an illustration of the use of the goal attainment scale and its value in treatment adjustment.

CASE ILLUSTRATION 7.2

GOAL ATTAINMENT SCALE: REDUCTION OF SMOKING

The client is a 47-year-old male who has been smoking cigarettes for over 30 years; as a result of a recent pulmonary exam that revealed early signs of lung damage, he has sought counseling support for his goal of smoking cessation. The counselor has an expertise and experience in working with individuals who have nicotine addiction. The counselor knows that the slowness with which some clients achieve total cessation—and the fact that for many there are periods of gain followed by regression relapse—often serve as points of frustration for the client. As such, the counselor was interested in developing and employing a measure that would enable the client and counselor to set reasonable subgoals for each session and assess progress toward those goals, adjusting goals and process as needed. The following reflects the goal attainment scale used three weeks into the behavioral modification program.

Goal Attainment Scale *Target: Smoking Reduction*	
+2	Client makes more than expected progress, reducing smoking by 51% or more from baseline average of five cigarettes a day.
+1	Client makes expected progress of 25% to 50% reduction of smoking behavior from baseline average of five cigarettes a day.
0	Client makes baseline of five cigarettes a day, with no improvement or less than 25% change in smoking behavior.
−1	Client exhibits an increase of 25% to 50% of smoking behavior over baseline of five cigarettes a day.
−2	Client exhibits an increase of over 51% of smoking behavior over baseline of five cigarettes a day.

The client collected the data daily over the course of the week between the third and fourth session. These data are reported as follows and reflected that the client had a total of +5 over the course of the seven days.

Client Self-Report

Monday +1
Tuesday +1
Wednesday + 2
Thursday +2
Friday +1
Saturday −2
Sunday 0

Analysis

These data suggested that the day of the counseling session and the day imme-diately following the session (Wednesday and Thursday) showed the best progress whereas the weekend, particularly Saturday on which there were times of heavy social interaction, was the most difficult for the client. With these data as the base, the counselor and client, feeling overall successful movement, changed the target goal of reducing the number of cigarettes and incorporated an alternative response behavior (chewing gum) to be used during the weekend.

Summative Evaluations and Outcome Measurement

Summative evaluation refers to the assessment of counseling outcome and sum-marizes the achievement of clients at a period of time. As discussed in Chapter 5, counselors need to assist their clients to move from presenting what is to envision-ing a preferred future and the articulation of desirable goals. When the goals of counseling are developed in clear, concrete, measurable terms, their achievement will be readily observable and thus serve as the outcome measure pointing to the effectiveness of the counseling. Consider the efforts of the counselor depicted in Case Illustration 7.3.

In the case, Marisa presented with a very vague and immeasurable goal of working to improve herself. Through the probing and reflecting of the counselor, this vague, general goal took more specific form. It is clear that Marisa wants to reduce her tendency to overreact with anger to frustrating situations. With this as a definition of the desired goal, both the counselor and client can devise methods for assessing the frequency and intensity of her incidence of expressions of anger and use those data to demonstrate the effectiveness of the counseling.

CASE ILLUSTRATION 7.3

The following is an excerpt from the intake session with a 33-year-old female who came to counseling because, as she noted, she "wanted to improve as a person." In this brief exchange, the counselor attempts to help the client more clearly define this goal—define it in a way that will allow both the counselor and the client to know if and when the goal was achieved.

Counselor:	So, Marisa, now that you are pretty established in your business and able to take time for yourself, you have decided to engage in counseling as a way to "improve as a person."
Marisa:	Yes, that's correct. I mean I have been fortunate in my career and I have taken steps to take care of myself physically, losing weight and exercising regularly, so I thought it was time to simply work on the psycho-emotional part of me.
Counselor:	I'm wondering; if you and I work together and are extremely successful at helping you achieve your goal, what might others notice that would let them know that something of significance had changed with you?
Marisa:	Well, I think the first thing they would notice is that I am much more at peace and generally more pleasant to be around.
Counselor:	That's good, but I wonder what they would actually see or experience that would let them know you are more at peace?
Marisa;	I would be able to relax, not always worry about work.
Counselor:	Good, anything else?
Marisa:	I would not let the little things of life—little frustrations, little irritants—get me upset and angry . . . that kind of thing.

Counselor: So, if I understand, you would think that our work together was successful if you found yourself more relaxed around your friends, enjoying their company rather than focusing on work and in general finding that you could accept the typical irritants and frustrations in life without getting angry?

Marisa: Yeah that's it . . . I really need to stop getting so upset and angry over dumb things. I think that is what I mean about relaxing.

Counselor: Marisa, that really helps. Could you describe a recent example of when you were not relaxed? You know, when you are being overly irritated and frustrated and angry about one of the typical irritants of life?

Marisa: Sure. Last night, we were out for appetizers and drinks—just me and really good friends—and we were having a good time. Well, when my order came the waiter had it all screwed up. Everybody got what they ordered except me. It really infuriated me. I went off on the waiter, complaining about his incompetence and demanding to see the manager. My voice was raised and I could feel my blood pressure going through the roof. I know my friends were totally embarrassed and even though I apologized I couldn't let it go, and it ruined my night.

Counselor: Well, let's pretend that you experience the same event, sometime in the very near future, but this time you are the relaxed person you wish to be. How might that look?

Marisa: Easy. I actually do this sometimes, just not enough. I would look at what the waiter brought and I would decide if I wanted that equally as much as what I ordered. If I did, I would keep it without a fuss, without saying anything, thinking, hey this is no big deal.

Counselor:	Okay . . . and if it wasn't something you wanted or liked?
Marisa:	I would simply get the waiter's attention and tell him this wasn't what I ordered and ask him to fix the order. And then I would probably share some of my friends' appetizers as I waited for mine. I would see it as really not a big deal . . . but something I wanted to correct.
Counselor:	So, Marisa, it seems that what you are hoping to do is first, increase your ability to keep your perspective on what is important and what is less important, and then employ strategies to correct situations you find undesirable without mentally judging them as personal attacks, injustices, or events deserving your angry response. It seems that the goal we are talking about is to help you reduce your tendency to overreact with anger to normal, nonthreatening yet frustrating situations. Does that sound right?
Marisa:	Absolutely. That's it. I really want to stop over-reacting with anger to all of these little things. You know I tend to take things as personal affronts. If I could learn to stay more objective I know I would be happier and more at peace.

While the case of Marisa illustrates the use of an operational definition of a specific client's goals as targets for outcome measurement, some counselors turn to more standardized measures as a means of assessing outcomes. For these measures to be of use, they need to possess certain psychometric characteristics. These characteristics include validity, reliability, and sensitivity to change.

Reliability refers to the consistency of measurement and is frequently evaluated through statistical tests of internal consistency, test-retest reliability, and inter-rater reliability. Because counselors assess the client at numerous points during the counseling process, it is important that the measure employed is stable and not affected by such irrelevant conditions of time of day, the fact of having previously taken the test, or whether or not the client ate breakfast. The second necessary characteristic is validity. As used here, *validity* refers to the extent to which a test measures the construct it is intended to measure. For example, if a counselor assesses a client for depression, a valid measure for depression would identify the presence of depression as opposed to other conditions such as anxiety or stress. Finally, for an assessment to be useful for counselors, it needs to be sensitive to change, noting even subtle changes in the construct under investigation.

There are a number of instruments counselors employ that possess these psychometric characteristics and target specific disorders or problems, such as depression (e.g., Beck Depression Inventory; Beck, Steer, & Brown, 1996), anxiety (e.g., Hamilton Anxiety Scale; Hamilton, 1959), or stress (e.g., Holmes and Rahe Stress Scale; Holmes & Rahe, 1967). While each of these scales has value for counselors, some researchers have suggested that practitioners use more global, self-reporting instruments, as efficient measures of outcome (see Lambert & Hawkins, 2004). Four of the more widely used global outcome instruments are presented in Table 7.1.

Table 7.1   Outcome Measures

Clinical Outcomes in Routine Evaluation–Outcome Measure (CORE-OM)

CORE-OM (Evans et al., 2002) is a 34-item self-reported scale that covers four domains: (1) well-being, (2) problems/symptoms, (3) life functioning, and (4) risk (to self and others). The scale has been demonstrated to be reliable and valid and sensitive to change. It is useful in a wide variety of settings.

Behavior and Symptoms Identification Scale (BASIS-32)

The BASIS-32 (Eisen, Grob, & Klein, 1986) is a self-report measure which uses a 5-point Likert scale and provides scores to measure each of the following: relation to self/others, depression/anxiety, daily living/role functioning, impulsive/addictive behavior, and psychosis.

Brief Symptom Inventory (BSI)

The BSI (Derogatis, 1993) is a 53-item scale that provides assessments for nine symptom subscales (somatization, obsessive-compulsive, interpersonal sensitivity, depression, anxiety, hostility, phobic anxiety, paranoid ideation, and psychoticism) and three global indexes (global severity index, positive symptom distress index, and positive symptom total index).

The Outcome Questionnaire (OQ-45)

The OQ-45 (Lambert et al., 1996) contains 45 Likert-scale items that measure symptoms of distress, interpersonal relations, and social role functioning.

ASSESSMENT AS A GUIDE TO PRACTICE DECISIONS

The use of formative and summative assessment processes provides data essential to practice decision making. As noted, formative assessment provides data that can be used not only to assess progress but also to provide direction for modification of a treatment plan. Formative assessments also enable a counselor to know when progress is blocked and when the needs of the client exceed the knowledge and the skill of the counselor. Under these conditions, the data provided by our ongoing formative assessment may suggest that the next step in our treatment plan is for counselors either to seek supervision or to prepare the client for an appropriate referral.

Supervision

The American Counseling Association (2005) *Code of Ethics* highlights the ethical necessity of assessing one's effectiveness and also provides direction for remediation when that effectiveness is less than desired. In Section C.2.d, Monitoring Effectiveness, it states: "Counselors continually monitor their effectiveness as professionals and take steps to improve when necessary. Counselors in private practice take reasonable steps to seek peer supervision as needed to evaluate their efficacy as counselors."

Supervision is essential for the ongoing professional development of a counselor. It is "an ongoing educational process in which one person in the role of supervisor helps another person in the role of the supervisee acquire appropriate professional behavior through an examination of the supervisee's professional activities" (Hart, 1982, p. 12). In counseling, supervision is a means of transmitting the counseling skills, knowledge, and attitudes of counseling to the next generation of counselors and ensuring clients receive a certain minimum quality of care while counselor trainees work with them to gain their skills (Bernard & Goodyear, 2009). Supervision is not only an intervention for beginning counselor trainees, but also a valuable tool for all counseling professionals for monitoring their therapeutic effectiveness and maintaining their professional competence. It is a process to be considered anytime when the data of formative assessments show that counseling progress is blocked and the needs of the client have exceeded the knowledge and the skill of the counselor. Under these conditions, the ethical, effective counselor needs to take reasonable steps to seek supervision from other professional counselors to facilitate her development of therapeutic and case management knowledge and skills.

Referral

Regardless of our training and our experience, there will be clients who may present with issues or needs that far exceed our ability to help. While it is desirable to recognize our limitations to effective practice and, as such, avoid engaging in a relationship with those whose situations require more than we are able to offer, this is not always possible. The benefit of ongoing formative evaluation is that it can bring to the counselor's awareness those situations in which more is required and thus indicate when referral is appropriate. Under these conditions, it is our ethical responsibility to make an appropriate, effective referral to an alternative resource or service. The ACA (2005) *Code of Ethics,* for example, states, "If counselors determine an inability to be of professional assistance to clients, they avoid entering or continuing counseling relationships. Counselors are knowledgeable about culturally and clinically appropriate referral resources and suggest these alternatives" (sec. A.11.b).

So, when should you as a counselor consider referral? Referrals should be made

1. When a client presents a problem or a request for information that is beyond the counselor's level of competency, for example, a counselor who has a client with obsessive-compulsive disorders but the counselor has never worked or had training with clients having such issue;

2. When the counselor notices some personality differences between the counselor and the client—differences that can't be resolved within the limited amount of time and resources and which the counselor feels will interfere with the client's effective progress;

3. When the counselor's values and worldviews come into conflict with the client's, for example, a counselor with strong religious convictions who may not feel comfortable with abortion as a woman's right or homosexuality as a lifestyle, and thus unable to facilitate the client's ability to consider all options;

4. When the counselor knows the client on other than a professional basis, for example, a friend's friend, neighbor, parent's student, and so on;

5. When the counselor finds that the client is reluctant to discuss important issues with the counselor for some reason, for instance, too personal due to gender differences; and

6. When the counselor realizes that the therapy has not progressed and believes that another approach or counselor may prove more effective.

When making a referral, the counselor should explain to the client the reasoning behind the referral. The counselor should answer all of the client's questions in order to insure that the client is not interpreting the referral as an abandonment or as evidence that the case is hopeless. The counselor should then provide all the information needed for the client to connect with the referred helper and, when needed, even offer to help the client make the initial contact. With the permission of the client, the counselor may contact the counseling professional to whom the referral was made and provide a summary of the case. The counselor should remember that the ultimate purpose of this referral is to meet the client's needs and satisfy the client's best interest.

How to Make a Referral

It is important that the concept of referral be seen and presented to the client as a statement of progress and not a failure. Without such self-awareness, counselors may resist the concept of referral, seeing it as an indication of their own limitations and a public statement of failure—and with this as their frame of reference, continue to treat even when the data suggest the treatment is ineffective. Referral, when done with the intent of providing the client with the most effective form of help, is a statement of progress and needs to be embraced as such.

For referral to be effective and truly advance the treatment, two conditions must exist: (1) the client is properly prepared, and (2) the referral is made to an appropriate source.

Preparing the Client. The client may receive the introduction of a change in plan and therapeutic relationship as a form of rejection—or worse, hopelessness—if not presented in the most effective way. The client needs to sense that the counselor is making the referral from the perspective of hope and positive expectations. It must be made clear to the client that the referral is a reflection of the counselor's increased awareness of client needs, and the service that will best assist in reaching the client's goals. As such, the counselor should:

- Present the goal of referral as the desirable next step to the helping process.
- Clarify for the client what referral is, while at the same time being sure to clearly highlight what it is *not*. It is important for the client to embrace the referral as a positive step rather than see it as a statement of personal failure, rejection, or hopelessness.
- Provide details about the referral source and the elements that make it the next step in the treatment plan, and answer any questions the client may have about the *what, why,* and *how* of the referral.
- Assist the client in making contact with the referral source and provide the client with support in taking this next step in treatment.
- Establish what, if any, continued role the original counselor will play in the helping process.
- Establish a means of follow-up to insure the initial contact was made and a relationship was established.

Referral Sources. The appropriateness of any particular referral sources is a function of the specific client characteristics and needs, and the accessibility to the needed helping agencies or professionals. It is useful, therefore, for counselors to develop a directory of potential resources to use when making a referral. Exercise 7.3 is provided to help you in the process of starting such a directory.

Exercise 7.3

RESOURCE DIRECTORY

Directions: The table below directs you to gather specific information about potential referral resources in your region or area for specific targets of concern. The targets identified are merely illustrative and a way of getting you started; they are not intended to be inclusive of the type of resource you may find valuable in your practice. The goal of this exercise is to provide you with an opportunity to begin a process of developing a comprehensive resource and referral directory. Upon completion you may want to share your data with your colleagues or classmates as a way of expanding the database.

Target Concern	*Resource Agency or Individual*	*Contact Information (e.g., location, phone, e-mail, fax, etc.)*	*Fee Structure and Payment Options (Insurance?)*	*Special Notes (e.g., intake contact person, waiting list, modalities used, personal notes on referral experience, etc.)*
Alcohol dependency/ Addiction				
Suicide risk/ideation				
Adolescent runaway				
Major depressive episode				
Eating disorder				
Career concerns				
Other (identify)				
Other (identify)				
Other (identify)				

Termination

Just as formative assessment data can provide direction for adjusting the counseling process, *summative assessment* data can serve as the marker for knowing when the relationship has served its purpose and termination is in order.

The American Counseling Association's (2005) *Code of Ethics* notes, in the Appropriate Termination section: "Counselors terminate a counseling relationship when it becomes reasonably apparent that the client no longer needs assistance . . ." (sec. A.11.c.). Clearly, the use of valid assessment procedures will enable the counselor and the client to identify when the " . . . client no longer needs assistance." Knowing when to end the counseling relationship is only one part of what has been termed *termination.* Knowing how to terminate is the second essential component.

When any relationship ends, including a counseling relationship, there are many emotions that those individuals involved in the relationship may experience. Termination is the final element of the counseling process and is just as important as each of the elements discussed to this point. Termination is a time to evaluate the work accomplished and celebrate the progress made. Furthermore, how termination is achieved can have a significant impact on how clients view their experience in counseling and the likelihood of their practicing what has been learned in counseling after sessions have concluded.

While termination may occur for a variety of reasons, ideally it is the process that occurs once the goals of counseling have been achieved or the problem for which a client has entered into counseling has become more manageable or is resolved. And as with the other elements of the counseling process, termination is not something that occurs at a fixed point in time or occurs as a one-time only process. Effective termination is an element that is introduced and revisited from the initial session on. The counselor and the client need to be clear, from the first contact, that the intent of treatment is to help the client function without the therapist (Kramer, 1990). Formative and summative assessments give form and direction to that intent.

Even though termination should be an indication of the success of counseling—a point of celebration—it is not unusual to find clients resisting termination. For many, counseling has been not only effective but truly a rewarding relationship. They may begin to experience anxiety anticipating that they will not be able to continue to function on their own or that they will forget everything they learned. It is also possible that the experience of being fully attended to and valued as an individual was so rewarding that the client is resistant to surrender the weekly meetings.

It is also not unusual for counselors to feel a reluctance to terminate a successful counseling relationship. They may have enjoyed working with a particular client, are proud of the success they have achieved, and as a result wish to maintain the relationship. Feeling needed and appreciated is a powerful enticement for a counselor and needs to be guarded against as a motive for continuing unneeded further counseling. The use of valid formative and summative measures will help guard against such self-serving motivations and provide clear evidence of the growth of the client—a point that should serve to reduce the client's own anxiety about termination.

Termination: A Process

Termination is a process, rather than a stage, and one that involves the accomplishment of a number of tasks. The followings are intended to assist you throughout this process:

Anticipate Termination. It is important to remind clients of the approaching end of the sessions with you. This should be done at least two to three sessions prior to the final one. This provides you an opportunity to ask clients to talk about relationships that have ended in their past, how they have ended, and how that might affect the end of this counseling relationship. You can also ask clients what they would like to focus on during their remaining time with you. A question to ask prior to the final one, which may help to prepare clients for the reality of the end, is "If this were our last meeting, how would that be for you?"

Wean. If you and your clients are not limited to a certain number of sessions, you have the option of spacing out your last few meetings. This is a good way to wean your clients of the relationship and foster in them a sense of confidence in their ability to handle things without seeing you on a weekly basis before the relationship abruptly ends.

Review Then and Now. Together it is helpful to review the specific conditions that brought the client to your service and the counseling relationship. In particular, you can contrast the client's current state and experience to the original conditions that led to the relationship, or to an ideal state of desired outcome. Very often, clients will forget the advances they have made, or neglect to give themselves credit for their accomplishments. Doing this with them can instill confidence and provide them with a positive perspective on what counseling helped them to do.

Review Strategies Employed and Insights Gained. Asking your clients what they learned, what they intend to do with what they have learned, what they found helpful about their sessions, and how they felt about their participation in the process are ways to review accomplishments made during counseling. Reviewing the tools and skills that the clients have acquired through the counseling process helps the clients to feel and be more self-sufficient in handling problems that might have previously brought them to counseling.

Transfer Support. As noted in the opening chapters, counseling and the counselor are only one of many processes and persons that can provide meaningful support and help to one in need. It is important to help the client identify those resources that exist naturally within his life that can be called upon for additional help and support (e.g., friends, family, community agencies, church, etc.).

Explore Feelings. Termination can be emotional for both the counselor and the client. It is important to allow the client to talk about her feelings surrounding termination. It is likely that she may have emotions to work through and time should be spent acknowledging and processing them.

It is also true that the counselor may also have feelings tied to the termination of a relationship with a particular client. It is normal to feel many emotions when ending a relationship with your clients. Acknowledge your feelings, your ambivalence about termination, while at the same time reminding yourself that the relationship was in service of the client and that your ultimate goal as a counselor was to "put yourself out of business."

Structure Follow-Up Carefully. The idea of having an open-door policy is one that should be considered with caution. Such an ill-defined avenue to continued contact may interfere with either you or the client coming to closure and termination. If follow-up is deemed to be useful for the purpose of maintaining the gains established, this follow-up, like all of the previous sessions should be formally structured, time and frequency limited, and focused on the specific goal of maintenance.

Termination is not meant to indicate the absolute cessation of professional contact between this counselor and this client. Termination is, however, a formal process that defines *this* counseling contract has reached its end. Clearly, there are times when a client needs additional support or information or may encounter an entirely different situation or problem and desire to reconnect with the counselor. There is no reason that such a recontracting for services can't occur. However, it is important for the counselor, along with the client, to identify the need, the value of a reconnection, and to rule out client dependency as a motive for such reconnection.

CHALLENGES TO ACCOUNTABILITY

The call to accountability is loud—it's clear—and as noted previously it comes from multiple sources—consumers, employers, third-party payers, and our own sense of ethical practice. In addition, it is clear that a good program of formative and summative assessment lays the foundation for effective practice decisions, including the *when* and *how* of referral and termination. Even with such a mandate and value for employing methods of accountability, the process of being accountable is not without its challenges.

Human Complexity

Clients seeking counseling support are, like all humans, complex and the issues they present are complicated—not easily narrowed down nor quickly lending themselves to the employment of a single notion of change. Consider the client who comes to the counselor's office for career planning. Certainly the counselor and client will pursue the client's interests, aptitudes, and abilities, as well as the data reflecting projected future employment trends and career growth areas. The counselor interested in assessing progress and outcome can certainly point to the client's increasing knowledge of career options along with his increased awareness of his own talents and interests and his selection of career to pursue as evidence of effectiveness. But the counselor is engaged with a person, not a problem.

The techniques and skills discussed in the previous chapters allow the counselor to create and maintain a working alliance in which clients not only share their story but in so doing experience acceptance, valuing of, and most often, insights about themself. Thus, the client seeking career counseling brings with him other issues, other concerns, and other desires which are often revealed within the counseling relationship. Further, the counseling, while contracted to assist the client with career direction, may have equally impacted other areas of the client's life and experience. In fact, it could be argued that it is impossible to surgically impact only the identified issue or concern in counseling, because again, counselors engage a person, not a problem.

The counselor working with the client around career issues may not only do well to assess the client's understanding and decisions regarding his career choice, but also respond to questions such as the following: How has the counseling impacted the client's sense of self-esteem, or his belief in his own competency and self-efficacy? How has the counseling elevated the client's awareness of other areas where personal growth is possible? How did working with the counselor on career issues help the client strengthen his own general problem solving and life- adaptation skills?

Areas of self-esteem, self-efficacy, growth, and prevention were not the targets for which the client sought assistance. However, the process and dynamics of the counseling he has experienced may have impacted those areas as well because, once again, counseling is with and of a person, not a problem.

Defining Issues and Outcome

While issues such as weight loss, smoking cessation, completion of homework, and even improved grades lend themselves to observation and measurement and thus allow for measures of progress and outcome, not all of the issues presented to counselors come in such neat, quantifiable packages. For emotional experiences such as anxiety, depression, and stress, which are not easily observed, counselors can rely on one of the numerous self-administered scales, surveys, and questionnaires that exist as means for assessing effectiveness of counseling.

But even with these added resources, some issues present challenges to both the counselor and the client in their attempts to assess. Consider goals such as personal betterment, increased wellness, congruency, self-actualization; or concerns ranging from feeling more comfortable in social settings to experiences of existential dread. How do we assess the impact of our counseling on these?

Counselors attempting to quantify thoughts, motivations, and attitudes of clients may employ goal scaling as a strategy for assessing progress and outcome (Kiresuk, Smith & Cardillo, 1994). As introduced in Chapter 6, the process is simple in that it requires the client and the counselor simply to articulate, in as much descriptive detail as possible, what it would look like if the client actually achieved the goal she desired. Using visual aids such as a picture of scale line or large thermometer (for children), the counselor places this description at the extreme point of the scale, for example at 10 on a scale line of 1 to 10. Next the counselor asks the client to identify where along the scale she feels she is at the present time (e.g., 3). Finally, the client is then asked to describe what it would look like if she was to move up one or two steps along the scale (e.g., to a 4 or 5).

These points on the scale, along with their descriptions, become the measures of progress and success. Figure 7.1 provides one illustration of a goal scale. In this case, the client was concerned that she felt like a doormat and would like to learn to speak up, especially at work. The first step to the scaling was for the counselor to ask her to respond to the following: "Let's assume that tomorrow when you go to work you have developed the attitudes and skills needed to be assertive, and you are excited about the opportunity to speak up and share your thoughts. How would others know you had this ability?" The elements of the client's description—"I would be able to interrupt a person (politely) rather than waiting for silence; I would be able to look at people in their eyes; I would be able to speak in a tone that is loud enough to be heard at the other end of the conference table; and I would simply state my position without apologizing for disagreeing or trying to justify it with lots of irrelevant background information"—were placed at 10 on the scale. Using this as the ultimate, ideal desired state and placing it at the 10 on a line scale, the counselor asked the client to identify where she would currently place herself, and why. The client responded by stating, "I would be at a 4—I always wait until someone asks my opinion and then I divert my eyes and usually give qualifiers such as 'I am not sure this is correct, but . . . ' and then I state what I feel." Finally, the counselor then asked the client what she would be doing or how she would appear if she were at a 5 or a 6 and the client responded: "I would probably still wait until the other person finished, and I would probably apologize a little for the interruption, but I would look at the person in the eyes as I shared my thoughts." These descriptions provided the markers to assess both progress and final outcome.

Goal scaling is just one tool that counselors can use to assist in their assessment of both progress and outcome, especially when the goals are not easily quantified. Another scale used for the assessment of a client's subjective experience of distress or disturbance is the Subjective Units of Distress Scale (SUDS; Wolpe, 1969).

The SUDS scale ranges from 0 to 10 in which each point along the scale reflects a client's subjective experience for intensity of distress. The client's self-assessment can serve as a benchmark for evaluation of progress and final determination of outcome. Figure 7.2 provides one illustration of a SUDS scale.

No Consensus

A review of outcome and effectiveness studies, as well as a sampling of clinical anecdotal reporting, reveals that counselors and researchers call upon a wide variety of measures to assess effectiveness. Some use measures of general distress

Figure 7.1 Sample of Goal Scale

Descriptions such as those listed within the three points of the scale serve as markers for both progress and final outcome. The client placed herself at a 4, along a scale that she hoped would lead to the description depicted at 10. The description listed at 6 served as both a goal for change and a measure of progress.

4 (B)	5	6	7	8	9	10
Need to be asked/eyes down and qualify my response.		Wait for other to finish, make eye contact, and apologize for interruption, not apologizing for what I want to say, just the fact that I interrupted.				Interrupt if important, eye contact, voice loud enough to be heard at end of table, no qualifiers.

Figure 7.2   Sample of a SUDS Scale

10 = Feeling unbearably bad, like I'm going to leap out of my skin. I feel overwhelmed, out of control, and ready to lose it completely.

9 = Feeling desperate, kind of freaked out, no control over emotions.

8 = Freaking out acting like a maniac.

7 = On edge, really testy, holding it together but barely.

6 = Really feeling like I need some help, and not sure what's going on or what could happen, nervous.

5 = Just not comfortable with myself, lots of unpleasant feelings although I am functioning.

4 = Handling things but not my usual self, upset and can't ignore the feelings and thoughts that are upsetting.

3 = Mildly upset, worried, bothered to the point that you notice it.

2 = Doing okay, knowing something is not quite right, but I have to think about it to notice it.

1 = Feeling basically good. Not quite 100% but doing okay.

0 = Totally at peace . . . relaxed . . . no real concerns or anxiety.

(e.g., Symptom Checklist-90-R; Derogatis & Unger, 2010) and others use specific indexes (e.g., Beck Depression Inventory; Beck, Ward, Mendelson, Mock, & Erbaugh, 1961) of outcome, and still others have emphasized behavioral observations (e.g., reactions after exposure to phobic stimulus) or measures of status (e.g., recidivism).

A key problem in measuring effectiveness is that while hundreds of measures have been created, no consensus exists about what measures are best or how these measures should be employed in practice or research. Further, the profession has yet to provide a standard to guide counselors in their selection of assessment measures.

Limited Training in and Valuing of Accountability and Outcome Assessment

Many counselors see the complex and dynamic nature of counseling as simply too prohibitive to assess. As discussed by Whiston (1996), the seemingly immeasurable nature of counseling often makes straightforward evaluations of its effectiveness difficult. Further, many counselor-training programs, event those providing training in research and program evaluation, often fail to provide direction and training in the art of assessing treatment effectiveness. As pointed out by Brot (2006), there is a need to focus counselor education on providing those in training with " . . . a practical application of accountability for demonstrating their effectiveness" (p. 180).

Counselors need to develop, value, and employ a framework for accountability. It is good for the profession and essential to effective, ethical practice.

COUNSELING KEYSTONES

- The call for counselor accountability comes from all who are stakeholders in what counselors do—client, employers, and third-party payers.
- The call for counselor accountability is a response to counselors' own ethical mandate to provide effective and efficient service.
- Counselors' response to the call for accountability is an opportunity to improve the practice.
- Counselors' response to the call for accountability is an opportunity to continue to reinforce counseling's position as a profession among all human service professions.
- Practice assessment is necessary as both a formative process guiding in-practice decisions and a summative activity documenting the outcome and achievements of counseling efforts.
- The very complexity of the human condition along with the intricacy of the issues presented within counseling oftentimes presents as a challenge to those seeking to assess progress and outcome.
- Counselors-in-training as well as those in practice need to embrace the value of assessment within practice and increase their knowledge and skills of the methods and instruments available for such assessment.

ADDITIONAL RESOURCES

Readings

Granello, D. H., & Yong, M. E. (2012). *Counseling today: Foundations of professional identity.* Upper Saddle River, NJ: Pearson.

Nassar-McMillan, S. C., & Niles, S. G. (2011). *Developing your identity as a professional counselor: Standards, settings, and specialties.* Belmont, CA: Brooks/Cole.

Roberts, A. R., & Yeager, K. R. (2004). *Evidence-based practice manual: Research and outcome measures in health and human services.* New York: Oxford University Press.

Web Resources

Accountability and Performance Indicators for Mental Health Services and Supports: A Resources Kit
www.phac-aspc.gc.ca/mh-sm/pdf/apimhss.pdf

Clinical Assessment Tools
www.ebrsr.com/~ebrsr/uploads/H_Clinical_Assessment_Tools.pdf

Encyclopedia of Psychology
www.psychology.org/links/Environment_Behavior_Relationships/Measurement/

Functional Analytic Psychotherapy (FAP)
http://functionalanalyticpsychotherapy.com/tools-for-therapists

What is psychological assessment?
www.psychpage.com/learning/library/assess/assess.html

REFERENCES

Adelman, H. S. (2002). School counselors and school reform: New directions. *Professional School Counseling, 5,* 235–248.

Albrecht, S. F., & Joles, C. (2003). Accountability and access to opportunity: Mutually exclusive tenets under a high-stakes testing mandate. *Preventing School Failure, 48,* 86–91.

American Counseling Association. (2005). *ACA Code of Ethics.* Alexandria, VA: Author.

American Psychological Association. (2006). Evidence-based practice in psychology. *American Psychologist, 61,* 271–285.

American School Counselor Association. (2004). *Ethical standards for counselors.* Alexandria, VA: Author.

American School Counselor Association. (2005). *American School Counselor association national model: A framework for school counseling programs.* Alexandria, VA: Author

Astramovich, R. L., & Coke, J. K. (2007). Program evaluation: The accountability bridge model for counselors. *Journal of Counseling & Development, 85,*162–172.

Barkham, M., Margison, F., Leach, C., Lucock, M., Mellor-Clark, J., Evans, C., Benson, L., Connell, J., Audin, K., & McGrath, G. (2001). Service profiling and outcomes benchmarking using the CORE-OM: Toward practice-based evidence in the psychological therapies. Clinical outcomes in routine evaluation-outcome measures. *Journal of Consulting and Clinical Psychology, 69,* 184–196.

Beck A. T., Steer, R. A., & Brown, G. K. (1996). *Manual for the Beck Depression Inventory-II.* San Antonio, TX: Psychological Corporation.

Beck, A. T., Ward, C. H., Mendelson, M., Mock, J., & Erbaugh, J. (1961). An inventory for measuring depression. *Archives of General Psychiatry, 4,* 561–571.

Bernard, J. M., & Goodyear, R. K. (2009). *Fundamentals of clinical supervision.* Needham Heights, MA: Allyn & Bacon.

Borders, L. D. (2002). School counseling in the 21st century: Personal and professional reflections. *Professional School Counseling, 5,* 180–185.

Brot, P. E. (2006). Counselor education accountability: Training the effective professional school counselor. *Professional School Counseling, 10*(2), 179–188.

Council for the Accreditation of Counseling and Related Educational Programs. (2001). *The 2001 standards.* Retrieved from www.cacrep.org/2001Standards.html

Dahir, C. A., & Stone, C. B. (2003). Accountability: A.M.E.A.S.U.R.E. of the impact school counselors have on student achievement. *Professional School Counseling, 6,* 214–221.

Danziger, P. R., & Welfel, E. R. (2001). The impact of managed care on mental health counselors: A survey of perceptions, practices, and compliance with ethical standards. *Journal of Mental Health Counseling, 23*(2), 137–150.

Derogatis, L. R. (1993). *BSI: Administration, scoring, and procedures manual* (3rd ed.). Minneapolis, MN: National Computer Systems.

Derogatis, L. R., & Unger, R. (2010). *Symptom Checklist-90-Revised.* Hoboken, NJ: John Wiley & Sons.

Eisen, S. V., Grob, M. C., & Klein, A. A. (1986). BASIS: The development of a self-report measure for psychiatric inpatient evaluation. *The Psychiatric Hospital, 17,* 166–171.

Evans, C., Connell, E., Barkham, M., Margison, F., McGrath, G., Mellor-Clark, J., & Audin, K. (2002). Towards a standardized brief outcome measure: psychometric properties and utility of CORE-OM. *British Journal of Psychiatry, 180,* 51–60.

Finn, C. E. (2002). Making school reform work. *The Public Interest, 148,* 85–95.

Gandal, M., & Vranek, J. (2001, September). Standards: Here today, here tomorrow. *Educational Leadership,* 6–13.

Gladding, S. T. (2011). *The counseling dictionary: Concise definitions of frequently used terms* (3rd ed.). Boston: Pearson.

Granello, D. H., & Hill, L. (2003). Assessing outcomes in practice settings: A primer and example from an eating disorders program. *Journal of Mental Health Counseling, 25,* 218–232.

Gysbers, N. C., & Henderson, P. (2000). *Developing and managing your school guidance program* (Third ed.). Alexandria, VA: American Counseling Association.

Hamilton, M. (1959). The assessment of anxiety states by rating. *British Journal Medical Psychology, 32,* 50–55.

Hart, G. M. (1982). *The process of clinical supervision.* Baltimore, MD: University Park Press.

Herr, E. L. (2002). School reform and perspectives on the role of school counselors: A century of proposals for change. *Professional School Counseling, 5,* 220–234.

Hill, C. E., & Kellems, I. S. (2002). Development and use of the Helping Skills Measure to assess client perceptions of the effects of training and of helping skills in session. *Journal of Counseling Psychology, 49,* 264–272.

Holmes, T. H., & Rahe, R. H. (1967). The social readjustment rating scale. *Journal of Psychosomatic Research, 11*(2), 213–218.

House, R. M., & Hayes, R. L. (2002). School counselors: Becoming key players in school reform. *Professional School Counseling, 5,* 249–256.

Houser, R. (1998). *Counseling and educational research: Evaluation and application.* Thousand Oaks, CA: Sage.

King, G., McDougall, J., Palisano, R., Gritzan, J., & Tucker, M. (1999). Goal attainment scaling: Its use in evaluating pediatric therapy programs. *Physical & Occupational Therapy in Pediatrics, 19*(2), 31–52.

Kiresuk, T. J., Smith, A., & Cardillo, J. E. (1994). *Goal attainment scaling: Applications, theory, and measurement.* Hillsdale, NJ: Lawrence Erlbaum.

Kramer, S. A. (1990). *Positive endings in psychotherapy: Bring meaningful closure to therapeutic relationships.* San Francisco: Jossey-Bass.

Krousel-Wood, M. A. (2000). Outcomes assessment and performance improvement: Measurements and methodologies that matter in mental health care. In P. Rodenhauser (Ed.), *Mental health care administration: A guide for practitioners* (pp. 233–253). Ann Arbor: University of Michigan Press.

Lambert, M. J., Bergin, A. E., & Garfield, S. L. (2004). Introduction and historical overview. In M. J. Lambert (Ed.), *Bergin and Garfield's handbook of psychotherapy and behavior change* (5th ed.). New York: Wiley.

Lambert, M. J., & Cattani-Thompson, K. (1996). Current findings regarding the effectiveness of counseling: Implications for practice. *Journal of Counseling & Development, 74,* 601–608.

Lambert, M. J., Hansen, N. B., & Finch, A. E. (2001). Patient-focused research: Using patient outcome data to enhance treatment effects. *Journal of Consulting and Clinical Psychology, 69,* 159–172.

Lambert, M. J., Hansen, N. B., Umphress, V. J., Lunnen, K., Okiishi, J., Burlingame, G. M., Huefner, J. C., & Reisinger, C. W. (1996). *Administration and scoring manual for the Outcome Questionnaire* (OQ 45.2). Wilmington, DE: American Professional Credentialing Services.

Lambert, M. J., & Hawkins, E. J. (2004). Measuring outcome in professional practice: Considerations in selecting and using brief outcome instruments. *Professional Psychology: Research and Practice, 35*(5), 492–499.

Lambert, M. J., & Ogles, B. M. (2004). The efficacy and effectiveness of psychotherapy. In M. J. Lambert (Ed.), *Bergin and Garfield's handbook of psychotherapy and behavior change* (5th ed., pp. 139–193). New York: Wiley.

Lusky, M. B., & Hayes, R. L. (2001). Collaborative consultation and program evaluation. *Journal of Counseling & Development, 79,* 26–38.

Makover, R. B. (1996). *Treatment planning for psychotherapists.* Washington, DC: American Psychiatric Association.

Mohr, D. C. (1995). Negative outcomes in psychotherapy: A critical review. *Clinical Psychology: Science and Practice, 2,* 1–27.

Mordock, J. B. (1994). Treatment planning in counseling. In J. L. Ronch, W. V. Ornum, & N. C. Stilwell (Eds.). *The counseling sourcebook: A practical reference on contemporary issues* (pp. 227–233). New York: Crossroad Publishing.

Myrick, R. D. (2003). Accountability: Counselors count. *Professional School Counseling, 6,* 174–179.

O'Donohue, W., Fisher, J. E., Plaud, J. J., & Curtis, S. D. (1990). Treatment decisions: Their nature and their justification. *Psychotherapy, 27,* 421–427.

Pekarik, G., & Guidry, L. L. (1999). Relationship of satisfaction to symptom change, follow-up adjustment, and clinical significance in private practice. *Professional Psychology: Research and Practice, 30*(5), 474–478.

Reed, G. M., & Eisman, E. J. (2006). Uses and misuses of evidence: Managed care, treatment guidelines, and outcomes measurement in professional practice. In C. D. Goodheart, A. E. Kazdin, & R. J. Sternberg (Eds.), *Evidence-based psychotherapy: Where practice and research meet* (pp. 13–35). Washington, DC: American Psychological Association.

Ridley, C. R., Li, L. C., & Hill, C. L. (1998). Multicultural assessment: Reexamination, reconceptualization, and practical application. *The Counseling Psychologist, 26*(6), 939–947.

Sexton, T. L. (1996). The relevance of counseling outcome research: Current trends and practical implications. *Journal of Counseling & Development, 74,* 590–600.

Shimokawa, K., Lambert, M. J., & Smart, D. W. (2010). Enhancing treatment outcome of patients at risk of treatment failure: Meta-analytic and mega-analytic review of a psychotherapy quality assurance system. *Journal of Consulting and Clinical Psychology, 78*(3), 298–311.

Tillett, R. (1996). Psychotherapy assessment and treatment selection. *British Journal of Psychiatry, 168*(1), 10–15.

Trevisan, M. S. (2001). Implementing comprehensive guidance program evaluation support: Lessons learned. *Professional School Counseling, 4,* 225–228.

U.S. Department of Education. (2001). No Child Left Behind Act of 2001 (H.R.1). Washington, DC: Author.

Weinrach, S. G., Thomas, K. R., & Chan, F. (2001). The professional identity of contributors to the Journal of Counseling & Development: Does it matter? *Journal of Counseling & Development, 79*(2), 166–170.

Whiston, S. C. (1996). Accountability through action research: Research methods for practitioners. *Journal of Counseling & Development, 74,* 616–623.

Wolpe, J. (1969). *The practice of behavior therapy.* New York: Pergamon Press.

Part III

Counselor as Professional

Counseling is more than a job—it is a profession. As professionals, counselors are empowered to make decisions that help expand the capacity of people to grow and develop (ACA, 2005). This is an awesome responsibility.

The chapters presented within Part III highlight the need for counselors to develop and maintain competence (Chapter 8), insure their own well-being (Chapter 9), and articulate the uniqueness of their professional orientation and services (Chapter 10), if they are to meet their professional responsibility and calling. Specifically, Chapter 8 makes the argument that while entry-level education is necessary for ethical and effective practice, it is not sufficient. To maintain competence, counselors need to engage in continuing professional development, and employ best-practice procedures. Chapter 9 introduces the reader to the signs, causes, and strategies necessary to prevent or intervene with two of the all too common examples of debilitating stress—professional burnout and compassion fatigue. Finally, Chapter 10 discusses what it means to be a counselor and what is meant by professional identity. The chapter engages the reader in reflections to help begin the articulation of one's own professional identity.

Chapter 8

Counselor Competence

An Ethical Precondition to Successful Intervention

Counselors practice only within the boundaries of their competence . . .

—American Counseling Association (2005, C.2.a)

INTRODUCTION

As noted in the opening quote, the American Counseling Association's (2005) *Code of Ethics,* in the Boundaries of Competence section, directs counselors to ". . . practice only within the boundaries of their competence, based on their education, training, supervised experience, state and national professional credentials, and appropriate professional experience" (C.2.a). While education, training, and credentialing would appear to be fundamental to one's competence and are certainly a necessary condition for competency, they are not the sufficient condition.

Counseling is a young profession, one that continues to develop methods and standards of practice. Ethical, competent counselors are aware of this developing knowledge base, engage in continuing education (ACA, 2005, C.2.f), and employ those emerging techniques, procedures, and modalities that have an empirical or scientific foundation (C.6.e).

Clearly, entry-level education, continuing professional development, and the employment of best-practice procedures are essential to professional competence. As such, each of these elements of competence serve as the focus for the current chapter. Specifically, after reading this chapter you will be able to do the following:

- Describe the core educational experiences that are foundational to competent practice.
- Explain the value and need for continuing education.
- Describe what is meant by evidence-based practice.

EDUCATION, TRAINING, AND SUPERVISION: FUNDAMENTAL TO COMPETENCE

While it should be obvious, counselors, as professionals, must be competent to provide the services they offer. The public, who entrust their well-being to counselors, are vulnerable and need to be protected from those who offer services that exceed their abilities. Failure of counselor competence, and the results incurred by one couple, is the focus of the book *A Heart Held Ransomed,* by Stephan Skotko and coauthored by Teila Tankersley (2011). The story is summarized in Case Illustration 8.1.

Because of this vulnerability, the American Counseling Association's (2005) *Code of Ethics* makes explicit this ethical responsibility by stating: "Counselors practice only within the boundaries of their competence based on their education, training, supervised experience, state and national professional credentials, and appropriate professional experience" (C.2.a).

CASE ILLUSTRATION 8.1

CALLING ONESELF COUNSELOR DOES NOT INSURE COMPETENCE: A SUMMARY OF ONE MAN'S HELLISH EXPERIENCE WITH "COUNSELING"

In 2008, Stephan Skotko and his wife of 23 years decided to seek out a family counselor. They were raising teenagers, his wife was suffering from depression, and they wanted to revive that spark that was missing from their marriage. He recounts his experience in his book *A Heart Held Ransomed.*

The counselor in this true-life case was Marion Knox, a self-professed family counselor and deliverance minister. Mr. Knox practiced a form of repressed memory therapy (RMT), which has a long controversial history. Sadly, the majority of Mr. Knox's clients following intensive repressed memory therapy began to believe that they had been ritually abused.

This was true for Stephan's children, who after going through RMT and being informed by Mr. Knox that their father had sodomized them, withdrew from their father, informed their mother of this "abuse"; their mother subsequently contacted police. It took months for the courts to finish their investigation and the case was eventually dismissed, as the allegations were unfounded, and the charges were officially dropped. In the meantime, Stephan had lost his job, his family, and his reputation because of these erroneous allegations, all in the name of therapy.

EDUCATION AND TRAINING: THE FUNDAMENTALS

To date, there is no single set of cognates and skills that have been defined as fundamental to the definition of initial training and education in counseling. However, two national bodies, the National Board of Certified Counselors (NBCC), and the Council for the Accreditation of Counseling and Related Educational Programs (CACREP) have set forth similar sets of common core experiences identified as foundational to counselor education.

The Council for Accreditation of Counseling and Related Educational Programs (2009), for example, posits that it is imperative students be prepared to be counselors first and counseling specialists second (p. 7). As such, CACREP provides a set of general standards and eight core areas it believes are fundamental to all counselor preparation, including the directive that counselor education programs should provide a minimum of 48 semester hours (or 72 quarter hours) of graduate studies. According to CACREP, these common core experiences include:

1. Professional identity

2. Social and cultural diversity

3. Human growth and development

4. Career development

5. Helping relationships

6. Group work

7. Assessment

8. Research and program evaluation

Each of these areas is more fully described in Table 8.1.

In addition to gaining fundamental knowledge and skills such as that outlined in Table 8.1, competent counseling requires the translation of knowledge to practice. As such, in addition to classroom work, CACREP and others (for example, NBCC) require supervised practicum and internship experiences.

Again, CACREP (2009) addresses this issue and distinguishes between practicum and internship experiences and the hours defined as minimum for each. Table 8.2 provides CACREP'S standard in regards to clinical experience.

With these cognates and skills identified as foundational to the development of a counselor's competency, assessing one's own training and experiences in this area is the first step to continued professional development. In Case Illustration 8.2, one student-counselor reflects on the value of these hands-on experiences as she approached the end of her training.

Table 8.1   Core Competencies (CACREP, 2009)

1. *Professional Identity.* Studies that provide an understanding of all of the following aspects of professional functioning:

   a. history and philosophy of the counseling profession, including significant factors and events;

   b. professional roles, functions, and relationships with other human service providers;

   c. technological competence and computer literacy;

   d. professional organizations, primarily ACA, its divisions, branches, and affiliates, including membership benefits, activities, services to members, and current emphases;

   e. professional credentialing, including certification, licensure, and accreditation practices and standards, and the effects of public policy on these issues;

   f. public and private policy processes, including the role of the professional counselor in advocating on behalf of the profession;

   g. advocacy processes needed to address institutional and social barriers that impede access, equity, and success for clients; and

   h. ethical standards of ACA and related entities, and applications of ethical and legal considerations in professional counseling.

2. *Social and Cultural Diversity.* Studies that provide an understanding of the cultural context of relationships, issues and trends in a multicultural and diverse society related to such factors as culture, ethnicity, nationality, age, gender, sexual orientation, mental and physical characteristics, education, family values, religious and spiritual values, socioeconomic status and unique characteristics of individuals, couples, families, ethnic groups, and communities including all of the following:

   a. multicultural and pluralistic trends, including characteristics and concerns between and within diverse groups nationally and internationally;

   b. attitudes, beliefs, understandings, and acculturative experiences, including specific experiential learning activities;

   c. individual, couple, family, group, and community strategies for working with diverse populations and ethnic groups;

   d. counselors' roles in social justice, advocacy and conflict resolution, cultural self-awareness, the nature of biases, prejudices, processes of intentional and unintentional oppression and discrimination, and other culturally supported behaviors that are detrimental to the growth of the human spirit, mind, or body;

   e. theories of multicultural counseling, theories of identity development, and multicultural competencies; and

   f. ethical and legal considerations.

Table 8.1

3. *Human Growth and Development.* Studies that provide an understanding of the nature and needs of individuals at all developmental levels, including all of the following:

a. theories of individual and family development and transitions across the life-span;

b. theories of learning and personality development;

c. human behavior including an understanding of developmental crises, disability, exceptional behavior, addictive behavior, psychopathology, and situational and environmental factors that affect both normal and abnormal behavior;

d. strategies for facilitating optimum development over the life-span; and

e. ethical and legal considerations.

4. *Career Development.* Studies that provide an understanding of career development and related life factors, including all of the following:

a. career development theories and decision-making models;

b. career, avocational, educational, occupational and labor market information resources, visual and print media, computer-based career information systems, and other electronic career information systems;

c. career development program planning, organization, implementation, administration, and evaluation;

d. interrelationships among and between work, family, and other life roles and factors including the role of diversity and gender in career development;

e. career and educational planning, placement, follow-up, and evaluation;

f. assessment instruments and techniques that are relevant to career planning and decision making;

g. technology-based career development applications and strategies, including computer-assisted career guidance and information systems and appropriate world-wide websites;

h. career counseling processes, techniques, and resources, including those applicable to specific populations; and

i. ethical and legal considerations.

5. *Helping Relationships.* Studies that provide an understanding of counseling and consultation processes, including all of the following:

a. counselor and consultant characteristics and behaviors that influence helping processes including age, gender, and ethnic differences, verbal and nonverbal behaviors and personal characteristics, orientations, and skills;

(Continued)

Table 8.1 Continued

   b. an understanding of essential interviewing and counseling skills so that the student is able to develop a therapeutic relationship, establish appropriate counseling goals, design intervention strategies, evaluate client outcome, and successfully terminate the counselor-client relationship. Studies will also facilitate student self-awareness so that the counselor–client relationship is therapeutic and the counselor maintains appropriate professional boundaries;

   c. counseling theories that provide the student with consistent model(s) to conceptualize client presentation and select appropriate counseling interventions. Student experiences should include an examination of the historical development of counseling theories, an exploration of affective, behavioral, and cognitive theories, and an opportunity to apply the theoretical material to case studies. Students will also be exposed to models of counseling that are consistent with current professional research and practice in the field so that they can begin to develop a personal model of counseling;

   d. a systems perspective that provides an understanding of family and other systems theories and major models of family and related interventions. Students will be exposed to a rationale for selecting family and other systems theories as appropriate modalities for family assessment and counseling;

   e. a general framework for understanding and practicing consultation. Student experiences should include an examination of the historical development of consultation, an exploration of the stages of consultation and the major models of consultation, and an opportunity to apply the theoretical material to case presentations. Students will begin to develop a personal model of consultation;

   f. integration of technological strategies and applications within counseling and consultation processes; and

   g. ethical and legal considerations.

  6. *Group Work.* Studies that provide both theoretical and experiential understandings of group purpose, development, dynamics, counseling theories, group counseling methods and skills, and other group approaches, including all of the following:

   a. principles of group dynamics, including group process components, developmental stage theories, group members' roles and behaviors, and therapeutic factors of group work;

   b. group leadership styles and approaches, including characteristics of various types of group leaders and leadership styles;

   c. theories of group counseling, including commonalties, distinguishing characteristics, and pertinent research and literature;

Table 8.1

   d. group counseling methods, including group counselor orientations and behaviors, appropriate selection criteria and methods, and methods of evaluation of effectiveness;

   e. approaches used for other types of group work, including task groups, psychoeducational groups, and therapy groups;

   f. professional preparation standards for group leaders; and

   g. ethical and legal considerations.

   7. *Assessment.* Studies that provide an understanding of individual and group approaches to assessment and evaluation, including all of the following:

   a. historical perspectives concerning the nature and meaning of assessment;

   b. basic concepts of standardized and nonstandardized testing and other assessment techniques including norm-referenced and criterion-referenced assessment, environmental assessment, performance assessment, individual and group test and inventory methods, behavioral observations, and computer-managed and computer-assisted methods;

   c. statistical concepts, including scales of measurement, measures of central tendency, indices of variability, shapes and types of distributions, and correlations;

   d. reliability (i.e., theory of measurement error, models of reliability, and the use of reliability information);

   e. validity (i.e., evidence of validity, types of validity, and the relationship between reliability and validity);

   f. age, gender, sexual orientation, ethnicity, language, disability, culture, spirituality, and other factors related to the assessment and evaluation of individuals, groups, and specific populations;

   g. strategies for selecting, administering, and interpreting assessment and evaluation instruments and techniques in counseling;

   h. an understanding of general principles and methods of case conceptualization, assessment, and/or diagnoses of mental and emotional status; and

   i. ethical and legal considerations.

   8. *Research and Program Evaluation.* Studies that provide an understanding of research methods, statistical analysis, needs assessment, and program evaluation, including all of the following:

   a. the importance of research and opportunities and difficulties in conducting research in the counseling profession;

(Continued)

Table 8.1 Continued

b. research methods such as qualitative, quantitative, single-case designs, action research, and outcome-based research;

c. use of technology and statistical methods in conducting research and program evaluation, assuming basic computer literacy;

d. principles, models, and applications of needs assessment, program evaluation, and use of findings to effect program modifications;

e. use of research to improve counseling effectiveness; and

f. ethical and legal considerations.

Source: Council for Accreditation of Counseling and Related Educational Programs. (2009). *2009 standards.* Retrieved from www.cacrep.org/doc/2009%20Standards%20with%20cover.pdf

Table 8.2 Practicum and Internship (CACREP, 2009)

Practicum

Students must complete supervised practicum experiences that total a minimum of 100 clock hours. The practicum provides for the development of counseling skills under supervision. The student's practicum includes all of the following:

1. 40 hours of direct service with clients, including experience in individual counseling and group work;

2. weekly interaction with an average of one (1) hour per week of individual and/or triadic supervision which occurs regularly over a minimum of one academic term by a program faculty member or a supervisor working under the supervision of a program faculty member;

3. an average of one and one half (1 1/2) hours per week of group supervision that is provided on a regular schedule over the course of the student's practicum by a program faculty member or a supervisor under the supervision of a program faculty member; and

4. evaluation of the student's performance throughout the practicum including a formal evaluation after the student completes the practicum.

Internship

The program requires students to complete a supervised internship of 600 clock hours that is begun after successful completion of the student's practicum (as defined in Standard III.G). The internship provides an opportunity for the student to perform,

Table 8.2

under supervision, a variety of counseling activities that a professional counselor is expected to perform. The student's internship includes all of the following:

1. 240 hours of direct service with clients appropriate to the program of study;

2. weekly interaction with an average of one (1) hour per week of individual and/or triadic supervision, throughout the internship, (usually performed by the on-site supervisor);

3. an average of one and one half (1 1/2) hours per week of group supervision provided on a regular schedule throughout the internship, usually performed by a program faculty member;

4. the opportunity for the student to become familiar with a variety of professional activities in addition to direct service (e.g., record keeping, supervision, information and referral, inservice and staff meetings);

5. the opportunity for the student to develop program-appropriate audio and/or videotapes of the student's interactions with clients for use in supervision;

6. the opportunity for the student to gain supervised experience in the use of a variety of professional resources such as assessment instruments, technologies, print and nonprint media, professional literature, and research; and

7. a formal evaluation of the student's performance during the internship by a program faculty member in consultation with the site supervisor.

Source: Council for Accreditation of Counseling and Related Educational Programs. (2009). *2009 standards.* Retrieved from www.cacrep.org/doc/2009%20Standards%20with%20cover.pdf

CASE ILLUSTRATION 8.2

FROM STUDENT TO PROFESSIONAL

It seems like only yesterday that I started this 2-year journey that has taken me from an overly confident "lay-problem solver" to a soon-to-be credentialed school counselor with both an increased sensitivity and appreciation for the complexity of the helping process. As I reflect on the journey, I can point to specific professors, courses, and even assignments that helped me gain the fundamental knowledge and skill that is required to be minimally prepared to enter this profession. But that knowledge, even those skills, remained as merely academic until I stepped into my

(Continued)

(Continued)

year-long internship experience. My year in the internship has moved me from being a student to becoming a beginning professional.

It is amazing to me to see how I have progressed. From my time as a first-year student asking too many closed-ended questions during my Fundamentals course to appearing as if I was in a daze when presented with the first seventh-grade client in my internships, to now as I approach the end of my training, feeling at ease and self-assured each time a student walks through my door. Now, don't get me wrong. I'm still a work in progress. My confidence comes not from an arrogant belief that I know it all and can do it all. On the contrary, this year at East Middle School has highlighted all that I do not know and the essential nature of a counselor's role as one demanding constant development and renewal. No, I'm not confident because I am a finished product. My comfort comes from the fact that I now know that even Mr. B. and all of the counselors at East, regardless of their years of experience, are also "unfinished." But they are true professionals and are committed to continuing to grow and support each other in that growth.

My internship experience gave me the opportunity to see the concepts learned in the classroom translated to application in the field. I was able to apply what I have learned in class in a practical setting, as well as get hands-on experience with what it's like to be a school counselor.

In the beginning, it was a bit confusing and even disheartening since it seemed like we had so much to do and so little time to do it. As the year progressed, I began to understand the culture of schools and was able to develop my own, efficient method of organizing the paperwork, getting students out of class, and working with teachers. The number of hats a counselor needs to wear is both a tad intimidating and yet affirming. Counselors are valuable and valued.

This year in internship helped me to begin to develop my counseling style; increase my comfort levels at working with teachers, parents, and most important, my students; and even start to see myself as a counselor.

However, with all that said, what I learned, more than anything, was that as a counselor I am part of larger whole…the profession of counseling. I attended both a state and the national ACA conference. The research presented—the discussions around professional identities and the organization of counselors to move as advocates for our profession—filled me with a desire to become active not just in helping my students but helping my profession gain the public recognition it deserves.

While I am excited about my upcoming graduation, I am really marking the time to the beginning of the next fall semester. But this fall I enter school, not as a student, but as an employee, a professional school counselor, and while anxious, I feel ready to meet the challenge.

Clearly, field placement serves an essential role in the formation of a counselor and the transition of an individual from student to professional. As such, Exercise 8.1 is provided to assist you in the process of reflecting upon your program of study and experience as it reflects these fundamental areas of competency and the impact of practical experience.

Exercise 8.1

PROGRAMMING FOR COMPETENCY

Directions: Below you will find a listing of the eight CACREP areas of general competency. Assuming you are currently in a counseling education program or considering engaging in one, you will find columns to equate your course work with CACREP areas and to plan for additional experiences if desired. Your course may address any one core experience in multiple courses or through a variety of experiences. You should list each.

CACREP Core Experiences	*My Program/Course(s) Addressing Each CACREP Competency Area*	*Plan for Additional Training and/or Supervision*
1. Professional identity	————————	————————
2. Social and cultural diversity	————————	————————
3. Human growth and development	————————	————————
4. Career development	————————	————————
5. Helping relationships	————————	————————
6. Group work	————————	————————
7. Assessment	————————	————————
8. Research and program evaluation	————————	————————
Practicum (100 hours)	————————	————————
Internship (600 hours)	————————	————————

In addition to enumerating core experiences seen as fundamental to counselor competency, CACREP posits additional training and experience for those pursuing specialization in areas such as career counseling, school counseling, student affairs, mental health counseling, and others. For those seeking additional information about the CACREP or NBCC standards, the websites are provided at the end of this chapter.

SUPERVISION: FACILITATING MOVEMENT OF STUDENT TO PROFESSIONAL

The hours of practicum and internships identified in Table 8.2 provide counseling trainees with the initial experience of moving from the classroom to the field of professional service. The supervision received during these experiences is essential to fostering the active, reflective learning that each practical encounter invites. It is during field experience that students begin to trust and value the process of sharing of cases and working with another professional, in supervision. This engagement in supervised practice is a significant component to the development of the professional counselor's competency (Milne & Oliver, 2000).

Supervision has been identified as second only to working directly with clients in contributing the professional development of counselors (Orlinsky, Botermans, & Ronnestad, 2001). Supervision not only assists in the development and application of counseling skills, but also serves to monitor competence and foster the development of the counselor's professional identity (Worthen & McNeill, 1996).

Working With Qualified Professional Supervisors

With client welfare as the primary concern of the professional counselor, counselors understand that they should not engage in counseling services or specific interventions for which they have not received proper education and clinical supervision. For example, a professional counselor who has no training in personality testing or IQ testing should never provide testing services for her clients. A counselor who does not have training in the area of eating disorders should never work with clients who seek help for their eating disorders. Or, a counselor trained and supervised in a particular technique must not attempt other techniques without first receiving proper training and supervision. Working with a supervisor trained and experienced within these areas of deficiency is essential to becoming a competent practitioner.

Engaging in supervision serves two functions in that it both safeguards the welfare of the client and ensures that the counselor develops and employs therapeutic skills competently. Working under supervision means that a counselor uses the services of a qualified counseling supervisor to review his or her work with clients on a regular basis.

Unlike in the academic arena of a graduate student receiving supervision, where a grade is often assigned, supervision for the professional in the counseling field may include coaching and a focus on professional development. Here, the supervisor acts not as a "boss," or an evaluator but as a consultant to the supervisee. The two engage in a more or less formal process of support and learning that enables counselor trainees to develop knowledge and competence while expanding their ability to assist their clients.

Peer Consultation: Supporting Competence

Previous chapters have invited you to participate in a variety of guided exercises in hope that such engagement would help make the concepts presented within the chapters come alive. In many of these exercises, it was suggested that you share your experience with a colleague or classmate. This process of sharing counseling experiences with a peer can prove to be a valuable tool for the maintenance of one's own competence. *Peer consultation* as supervision has been defined as ". . . a structured, supportive process in which counselor colleagues (or trainees), in pairs or in groups, use their professional knowledge and relationship expertise to monitor practice and effectiveness on a regular basis for the purpose of improving specific counseling, conceptualization and theoretical skills" (Wilkerson, 2006, p. 62). Implicit in this definition is that peer consultation is nonhierarchical in nature and thus the use of the term *consultation* appears more appropriate than supervision.

The idea of peer consultation is not new. In fact, the benefits of such an interchange were highlighted by Benshoff and Paisley in the early 1990s. These authors suggested that peer consultation achieves the following:

1. Increasing interdependency between colleagues thus reducing dependency on "expert" supervisors;

2. Increasing responsibility of counselors for assessing their own skills and those of their peers and thus encouraging the structuring of their own professional growth;

3. Providing counselors more options in choosing peer consultants; and

4. Assisting with the development of not only counseling skills and self-confidence but also consultation and supervisory skills.

In contrast to traditional models of counseling supervision, the emphasis in peer consultation is on helping each other to reach self-determined goals rather than on evaluating each other's counseling performance. This lack of evaluation and the egalitarian, nonhierarchical relationship that is created between peer consultants offers opportunities for different types of experiences than those with designated counseling supervisors. As noted by Benshoff and Paisley (1996), peer consultants can assume greater responsibility for providing critical feedback, challenge, and support to a chosen colleague. Feedback from those who have participated in peer consultation consistently reflects a sense of empowerment that comes from setting one's own goals. This empowerment suggests that the process of peer consultation works, and those who employ peer consultation find structure and direction for themselves within the framework of the model (Benshoff & Paisley, 1996).

Case Illustration 8.3 provides the reflection from one mental health counselor who worked in a community mental health agency located in a rural area. As evident, the peer supervision proved essential to the counselor's continued growth and development.

CASE ILLUSTRATION 8.3

GROWTH THROUGH PEER SUPERVISION

I just completed our weekly peer supervision session and cannot express the gratitude I have for my colleagues—Gary and Denise—for their sharing of their insights and suggestions. The idea of getting together to review each other's cases and treatment plans, as well as simply share any emotional challenges we experienced during the week, has been a godsend.

We are pretty isolated out here—and I guess the good news is that we could pretty much do whatever we want to do, with really no "boss" looking over our shoulder. Our agency does have a coordinator, but he works 25 miles away and visits only once a month. As long as we keep records of the number of clients "seen," actual effectiveness seems less important to the granting bodies than numbers. As such, I could see where it would be easy to simply fall into a production line mentality—doing the same thing to each client who walked through the door. But it was amazing. From the first day on the job, we all had the exact same sense of counseling and what it is to be professional and effective.

We come from different graduate programs and have had different training and theoretical emphasis throughout our programs. As such, it was not unusual to find us getting into some debates about which treatment model is best for which presenting concern. It was some of these initial lunchtime debates that led the three of us to agree to have regular meetings where we would take turns leading the discussions and case presentations. The goal of these meetings was simply to support and foster each other's professional development. The format for our meetings is the same each week, unless something exceptional happened during the week or someone had an urgent issue or need.

Last week, I led the group and followed the typical format we had established:

1. First, we did a check-in. This is just taking a minute to see if everyone is okay—emotionally and mentally available and ready to proceed. This is a time when, if one of us is struggling, we will change the agenda and help with the issue that the person is attempting to handle.

2. Next we do follow-up. This is when we share anything that we may have learned from the last session and what we may have done with it. For example, we may have read an article or tried what was suggested, so we allow time to process that.

3. Finally, we do a case presentation. This is the meat of our time together. The session leader, that was me this week, discusses one of the cases he or she is working with. The focus can be on some problem the counselor is encountering, or simply sharing the case conceptualization and treatment plan for alternative perspectives.

In my session, I shared a personal situation I was having with a new client. The client was mandated to counseling because his boss discovered pornographic images and videos on his work computer. The intake revealed that this was not a singular event but rather the client was, by his own admission and with ample evidence, addicted to pornography. The client felt that he would not be able to continue working where computer access would be available. While initially horrified at being discovered, he expressed both a gratitude about being in counseling and a real sense of hope and desire to change.

I know that I am not trained in working with such addictions and, thus, I had planned to prepare the client for referral to a clinician in the next town who specializes in this area. My issue wasn't what to do, but more the personal, emotional reaction I was having in regards to this client.

I clearly felt—and as I discussed the case, the others picked up—disgust with this behavior. While I could intellectually state that I was not disgusted with the client and that I understood this was a real addiction, it was clear to me, and apparently evident in my tone and demeanor, that the behavior was tainting my ability to remain objective and stay nonjudgmental. My goal for this supervision was to be able to regain my professional objectivity and empathic caring for this client so that I could present the referral as a caring, treatment strategy and not come across as if I was rejecting him.

(*Continued*)

(Continued)

Our discussion was invaluable. My colleagues were supportive and affirming. They helped me reframe the client's issues and see the situation as truly something that he was struggling with and for which he now sought help. Our discussion helped me realize that he was victimized by his own addiction. It helped me highlight the fact that he had shown a relief about being "forced" to counseling and a sense of hope about conquering his addition. With this new perspective, I felt confident that I could focus on his desire to gain control over his addiction and not focus on the incident that forced the referral. Helping me shift my attention from a problem focus to a goal focus really did help me reduce my emotional reaction.

The fact that we are peers helped me to be open and be completely honest. I know that they personally wouldn't judge me and that while their issues were different than mine, we all have personal issues that need to be monitored so that they don't negatively impact our professional work. Peer supervision—or consultation or mentoring, whatever one wants to call it—is for me a professional lifesaver.

CONTINUING EDUCATION: AVOIDING TECHNICAL OBSOLESCENCE

While initial training and credentialing are fundamental to a counselor's competence, the ever-changing nature of our profession and the increasing knowledge base from which we operate invite what is known as technical obsolescence among those in practice. Willis and Dubin (1990) defined *technical obsolescence* across professions as ". . . the discrepancy between a professional's body of knowledge, skills, and abilities and the individual's capability to perform the required tasks at hand as well as those planned for the future" (p. 10).

Given the danger of such obsolescence, counselors have the mandate—both ethical and, in many states, legal—to maintain competence by way of engaging in programs of continuing education. The American Counseling Association, for example, in the Continuing Education section in the *Code of Ethics* (2005) directs counselors to ". . . recognize the need for continuing education to acquire and maintain a reasonable level of awareness of current scientific and professional information in their fields of activity" (C.2.f). But the acquisition of knowledge regarding the current state of the profession is not all that is required. These same ethical standards direct counselors to ". . . take steps to maintain competence in the skills they use, be open to new procedures, and keep current with the diverse populations and specific populations with whom they work" (C.2.f).

This need for continuing education is widely regarded as critical to a practitioner's ongoing competence (Rubin et al., 2007). However, while valued and widely shared as a commitment to competence, there is considerably less consensus regarding how best to accomplish this goal.

In stark contrast to academic training programs, engagement in continuing education experiences is largely self-regulated (Daniels & Walter, 2002). Counselors are left to select their continuing education experiences presumably on the basis of their self-assessed needs and interests. Thus, in responding to this call for continuing education, counselors must assess their professional skills and needs, recognize key areas of growth and development in the field, and pursue the completion of continuing education experiences that address their acknowledged areas of need and workplace demands.

With the aforementioned as a caveat, it may be assumed that there are several broad topic areas that counselors may consider as they continue their pursuit of competence. While not intended to be an exhaustive list, some potential areas for continuing education include: the area of multicultural competence, the role of technology in practice, the revised ethical standards and current legal issues, and the concept of best practice and use of evidence-based practice.

BEST PRACTICE AS EVIDENCE BASED

The continued pursuit of knowledge about the state of the profession serves as a portal to the increased awareness of *best practice,* which includes both procedures and intervention strategies. The counseling process and outcome research has grown into an undeniably reliable, valid, and necessary source of clinical practice knowledge. This large and ever-increasing body of applicable and relevant research is an invaluable source of guidance for both the general practice of counseling and the application of counseling to specific problems and populations (Sexton, 1996).

Evidence-Based Practice: A Matter of Ethics

In this so-called era of accountability, with concerns for service costs and intervention effectiveness, research supporting best practice is a primary factor in much clinical decision making. In addition to being a response to these real-world pressures, the interest in evidence-based practice finds support within the ethical code of the American Counseling Association (2005), in the Scientific Bases for Treatment Modalities section, which directs counselors to ". . . use techniques/ procedures/modalities that are grounded in theory and/or have an empirical or scientific foundation" (C.6.e).

From Theory to Empirically Supported and Evidence-Based Techniques

In recent years, a shift has occurred away from seeking a theory that is universally applicable to all clients and all issues of concern toward the promotion of specific approaches for specific problems based on empirical support for those treatments (Deegear & Lawson, 2003). The use of these *evidence-based interventions* has been supported by the surgeon general (U.S. Public Health Service, 2000) and a variety of those within the helping profession (e.g., Brown & Trusty, 2005). The use of such empirically supported techniques is based on the belief that well thought and carefully designed and implemented interventions will increase the likelihood that counselors' efforts will prove effective. Research highlights the fact that those treatments supported by a substantial number of research studies are more likely efficacious than those without such support (see Massey, Armstrong, Boroughs, Henson, & McCash, 2005; Nathan & Gorman, 2002). Thus, while not restricting one's choice of intervention to those with empirical support, it is suggested that counselors, in their attempt to provide interventions with the most reasonable chance for success, would do well to review the research on best practice.

Developing plans for the continued development of a counselor's knowledge and skill as it reflects the best of our science and our art—the best of practices—is the hallmark of competency. Exercise 8.2 is presented to help you increase your awareness of evidence-based practice.

Exercise 8.2

A BRIEF REVIEW OF THE LITERATURE

While different counselors may employ a specific theory of counseling, for example, solution focused or cognitive-behavioral, when addressing client needs, it is important for counselors to periodically turn to the research to see if there are specific techniques or strategies that have proven support for their efficacy. Under these conditions, the treatment of choice may be that which has evidence supporting its effectiveness.

Directions: Below you will find a number of reasons a client may seek counseling. As you will note, within each referral there are a number of words italicized. It is suggested that you select a reason for referral and use the italicized words to do a search of the literature to reference the current state of evidence supporting any one approach. Share your findings with your colleagues or classmates.

Referral

1. A 28-year-old male exhibiting *OCD* around the issue of germs and hand washing

2. *A first-grade* student exhibiting *separation anxiety* during the first week of school

3. A 61-year-old woman experiencing *depression following the death* of her spouse of 40 years

4. A fifth-grade student making *noises* within the classroom as *apparent attention getting*

5. A 20-year-old obese college student seeking to *lose weight*

6. A *4-year-old* child brought to counseling and presenting as *oppositional-defiant*

7. A 48-year-old executive referred by his family physician because of *chronic stress*

8. A senior in high school referred for *explosive temper* and *physical aggression*

9. A man with an *irrational fear* of elevators and close spaces who has just been transferred to work in a building where elevator transport is essential

10. A tenth-grade male who is being verbally *bullied*

A FINAL THOUGHT

Counseling is a profession requiring responsible—that is, ethical—and competent decision making on the part of those engaged in the profession. This ability for competent practice may have a beginning in a book, an experience, or a formal training program, but it is a process without end. As suggested throughout this chapter, professional competency is an ongoing quest, one to be pursued by all who call themselves *counselor.*

COUNSELING KEYSTONES

- The American Counseling Association's (2005) *Code of Ethics* directs counselors to " . . . practice only within the boundaries of their competence . . ."
- Entry-level education, continuing professional development, and the employment of best-practice procedures are essential to professional competence. The Council for Accreditation of Counseling and Related

Educational Program and the National Board of Certified Counselors present a similar set of core competencies which cover: professional identity, social and cultural diversity, human growth and development, career development, helping relationships, group work, assessment, and research and program evaluation.

- Transforming classroom learning to practice requires participation in supervised practicum and internship experiences.
- Most states have laws mandating professional counselors to engage in continuing education experiences as a requirement for maintaining their licenses and certifications.
- Beyond the legal requirement for continuing education, it is the ethical responsibility of all professional counselors to engage in life-long professional development.
- While there is some debate about the cost and benefit of employing empirically supported interventions, the use of these evidence-based interventions has been supported by the surgeon general and a variety of those within the helping profession.

ADDITIONAL RESOURCES

Readings

Carey, D., Carey, J. C., & Hatch, T. (2007). *Evidence-based school counseling: Making a difference with data-driven practices.* Thousand Oaks, CA: Corwin.

Hodges, S. (2011). *The counseling practicum and internship manual: A resource for graduate counseling students.* New York: Springer.

Ladany, N. (2010). *Counselor supervision.* New York: Routledge.

Sue, D., & Sue, D. M. (2008). *Foundations of counseling and psychotherapy: Evidence-based practices for a diverse society.* Hoboken, NJ: John Wiley & Sons.

Web Resources

The National Board for Certified Counselors, Inc. and Affiliates (NBCC)
www.nbcc.org

This independent not-for-profit credentialing body for counselors was incorporated in 1982 to establish and monitor a national certification system, to identify those counselors who have voluntarily sought and obtained certification, and to maintain a register of those counselors.

Council for Accreditation of Counseling and Related Educational Programs (CACREP)
www.cacrep.org

CACREP's mission is to promote the professional competence of counseling and related practitioners through (1) the development of preparation standards, (2) the encouragement of excellence in program development, and (3) the accreditation of professional preparation programs.

REFERENCES

American Counseling Association. (2005). *Code of ethics.* Alexandria, VA: Author.

Benshoff, J. M., & Paisley, P. O. (1996). The structured peer consultation model for school counselors. *Journal of Counseling & Development, 74*(3), 314–319.

Brown, D., & Trusty, J. (2005). School counselors, comprehensive school counseling programs, and academic achievement: Are school counselors promising more than they can deliver? *American School Counselor Association, 9*(1), 1–8.

Council for Accreditation of Counseling and Related Educational Programs. (2009). *2009 standards.* Retrieved from www.cacrep.org/doc/2009%20Standards%20with%20cover.pdf.

Daniels, A. S., & Walter, D. A. (2002). Current issues in continuing education for contemporary behavioral health practice. *Administration and Policy in Mental Health, 29,* 359–376.

Deegear, J., & Lawson, D. M. (2003). The utility of empirically supported treatments. *Professional Psychology: Research and Practice. 34*(3), 271–277.

Massey, O. T., Armstrong, K., Boroughs, M., Henson, K., & McCash, L. (2005). Mental health services in schools: A qualitative analysis of challenges to implementation, operation and sustainability. *Psychology in the Schools, 42*(4), 361–372.

Milne, D. L., & Oliver, V. (2000). Flexible formats of clinical supervision: Description, evaluation and implementation. *Journal of Mental Health, 9,* 291–304.

Nathan, P. E., & Gorman, J. M. (Eds.) (2002). *A guide to treatments that work* (2nd ed.). New York: Oxford University Press.

Orlinsky, D. E., Botermans, J. F., & Ronnestad, M. H. (2001). Towards an empirically-grounded model of psychotherapy training: Five thousand therapists rate influences on their development. *Australian Psychologist, 36,* 139–148.

Rubin, N. J., Bebeau, M., Leigh, I. W., Lichtenberg, J., Smith, I. L., Nelson, P. D., et al. (2007). A history of the need for competency assessment. *Professional Psychology: Research and Practice, 38*(5), 452–462.

Sexton, T. L. (1996). The relevance of counseling outcome research: Current trends and practical implications. *Journal of Counseling & Development, 74,* 590–600.

Skotko, S., & Tankersley, T. (2011). *A heart held ransomed.* Charleston, SC: CreateSpace Independent Publishing Platform.

U.S. Public Health Service. (2000). *Report on the surgeon general's conference on children's mental health: A national action agenda.* Washington, DC: U.S. Government Printing Office.

Wilkerson, K. (2006). Peer supervision for the professional development of school counselors: Toward an understanding of terms and findings. *Counselor Education & Supervision, 46,* 59–67.

Willis, S. L., & Dubin, S. S. (Eds.). (1990). *Maintaining professional competence: Approaches to career enhancement, vitality and success throughout a work life.* San Francisco: Jossey-Bass.

Worthen, V., & McNeill, B. W. (1996). A phenomenological investigation of ''good'' supervision events. *Journal of Counseling Psychology, 43,* 25–34.

Chapter 9

Care for the Counselor

The act of caring for others can distract us from the necessity of caring for self.

—Gerry Corey (2010)

INTRODUCTION

Gerry Corey (2010), in his keynote address for the American Counseling Association Pittsburgh Conference stated: "There is a good deal of stress that goes along with being a counseling professional." Corey's comments certainly reflected the reality experienced by most serving as professional counselors. Counseling can be stressful for the counselor and this stress can interfere with the counselor's effectiveness and competence.

The American Counseling Association's (2005) *Code of Ethics* reminds us that counselors need to be " . . . alert to the signs of impairment from their own physical, mental, or emotional problems and refrain from offering or providing professional services when such impairment is likely to harm a client or others" (C.2.g). As such, understanding the signs of debilitating stress, the causes for debilitating stress, and strategies for intervening with or preventing the occurrence of debilitating stress is not simply a good idea—it is an ethical mandate. The current chapter addresses the signs, causes, and strategies necessary to prevent or intervene with two of the all too common examples of debilitating stress—professional burnout and compassion fatigue.

Specifically, after reading this chapter, you will be able to do the following:

- Describe the difference between professional burnout and compassion fatigue.
- Describe the behavioral indicators of professional burnout and compassion fatigue.
- Describe steps that can be taken to reduce the possibility of experiencing professional burnout and compassion fatigue.
- Develop an initial wellness and care-of-self plan.

PROFESSIONAL BURNOUT

Many counselors approach their role as care provider in ways that are often costly to their own well-being and mental health (Lee et al., 2007; O'Halloran & Linton, 2000). Counselors, by the very nature of the work they do, and how they do it, are vulnerable to the effects of stress (Yassen, 1995): Counselors are engaged in work that involves them in emotionally demanding relationships with their clients (Bakker, Van der Zee, Lewig, & Dollard, 2006; Renzi, Tabolli, Ianni, Di Pietro, & Puddu, 2005). Confidentiality, isolation, shame, and additional considerations lead counselors to overpersonalize their own sources of stress, when in reality they are part and parcel of the common world of psychological work (Norcross, 2000). These conditions, along with the cumulative effect of witnessing and engaging with humans who are suffering, can take its toll on the counselor (O'Brien 2011, Webb, 2011). It is a toll that has been identified as *professional burnout* (Evans & Villavisanis, 1997; Pines & Aronson, 1981, Schaufeli, 2003).

Burnout is a state of physical, emotional, intellectual, and spiritual exhaustion characterized by feelings of helplessness and hopelessness. Burnout is "a gradually intensifying pattern of physical, psychological, and behavioral responses to a continual flow of stressors" (Gladding, 2011, p. 24) and consists of emotional exhaustion, the loss of a sense of accomplishment in one's work, and a depersonalization of those served (Maslach & Jackson, 1986). Some characteristics of burnout include apathy, fatigue, anger, and conflict (Gladding, 2011). Consider the story of Dr. G. in Case Illustration 9.1, a competent, well-respected professional who failed to care for himself as much as he cared for his clients.

Causes

There is no one single cause of burnout; however, a number of factors have been found to contribute to its occurrence. These factors may be work-related, lifestyle, or certain personalities. Research has identified two major factors of burnout—bureaucratic atmosphere and overwork.

For counselors, the work-related causes of burnout can be working in a highly pressured environment, little support from a supervisor, no recognition or reward for high effective job performance or job satisfaction, role conflict, role ambiguity, or interpersonal conflicts (Lee & Ashforth, 1996; Wilkerson & Bellini, 2006). Causes of burnout due to lifestyle may include seeing too many clients and having little personal time, being overcommitted, taking too many responsibilities with little or no support and resources, or having little sleep. Causes of burnout due to personality may consist of perfectionism, being a high achiever, or seeking power and control over things and other individuals.

CASE ILLUSTRATION 9.1

DR. G.

It happened so slowly that his colleagues, his friends, and his family only understood it in retrospect. Dr. G. was a successful professional counselor with a thriving practice of 20 years. He was well known in the community and an active church member, a husband, and model parent. Dr. G. was noted throughout the community for his pleasant smile and uplifting spirit and his engagement with a variety of youth organizations. All in all, he was the picture of health—physically and mentally. That all being said, how could his life unravel as unexpectedly as it did?

No one saw it coming, not his colleagues, not his friends, not his family. However, now in retrospect, it all made sense. Here was a man with a caseload of 30 to 35 clients a week. He worked mainly with clients experiencing depression and was somewhat of a workaholic, scheduling clients back to back throughout the day and often failing to take time for lunch, or small coffee breaks. He enjoyed his work, at least during the early years of his 20-year practice. But as he describes it, now he began to find that there were times when he hoped clients would cancel. He found himself wanting to leave his office and simply be alone, having had, as he states, ". . . enough human interaction for that day."

Dr. G. began to withdraw from his youth coaching activities and removed his name from his church council. His wife explained that he had begun to become quiet—absorbed in his thoughts or would simply sit and stare at whatever was on the television. While she was concerned that he was not as engaged with the children and their school activities as he once was—and that their own levels of intimacy had fallen—she simply dismissed it as a result of him being concerned over some difficult clients.

Over the course of the last year, Dr. G. gained weight as a result of poor eating habits and a developing habit of multiple cocktails in the evening. He started to find excuses for not attending family functions, such as a nephew's wedding and a father-in-law's 92nd birthday. The smile that seemed to be his hallmark was replaced by an emotionless expression. The physical changes could not go unnoticed and were only the outward signs of the changes going on within.

Dr. G. began to miss appointments, having failed to record them. He often booked more than one client at the same timeslot and even began mixing clients' names and information in his mind as he engaged with the clients. The once vibrant and competent help giver was now in need of help himself.

(Continued)

(Continued)

It was the occasion of a multiple booking—three clients all showing up for the same appointment—that caused his colleague to finally confront him about the physical changes exhibited, his apparent social disengagement and withdrawal, and now his professional miscues. Through that and a follow-up discussion, Dr. G. was helped to see that he was "burned out," that he was experiencing depression, and that he needed to commit to his own health.

A 6-month sabbatical in which he engaged in his own personal counseling and contracted with a personal trainer and nutritionist brought Dr. G. back to his previous self, but this time with an awareness that no one—not even he—is invincible and immune from burnout.

Moreover, the very nature of the counselor's engagement with constant empathy, heightened interpersonal sensitivity, and the real restriction that theirs is a relationship of one-way caring are characteristics that increase a counselor's vulnerability to burnout (Skovholt, 2001). Further, counselors often experience long work hours, days working in isolation of professional exchange, assignment of inordinately large caseloads, or schedules that are so tight as to prevent normal self-care activities. These are all systemic factors that increase a counselor's vulnerability to burnout. Additional factors increasing the possibility of burnout can be found in Table 9.1.

Warning Signs

Burnout can have a cumulative effect; thus, the earlier in the developmental sequence that one can take note of the symptoms or warning signals, the easier the intervention may be. Those in the initial stages of burnout often report feeling less valued, enthusiastic, competent, connected, idealistic, involved, energetic, and creative (Jevne & Williams, 1998). Symptoms of burnout for counselors may also include feeling tired most of the time, decreased empathy, decreased self-esteem, sense of doubt about self effectiveness with clients, feeling alone, sleep disturbances, stomach pains, fatigue, withdrawing from own responsibilities, procrastinating on paperwork and projects, and isolating self from colleagues. These are early warning signs.

We have collected a number of the typical complaints or descriptors employed by counselors experiencing burnout and have presented those in Exercise 9.1. It is suggested that you employ the scale throughout your training and practice to monitor the degree to which these early indicators may be present in your own experience.

Table 9.1 Factors Contributing to Burnout

1. *Unrealistic expectations.* It is important to set high hopes for what can be achieved in counseling while at the same time having a realistic awareness of the limits of counseling and the power of the counselor.

2. *Overpersonalization.* Counselors need to resist the invitation to take on total responsibility for the progress of the counseling and the actions and experiences of the client.

3. *Loss of objectivity.* While caring deeply for the client, counselors need to care from a professional stance—one insuring objectivity and appropriate emotional distance. Counselors who closely identify with the client's problem not only lose the ability to view the situation and process objectively but invite burnout.

4. *Task overload.* Burnout is nurtured by simply having too much to do given the realities of time and energy. With task overload, counselors will experience physical and psychological exhaustion making them susceptible to burnout.

5. *Failure to care for self.* Burnout is often experienced by counselors who are unable or unwilling to say yes to self-care, be it in the form of scheduling breaks throughout the day or engaging in healthy life patterns.

6. *Isolation and lack of support.* Counseling can be an isolating experience—one in which the counselor is in fact "going it alone." Counselors who fail to engage in supervision, collegial dialogue, and even personal therapy can feel burdened by the responsibility they have taken on without the support they need. This is a condition ripe for burnout.

Exercise 9.1

MONITORING SIGNS OF BURNOUT

Directions: Below you will find a list of symptoms or characteristics associated with the experience of burnout. It is important to note that this is not presented as a diagnostic instrument, but rather a simple checklist that may be of value in alerting you to signs that have been found to be associated with burnout.

Over the past month, which, if any, of the following have you experienced?

(Continued)

(Continued)

If you find that there are a number of the followings that you have encountered, it is suggested that you share your findings with a colleague, an instructor, a supervisor, or a mental health specialist.

_____I have felt tired or sluggish much of the time, even when I'm getting enough sleep.

_____I have felt detached, and it seems like I don't really care about the problems and needs of other people.

_____I have felt drained, and even routine activities feel like an effort.

_____I have felt burdened by responsibilities and pressures.

_____I have felt apathetic and uncaring, even while interacting with a client.

_____I have had difficulty paying attention in class or in sessions.

_____I have been forgetting assignments, appointments, etc.

_____I have been experiencing more than usual physical problems like stomachaches, headaches, lingering colds, and general aches and pains.

_____I have been avoiding people and don't even enjoy being around close friends and family members.

_____I don't seem to laugh as much as usual.

_____I feel increasingly sad or irritable.

Prevention and Intervention

The developmental nature of burnout suggests that recognizing its onset is clearly the first step to intervention. However, recognition, while necessary, is not sufficient. There are a number of self-care strategies that have been identified as having the potential to reduce the possibility of burnout and intervene in when burnout is being experienced. The strategies identified to prevent and to intervene burnout often target our cognitions, emotions, and behaviors. Some characterize these strategies as cognitive self-care, emotional self-care, physical or behavioral self-care (Baird, 2008) and others organize them into physical self-care, psychological self-care, emotional self-care, spiritual self-care, and professional self-care (Pearlman & Saakvitne, 1995). Table 9.2 highlights a number of actions that should be incorporated in every counselor's repertoire as a step toward self-care and the fostering of competency in practice.

Table 9.2   Reducing the Possibility of Professional Burnout

Assess and Monitor current well-being and signs of Burnout

- Increase awareness through self-assessment
  - Assess history of trauma . . . know triggers and take steps (therapy) to reduce potency
  - Assess stress load in and out of the work environment
  - Look for subtle behavioral changes
- Employ self-assessment instruments such as "ProQOL" . . . B. Hudnall Stamm available online at http://www.proqol.org/.

Invest in Wellness

- *Physical—Take care of the basics:*
  Sleep 8 hours
  Eat nutritional meals—avoid quick pick-me ups
  Exercise—even brisk walks; drink water
  Pacing—take more time to transition place to place, task to task

- *Cognitive*
  Allow for an interior life—read for relaxation
  Solitude-Silence: take time away from the 'noise' of life, practice Mindfulness/ Meditation
  Leave Work at work—can be involved not overinvolved
  Reduce private irrationality—challenge dysfunctional thoughts especially those that place you in a 'must be the savior, rescuer mind set'

- *Social*
  Engage/Talk to friends—about life outside of work
  Laugh—it helps with perspective
  Engage in personal growth through therapy, supervision or even encouragement circles (peers)

- *Spiritual*
  Take time for reflection . . . on the gifts as well as challenges you have been given
  Read materials that inspire
  Connect with a Spiritual Community

- *Systemic*
  Challenge toxicity: look at caseload, schedule and process for starting and ending day and time between!
  Invite collegial support (supervision, growth, escape)
  Challenge climate . . . one of hope or negativity

COMPASSION FATIGUE

Empathy—one's capacity to share another's feelings, to feel the person's pain, joy, fear, and other emotions in oneself (Hein & Singer, 2008; Hoffman, 1997)—is a hallmark of counseling. As touched upon in the Introduction, being empathically engaged as a counselor in a deeply personal and intimate relationship with clients who share their suffering can take a toll (Figley, 1995). Counselors care—and often it is this caring that leads a counselor to embrace more responsibilities for the well-being of the client than what is reasonable. With this exaggerated sense of responsibility, the counselor often embraces unrealistic demands and, with that, the experience of destructive stress. These conditions, as explained in the previous section, can result in professional burnout. And while all counselors are susceptible to the experience of professional burnout, those counselors who work in crisis situations with clients traumatized by violence, natural disasters, or war exhibit a unique type of burnout called *compassion fatigue.*

Compassion fatigue, or CF, is defined as "a state of exhaustion and dysfunction—biologically, psychologically, and socially—as a result of prolonged exposure to compassion stress" (Figley, 1995, p. 253). As noted by Gladding (2011), it is secondary traumatization experienced by professional counselors after a prolonged exposure to clients who have experienced tragedies or trauma. Whereas burnout is characterized by emotional exhaustion and lack of self-efficacy, CF is characterized by fear and anxiety (Killian, 2008).

Compassion fatigue is unlike typical burnout in that it emerges suddenly with little warning and tends to be more pervasive than burnout. In addition to the regular symptoms typically experienced with burnout, those with compassion fatigue often experience symptoms that parallel those with post-traumatic stress disorder (PTSD). When working with survivors of traumatic events, counselors sometime experience countertransference reactions that mimic the symptoms of PTSD (Pearlman & Saakvitne, 1995; Wilson & Lindy, 1994). As such, compassion fatigue has also been termed secondary post-traumatic stress disorder (Figley, 1995; Trippany, Wilcoxon, & Satcher, 2003).

Symptoms

Counselors experiencing compassion fatigue report symptoms very similar to those who have post-traumatic stress syndrome, including: a loss of meaning and hope, strong feelings of anxiety, difficulty concentrating, being jumpy or easily startled, irritability, difficulty sleeping, excessive emotional numbing, and intrusive images of their client's traumatic material. Emotional symptoms associated with compassion fatigue vary from increased anxiety, guilt, powerlessness, anger, rage, numbness, fear, helplessness, and sadness (Dutton & Rubinstein, 1995); and somatic symptoms vary from shock, sweating, rapid heartbeat, breathing difficulties, and dizziness to increased medical problems. Figley (2002) identified symptoms of CF across seven domains: (1) *cognitive* (e.g., decreased concentration), (2) *emotional* (e.g., anxiety, guilt, sadness), (3) *behavioral* (e.g., appetite changes, sleep disturbances), (4) *personal relations* (e.g., mistrust, isolation, loneliness), (5) *somatic* (e.g., aches and pains, impaired immunity), (6) *work performance* (e.g., low motivation, absenteeism), and (7) *spiritual* (e.g., questioning one's belief systems and values).

Over time, these experiences morph into the counselor's reduced empathy, diminished sense of personal safety, reduced sense of control and hopelessness, and increased involvement in escape activities, including chronic overeating, and drug or alcohol use (VandeCreek & Jackson, 2000). Those individuals who experience compassion fatigue may also become withdrawn from personal relationships, have decreased interests in intimacy and sex, abuse drugs, display mistrust, and complain of loneliness or increased personal conflicts (Beaton & Murphy, 1995).

Case Illustration 9.2 illustrates how the symptoms outlined here were clearly evident in the case of Julian H., who was a counselor working with abused and victimized children. Her 3-year experience apparently took a toll and tested the limits of her empathy.

Clearly, the experience of compassion fatigue not only has potentially devastating effects on the counselor, but also interferes with, if not totally impedes, a counselor's ability to provide competent, effective service to the client.

CASE ILLUSTRATION 9.2

JULIAN H.

The A.B.S. Child Care Center is a community mental health center that works specifically with women and children who are victims of abuse and violent crime. Julian H. was a counselor with a master's degree who started work at the center immediately following her graduation 3 years earlier. Her specialty was working with children under the age 5.

Julian took the job because she felt a calling to youth services and truly felt as if she had the energy and the training to make a difference. This is the third year of her employment and she has worked with well over 200 cases. During that time, she had seen what she felt was all that could be seen. From babies abandoned in trash cans to women and children being sexually abused, burned, and physically tortured. All

(Continued)

(Continued)

of the clients' stories were tragic. Yet, in spite of the inhumanity of the presenting stories, Julian H. felt as if the clients' presence at the center was a hopeful sign and with that hope she actively, creatively, and effectively intervened.

Liz, a sweet little 4-year-old with red hair and emerald green eyes, was just another client, another sweetie who was dealt a very bad hand in life. At least that is what Julian remembers thinking as she began her work with Liz.

But this time, something was different. It wasn't the story that included sexual abuse, confinement in a bedroom closet, threats to her life, and even physical abuse, that was different—it was Julian and something occurring within.

From the initial intake, Julian felt different about this case. She could not stop thinking about this sweet little girl. She would talk almost incessantly about the case (without revealing identifying information) to her roommate. She found that even on her days off she stopped by to just "see how Liz was doing." She even found herself waking from sleep with dreams about Liz's travails or things that she, Julian, should have done.

Within a month of the initial intake, Julian found that she could concentrate on little else other than Liz. She found herself sad and often feeling guilty about leaving work and living in a comfortable apartment "while Liz was in a shelter." Her appetite diminished, her engagement in social and recreational activities ceased, and much of her non-Liz work assignments seemed to suffer. Her inability to provide Liz with initial relief and a life she deserved, while unrealistic, seemed to send Julian into a spiritual and professional crisis. She began questioning not only her own desire to be a counselor but her belief in the general good of humanity. She became cynical and negative, and the once sweet, caring person now exhibited reduced capacity for empathy, a reduced sense of control, and a general sense of hopelessness.

This sudden change in Julian's personality and interpersonal style was apparent. Because of both the rapidity of its onset and the dramatic level of change exhibited, Julian's supervisors were able to step in and intervene, giving Julian the support needed and the structure and treatment that allowed her to return to being a fully and more healthy functioning professional counselor.

Causes

Researchers in this area may differ in their focus or what term they use to describe the phenomenon, but one common theme emerges: work that is focused on the relief of clients' emotional suffering typically results in the absorption of information about human suffering (Figley, 1995). The ability of a counselor to connect empathically with the lived experience of the client—while therapeutic for the client—can introduce the counselor to the client's pain and with that connection a vicarious experience of the impact that such pain has on one's life. Our empathy with pain has an impact, one that often results in compassion fatigue. Stebnicki (2000) attributed CF to the "empathic connection [human service professionals] maintain with their clients" (p. 23). Paradoxically, the more empathic providers are toward their clients, the more likely they are to internalize their clients' trauma. While engagement with those experiencing trauma is certainly a key factor in the creation of compassion fatigue, a number of other factors have been identified which serve as contributing factors to the development of compassion fatigue. For example, working in professional isolation, working with difficult clients, working long hours, and working in situations where measures of success are ambiguous and where there is little reciprocated giving all appear to set the stage for compassion fatigue.

Prevention and Intervention

If addressed in the early stages, there can be complete and rapid recovery. As such, early recognition and improved self-care both in and out of the workplace are essential to creating and maintaining counselor wellness and thus the avoidance of compassion fatigue. Individuals differ in their responses to stressors; some are able to tolerate exposure to stressors without negative manifestations while others are not. Differences in coping techniques to handle stressors can play an important role in compassion fatigue.

It is crucial for counselors to engage in strategies and activities that replenish themselves—physically, socially, psychologically, and spiritually. Evidence suggests that counselors who engage in career sustaining behavior and are committed to personal emotional wellness are better protected from burnout or compassion fatigue (Rupert & Kent, 2007).

The literature on compassion fatigue (Linley & Joseph 2007; Nelson-Gardell & Harris 2003; Trippany, Kress, & Wilcoxon, 2004; Ulman, 2008) suggests that the remedy for it lies in the employment of various forms of self-care, or nurturing activities, including the following:

- Find ways to soothe the self as with meditation, yoga, spirituality, or connecting with nature.
- Find things to laugh and cry about.
- Attend to your need for relaxation, exercise, and diet.
- Lead a more balanced life.
- Maintain social supports.

While each of these recommendations are both understood and embraced as intuitively appealing concepts, counselors may fail to implement them as a lifestyle. And yet, the need for counselors to commit to a program of self-care cannot be underestimated as it not only serves the well-being of the counselor but positions the counselor to better provide competent care for the client. One specific set of recommendations provided by Gentry (2002, pp. 27–61) for preventing the development of compassion fatigue included the following:

- Become more informed about the nature of compassion fatigue.
- Join a traumatic stress study group.
- Begin an exercise program.
- Teach your friends and peers how to support you.
- Bring your life into balance.
- Develop your spiritual connections.
- Develop an artistic or sporting hobby.
- Be kind to yourself.
- Seek short-term counseling or therapy.
- Have periodic or regular professional supervision, especially during a rough time.
- Collectively, the prescription is for all counselors to engage in a program of personal well-being as an essential ingredient to professional competence.

PERSONAL WELL-BEING: FUNDAMENTAL TO COMPETENCE

In responding to professional burnout and compassion fatigue, the call is for counselors to develop and engage in programs of self-care and personal well-being. The American Counseling Association, for example, recognized the realities experienced by counselors and the potential for these to result in counselor impairment. As such, the Governing Council of the ACA established a Task Force on Impaired Counselors in 2003. The focus of this task force was to increase awareness of the potential of impairment and develop intervention strategies and resources to help impaired counselors. One of the struggles in making the case for a wellness effort among counselors is that often counselors do not practice what they preach (O'Halloran & Linton, 2000). But engaging in self-care and wellness is not simply a good idea—it is an ethical mandate.

As mentioned in the Introduction to this chapter, Gerald Corey, in his keynote address for the American Counseling Association Pittsburgh Conference (2010), called the pursuit of wellness and self-care practices an ethical imperative. The perspective he took is one echoed here—self-care must be a priority for counselors as it is essential to the maintenance of competent, effective practice. Put simply, one cannot foster health and well-being in another if such is lacking in oneself.

When thinking about self-care, we are challenged to be broad in our conceptualization including strategies that care for mind, body, and spirit. As noted by Norcross and Guy (2007), in their book *Leaving It at the Office: A Guide to Psychotherapist Self-Care,* a good plan starts with a comprehensive self-assessment of how well one is taking care of oneself in specific areas. Such an assessment will help identify areas that can be targeted for self-care programming. Exercise 9.2 invites you to engage in just such a self-assessment activity. The hope is that you will use the self-assessment as the first step to the development of a plan for maintaining your own personal well-being. In developing a personal self-care program, one should be as holistic and expansive as possible in finding ways to maintain well-being across multiple domains. For example, Pearlman and MacIan (1995) note the ten most helpful activities that trauma therapists use to promote wellness. They include (1) discussing cases with colleagues; (2) attending workshops; (3) spending time with family or friends; (4) travel, vacations, hobbies, and movies; (5) talking with colleagues between sessions; (6) socializing; (7) exercising; (8) limiting caseload; (9) developing spiritual life; and (10) receiving supervision. These are strategies that cut across the domains of wellness and match perfectly to the causes of counselor vulnerability.

As implied, care of self is not just a good idea; it is a precondition to being an effective, ethical practitioner. Self-care should not, and cannot, begin once you have begun your professional life. Even for those who are new to the field, the danger of overextension, emotional exhaustion, burnout, and compassion fatigue exists. So it is important *not* to wait until you are in the field as a professional to begin monitoring your own well-being and planning for its maintenance. So what's next? Use Exercise 9.2 to begin the process of planning for your own well-being.

COUNSELING KEYSTONES

- Counseling can be stressful for the counselor and this stress can interfere with the counselor's effectiveness and competence.
- Burnout is a state of physical, emotional, intellectual, and spiritual exhaustion characterized by feelings of helplessness and hopelessness.
- The counselor's engagement with constant empathy, heightened interpersonal sensitivity, and the real restriction that theirs is a relationship of one-way caring are characteristics that increase a counselor's vulnerability to burnout.
- The initial stages of burnout often report feeling less valued, enthusiastic, competent, connected, idealistic, involved, energetic, and creative.
- Compassion fatigue (CF) is defined as "a state of exhaustion and dysfunction—biologically, psychologically, and socially—as a result of prolonged exposure to compassion stress" (Figley, 1995, p. 253).

Exercise 9.2

SELF-CARE ASSESSMENT WORKSHEET

This assessment tool provides an overview of effective strategies to maintain self-care.

After completing the full assessment, choose one item from each area that you will actively work to improve.

Using the scale below, rate the following areas in terms of frequency:

5 = Frequently

4 = Occasionally

3 = Rarely

2 = Never

1 = It never occurred to me

Physical Self-Care

____ Eat regularly (e.g. breakfast, lunch, and dinner)

____ Eat healthy

____ Exercise

____ Get regular medical care for prevention

____ Get medical care when needed

____ Take time off when needed

____ Get massages

____ Dance, swim, walk, run, play sports, sing, or do some other physical activity that is fun

____ Take time to be sexual—with yourself, with a partner

____ Get enough sleep

____ Wear clothes you like

____ Take vacations

____ Take day trips or mini-vacations

___ Make time away from telephones

___ Other:

Psychological Self-Care

___ Make time for self-reflection

___ Have your own personal psychotherapy

___ Write in a journal

___ Read literature that is unrelated to work

___ Do something at which you are not expert or in charge

___ Decrease stress in your life

___Let others know different aspects of you

___ Notice your inner experience—listen to your thoughts, judgments, beliefs, attitudes, and feelings

___ Engage your intelligence in a new area, e.g., go to an art museum, history exhibit, sports event, auction, theater performance

___ Practice receiving from others

___ Be curious

___ Say no to extra responsibilities sometimes

___ Other:

Emotional Self-Care

___ Spend time with others whose company you enjoy

___ Stay in contact with important people in your life

___ Give yourself affirmations, praise yourself

___ Love yourself

___ Re-read favorite books, re-view favorite movies

___ Identify comforting activities, objects, people, relationships, places and seek them out

___ Allow yourself to cry

(Continued)

(Continued)

___ Find things that make you laugh

___ Express your outrage in social action, letters and donations, marches, protests

___ Play with children

___ Other:

Spiritual Self-Care

___ Make time for reflection

___ Spend time with nature

___ Find a spiritual connection or community

___ Be open to inspiration

___ Cherish your optimism and hope

___ Be aware of nonmaterial aspects of life

___ Try at times not to be in charge or the expert

___ Be open to not knowing

___ Meditate

___ Pray

___ Sing

___ Spend time with children

___ Have experiences of awe

___ Contribute to causes in which you believe

___ Read inspirational literature (talks, music, etc.)

___ Other:

Workplace or Professional Self-Care

___ Take a break during the workday (e.g., lunch)

___ Take time to chat with coworkers

___ Make quiet time to complete tasks

___ Identify projects or tasks that are exciting and rewarding

___ Set limits with your clients and colleagues

___ Balance your caseload so that no one day or part of a day is "too much"

___ Arrange your work space so it is comfortable and comforting

___ Get regular supervision or consultation

___ Negotiate for your needs (benefits, pay raise)

___ Have a peer support group

___ Develop a nontrauma area of professional interest

___ Other:

Balance

___ Strive for balance within your work life and workday

___ Strive for balance among work, family, relationships, play and rest

Source: From *Transforming the Pain: A Workbook on Vicarious Traumatization* by Karen W. Saakvitne Laurie Anne Pearlman. Copyright © 1996 by the Traumatic Stress Institute/Center for Adult & Adolescent Psychotherapy LLC. Used by permission of W.W. Norton & Company, Inc.

- Compassion fatigue is unlike typical burnout in that it emerges suddenly with little warning and tends to be more pervasive than burnout.
- Counselors experiencing compassion fatigue report symptoms very similar to those who have PTSD.
- It is crucial for counselors to engage in strategies and activities that replenish themselves physically, socially, psychologically, and spiritually.
- In developing a personal self-care program, counselors should be as holistic and expansive as possible in finding ways to maintain well-being across multiple domains.

ADDITIONAL RESOURCES

Readings

Baker, E. K. (2003). *Caring for ourselves: A therapist's guide to personal and professional well-being.* Washington D.C.: American Psychological Association.

Conyne, R. K., & Bemak, F. (2005). *Journeys to professional excellence: Lessons from leading counselor educators and practitioners.* Alexandria, VA: American Counseling Association.

Corey, G. (2009). *The art of integrative counseling* (2nd ed.). Belmont, CA: Brooks/Cole.

Corey, G. (2010). *Creating your professional path: Lessons from my journey.* Alexandria, VA: American Counseling Association.

Domar, A. D. & Dreher, H. (2000). *Self-nurture: Learning to care for yourself as well as you care for everyone else.* New York: Penguin Books.

Geller, J. D., Norcross, J. C., & Orlinsky, D. E. (Eds.). (2005). *The psychotherapist's own psychotherapy: Patient and clinician perspectives.* New York: Oxford University Press.

Kottler, J. A. (2012). *The therapist's workbook: Self-assessment, self-care and self-improvement exercises for mental health professionals* (2nd ed.). Hoboken, NJ: John Wiley & Sons.

Norcross, J. C., & Guy, J. D. (2007). *Leaving it at the office: A guide to psychotherapist self-care.* New York: Guilford Press.

Skovholt, T. M., & Jennings, L. (2004). *Master therapists: Exploring expertise in therapy and counseling.* Boston: Pearson Education.

Stebnicki, M. A. (2008). *Empathy fatigue: Healing the mind, body, and spirit of professional counselors.* New York: Springer.

Web Resource

ACA's Taskforce on Counselor Wellness and Impairment
www.counseling.org/wellness_taskforce/index.htm

REFERENCES

American Counseling Association. (2005). *Code of ethics.* Alexandria, VA: Author.

Baird, B. N. (2008). *The internship, practicum, and field placement handbook: A guide for the helping professions* (5th ed). Upper Saddle River, NJ: Pearson/Prentice Hall.

Bakker, A. B., Van der Zee, K. I., Lewig, K. A., & Dollard, M. F. (2006). The relationship between the big five personality factors and burnout: A study among volunteer counselors. *The Journal of Social Psychology, 126,* 31–50.

Beaton, R. D., & Murphy, S. A. (1995). Working with people in crisis: Research implications. In C. R. Figley (Ed.), *Compassion fatigue: Secondary traumatic stress in helpers* (pp. 5181). New York: Brunner/Mazel.

Corey, G. (2010). *The counselor as a person and as a professional.* Keynote address for the American Counseling Association Pittsburgh Conference. Retrieved from www.counseling.org /handouts/2010/Keynote-Speaker-Gerald-Corey.pdf

Dutton, M. A., & Rubinstein, F. L. (1995). Working with people with PTSD: Research implications. In C. R. Figley (Ed.), *Compassion fatigue: Secondary traumatic stress disorder in helpers* (pp. 82–100). New York: Brunner/Mazel.

Evans, T. D., & Villavisanis, R. (1997). Encouragement exchange: Avoiding therapist burnout. *The Family Journal: Counseling and Therapy for Couples and Families, 5,* 342–345.

Figley, C. R. (1995). *Compassion fatigue: Coping with secondary traumatic stress disorder in those who treat the traumatized.* New York: Brunner/Mazel.

Figley C. R. (Ed.). (2002). *Treating compassion fatigue.* New York: Brunner-Routledge.

Gentry, J. E. (2002). Compassion fatigue: The crucible of transformation. *The Journal of Traumatic Stress, 1*(34), 37–61.

Gladding, S. T. (2011). *The counseling dictionary: Concise definitions of frequently used terms.* Upper Saddle River, NJ: Pearson Education.

Hein, G., & Singer, T. (2008). I feel how you feel but not always: The empathic brain and its modulation. *Current Opinion in Neurobiology, 18*(2), 153–158.

Hoffman, M. L. (1997). Varieties of empathy-based guilt. In J. Bybee (Ed.), *Guilt in children* (pp. 91–112). New York: Academic Press.

Jevne, P., & Williams, D. R. (1998). *When dreams don't work: Professional caregivers and burnout.* Amityville, NY: Baywood.

Killian, K. D. (2008). Helping till it hurts? A multimethod study of compassion fatigue, burnout, and self-care in clinicians working with trauma survivors. *Traumatology, 14,* 32–44.

Lee, J., Nam, S., Park, H. R., Kim, D. H., Lee, M. K., & Lee, S. M. (2007). The relationship between years of counseling experience and counselors' burnout: A comparative study of Korean and American counselors. *The Korean Journal of Counseling and Psychotherapy, 20,* 23–42.

Lee, R. T., & Ashforth, B. E. (1996). A meta-analytic examination of the correlates of the three dimensions of job burnout. *Journal of Applied Psychology, 81*(2), 123–133.

Linley, P. A., & Joseph, S. (2007). Therapy work and therapists' positive and negative well-being. *Journal of Social and Clinical Psychology, 26*(3), 385–403.

Maslach, C., & Jackson, S. E. (1986). *Maslach Burnout Inventory: Manual* (2nd ed.). Palo Alto, CA: Consulting Psychologists Press.

Nelson-Gardell, D., & Harris, D. (2003). Childhood abuse history, secondary traumatic stress, and child welfare workers. *Child Welfare Journal, 82*(1), 5–26.

Norcross, J. C. (2000). Psychotherapist self-care: Practitioner-tested, research-informed strategies. *Professional Psychology: Research and Practice, 31,* 710–713.

Norcross, J. C., & Guy, J. D. (2007). *Leaving it at the office: A guide to psychotherapist self-care.* New York: Guilford Press.

O'Brien, J. M. (2011). Wounded healer: Psychotherapist's grief over a client's death. *Professional Psychology Research and Practice, 42,* 236–243.

O'Halloran, T. M., & Linton, J. M. (2000). Stress on the job: Self-care resources for counselors. *Journal of Mental Health Counseling, 22,* 354–364.

Pearlman, L. A., & MacIan, P. S. (1995). Vicarious traumatization: An empirical study of the effects of trauma work on trauma therapists. *Professional Psychology: Research and Practice, 26,* 558–565.

Pearlman, L. A., & Saakvitne, K. W. (1995). *Trauma and the therapist: Countertransference and vicarious traumatization in psychotherapy with incest survivors.* New York: Norton.

Pines, A. M., & Aronson, E. (1981). *Burnout: From tedium to personal growth.* New York: Free Press.

Renzi, C., Tabolli, S., Ianni, A., Di Pietro, C., & Puddu, P. (2005). Burnout and job satisfaction comparing healthcare staff of a dermatological hospital and a general hospital. *Journal of the European Academy of Dermatology & Venereology, 19,* 153–157.

Rupert, P. A., & Kent, J. S. (2007). Gender and work setting differences in career-sustaining behaviors and burnout among professional psychologists. *Professional Psychology: Research and Practice, 38,* 88–96.

Schaufeli, W. B. (2003). Past performance and future perspectives of burnout research. *South African Journal of Industrial Psychology, 29,* 1–15.

Skovholt, T. M. (2001). *The resilient practitioner: Burnout prevention and self-care strategies for counselors, therapists, teachers, and health professionals.* Boston: Allyn & Bacon.

Stebnicki, M. A. (2000). Stress and grief reactions among rehabilitation professionals: Dealing effectively with empathy fatigue. *Journal of Rehabilitation, 66,* 23–29.

Trippany, R. L., Kress, V. E. W., & Wilcoxon, S. A. (2004). Preventing vicarious trauma: What counselors should know when working with trauma survivors. *Journal of Counseling & Development, 82*(1), 31–37.

Trippany, R. L., Wilcoxon, S. A., & Satcher, J. F. (2003). Factors influencing vicarious trauma for therapists of survivors of sexual victimization. *Journal of Trauma Practice, 2,* 47–60.

Ulman, K. H. (2008). Helping the helpless. *Group, 32*(3), 209–221.

VandeCreek, L., & Jackson, T. L. (Eds.) (2000). *Innovations in clinical practice: A sourcebook* (pp.441–453). Sarasota, FL: Professional Research Press.

Webb, K. M. (2011). Care of others and self: A suicidal patient's impact on the psychologist. *Professional Psychology: Research and Practice, 42,* 215.

Wilkerson, K., & Bellini, J. (2006). Intrapersonal and organizational factors associated with burnout among school counselors. *Journal of Counseling & Development, 84*(3), 440–450.

Wilson, J., & Lindy, J. (1994). *Countertransference in the treatment of PTSD.* New York: Guilford Press.

Yassen, J. (1995). *Compassion fatigue: Coping with secondary traumatic stress disorder in those who treat the traumatized.* Philadelphia: Brunner/Mazel.

Chapter 10

The Unfolding Professional Identity

So what is counseling? How is a counselor different than
other mental health specialists?

INTRODUCTION

The opening questions are simple, but they demand more than simple answers. What makes a counselor different from other professional helpers? This is not only an interesting question, but one which needs to be answered by counselors themselves. It is also a question that deserves to be answered for those whom we serve.

Answering the questions of "What is counseling?" and "What makes a counselor different?" is pivotal to survival of the profession and the ongoing development of each of its members. The unfolding answers to these questions, which each professional counselor comes to embrace, give shape to that counselor's *professional identity.*

Because we have discussed what counseling is in Chapter 2 and what counseling entails thoroughly in other previous chapters, the current chapter discusses what it means to be a counselor and what is meant by professional identity. Clarity around these two issues is important not only for the individual counselor, but also for the profession as a whole.

The current chapter outlines a number of the components that contribute to the formation of one's professional identity and will help you begin to outline a program or plan to facilitate the development of your own professional identity. Specifically, at the end of this chapter you will be able to do the following:

- Describe what is meant by a counselor's professional identity.
- Identify the components that contribute to one's professional identity.

- Develop an initial plan for assessing the current state of your unfolding professional identity and establishing additional steps aimed at facilitating the further development of your professional identity.

THE *WHY* OF PROFESSIONAL IDENTITY

The development and articulation of a counselor's professional identity is an important issue, not just for counselors but for every member of this unique discipline. The professional identity of counselors serves both the individual counselors and the counseling profession as a whole (CACREP, 2009; Gale & Austin, 2003; Myers, Sweeney, & White, 2002).

Value for the Individual Counselor

At the most basic level, a professional identity serves as a template for what we do, and similarly, what we choose not to do as professional counselors. One's professional identity serves as a frame of reference, a lens, through which to make sense of one's professional work. Professional identity contributes to our sense of belonging—to being part of something larger than ourselves (i.e., our profession) and to our uniqueness, distinguishing us from others of similar helping professions (Heck, 1990, as cited in Pistole & Roberts, 2002, p. 1), for example, social workers, psychologists, or other mental health professionals.

In addition to providing the counselor with both a connection point to others in the profession and a reference of distinction from other helpers, a strong professional identity helps to increase the public's knowledge and understanding of the counseling profession (Remley & Herlihy, 2007).

Value for the Counseling Profession

Our profession is relatively young when compared to other mental health professions such as psychiatry and psychology (Remley & Herlihy, 2007). As a young profession, we are still trying to articulate that which binds us as well as that which distinguishes our profession from these other professions. There have been numerous calls from professional groups and individuals for the development of a unified professional identity (e.g., ACA, 2009; CACREP, 2009; Calley & Hawley, 2008) as a means of strengthening the entire profession, enhancing advocacy efforts, and providing standards for training and professional development. Some have gone as far as to suggest that a professional identity is essential to the maintenance of the professional status of counseling and our ability to stand among the other professions in the helping field (Myers, Sweeney, & White, 2002). Articulating the unique contributions of the counseling profession—when contrasted to other professional helpers such as psychologists, social workers, psychiatrists, and so on—is not only essential to the argument for our profession's existence (Myers et al., 2002), but necessary in the fight to gain parity with and independent recognition from other mental health professions (Calley & Hawley, 2008).

THE *WHAT* OF PROFESSIONAL IDENTITY

While those within the profession support the need and value of having a professional identity, individually and collectively as counselors, there is no one, comprehensive, singularly accepted definition of what constitutes a professional identity.

There have been numerous attempts to define professional identity (e.g., Gray, 2001; Puglia, 2008; Weinrach, Thomas, & Chan, 2001). Nugent and Jones (2009) defined it as the integration of professional training with personal attributes in the context of a professional community. One professional organization, the Council for Accreditation of Counseling and Related Educational Programs (CACREP) has not only made the issue of counselor professional identity prominent within its 2009 Standards, but has also attempted to provide a definition of what constitutes professional identity.

CACREP (2009) provides a description of professional identity, which includes knowledge and understanding of (a) history and philosophy, (b) roles and functions, (c) advocacy, and (d) ethical standards of professional organizations and credentials (sec. II.G.1). We have adopted these components as the core to what is being presented here as professional identity. However, in addition to these components, we wish to add another component, one articulated by Remley and Herlihy (2007), and that is the component of *professional pride.* As will be discussed, this element reflects the counselor's sense of pride both in the profession and membership within that profession. Each of these components is more fully described in the following sections.

History

Counselors with a strong professional identity have knowledge of the history of the counseling profession (Remley & Herlihey, 2007). Having an awareness of the evolution of the profession helps a counselor to understand the profession's connection to other fields and disciplines, while at the same time understanding and valuing that which makes counseling unique from these other disciplines. This history sets the context for a counselor's understanding of what she is joining and what she is about to represent. For many counselors in training, introduction to the profession's history takes place in one of the early courses such as the Introduction to Counseling or Orientation to the Profession courses. Exercise 10.1 will help you begin to develop and engage this component of professional identity.

Philosophical Foundations

Along with a strong grasp of the counseling profession's history and knowledge, understanding of the counseling philosophy is also necessary for the achievement of a strong professional identity (Remley & Herlihy, 2007). As a profession, counseling is unique among helping professions in that it is founded on a set of four fundamental philosophical perspectives: (1) developmental perspective (Myers, Sweeney, & Witmer, 2001; Remley & Herlihy, 2007), (2) wellness perspective (Myers, Sweeney, & Witmer, 2001; Remley & Herlihy, 2007), (3) prevention, and (4) empowerment (McWhirter, 1991; Remley & Herlihy, 2007). A review of the marketing blogs provided by professional counselors highlights the emphasis on these four elements. Case Illustration 10.1 provides

---

Exercise 10.1

REFLECTING ON THE HISTORY

Directions: As you proceed through your training, it will be important for you to be able to answer each of the following. This is not intended as an academic test but is meant as an exercise to help you connect with the profession in which you are becoming a member.

1. Identify one individual whom you would hold up as having made a significant impact on the emergence of the unique profession of counseling.

2. What significance did vocational guidance play in the formulation of a new profession of counseling?

3. What was the significance of Sputnik to the ongoing development of counseling as a profession?

4. Identify one federal legislation that proved significant to the development of counseling.

5. What is meant by the term *credentialing,* and in what ways has the profession been credentialed?

a brief sampling of some real marketing statements from professional counselors across the nation.

Developmental Perspective. Counselors approach the helping process from an educational-developmental perspective. While most other mental health professionals view mental or emotional problems as "illnesses" and an extension of the medical

---

CASE ILLUSTRATION 10.1

COUNSELOR UNIQUENESS

Each of the following is a statement extracted from marketing blogs and professional counselors' self-descriptions. Each emphasizes a unique element of a counselor's approach to helping.

Developmental Focus

- I believe that each of us experience challenges in our road of life—counseling is one support to guide us through these difficult times and prepare us for addressing the next.
- My goal is to help my clients not only resolve a current concern, but do so in a way that is growthful.
- As we walk through life, we are affected by so many events that can change us. Sometimes the change is in the wrong direction, and it is difficult to find your way back. As your therapist, I can help you return to the person you once were, or help you to be the person you can be. Everyone needs help sometimes; you are just the courageous one who chooses to seek it.

Wellness Perspective

- My groups focus on promoting health and well-being.
- Counseling is not just for those experiencing a life crisis or a current difficulty—counseling is an opportunity to learn new skills, gain new insights, and position oneself for increased health and wellness.
- An understanding of the creative mind and its importance to emotional health continues to inform my work.
- Working together, we can help you find your way back to the path for growth and emotional well-being.

(Continued)

(Continued)

Prevention Emphasis

- It is not sufficient to simply wait for problems to arise—I feel an obligation to engage in advocacy for programs of education and mental health.
- I believe counseling is both remedial—in helping one move from distress—and more important, preventive in helping the client learn both the factors contributing to the initial distress and developing the skills to avoid or prevent those factors from reemerging.
- My parenting groups are intended to help parents manage the stress of parenthood while at the same time incorporating practices which will help develop healthy, resilient children.

Empowerment

- While I am a counselor, I don't believe I know what is best. There is no right way of viewing circumstances. Rather I focus on the client's positive characteristics, strengths, and resources.
- As the counselor, I'm not in a hierarchical relationship with my client; rather I believe we are two people journeying through life and that working collaboratively can make that journey more effective.

model perspective, counselors view such problems as a part of the normal process of living. This view positions counselors to approach their work with clients more positively, viewing the clients' difficulty as a reflection of developmental block rather than an indication of severe pathology.

Wellness Perspective. Counselors value the goal of helping each person achieve positive mental health (Remley & Herlihy, 2007). To this end, counselors focus on the client's strengths as opposed to seeing the client as being problematic or only having problems. Counselors believe in the value of counseling not just for those experiencing blocks in their development, but for all who seek to unfold their potential. Further, this wellness perspective directs counselors to view the client holistically, including his behavioral, spiritual, systemic, cultural, psycho-social, and emotional components.

Prevention. Like other helping professionals, counselors not only have the knowledge and skills to intervene at times when clients are experiencing difficulty, but also philosophically value the provision of preventive care over mere remediation (Remley & Herlihy, 2007). Counselors employ programs and strategies such as guidance curriculum, resiliency training, premarital communication training, and so forth, which are focused on helping clients develop the knowledge and skill that will help them prevent potential problems.

Empowerment. Counselors seek to assist those individuals and groups who feel powerless and marginalized to gain not only awareness of those external influences on their lives which are creating a sense of powerlessness, but control over their lives (Puglia, 2008). This goal of promoting client personal power extends to the relationship between the counselor and the client. Counselors seek to promote client independence and to that end employ knowledge and skills that not only assist the client at the moment, but also help her develop the tools necessary to be more able to solve problems and navigate life's challenges on her own (Remley & Herlihy, 2007).

It is important for each member of the counseling profession to know the unique components of the profession's philosophical stance, but knowing alone is insufficient. Similarly, it is not sufficient for a counselor-in-training simply to "know" these unique perspectives. As one's professional identity develops, each of these components must and will become assimilated as personal values, which will give shape to the professional decisions and practices of each of us as counselors. Exercise 10.2 will help you review your own understanding and valuing of these philosophical positions.

Exercise 10.2

OWNING THE COUNSELING PHILOSOPHY

PART I. PHILOSOPHICAL PERSPECTIVE IN ACTION

Directions: Using information you learned in class, programs, and research you may have reviewed, or through discussion with a professional counselor, identify how each of the following would look or take shape in practice.

Developmental Perspective

(Continued)

(Continued)

Wellness Perspective

Prevention Perspective

Empowerment Perspective

PART II. ASSESSING YOUR CURRENT ASSIMILATION OF THE PHILOSOPHICAL PERSPECTIVES

Directions: Use the following scale to assess your knowledge and personal valuing of each of the philosophical perspectives. 1 = none, 5 = mastery (knowledge) or fully value.

	Understanding of What Is Meant by Each of the Following Philosophical Perspectives	*Personal Valuing—Degree to Which You Hold These Perspectives as Something to Be Truly Valued and Embodied in Practice*
Development	_____	_____
Wellness	_____	_____
Prevention	_____	_____
Empowerment	_____	_____

Roles and Functions

Another element in the development of a professional identity is knowing and embracing the unique roles and functions performed by members of a profession (Remley & Herlihy, 2007). While embracing a common set of values and philosophical assumptions, counselors give form to these in a wide variety of settings (e.g., schools, businesses, private practices, hospitals), providing a multitude of services (growth and remediation) to all types of clients.

The expanse of the counselor's role and function can be gleaned from a review of CACREP's scope of accreditation which includes: (1) addictions counseling; (2) career counseling; (3) clinical mental health counseling; (4) marriage, couple, and family counseling; (5) school counseling; (6) student affairs and college counseling; and (7) counselor education and supervision (CACREP, 2009). Further, a review of the listing of divisions found within the American Counseling Association (ACA) speaks to the variety of interests counselors serve. (See Figure 10.1.)

In appreciation of both the connectedness and uniqueness of counselors specializing in different areas, complete Exercise 10.3.

Figure 10.1 ACA Divisions

American College Counseling Association (ACCA)

American Mental Health Counselors Association (AMHCA)

American Rehabilitation Counseling Association (ARCA)

American School Counselor Association (ASCA)

Association for Adult Development and Aging (AADA)

Association for Assessment in Counseling and Education (AACE)

Association for Counselors and Educators in Government (ACEG)

Association for Counselor Education and Supervision (ACES)

Association for Creativity in Counseling (ACC)

Association for Humanistic Counseling (AHC)

Association for Lesbian, Gay, Bisexual, and Transgender Issues in Counseling (ALGBTIC)

Association for Multicultural Counseling and Development (AMCD)

Association for Specialists in Group Work (ASGW)

(Continued)

Figure 10.1 Continued

Association for Spiritual, Ethical, and Religious Values in Counseling (ASERVIC)

Counselors for Social Justice (CSJ)

International Association of Addictions and Offender Counselors (IAAOC)

International Association of Marriage and Family Counselors (IAMFC)

National Career Development Association (NCDA)

National Employment Counseling Association (NECA)

Exercise 10.3

ROLE AND FUNCTIONS OF COUNSELORS

Directions: In order to get a feel for the uniqueness and yet common bonding of counselors operating in specialty areas, you are to complete the following:

Part 1

Select any two of the divisions of ACA and review their mission and purpose. Because one of the characteristics of professional identity is engagement in the profession, it would be helpful to select two divisions that on the surface you feel you may someday wish to be a member of.

Part 2

Using the different specialty areas identified by CACREP, contact a counselor certified in one of these specialty areas and ask how he or she incorporates the four philosophical perspectives of development, wellness, prevention, and empowerment within his or her practice.

Advocacy and Professionalism

As members of a profession, counselors exhibit professionalism and engage in those activities that advocate for the profession and its advancement. For any profession not only to survive, but to thrive, it needs its members as professionals to advocate for it (Myers & Sweeney, 2004). With the unfolding of professional identity, each counselor will be knowledgeable about the issues confronting the profession and motivated to act as an advocate for the profession. Acting as an advocate may simply require a counselor to educate others on the role and function of counselors, along with their unique contribution to the well-being of their clients. This is certainly true for the elementary school counselor illustrated in Case Illustration 10.2.

CASE ILLUSTRATION 10.2

ADVOCATING FOR AN EXPANDED ROLE DEFINITION

Josh was in his first year as an elementary school counselor in a rural area of Pennsylvania. The school district in which he was working had a total of five counselors (one elementary, two in middle school, and two for the high school). The area was not really psychologically sophisticated and the employment of counselors was a recent development in the district, only being instituted 4 years prior to Josh's employment.

While Josh experienced many of the common tasks assigned to most elementary school counselors, he was shocked by the number of cases of corporal punishment (spanking) that his students would report. It appeared that physical discipline was commonplace and generally accepted not just by parents, but also by many of the teachers.

Josh approached his principal regarding his concern and was politely told that this was the way things were done, and the state allowed school personnel to employ mild corporal punishment in certain circumstances. Further, the principal explained that counselors were there to deal with so-called problem kids and that is where his focus should be.

The answer was not satisfactory and was not the end to this issue. Josh felt, as a counselor, that his job should be restricted to those needing remediation. He believed that his role was one that should promote growth and wellness for all students and he knew from his studies that there were more positive, effective ways than discipline and that corporal punishment can have lasting negative effects on children. He felt compelled to try to address this issue and to change the attitude toward spanking.

Working with the National Center for the Study of Corporal Punishment and the Center for Effective Discipline, he gathered educational materials and research support for a program that he sought to introduce. With the materials gained through these organizations, Josh developed a proposal for a parent education program that he submitted to the principal for approval and then to a grant agency for financial support.

(Continued)

(Continued)

This parent education program was the first of its kind in the district. The principal, while very pleased—actually excited—about the possibility of grant monies, was skeptical about the value of the program and even the fact that a counselor should be running a parent-education program. He was surprised by the proactive, advocacy, and educational focus of Josh's program; it did not fit the remedial role counselors served. He, and others, narrowly believed that counselors dealt with children with mental and behavioral problems, so Josh's proposal was stretching that view of the profession.

While many of the teachers felt that Josh was wasting his time and that this was just the "way things were," Josh was not dissuaded. The program, which started with only 6 parents the first year, within 3 years, was servicing over 30 parents each quarter.

The program was not only successful in introducing parents to an alternative form of discipline, but a wonderful vehicle to educate school administration and teachers to the proactive, preventive services a counselor could provide. Josh advocated not only for his students, but his profession.

A counselor's professional identity is strengthened by active participation in national, state, and local professional organizations. This participation can take the form of attending professional conferences, and supporting and advocating legislation and political action that not only support the profession but also support client access to services.

Active participation in professional organizations need not wait for a counselor to be fully credentialed. Counselors-in-training are also encouraged to participate in the work and activities of professional organizations. The American Counseling Association (2012), for example, provides the means for students to have a strong voice in the future of our profession, as do the American School Counselor Association (2011) and the American Mental Health Counselors Association (2012).

As you begin your journey along the path of developing a professional identity, membership and active involvement in the organization that best reflects your professional identity will be essential and, as such, it should start now.

Ethics

As with all professions, counseling and counselors have adopted a set of general principles of conduct as guides to professional practice. These ethical codes of behavior as established by the ACA (2005), ASCA (2010), and AMHCA (2010) serve not only to guide professional decisions and behavior but also to function as a covenant to those we serve (Ponton & Duba, 2009). Promulgating the ethical principles of our profession helps those whom we serve know what to expect, and protects them if these expectations are violated.

But as with the four philosophical perspectives previously discussed, the real value of our professional ethics is experienced when the principles are assimilated not only as the rule of professional conduct but as personal values that are part and parcel of one's professional identity. While each of the various counselor professional organizations (e.g., ACA, ASCA, AMHCA) has honed specific rules of conduct and ethical guidelines of practice, in general they abide by the five general moral principles of (1) autonomy, (2) justice, (3) beneficence, (4) non-malfeasance, and (5) fidelity. Exercise 10.4 will introduce you to these five moral principles and

---

Exercise 10.4

EMBRACING THE FUNDAMENTALS OF ETHICAL PRACTICE

Directions: Read the description of each of the five moral principles and describe an example of how your behavior in working with a faculty member, a colleague, a peer, or a real or simulated client reflected your employment of that principle.

Principle	*Personal Example*
Autonomy is the principle that addresses the concept of independence, allowing an individual the freedom of choice and action.	_____ _____ _____
Non-malfeasance is the concept of not causing harm to others and includes both not inflicting intentional harm and not engaging in actions that risk harming others.	_____ _____ _____ _____
Beneficence directs us to be proactive to do good and when possible prevent harm.	_____ _____
Justice is treating all individuals the same or if differently, being able to justify the need for such differential treatment.	_____ _____ _____
Fidelity includes the idea of being loyal, faithful, and honoring commitments so that others can trust us.	_____ _____ _____

give you the opportunity to assess the degree to which you try to incorporate these in your work with teachers, colleagues, peers, and clients.

Professional Pride

While each of the previous components have been identified by CACREP as essential to the development of a counselor's professional identity, we wish to add the component of professional pride to this listing of components. Remley and Herlihy (2007) posited that a sense of pride, not just in the profession, but in who one is as a professional, is also important to professional identity. Case Illustration 10.3 provides one counselor's manifestation of that pride.

CASE ILLUSTRATION 10.3

MY CHOICE

You know it still makes me laugh, each time I think of it. I graduated from an Ivy League school as a psychology major. I had honors and my professors were very supportive of my continuing on into a doctoral program in clinical psychology. It was certainly affirming—even an honor—but I did some research and really thought (and prayed) about my future and my career path. I can remember the first time I received the reaction—it caught me off guard but in retrospect I'm glad I received it.

I was finishing my final in my Physiological Psychology course when my professor asked me if I had thought about a clinical program I would pursue. I told him I thought a lot about it, and I decided that I was going to pursue a degree in counseling education. I thought I was speaking a foreign tongue. He actually laughed!

His first response was, "You're not serious?" But I assured him that I was. What followed was a 10-minute attack against counseling, testimonials regarding the value of psychology, and a challenge to whether I was wasting my talent. To be honest, it shook me a bit and gave me pause to rethink my decision.

Following that experience, I went to talk to the career counselor at the student services center and the more I talked and the more I learned about the philosophy, the history, and the focus of both clinical psychology and counseling, the more I felt called to the doctoral program in counselor education that I had initially chosen. Well, that resolved the first challenge to my choice . . . and it was my choice and I was happy with it.

But more, much more, was to follow and it all resounded the same type of messages. Why counseling? Can't make it in psychology? Grades, GREs not good enough? Taking the easy route . . . just chatting with people rather than doing the hard work of helping? And so it went, from friends and family.

Each question—each challenge—while initially catching me off guard, pushed me to investigate my chosen profession and the more I did the more I realized it was the right profession for me. I loved the emphasis on human development, wellness, preventive service, and even social advocacy and the belief in the human potential. I am not suggesting there are not those in clinical psychology that own these values, these perspectives, but each is the hallmark of all within counseling and that is a group I look forward to calling my group.

I start the program in a month; the questions and the challenges have stopped, but my sense of commitment to the decision and my belief that it was my choice are stronger now than ever before. It was—it is—my choice, and I am proud to be on the path to becoming a counselor.

Certainly those who have strong professional identity as a counselor can speak to their pride of membership, affirm the "rightness" of their vocational choice, and in general, communicate a sense of pride about being a counselor. Counselors with a strong professional identity are not only comfortable talking about their profession, but also quick to defend the profession against misinformation or unjust characterizations.

DEVELOPING COUNSELOR PROFESSIONAL IDENTITY

It is clear that the development of a counselor's professional identity is essential not only to a counselor's practice, but perhaps to the very future of the profession (Calley & Hawley, 2008). This development begins with the counselor's first experience in training and continues throughout his professional career (Brott, 2006; Remley & Herlihy, 2007). According to Auxier, Hughes, and Kline (2003), the development of one's professional identity is an ongoing process through which the counselor identifies, clarifies, and then reclarifies this identity.

A number of researchers have attempted to identify how this professional identity is developed (e.g., Auxier et al., 2003; Skovholt & Ronnestad, 1992). While there is no one definitive explanation on how a counselor's professional identity develops, it appears that the development proceeds from a general naïveté about what it means to be a counseling professional to eventually seeing oneself as a member of the counseling profession. Skovholt and Ronnestad (1992) suggested that counselors' development "involves a movement from reliance on external authority to reliance on internal authority and that this process occurs through the individual's interaction with multiple sources of influence over a long period of time" (p. 514). However, these authors were speaking of development in the broadest sense of that term, and not specifically to the development of professional identity. It is fair to assume that the movement they speak of, that is, moving from reliance on external authority to reliance on internal authority, reflects a parallel shifting from seeing the others (i.e., teachers, supervisors, etc.) as professional to seeing one's self as no longer just a student, but now a professional.

If we reflect on the traditional model of training and educating professional counselors, we can see the structure that can foster this development of the internalized sense of self as professional. Auxier, Hughes, and Kline (2003) noted that counselor identity develops as a result of the counselor-in-training moving from conceptual learning by way of traditional academic presentations and assignments to experiential learning where practicum and internships provide hands-on learning, and then finally experiencing formation as a result of external evaluation. This last component, external evaluation, includes the processes of receiving feedback from peers, supervisors, professors, and clients regarding each counselor's professional behavior. According to Auxier and colleagues (2003), it is this feedback that is integral to the identity development of counselors because it constantly challenges the participants' self-concepts as counselors. This self as a professional is tested via feedback from others and evolves as new input is compared to previous views, evaluated, and internalized or rejected (Auxier et al., 2003).

ASSESSING UNFOLDING PROFESSIONAL IDENTITY

As we draw to the end of the current textbook—an experience that should have contributed to the beginning steps of the development of your professional identity—it is important that you stop and assess where you are and where you need to go in order to facilitate the unfolding of your own identity as a professional counselor. To this end, we conclude this chapter with Exercise 10.5, Taking a Snapshot of Your Professional Development.

Exercise 10.5

TAKING A SNAPSHOT OF YOUR PROFESSIONAL DEVELOPMENT

Directions: Below are a series of questions that, while not inclusive of all the ways to assess a particular component of one's professional development, will provide a snapshot of your own developing professional identity. Individuals with well-developed professional identities will be able to answer yes to each of the items listed. Clearly, many of the answers to these questions are not in the text, but for your exploration of outside research. There is no passing or failing. Review your answers and then commit to a plan that will help you further develop your understanding and ownership of each of the these components.

History

1. Can you explain why Frank Parsons has been called the "father" of counseling?

2. Can you explain how funding of NDEA promoted the growth of counseling as a profession?

3. Can you describe Jesse B. Davis's contribution to the profession?

4. Can you describe what the APGA is and the significance of its establishment to the development of our profession?

Philosophy

1. Can you distinguish philosophical perspective of counseling versus psychology? Psychiatry?

2. Can you contrast counseling's view of a client's presenting issue from what has been termed the medical model?

3. Can you give an example of how counselors embody the philosophical principle of wellness?

(Continued)

(Continued)

4. Can you give an example of how counselors embody the philosophical principle of prevention?

5. Can you explain how psycho-education reflects a philosophical perspective of counselors?

Role and Function

1. Can you list at least three (3) specializations certified by CACREP?

2. Can you list the various settings in which professional counselors are employed?

3. Have you begun to identify the area of specialization, setting, or population that will characterize your professional life?

4. Do you value working as an advocate for prevention and wellness, regardless of the setting, specialization, or population served?

5. Do you (or will you) approach services with a goal of empowerment of the client?

Ethics

1. Do you understand and abide by the ACA code of ethics?

2. Do you feel comfortable in your knowledge of ethical, legal, and professional standards for counselors?

3. Do you seek appropriate supervision and legal consultation when necessary?

4. Are you familiar with the concept and limits of confidentiality?

5. Do you understand the danger of boundary crossing and boundary violations?

6. Do you know the limits of your own competence and use those limits as the parameters for your own practice?

7. Do you intend to continue engaging in professional growth activities even after your formal education has been completed?

Pride

1. Do you feel excited when you think of becoming a counselor?

2. Are you eager to share with friends and family your ongoing development as a counselor?

3. Is counseling your profession of choice?

4. Do you value engaging in prevention service as well as remedial service?

5. Have you participated in any national, regional, state, or local counseling association activities?

6. Are you a student member of a counseling association?

7. Do you correct anyone who suggests that you are studying to be a therapist, psychologist, or psychoanalyst, and point to the unique value of being a counselor?

COUNSELING KEYSTONES

- At the most basic level, a professional identity serves as a template for what counselors do and, similarly, what they choose not to do as professional counselors.
- A strong professional identity helps to increase the public's knowledge and understanding of the counseling profession.
- A unified professional identity serves as a means of strengthening the entire profession, enhancing advocacy efforts, and providing standards for training and professional development.
- Counselors with a strong professional identity will have knowledge of the history of the counseling profession.
- As a profession, counseling is unique among helping professions in that it is founded on a set of four fundamental philosophical perspectives: developmental perspective, wellness perspective, prevention, and empowerment.
- Counselors with strong professional identity know the unique roles and functions performed by members of the profession.
- As members of a profession, counselors exhibit professionalism and engage in those activities that advocate for the profession and its advancement.
- Counselors with strong professional identity not only know and abide by the code of ethics of their profession, but have also assimilated the fundamental moral principles of autonomy, justice, beneficence, non-malfeasance, and fidelity that serve as the foundation for the ethics of practice.
- Counselors with strong professional identity have a sense of pride, not just in the profession, but in whom they are as professionals.
- Counselor identity develops as a result of the counselor-in-training moving from conceptual learning by way of traditional academic presentations and assignments to experiential learning whereby practicum and internships

provide hands-on learning, and then finally experiencing formation as a result of external evaluation.

- Professional identity continues to evolve throughout one's professional career.

ADDITIONAL RESOURCES

Professional Associations

Membership and participation in a professional organization may be the best resource for supporting the ongoing development of one's professional development.

American Counseling Association

www.counseling.org

American School Counselor Association

www.schoolcounselor.org

American Mental Health Counselors Association

www.amhca.org

Readings

Calley, N. G., & Hawley, L. D. (2008). The professional identity of counselor educators. *The Clinical Supervisor, 27,* 3–16.

Granello, D., & Young, M. E. (2012). *Counseling today: Foundations of Professional Identity* (MyHelpingLab Series). Columbus, OH: Merrill.

Nassar-McMillan, S., & Niles, S. C. (2010). *Developing your identity as a professional counselor: Standards, settings, and specialties.* Belmont, CA: Brooks/Cole.

REFERENCES

American Counseling Association. (2005). *ACA code of ethics.* Alexandria, VA: Author.

American Counseling Association. (2009). *20/20 statement of principles advances the profession.* Retrieved from www.counseling.org/PressRoom/NewsReleases.aspx?AGuid=4d87a0ce-65c0–4074–89dc-2761cfbbe2ec

American Counseling Association. (2012). *Role in ACA.* Retrieved from www.counseling.org /Students/RoleInACA/TP/Home/CT2.aspx

American Mental Health Counselors Association. (2010). *Code of ethics.* Retrieved from www .amhca.org/assets/news/AMHCA_Code_of_Ethics_2010_w_pagination_cxd_51110.pdf

American Mental Health Counselors Association. (2012). *Student benefits.* Retrieved from www .amhca.org/become/student.aspx

American School Counselor Association. (2010). *Ethical principles for school counselors.* Retrieved from www.schoolcounselor.org/files/EthicalStandards2010.pdf

American School Counselor Association. (2011). *School counselors and members.* Retrieved from www.schoolcounselor.org/content.asp?pl=325&contentid=325

Auxier, C. R., Hughes, F. R., & Kline, W. B. (2003). Identity development in counselors-in-training. *Counselor Education and Supervision, 43,* 25–38.

Brott, P. (2006). Counselor education accountability: Training the effective professional school counselor. *Professional School Counseling, 10,* 179–188.

CACREP (2009). *2009 standards.* Retrieved from www.cacrep.org/doc/2009%20Standards%20 with%20cover.pdf

Calley, N. G., & Hawley, L. D. (2008). The professional identity of counselor educators. *The Clinical Supervisor, 27,* 3–16.

Gale, A. U., & Austin, B. D. (2003). Professionalism's challenges to professional counselor's collective identity. *Journal of Counseling & Development, 81,* 3–10.

Gray, N. D. (2001). *The relationship of supervisor traits to the professional development and satisfaction with the supervisor of post-master's degree counselors seeking state licensure* (Unpublished doctoral dissertation). University of New Orleans, LA.

McWhirter, E. H. (1991). Empowerment in counseling. *Journal of Counseling & Development, 69,* 222–227.

Myers, J. E., & Sweeney, T. J. (2004). Advocacy for the counseling profession: Results for a national survey. *Journal of Counseling & Development, 82,* 466–471.

Myers, J. E., Sweeney, T. J., & White, V. E. (2002). Advocacy for counseling and counselors: A professional imperative. *Journal of Counseling & Development, 80,* 394–402.

Myers, J. E., Sweeney, T. J., & Witmer, J. M. (2001) Optimization of behavior: Promotion of wellness. In D. C. Locke, J. E. Myers, & E. L. Herr (Eds.), *The handbook of counseling* (pp. 641–652). Thousand Oaks, CA: Sage.

Nugent, F. A., & Jones, K. D. (2009). *Introduction to the profession of counseling* (5th ed.). Upper Saddle River, NJ: Pearson.

Pistole, M. C., & Roberts, A. (2002). Mental health counseling: Toward resolving identity confusions. *Journal of Mental Health Counseling, 24,* 1–19.

Ponton, R. F., & Duba, J. D. (2009). The ACA code of ethics: Articulating counseling's professional covenant. *Journal of Counseling & Development, 87,* 117–121.

Puglia, B. (2008). *The professional identity of counseling students in master's level CACREP-accredited programs* (Unpublished doctoral dissertation). Old Dominion University, Norfolk, VA.

Remley, T., & Herlihy, B. (2007). *Ethical, legal, and professional issues in counseling* (2nd ed.). Upper Saddle River, NJ: Prentice Hall.

Skovholt, T. M., & Ronnestad, M. H. (1992). Themes in therapist and counselor development. *Journal of Counseling & Development, 70,* 505–515.

Weinrach, S. G., Thomas, K. R., & Chan, F. (2001). The professional identity of contributors to the Journal of Counseling & Development: Does it matter? *Journal of Counseling & Development, 79,* 166–170.

Part IV

Applying What We Know

What follows are three counseling sessions with verbatim interaction between counselor and client. In addition, the counselor in each case provides reflections on the decisions he or she made within the counseling session that led to the intentional employment of specific actions. While brief, it is hoped that in reviewing each case you will not only see the skills described within the previous chapters take form in an actual session, but also will understand the intention, the reflection, that served as the basis for the engagement of those skills.

This is the counseling process—an intentional process seeking to facilitate desired change.

Chapter 11

Samantha: Finding It Hard to Say Goodbye

BACKGROUND

The Client

Samantha (Sam) is a 4-year-old Caucasian female, who is enrolled in the St. Jude Preschool. This is the first experience Samantha has had with a full day of schooling and in the first few days of the program, she has shown increasing reluctance to separate from her parents or to stay in the classroom. Samantha screams and sits on the floor crying as her parents attempt to walk out the door. She will run after them as they attempt to leave, crying and grasping on to them. If not restrained by the teacher's assistant, Samantha would attempt to run after the car as her parents drove away.

The Helper

Ms. Kim is a licensed counselor whom the school has hired to provide counseling and psycho-educational support to all of the students. Mrs. Morton is the master teacher for the preschool and she requested Ms. Kim to see Samantha with the goal being to help Samantha separate from mom and dad and engage with the other children in the classroom.

TIME TO REFLECT

What We Know

- Samantha is crying and attempting to stay with parents.
- Samantha is 4 years old.
- This is Samantha's first full-day experience with school.

Procedural Thinking (given this, then the helper will . . .)

- Would you see Samantha by herself or with her parents?
- How would you build a working alliance with Samantha?
- What are your initial ideas about the nature of the "problem" and the steps that could be taken to help resolve it?

Ms. Kim's Reflections Prior to Meeting Samantha

After reviewing the brief background on Samantha's presenting problem, Ms. Kim established a number of initial hypotheses about what might be going on and how best she should approach the first contact with Samantha. The following thoughts served as the basis for her initial plan.

1. *The parents have brought Samantha to school and have forced themselves to separate. It is clear that this is difficult for them. Mom and dad need to see that responding to Samantha's request for contact or for removal from the class is only strengthening her tendency to throw a tantrum. I may need to go slow with the separation for both Samantha and her parents.*

2. *The other children in the class have all had prior preschool experience and when Samantha comes to class they are all actively engaged in independent play activities. Since this is Samantha's first experience with school and most of her social interaction has been with her parents, I wonder if she lacks the social skills necessary to join in.*

3. *This is Samantha's first experience in a formal schooling environment and her first full-day separation from her parents. I wonder if there is separation anxiety or if her tantrums are simply ways she gets what she wants—parent attention.*

4. *I also wonder if Samantha and her parents are at the precontemplative or contemplative stage (Prochaska's stage of change model).*

With these thoughts guiding her actions, Ms. Kim decided that she would like to observe Samantha before even sitting with her or her parents. Her goals in observing Samantha were to achieve the following:

1. *See how Samantha's tantrums worked. What were the cues that started them and what if any were the payoffs?*

   My initial thoughts are that Samantha has gotten the attention she desires by acting out and throwing a tantrum. If that is the case, then it will be important to make sure that tantrums don't work but engaging in the classroom does.

2. *Observe if Samantha had the social skills to interact with her peers.*

   Her ability to interact with adults and her play group at home suggests she knows how to interact, but because the children are already engaged in activities she may be having a problem breaking into the circle. If that's the case, we can structure the activities to encourage inclusion.

With these thoughts as a foundation, Ms. Kim's actions were to gather observational data (rather than seeking information from Samantha or her parents) as a way to identify the nature of the issue and develop an initial plan for addressing this issue. Ms. Kim observed Samantha for 3 days and was able to identify both some strengths and challenges.

Her observations revealed the following:

1. Samantha enters the classroom holding her mother's hand. She is calm, smiling, and even says hello to Mrs. Morton.

2. After Samantha takes off her coat and places her things in the cubby, her mother gives her a hug and says goodbye. On each of the 3 days of observations, this was immediately followed by Samantha falling to the ground and screaming "no . . . no. . . . don't go. . . ."

3. Her parents' reactions to these outbursts were to pick up Samantha and try to comfort her by telling her it will be okay, that they will be back soon, and not to cry.

4. In response to this, Samantha only cried more and pleaded to leave with them.

5. When Mrs. Morton approached Samantha, she kicked and screamed that she hated school.

6. With the teacher's encouragement, the parents left, and Samantha continued to stand by the door (which was locked) crying and calling out for her mother and father. The teacher ignored this behavior and returned to the classroom.

Samantha continued this behavior for 10 minutes on Monday, 12 minutes on Tuesday, and 8 minutes on Wednesday.

7. Following these periods of acting out, Samantha would slowly join in with the class activities.

8. Samantha was actively engaged in the classroom for the remainder of the day but returned to crying and clutching once her parents returned to pick her up.

9. The pattern was consistent for the three days of observations.

TIME TO REFLECT

Given the data that Ms. Kim has gathered, have you changed your thoughts about how you would proceed in developing a working alliance with Samantha and how you would begin to explore the nature of the problem and the resources the helpee brings to the situation?

Ms. Kim's Reflections

In reviewing the data, I felt that Samantha had the appropriate social skills to engage with her peers, but that she had learned to use the tantrum behavior as a means of gaining parental attention, and when those behaviors did not work (on the teacher) she would eventually (approximately 10 minutes) stop and engage in more appropriate social behavior.

Further, given the age of the helpee (age 4) and the fact that this appears to be an issue of behavior management (that is, eliminating the tantrum behavior and increasing the speed with which Sam engages with her peers), I decided to employ a behavioral approach to treatment. With this, I decided to use a process of extinguishing the acting out (that is, reducing it by ignoring it), while at the same time reinforcing (using rewards) the increased speed with which she joined her peers in independent play.

Apparently Samantha is at the precontemplative stage, because she is not aware of the issue and does not accept the change, while her parents recognize the need for change but they don't know how to make it happen. I wanted to explain the plan to Samantha and her parents, and chose to do that during her initial contact.

In order to help Samantha move from the stage of precontemplation to the stage of contemplation, I want to see her with her parents in the room as a way to reduce her initial anxiety and establish a positive experience in the relationship. I think it is important that the parents understand what I will be proposing and agree to participate, because they know the benefits of the change and are considering change although they don't know where to start. It is my expectation that the plan I am proposing will help the parents move from the stage of contemplation to the stage of action.

WHAT HAPPENED?

Guided with Prochaska's model of change, Ms. Kim not only has developed a hypothesis about the nature of the problem, but also formulated a plan for intervening. She has done this and she has yet to meet the helpee. What happened to building a working alliance, using skillful questioning to assist the helpee to share her concerns? Where is the use of path finding for the development of solutions?

It is quite possible that these skills will still be employed. It is important to remember, as we explained in the early chapters, helping is *not formulaic*. Helping is a process that incorporates elements such as relationship building, exploration, focusing, and problem solving, but these are elements, not stages, and as such, can be inserted at multiple points along the helping process. In the current case, the helper felt that observational information was more useful than the information she would have gleaned from face-to-face discussion with Samantha. However, that doesn't mean, even with a problem-solving plan in hand, that she won't recycle and begin to develop a working relationship with Samantha.

FIRST SESSION: INITIAL CONTACT

Ms. Kim:	Hello Mr. and Mrs. Wilkes, and hi Samantha (looking at Samantha), my name is Ms. Kim.
Mr. Wilkes:	Sam . . . say hello.
Samantha:	Hello.
Ms. Kim:	(focusing on Samantha) Sam, I am very happy to meet you. You know, I was in school yesterday and the day before, and . . .
Samantha:	(interrupting) I saw you.
Ms. Kim:	(sitting next to Samantha) You did? Wow, that's neat. Well, I saw you too and I was sad to see how upset you were when your mom and dad had to leave to go to work.

Samantha:	(starts to tear up)
Mrs. Wilkes:	(grabbing Samantha's hand) It's okay, dear.
Ms. Kim:	Actually (turning to Mr. and Mrs. Wilkes), it seems to me after watching for 2 days that Sam does really very well once she settles in . . . and in fact, it didn't take her all that long to settle in . . . on the average about 10 minutes.
	(turning back to Samantha) Sam, when I was watching yesterday, I was really surprised at how well you did with the collage you were making. You seemed to be having a lot of fun.
Samantha:	I like using the scissors, and all the pictures . . . it was really fun.

TIME TO REFLECT

If Ms. Kim's goal at this early stage of interacting with Samantha was to foster a positive, supportive relationship, what skills was she employing to achieve this goal? What would you do next as a way of moving toward a working alliance?

Ms. Kim's Reflections

I deliberately ignored the little tearing and redirected Sam to a positive school experience, the collage. I think it is important that we highlight the positive experiences in school as a way of making the engagement in these activities a payoff for doing the difficult thing of separating from her parents. I also deliberately chose to sit in the little chair next to Sam so that we could be in eye contact—and I would be seen as an ally, a collaborator, rather than another authority figure. Finally, I wanted to do a lot of reflection on positive experiences that she shares as a way not only to show her I am attending and I care, but as a way to build the data about how positive school really is for her.

Ms. Kim:	So, is it fun to use the scissors and the pictures to make the collage? You really looked like you were having fun and even now you seem really excited talking about it, I can hear it in your voice . . . I guess it was fun.

Ms. Kim uses a reflection of both content and feeling as a skill to demonstrate her attending.

Ms. Kim:	You also seemed to be having fun working with your table partner.
Samantha:	That is Louisa . . . she's my friend . . . she's good at coloring.
Ms. Kim:	Louisa is your friend? Would you tell me about her?

Ms. Kim uses an open-ended question to engage Samantha and invite her expansion on the topic.

TIME TO REFLECT

Ms. Kim has spent a few moments focusing on the collage and now inviting Samantha to expand on her relationship with her friend Louisa. She has not addressed the tantrums. Given the presenting concern and the information we have to this point, why might she be doing this?

Ms. Kim's Reflections

My observations suggested that Sam is actually really enjoying school and that it is just the separation causing the problem, a problem that only lasts about 10 minutes. So I really want to intervene, even at this early stage in the relationship by trying to refocus Sam and her parents on this reality as a way to place the problem in the proper context—it is manageable. I wanted to focus on the positive rather than the tantrums to create a positive experience between Sam and myself and help her move from the precontemplative stage to contemplative stage and then to the stage of action.

Samantha:	Louisa is my bestest friend but so are Raul, James, and Sarah.
Ms. Kim:	Wow, you have four bestest friends here at school—Louisa, Raul, James, and Sarah!

Ms. Kim uses a paraphrase to show attending, but also highlights the four friends, emphasizing again the positive nature of the school experience.

Ms. Kim: Sam, I am wondering, would you tell me what other things you and your four "bestest friends" like to do at school?

Ms. Kim uses an open-ended question to invite Samantha's exploration and elaboration, again highlighting the positive quality of school as a beginning intervention to changing her attitude.

Samantha: (sounding excited) We do everything—we play with the kitchen and we sit together at story time . . . oh . . . oh . . . and play in the playhouse outside and . . . and . . . we always have snack and lunch . . . and . . . and . . . do you want to see my cubby? It's right next to Sarah's.

Ms. Kim: Wow, you certainly do a lot of fun things at school, things like playing in the kitchen and having story time and playing in the playhouse . . . that sounds like you have a lot a fun at school.

Ms. Kim paraphrases again, highlighting the positive.

Samantha: Uh, huh.

Ms. Kim: But then I'm really confused . . . maybe you can help me?

Samantha: Help you?

Ms. Kim: Well, you are telling me about all the fun things you do and all the friends you have and . . .

Samantha: That's just my bestest friends. I have other friends here, like Renee and Tomica and Sean and Robert. . . .

Ms. Kim: Wow, you sure do have lots of friends and I guess that is what I am confused about. I mean you have all of these friends and you do all of these fun things and you seem to have so much fun at school . . . but when I watched you the other day, you seemed soooooo upset and crying, like something was wrong?

This is a confrontation, and invites Samantha to elaborate on what is happening.

Samantha:	(looking as if she is about to cry) But I don't want to be here by myself; I want to be with my mommy and daddy . . . why can't they stay?
Ms. Kim:	Oh, I think I understand. You really like your friends and you like the activities here in school, but you also like being with your mommy and daddy and so it is hard to say goodbye. Do I have it right?

Ms. Kim provides a reflection as a way of demonstrating understanding.

Samantha:	(holding back tears) Yes.

TIME TO REFLECT

Ms. Kim seems to have established a comfortable relationship with Samantha, and Samantha is certainly engaging. Now that the confrontation has led to a clarification that it is not school that Samantha is upset about—instead, it is wishing to be in school but with her parents, thus having the best of both worlds. Where would you go next and how would you get there?

Ms. Kim's Reflections

At this point, I wanted to support Sam and being nonjudgmental allowed her to feel free to share her feelings. But by sharing my confusion, I wanted to have the opportunity to highlight that she does like school—that is, not even missing her parents (because she gets involved in school) but just the initial saying goodbye is what troubles her. I wanted to get her (and her parents) to understand this so that my suggested plan would make more sense. I guess this is a clarification but my hope is that it will work as the beginning of my intervention and move her from the stage of precontemplation to the stage of contemplation.

Ms. Kim:	Okay, thanks, now that makes sense, because what I noticed was that it was hard to say goodbye.
	But I was so proud of you for working hard to calm yourself down after your mom and dad left, and when you finally got calm you went right over to your friends and started coloring and that seemed to help a whole lot.

How did you feel once you were able to join your friends and play with them?

Ms. Kim poses an open-ended question aimed at confirming the positive experience following the upset.

Samantha: (now refocused) It was fun . . . I wasn't sad anymore.

Ms. Kim: You weren't sad anymore?

Ms. Kim uses Samantha's words as a minimal encourager to expand.

Samantha: Uh, huh. I like playing with my friends and we laugh and we have lots of fun and I like that.

Ms. Kim: That gives me an idea, but let me make sure I really understand, okay?

Samantha: Okay.

Ms. Kim: So when you first come to school, you are happy to see your friends, and then your mom and dad have to say goodbye to go to work and then you get very sad, but after a few minutes you calm yourself down and then you go play with your friends, and the rest of the day is fun. Is that right? *(summarizing)*

Samantha: Uh, huh.

Ms. Kim: So you really have fun at school . . . it is just that few minutes of saying goodbye that is so upsetting?

Samantha: Uh, huh.

Ms. Kim: Boy, if we could make it so that saying goodbye was not so sad, school would really be fun for you, wouldn't it?

Ms. Kim poses a closed-ended question, but invites Samantha to take ownership.

Samantha: (looking unsure) Uh, huh.

Ms. Kim: I have an idea that may help it become easier to say goodbye and help you be with your friends as soon as you come into the classroom. How would you feel if we could do that?

Ms. Kim uses an open-ended question to engage Samantha.

Samantha:	(smiling) I would like that.
Ms. Kim:	You actually sound like you would like that . . . and I saw you smile!

Ms. Kim uses a reflection of feelings and nonverbals.

Ms. Kim's Reflection

I really feel that I understand the situation and that Sam and her parents are on the same page. So I want to suggest using a token system for reinforcing her engaging with friends and separating calmly from her parents to help her move from the stage of contemplation to the stage of action.

Ms. Kim:	Sam, I was thinking that tomorrow when you come to school, that I could meet you when you come in, and we could do a couple of things. First, I would like your mom and dad to stay for about 5 minutes and while they are here, you and I could color a picture together. How does that sound?
Samantha:	My mom and dad will stay?
Ms. Kim:	Yes, for a little while . . . just about 5 minutes or so. And then after a few minutes your mom and dad will have to go to work and they will say goodbye.
Samantha:	(getting upset) But I don't want them to leave me here. . . .
Ms. Kim:	Remember, we said that it is hard to say goodbye, so I thought if you needed to stay with me and color for a little while after they leave, we could do that. How would you feel about coloring with me? *(open-ended question)*
Samantha:	Okay, but I like coloring with Louisa.
Ms. Kim:	That's right . . . I forgot . . . so really, we—you and I—can say goodbye to your mom and dad and then maybe I could go over with you to the table where Louisa is coloring? How about that? *(open-ended question)*

Samantha:	Okay, but I don't like it when mommy and daddy leave.
Ms. Kim:	I know, but you know what? I have an idea about what we can do to help that be a little better and get you over to play with Louisa and your friends as fast as you can. Want me to tell you? *(closed-ended question)*
Samantha:	Uh, huh.
Ms. Kim:	When your mom and dad say goodbye, I am going to start this timer (showing her the stopwatch) and if you can join your friends right after you say goodbye to your mom and dad, we are going to give you 5 points (pointing to a chart that has the 5 days of the week listed down the left side and columns marked at the top as 5 points, 3 points, 1 point).
Samantha:	Points?
Ms. Kim:	Yeah, I know, I didn't explain it very well. So here's what I was thinking. Since it is hard for you to say goodbye, we could reward you for working hard at learning to be calm when your mom and dad leave. I thought we could reward you with points every time you calm down and go play with your friends. Now at the end of the week, we could show your mom and dad how many points you earned and depending on how many points you earned, they would give you a special treat . . . like maybe take you for ice cream, or get you a coloring book, or maybe let you pick what you would like for dinner, or pick a game to play at home . . . that kind of thing.
Samantha:	Oh, I know (turning toward her mom) like our chore chart.
Ms. Kim:	(looking at Samantha) Chore chart?

Ms. Kim uses a reflection of her words as an invitation for clarification and elaboration.

Samantha:	When I pick up my toys, brush my teeth . . . I forget all the things (again looking at her mom) I get stars for doing them, and then if I get 20 stars in the week I get to pick a movie for movie night, and if I get 15 stars, I get to stay up a little later on Saturday night and if I get 10 stars, I forget what I get (again looking at mom who says "You can pick a game for us all to play") yeah . . .

Ms. Kim's Reflection

This was unexpected but certainly welcomed. Both Sam and her parents are familiar with a token system, and clearly see its value. That should make its use in this situation a lot easier for them to accept.

Ms. Kim:	Wow, what a great idea, and yep, that's what I was thinking here. So I will get you stars rather than points. How does that sound?

Ms. Kim uses a combined reflection and paraphrase to demonstrate attending, and asks an open-ended question to engage Samantha.

Samantha:	I'd like that.
Ms. Kim:	Okay, so here's what I will do. I am going to write down on this paper how you can earn stars and tomorrow you and I can practice these so that you can begin to earn stars (writing and saying the following)

1. So if you say goodbye to mom and dad with no tears and go right into the classroom and begin to play, you get 5 stars.

2. If you say goodbye, but need up to 5 minutes (pointing to her stopwatch) to calm down before joining your friends, you will get 3 stars.

3. And if you take more than 5 minutes to join your friends, you will get 1 star.

How does that sound? *(open-ended question)*

Samantha:	I can't remember all that . . .

Ms. Kim:	That's okay. You don't have to remember all of this. Maybe tomorrow, since you are so good at using scissors and making collages, we could make up a chart that shows all the stars. How about that? *(open-ended question)*
Samantha:	That would be fun. We could use the color pencils and the stickums. I like the stars cause I'm good at earning stars . . . right mom? (Mrs. Wilkes nods, smiles and says yes)

Ms. Kim's Reflection

I decided to make a system where she would always get at least one star, because I wanted this to be a positive experience and my observations suggested that she wants to calm down in order to be with her friends, so that stars will really be secondary to playing. I am happy that she wants to help me make the chart; that will make it our plan and not just mine.

Ms. Kim:	That's great. I know you will earn lots of stars! Now, maybe what you and mom and dad can do is to make up a list of things you can get or do with your stars, just like you do with your chore chart.
Ms. Kim:	(looking at Mr. and Mrs. Wilkes): If all goes well, Sam would earn 5 points a day for a maximum of 25 points. So do you think you could come up with a list of treats and privileges that she could exchange her stars for, 1 to 25?
Mr. Wilkes:	(looking at Samantha) Oh yes . . . what do you think, Sam? We could come up with some good ideas?
Samantha:	(smiling) Do I get stars today?
Ms. Kim:	Sure . . . in fact, that reminds me. Maybe it is a good time to say goodbye to mom and dad, and I'll start the timer right now to see if we can earn some stars starting now. Okay?
Samantha:	Okay (getting up going over and hugging mom, then dad) goodbye.

Ms. Kim:	Wow, that was super. See you Mr. and Mrs. Wilkes . . . it looks like Sam is on her way to earning 5 points today.
Mr. and Mrs. Wilkes:	(get up, looking a little shocked, and exit) See you Sam . . . have fun today.
Ms. Kim:	(after they leave) Sam, how are you doing? *(open-ended question)*
Samantha:	(looking a little tearful and with a quiver in her voice) Okay.
Ms. Kim:	I know it is hard . . . but you are doing super today! This is definitely a 5 point . . . oops, 5 star day!

Ms. Kim uses a reflection of feelings, focusing on nonverbals. Further, Ms. Kim employs an affirmation as encouragement for Samantha and her efforts to this point.

Samantha:	(smiles)
Ms. Kim:	Let's go see what Louisa is doing.

TIME TO REFLECT

Now that the case illustration has come to its conclusion, we invite you once again to review the case, but this time, rather than focusing on skills employed or intervention attempted, we suggest you focus on identifying each of the following:

1. Evidence of the helper's genuineness and unconditional prizing of the helpee.

2. Evidence of the helper's respect for the autonomy and independence of the helpee.

3. Evidence of the helper's interest in wellness, prevention, and empowerment for the helpee.

The dispositions of genuineness and unconditional prizing are characteristics of the effective helper and evidence for respect of autonomy, while interest in promoting wellness, prevention, and empowerment are characteristics of a helper whose professional identity is that of a counselor.

CONCLUSION

This may not have been the type of helping or counseling you were expecting. There was not a lot of history taking or extensive analysis of the problem (tantrum behavior) and even the interaction with the helpee (Samantha) was relatively brief and remained in a here-and-now level of discussion, with most of the focus on behavior and not feelings. This is because this helper, Ms. Kim, employed a behavioral theory as her lens for making meaning out of the situation with Samantha.

While this was a very brief interaction, it is clear that Samantha understood both the goal (i.e., to separate calmly and join friends) and the plan (the token system with stars). Further, it was clear that with this little plan in place, as well as the presence, understanding, and support of Ms. Kim, Sam began engaging in the new behavior. It would appear that this session, using the transtheoretical model as an orienting framework, was successful in not only developing a working relationship, but also in identifying achievable goals and engaging in a strategy, which at least at the moment, appears to hold hope for helping this helpee reach her goals.

Chapter 12

Jamal: The Gym Teacher's Concern

BACKGROUND

As she opened her office, Ms. Sarah Greene, the ninth-grade counselor, reviewed the note that someone had placed under her door.

Date: Friday, October 29, 2012
Subject: Issue With Jamal Thomas

Hi Sarah,

Sorry I didn't come to you directly yesterday, but I was on my way to a meeting with my quarterback, and had to go over some plays for the game this week.

I'm having an issue with one of your students, Jamal Thomas. He's been a real pain in the butt lately. He's been skipping class, not dressing, and is just not involved during my class. I don't get it! His older brothers are two of my favorite athletes. Can you bring him in to straighten him out, look at his grades, and see what's going on with him?

We're in the middle of another huge season and I don't have the time to babysit him and figure out what's going on. You can see his grades in the online grade book, and it appears that he's definitely not going to make it this semester. Hopefully he'll get on board for the next marking period.

Thanks!

Jack

Ms. Green's Reflection

Ms. Green reflected on the referral with the following thoughts serving the basis for her initial formulation of a helping plan.

1. *Since the referral came from the teacher, I'm wondering where Jamal is along the continuum of change (Prochaska's stages of change model). Is he aware of a problem (precontemplation or contemplation)?*

2. *We are only 3 weeks into the first marking period. I wonder if Jamal is having trouble adjusting to high school.*

3. *I know Jamal's brothers but I haven't met Jamal. I wonder what is in his cumulative file.*

Even though Ms. Greene did not have a history or even a familiarity with Jamal prior to this referral, she new the value of having some information to ground her initial reflections and planning. As such, Ms. Greene decided to first check the file to see what she could learn about Jamal prior to requesting a meeting. The following were the data she reviewed and what she concluded.

1. *Jamal is enrolled in the college-prep track of classes and his grades at this point are all in the A, A- range, with the exception of physical education where he has a D as a result of nonattendance or failing to dress for class.*

2. *He has no discipline actions against him up to this point.*

3. *He is a member of the French club, the Glee Club, the Helping Hands' Club, and is currently the secretary for the freshman class.*

4. *Jamal appears appropriately placed in his classes and according to the grades and teacher comments is certainly a model student. I wonder if there is something about gym or Jack's style that is contributing to the current problem.*

    It doesn't appear he is any problem in class. I'm surprised Jack didn't report him for cutting class. I know Jack likes to handle his own problems but I hope that is not sending Jamal a message that it doesn't matter if he goes to class.

    It appears he is active and engaged in school and certainly is liked by his classmates.

    The picture Jack is painting doesn't seem to fit these data—there is something unique about phys. ed. that seems to be somehow contributing to this issue. I guess I need to meet with Jamal to get his side of the story, but I must remember that he may be in the precontemplative stage of change and not completely understanding or accepting there is a problem; therefore I need to go slow!

Ms. Green is using the transtheoretical model of change to anticipate where Jamal may be along a continuum of change.

PRECONTACT PREPARATION

TIME TO REFLECT

Given the material presented, what are your initial hypotheses about what may be going on? Also, what thoughts might you have regarding how you would want to approach Jamal at this initial contact? What goals would you set for yourself?

In preparation for meeting with Jamal, Ms. Greene thought about her goals for the sessions. Being concerned that this was not Jamal's idea she wanted to achieve the following:

1. *Go slow—focus on building a safe, trusting environment, especially given that she knows Jamal's family, to emphasize the conditions of confidentiality.*

2. *Invite Jamal to share his perspective and, if need be, highlight the reality of the problem at hand.*

3. *Identify at least an initial goal and purpose of continuing to meet.*

4. *Respond to any of Jamal's questions or concerns.*

INITIAL CONTACT

Ms. Greene:	Good morning, Jamal. Thank you for coming down (extending her hand in a gesture of welcome).
Jamal:	Good morning (looking a little confused).
Ms. Greene:	You can have a seat either on the chair or the little beanbag, whichever you like.
Jamal:	(sitting in the chair, remains silent)

TIME TO REFLECT

If the goal is to work on relationship building, how would you respond to Jamal's silence?

Ms. Green's Reflection

Jamal is certainly a polite young man. He is very well kempt, nicely dressed. He looks a little confused and anxious. So I won't let him sit in silence too long; his silence doesn't appear to be a form of resistance or an opportunity for him to get in touch with his own issues. He seems simply unsure why he is here and he is waiting for some direction.

Ms. Green:	I'm Ms. Green and I'm the ninth-grade guidance counselor.
Jamal:	(still quiet)
Ms. Green:	Do you have any idea why I asked to talk with you?
Jamal:	I assume it has to do with phys. ed. class.
Ms. Green:	Yes, that is it. Mr. Abbott said he was concerned about your participation in class and was worried that you had cut class a couple of times. What is your experience in that class? *(open-ended question)*
Jamal:	I'm not sure what you mean?
Ms. Green:	Well, I am a bit confused because it is clear that you are a good student in all of your other classes and you seem to be active in extracurricular activities. So I was trying to figure out why there is this difficulty in Mr. Abbott's class?

Ms. Green employs a challenge, a confrontation, noting the inconsistency between Jamal's history as a good student and his current, out of character, difficulty with Mr. Abbott. Her use of a challenge was her attempt to move Jamal from the precontemplation to contemplation stage of change, and to see the existence of a problem that he will own.

Jamal:	It's really not something I want to talk about (looking down).
Ms. Green:	Jamal, I can see it is a bit uncomfortable for you to discuss this *(reflecting the nonverbals)* and I certainly don't want to force you to do something you don't want to do, but I would really like to help if I can.
Jamal:	(remains quiet)
Ms. Green:	You are doing so well in everything else, and it would be a shame to have this one class bring your overall grades down.

Ms. Green highlights consequences as a way of inviting Jamal's ownership, or contemplation.

Jamal:	(appearing anxious, a bit embarrassed) It's just, well, I don't know how to explain it . . . or what people would think . . .
Ms. Green:	What people would think? *(paraphrasing)*
Jamal:	It's just embarrassing.
Ms. Green:	You know, in case you are worried, that I would not tell Mr. Abbott or anyone else. I want you to know that whatever you share with me will be kept in confidence, just between you and me. The only time I would break that confidence is if I thought you were placing yourself in danger or going to hurt someone else, and even then I would let you know that I had to disclose that information and to whom.

Ms. Green, in attempt to build safety into the relationship, provides the boundaries of confidentiality.

Jamal:	I know about confidentiality. It's not that—it's just hard to talk about. It's kind of embarrassing . . . kind of personal, a guy kinda of thing.
Ms. Green:	Guy stuff? *(paraphrasing)*

| Ms. Green: | Would you feel more comfortable talking to Mr. Benson . . . since he's a guy? |

Ms. Green is reflecting her understanding of the male concern, asking a closed-ended question.

| Jamal: | Not really—it's not that. I don't know. |
| Ms. Green: | Well, I have an idea. Maybe you could tell me how you did in phys. ed. in middle school. |

Ms. Green poses an open-ended question to invite Jamal to elaborate and engage.

| Jamal: | I did well. I liked phys. ed and gym last year. |
| Ms. Green: | So you liked gym and PE last year? *(paraphrasing)* That's interesting. I wonder what the difference is between that class and the one you're taking now? What are your thoughts about the difference that may explain the difficulty in high school phys. ed.? |

Ms. Green begins by paraphrasing, and then expresses confusion to offer a subtle confrontation. She concludes with an open-ended question.

| Jamal: | It's not harder or anything like that . . . and really I don't have a problem with Coach Abbott. It is just in middle school we didn't have to take showers after class. |
| Ms. Green: | So if I understand, it isn't the course content or the way Mr. Abbott teaches . . . it's the requirement to take a shower after class that is the concern? |

Ms. Green uses a summary to demonstrate attending.

| Jamal: | I know that's weird . . . I feel stupid. |
| Ms. Green: | Actually, it doesn't sound so weird and you are certainly not stupid. I've actually heard similar things from other students. |

Ms. Green intervenes by normalizing Jamal's concern.

Jamal:	Really?
Ms. Green:	Yep. While I have heard it from both guys and girls, the girls really complain about the shower. They don't have time to dry their hair—you know how the girls are?
Jamal:	Yeah (smiling). It's not that (looking down and appearing anxious).
Ms. Green:	I know it can be different and rougher for boys, sometimes. I know that the boys can sometimes get kind of rowdy in the locker room—hitting each other with towels and things like that . . .
Jamal:	I . . . it's . . . well . . . I just don't like the shower . . .
Ms. Green:	The shower?

Ms. Green uses Jamal's words as a continuation or minimal encourager, seeking clarification.

Ms. Green's Reflection

I could sense that the problem was not the shower. I was hypothesizing it had something to do with a discomfort being naked among the other students but felt that raising that as a possible issue that may be too sensitive given the newness of our relationship. So my reflection focused on the shower to give Jamal freedom to expand as he felt comfortable.

Jamal:	It's not the shower . . . it's just everyone showers together.
Ms. Green:	Uh huh.

Ms. Green provides a minimal encourager to prompt Jamal to continue.

Jamal:	It just seems weird.
Ms. Green:	Weird?

Ms. Green uses Jamal's word as an invitation for continuation—a minimal encourager seeking clarification.

Jamal:	Uncomfortable . . .

Ms. Green:	Jamal, I really appreciate you trying to help me understand and I can tell by your expression, looking down and the difficulty finding that word you want to use, that this is difficult and somewhat uncomfortable for you. *(reflecting feelings)* If I heard you correctly, it's not the course material or the teacher; it is your discomfort with taking a shower with the other boys after class. Is that what you are saying? *(summarizing)*
Jamal:	Well kind of . . .
Ms. Green:	Kind of . . . *(seeking clarification and elaboration)*
Jamal:	I am just really a private person and I just don't like having everybody looking at me.
Ms. Green:	I think I understand. Taking a group shower is not something that you are used to, nor are you comfortable with that. *(reflecting content)* Is that correct?
Jamal:	Yeah . . . is that weird?
Ms. Green:	Is valuing your personal privacy, and preferring not to be in a group shower, weird?

   As an intervention, Ms. Green challenges Jamal to reconsider his own interpretations, helping Jamal move from the stage of contemplation to the stage of preparation.

Jamal:	(smiling) Wow—hearing the way you say it . . . I guess it isn't so weird, but it is a problem.
Ms. Green:	Well, it does appear to be a problem on at least two levels. First, it makes you feel really uncomfortable and that's not fun. And the way you are trying to solve the problem, by cutting, is causing a second problem . . . failing grades.
Jamal:	Yeah, but I don't know what else to do.
Ms. Green:	What else to do?

Ms. Green uses a reflection as a minimal encourager to invite Jamal to expand on his comment and thus provide more elaboration and clarity regarding the real concern.

Jamal:	Yeah, I don't know how not to feel uncomfortable and I don't know what I can do to pass the class without showering.
Ms. Green:	That is really good . . . how about we look at both of these to see if we can come up a way of helping
Jamal:	Okay.

Ms. Green's Reflection

It was not easy for Jamal, and my decision to go slow has paid off. He has now presented his concerns, rather than focus on Mr. Abbott's concerns. He is now at the stage of preparation because he is owning the problem and now appears able and willing to look for solutions. I think we have moved into a stage of change where we can begin preparing some actions.

Ms. Green:	Jamal, regarding the discomfort, I know from talking to other students over the years that sometimes this is the result of them thinking that they look different or that they are afraid others will make fun of them.
Jamal:	Yeah, well it's just that I'm younger than the other guys and . . . (becomes silent).

Ms. Green's Reflection

It is clear that this is hard for Jamal to share, but even though he is silent, he doesn't look confused like he did the first time he went silent when we first sat down, and he doesn't look like he is upset or really overly anxious, so I chose to sit in the silence.

Jamal:	I kind of feel . . . or look . . . I don't know . . . just younger.
Ms. Green:	Jamal, I know that you skipped a grade and are probably the youngest boy in your class. I also

know that boys and girls in the ninth-grade develop physically at different rates, and that's normal.

Jamal: I know that . . . in fact that is what we are talking about in class but it still feels weird. . . . I feel weird . . . I don't know.

Ms. Green: You know, it seems like there could be a couple of things going on here?

Jamal: Really?

Ms. Green: Well, let's see what you think. It seems that because you are younger than some of the other boys in class, that perhaps they are at a different point in their physical development than you?

Jamal: Yeah.

Ms. Green: Jamal, that by itself is not a problem—it's normal, and everyone gets to where they need to get in their physical development at their own time. Is that your concern?

Ms. Green uses a closed-ended question to obtain specific information.

Jamal: No, my brothers helped me understand that stuff, and they told me that they were late developers but boy are they built now!

Ms. Green: Okay, so we know that things will eventually work out on that level . . . so you are not really concerned with your own development, but let me guess, you are just concerned that other guys may not be as understanding and you will get teased?

Jamal: Yeah, there are some real jerks in my class and I've seen them rip on some of the other guys really bad.

Ms. Green: So in order to avoid the possibility of being ripped on your solution is to cut class or not dress?

Ms. Green uses Jamal's words to demonstrate understanding, and then offers an interpretation.

Jamal:	Yes (looking very confused).
Ms. Green:	Well, I can sense what a dilemma this is? On the one hand your strategy works if your goal is to avoid showering . . . but it comes at quite a cost . . . failing? I wonder if we could think of another solution that would be less costly to you.

Ms. Green first demonstrates empathy, and then uses interpretation to help Jamal see two sides of his behavior and his ineffective solution to deal with his concern. Her closing statement is intended to help Jamal move to the stage of action.

Jamal:	That would be great . . . but what?

Ms. Green's Reflection

Jamal was really engaged and eager to find an alternative solution, but I thought it was important that the solution come from both of us and not just me. I wanted to be sure he not only understood the solution, but owned it.

Ms. Green:	Slow down tiger . . . I am not the answer lady (smiling).
Jamal:	(smiling) Boy that would be great if you were!
Ms. Green:	Well, maybe I'm not the answer lady but I really feel we could be the answer team!
Jamal:	Thanks.
Ms. Green:	So, I have an idea. I know tomorrow we are on Schedule A and you don't have phys. ed., so why don't we get together during your study hall and we will start to brainstorm some creative solutions? How would you feel about that?

Ms. Green introduces brainstorming as a path-finding strategy and helps Jamal move to the stage of action.

Jamal:	Yeah, that would be great . . . thanks.
Ms. Green:	But I'm also wondering . . . I wonder if it would be worthwhile to talk to your brothers and see

how they dealt with the teasing. You know they may have some ideas that we could use.

Ms. Green is helping Jamal move to the stage of action.

Jamal: I can talk to them tonight. I know Damian would be willing to help.

Ms. Green: Then . . . that's your homework . . . talk to Damian and we will meet tomorrow during the third period.

Jamal: Thanks Ms. Green, I appreciate your helping.

Ms. Green: Thank you Jamal, for sharing with me. And just so we are on the same track what we have discovered is that you are comfortable with your own physical development but that because you are a little younger than the other guys, that you are worried about possible teasing or being ripped apart by some of the guys. So your solution to this point has been simply not to shower . . . and as we know that is a costly solution. How's that?

Ms. Green first emphasizes the helping alliance, and then offers a summary to promote understanding. She poses an open-ended question at the end for further confirmation.

Jamal: Right on (smiling)!

Ms. Green: Super. See you tomorrow.

SESSION II

Ms. Green: Good morning Jamal, come on in.

Jamal: Good morning, Ms. Green.

Ms. Green: Well? How did your homework work out? *(open-ended question)*

Jamal: (smiling) Damian is really cool. You know he is the quarterback on our football team?

Ms. Green:	Yes, I do. I love going to the games.
Jamal:	(smiling) He said he used to come down and talk to you all the time and that you were really cool.
Ms. Green:	(smiles)
Jamal:	He also said he talked to you about the same thing when he was in ninth grade. You didn't say anything about that yesterday.
Ms. Green:	Remember I told you that what we talk about is confidential . . . well that is true for any of the students I talk with.

Ms. Green emphasizes confidentiality to support the safety of this helping relationship.

Jamal:	Well, Damian told me that I should try not to worry about what the other guys may say . . . it's just words.
Ms. Green:	He told you to try not to worry about their words. *(paraphrasing)* That certainly sounds like good advice. How do you feel about that suggestion? *(open-ended question)*
Jamal:	I know it makes sense but . . . it is hard not to feel embarrassed.
Ms. Green:	It is hard not to feel embarrassed. *(reflection/ paraphrase)* Did you and Damian talk about other ideas? *(closed-ended question)*
Jamal:	Damian said that when he had Mr. Abbott he went and talked to him about the same kinds of stuff and that Mr. Abbott was really cool about it.
Ms. Green:	Cool about it?

Ms. Green is reflecting Jamal's words as a minimal encouragement for elaboration.

Jamal:	Yeah, Damian said in his class, Mr. Abbott broke the class into two teams and that he used them to do different activities or games, like volleyball or softball, but then he would also have them shower by team.

Ms. Green:	And Damian said that helped?
Jamal:	Yeah, Damian said that Mr. Abbot kind of set up the teams so that the younger guys were on one team and the older or older looking guys were on another team.
Ms. Green:	So Mr. Abbott split his class up into teams that competed and then he used that somehow to separate the showering? *(paraphrasing)* And Damian said that helped?
Jamal:	Damian said that he didn't realize it at the time but now he understands that Mr. Abbott put all the jerks in the same team so there was less teasing of the guys on the other team.
Ms. Green:	Oh, so Mr. Abbott kind of grouped the guys as a way of reducing the teasing. Hmm . . . what do you think?
Jamal:	I think that would work . . . cause we all wear towels as we get out of the shower and Mr. Abbott is always in the locker room so that there is no horseplay or towel snapping, that kind of stuff. There are a lot of guys in class who seem to be self-conscious like me, so we wouldn't tease each other . . . it's just some of jerks . . . sorry, I mean just some of the guys.
Ms. Green:	Well, it certainly seems like you and Damian really did do some great problem solving and you have certainly given it a lot of thought in relationship to the different guys in your class—identifying those who are similarly uncomfortable. *(paraphrasing)* What do you think we need to do next? *(open-ended question)*
Jamal:	Talk to Mr. Abbott.
Ms. Green:	Talk to Mr. Abbot? *(reflecting content)* How would you like me help?
Jamal:	I'm not sure if he likes me . . . especially after

	I have cut his class . . . so I am wondering, would you talk with him?
Ms. Green:	I certainly could do that, but you know Jamal, you have really approached this problem very maturely and you came up with a great solution, so I would like you to get the credit.
Jamal:	I don't know.
Ms. Greene:	I can see you are apprehensive *(reflecting feelings)*, but remember Damian said Mr. Abbott was really cool. *(confrontation)* So, how about if we meet together and I let him know that you really want to do well in class and you came up with an idea that you would like to share?
Jamal:	Okay, as long as we do it together. I think that would be okay . . . actually I think if I tell him Damian told me that is what he did for his class that he may be okay with that . . . he really likes my brother! You know Damian is playing quarterback?
Ms. Green:	Yes, remember I said I go to the games! Jamal, you are something special—that's a great idea. You know, we have 15 minutes left in this period, and this is Mr. Abbott's prep time. How about if I go there to see if he can come down now? *(open-ended question)*
Jamal:	Wow, that would be great, since we have gym tomorrow.

Ms. Green's Reflection

Jamal is really a great kid with lots of potential. I certainly would like to work with him to help him truly learn not to care about comments from others—how he separates his self-worth from the evaluation of others—but that is a big task. Actually, that is something all the students could learn, but for now I feel good that he is not concerned about the rate of his own physical development and that the issue is really on simply reducing the chances of being teased. His willingness to share with me, Damian, and now Mr. Abbott suggests he has a real good sense of self and feels good about himself. Knowing Mr. Abbott, I expect he will be more than happy to work on this and will be happy that Jamal took charge.

TIME TO REFLECT

As we suggested at the end of Chapter 9, it would be beneficial for the development of your own professional identity to revisit the case, but again, rather than focusing on identification of skills employed, look for evidence of this counselor's employment of the fundamental underlying ethical practice as well as promoting the unique goals of development, wellness, prevention, and empowerment.

CONCLUSION

The current case presents a more typical interaction of a helper and helpee, in that the helper needed to establish a working relationship and use the skills of helping to facilitate the helpee's identification of the problem, the establishment of goals, and the generation of paths to a solution. Throughout the brief contact, Ms. Green demonstrated her ability to attend and to "step into Jamal's world" (empathy) through her use of paraphrase and reflection of feelings. She was quite adroit at using minimal encouragers to invite Jamal to elaborate and further explore the issue, and was very skilled at using silence to assist the helpee. Overall, within two brief encounters, Ms. Green was able to assist the helpee move along the continuum of change from a precontemplative stage through to the action stage. It is assumed that Jamal, like his brother Damian, will find Ms. Green a valuable resource throughout his high school career.

Chapter 13

Mrs. Ayame Hoshi: Feeling as Half of a Person

BACKGROUND

The Client

Mrs. Ayame Hoshi is a 57-year-old, second-generation Japanese-American woman who came to counseling following her husband's announcement that he was no longer in love with her, and was going to seek a divorce. Mrs. Hoshi was married for 35 years, has two grown children, Cho, who is married with two children of her own; and Ken, who is single and is currently a physician specializing in neurosurgery.

Mrs. Hoshi's husband is 60-years-old and is a successful plastic surgeon; up to this point, Mr. Hoshi has not given Mrs. Hoshi any evidence of being dissatisfied with their marriage. He has explained to her that he "loves her" but is no longer "in love" with her and has, over the course of the past year, fallen in love with a colleague.

TIME TO REFLECT

Assuming that you were the helper in this situation, what concerns of competence might you have? For example, are there possibly culture differences that may hinder your helping? Does the possibility that the client is severely depressed suggest a need for referral? What other issues can you identify that would suggest working with this client or referring her to another?

INTAKE SESSION

Dr. Abrams:	Good morning, Mrs. Hoshi, please come in. Please take a seat (pointing to the chair).
Mrs. Hoshi:	Good morning, Doctor (with her eyes looking down).
Dr. Abrams:	Thank you for taking the time to read the information about our practice and completing the background information sheet. Did you have any questions about the information on our practice?

Dr. Abrams asks a closed-ended question for confirmation.

Mrs. Hoshi:	(still with eyes cast down) No Doctor, it was very clear.
Dr. Abrams:	I do want to make sure that you understand the issue of confidentiality and the fact that I will not disclose anything we talk about without your permission or a court order. The one area of exception is that if I think you endanger yourself or another I will take whatever steps are needed to protect you. Is that clear? *(closed-ended question for confirmation)*
Mrs. Hoshi:	Yes, I am familiar with the limits of privilege. My husband (starting to weep) is a physician and I am a lawyer, even though I've never practiced.
Dr. Abrams:	I can see that this is upsetting.

Dr. Abrams uses Mrs. Hoshi's nonverbal as the data from which to reflect the implied feelings being shared.

Mrs. Hoshi:	(quietly weeps and reaches for a tissue)

Dr. Abrams's Reflection

I chose to sit in silence and allow Mrs. Hoshi all the time she needed, feeling that it was important that she vent her feelings. The business part of the session didn't allow her to be in the moment and genuine. I sat, not interrupting her nor offering a tissue (they were on the desk beside her). I wanted her not to feel judged but I also wanted to demonstrate empathy and that's why I reflected after a few moments. Meanwhile, I wanted to see where Mrs. Hoshi was in terms of her stage of change based on Prochaska's model.

Dr. Abrams: I can see how upsetting this is for you. I truly appreciate your willingness to share with me, and Mrs. Hoshi, I want you to relax and take as much time as you need. There is no rush—I am here with you.

Dr. Abrams is reflecting Mrs. Hoshi's feelings, being nonjudgmental and genuinely expressing concern.

Mrs. Hoshi: (now with full tears) I just don't know what to do—I'm lost, and everything is falling apart (stops and returns to silence, and while crying, reaches for the tissue on the table next to her seat).

Dr. Abrams: (allows the silence but sits forward in his chair)

Dr. Abrams's adjustment in his body language nonverbally conveys that he is fully attending.

Mrs. Hoshi: (begins to gather herself) This is not the way it was supposed to be. Everything we have worked for is destroyed. I don't know what to do . . . who I am . . . I am so afraid (again breaks down in tears).

Dr. Abrams: Mrs. Hoshi, you appear overwhelmed and if I sense correctly, your words and tone of voice suggest you are feeling hopeless?

Dr. Abrams demonstrates empathy by reflecting Mrs. Hoshi's feelings.

Mrs. Hoshi: It is hopeless. What am I to do? (falls silent)

Dr. Abrams: Mrs. Hoshi, it seems that the news that your husband was unhappy in the marriage and was seeking a divorce took you by surprise.

Dr. Abrams shares an interpretation of information implied but not explicitly stated.

Mrs. Hoshi:	Yes, it was totally unexpected, it makes no sense (crying).
Dr. Abrams:	(continuing) It was a surprise, unexpected. (*reflecting content and paraphrasing*) . . . And something like this can at first seem unbearable, as if life itself is over . . .
Mrs. Hoshi:	Yes . . . it is!
Dr. Abrams:	I am a little confused. Are you saying that you are thinking about hurting yourself or that your life is over because your marriage is ending?

Dr. Abrams seeks clarification by using a confrontation.

Mrs. Hoshi:	It feels that way . . . I am not going to hurt myself—I could never do that to my children or grandchildren . . . but it feels so horrible.
Dr. Abrams:	I can only imagine how horrible it does feel, but I am glad you are able to see that even though your marriage is ending, you still have much to be enjoyed in your life—your children, your grandchildren.
Mrs. Hoshi:	I do love them so much. I enjoy them every day, but . . . but what am I to do . . . who am I? I'm a half person, no longer a we—a husband and wife—I'm by myself. (crying)
Dr. Abrams:	(allows her to cry for a minute, sitting in silence)

Dr. Abrams's Reflection

It is apparent that Mrs. Hoshi is at the stage of contemplation due to that she has already been aware of her issue and is intending to start the healthy behavior. It also seems to me that Mrs. Hoshi is in crisis and, as a result, is unable to separate what the reality of this divorce means, and will mean, from her somewhat catastrophic view of the situation. This is not really the time to confront her; our relationship is not that strong and she needs to express her feelings, but I want to continue to challenge her to see the facts—see the reality, which while very difficult and sad, is not a catastrophe and can be something for which we can figure out how to best cope. By doing so, I intend to help her move from the stage of contemplation to the stage of action.

Mrs. Hoshi: I know I'm not by myself. As I said, I have my children, and they are very supportive, and all my church friends, it's just . . . it's just . . . why is this happening (begins to cry)?

Dr. Abrams: You know, Mrs. Hoshi, you just did a very interesting thing, something that is really helpful . . . to me and can be helpful for you.

Mrs. Hoshi: (appearing confused, and stops crying) I don't know what you mean.

Dr. Abrams: Well, when you first started to talk about your husband's decision, you described yourself as being totally alone—all by yourself—not even a person, only half a person.

Mrs. Hoshi: That's how it feels.

Dr. Abrams: I am sure it does, and that is a horrible feeling. But Mrs. Hoshi, that feeling is coming from the fact that at that moment, you were believing all of that to be true and if it were absolutely, factually true that you were totally alone and only half of a person, that would be horrible.

Mrs. Hoshi: It feels so horrible . . .

Dr. Abrams: And if it were true that you were absolutely all alone in this world and that you were only a half a person, it should feel horrible and would feel horrible—unbearable for anyone for whom that were true, but Mrs. Hoshi that's not true. You are *not* alone, and you are certainly a whole person.

Mrs. Hoshi: I know . . .

Dr. Abrams: And that's what I meant when I said you did something really helpful. When you were saying those things and believing them and feeling so horrible, you actually challenged yourself. You reminded yourself that you have family who love and support you and that you have friends at church, and for that brief moment of returning to what is real and factual you actually began to feel better.

Dr. Abrams is beginning a plan to help Mrs. Hoshi, a plan that comes from a cognitive theory.

Mrs. Hoshi:	Yes I did, but he doesn't want me . . .
Dr. Abrams:	I can hear how sad that makes you. After all, you were married for 35 years. *(showing his empathy)*
Mrs. Hoshi:	(looking down) Yes . . .
Dr. Abrams:	But Mrs. Hoshi, could you imagine how much worse—how much more sad—a person would be if not only had her husband left her, but everyone else in her life, and all the people who might someday be in her life, left her and she was totally alone?

Dr. Abrams asked a closed-ended question, but it is also a subtle confrontation to how Mrs. Hoshi is thinking.

Mrs. Hoshi:	(looking up) That does sound silly . . .
Dr. Abrams:	But when we believe that to be true, it doesn't feel silly. It feels overwhelming and hopeless. So, I'm wondering if it would help if we began at the beginning but with one rule.
Mrs. Hoshi:	A rule?
Dr. Abrams:	Well, not really a rule, but maybe a permission. I would like your permission to challenge you if you start to describe something or state something to be true when that something doesn't seem to make sense to me or doesn't seem to reflect the facts—the reality.

This is an intervention and pathway to helping, even at this early point in the relationship.

Mrs. Hoshi:	You mean like when I said I'm all alone . . .
Dr. Abrams:	That is a perfect example, because we both know that's not true, but it is not just about being factual, but recognizing that distorting those facts often results in us feeling really bad and hopeless.

Mrs. Hoshi:	I understand, and you are right. I mean, as soon as I thought about my children and the people at church, I recognized I have a lot of support, but truthfully, the last couple of years with my husband so engaged at work, I've actually spent more time with these friends than with him.

SUMMARY OF THE MIDDLE OF THE SESSION

Because Mrs. Hoshi was at the stage of contemplation, Dr. Abrams used skills of attending and encouragement to engage and help her share what happened during the majority of the session. Throughout the interaction, his tone and his style reflected his genuine, nonjudgmental concern for Mrs. Hoshi and he conveyed that through his accurate reflections of her content and feeling. Being nonjudgmental of her as a person, however, did not stop Dr. Abrams from challenging (judging) her thoughts as they failed to reflect reality. Dr. Abrams viewed this challenging, even at the early stages of helping as an intervention or helping strategy and moved Mrs. Hoshi to the stage of preparation. Throughout the session, Dr. Abrams helped Mrs. Hoshi to focus on identifying the specific concerns she had such as lack of social supports, concerns about finances, and questions about her own lovability. Each time Mrs. Hoshi distorted reality, as was the case when she said, " . . . if he doesn't love me, no one will," Dr. Abrams would invite her to think about what she said and test it against the evidence. This type of intervention or helping strategy is illustrated in the brief exchange about her lovability.

EMPLOYING COGNITIVE INTERVENTION

Mrs. Hoshi:	(crying) I just feel so unlovable.
Dr. Abrams:	Unlovable?

Dr. Abrams offers a minimal encourager for clarification and exploration.

Mrs. Hoshi:	I mean clearly he doesn't love me—he said so— he said he was no longer in love with me.
Dr. Abrams:	So it is true, it is factual, that he said he was not in love with you?

Dr. Abrams is paraphrasing and seeking clarification.

Mrs. Hoshi:	Yes, he said it.
Dr. Abrams:	And because one person no longer feels love toward you, that means that everyone else who loved you—like your children, grandchildren, dear friends—now will follow his lead and also no longer love you?

Dr. Abrams uses a confrontation of Mrs. Hoshi's thinking as an intervention.

Mrs. Hoshi:	No . . . I know . . . that's silly . . . but clearly he doesn't find me attractive.
Dr. Abrams:	Given what you have told me he said, it sounds accurate that sadly he is no longer in love with you, but isn't that where the conclusions stop? It doesn't mean your children find you unlovable, or your friends see you as undesirable, does it?

Dr. Abrams poses a closed-ended question, but uses it as a confrontation to Mrs. Hoshi's distorted thinking. This is an intervention or solution strategy.

Mrs. Hoshi:	(smiling) No, actually, one of the widowed men at church has shown interest in me for the past year, but it was just platonic.
Dr. Abrams:	Okay, so when we really stop and challenge our conclusion with the evidence, sometimes we find that we are drawing some pretty distorted conclusions, and these can really hurt us, and stop us from problem solving. I mean, there is a big difference from being the one human being in the whole human race who is unlovable versus being quite sadly, the one of many, many individuals who are confronted with divorce or the loss of a spouse.
Mrs. Hoshi:	I know you are right, Dr. Abrams, but it just feels like everything is falling apart . . . wait, wait . . . I know it's not, but it just seems like so much to figure out.
Dr. Abrams:	Mrs. Hoshi, that was really good the way you challenged yourself. While it might feel like everything is falling apart, in reality it is not,

and in fact many things, like your relationships with the children and friends and your health and even the things you enjoy, still are intact. It's the marriage that is ending, not your life, and not the person you are . . .

Mrs. Hoshi: I know, but still there are many things I am going to have deal with, that I have to figure out. It just seems like so much and I'm not sure where to start.

Dr. Abrams: Mrs. Hoshi, I can hear the concern in your voice and it does appear there are a lot of things that will need to be addressed or resolved.

Dr. Abrams is reflecting both verbal and nonverbal messages to demonstrate attending.

Mrs. Hoshi: . . . and where to start?

Dr. Abrams: Well, Mrs. Hoshi, let's look at the start you have already taken today. Yes, it is clear you are both shocked and truly sad—grieving the end of your marriage—but you have done a super job not letting your thoughts distort the reality, making the experience feel even more overwhelming. So just being able to stay focused on the facts of what is, and not getting lost in all the what may be, or exaggerating the what will happen now, seems to be a really good start.

Dr. Abrams is providing encouragement and demonstrating his valuing, or prizing, of Mrs. Hoshi.

Mrs. Hoshi: I agree and actually I do feel a lot more in control right now than I have for the past 10 days.

Dr. Abrams: So, you did take a real big step and that's super. But there will be a lot of questions or things that will need to be decided, and maybe having support would be helpful.

Mrs. Hoshi: I would like to continue to see you for awhile, just to help me keep focused.

Dr. Abrams:	I would be honored to work with you and we can set up another appointment, but before we end, do you have any questions?
Mrs. Hoshi:	No . . . except . . . (hesitates, with a long pause)
Dr. Abrams:	Except?
Mrs. Hoshi:	Well, if something comes up or I have questions or get back into that thinking, could I contact you?
Dr. Abrams:	(handing her a card) Absolutely. You can call or if you prefer, this is a private e-mail that I use for clients. You could write if that would help.
Mrs. Hoshi:	Thank you.
Dr. Abrams:	You are welcome. If there is nothing else, then I have a homework assignment for you (smiling).
Mrs. Hoshi:	Homework?
Dr. Abrams:	I would like you to buy a little notebook and do two things over the next week (grabbing a tablet from the desk, and beginning to write). First, I would like you to make a list of things that come to mind that you are concerned about—practical things, real, factual things.

Dr. Abrams is introducing a problem-solving strategy.

Mrs. Hoshi:	You mean like how am I going to pay the bills?
Dr. Abrams:	Yep, that's a good one. Now you don't have to sit and try to generate these items, but as they come up in your thinking, I want you to simply list them. We can look at them together and identify any, if there are any, that you may want some help in resolving. Okay?
Mrs. Hoshi:	Yes, I think that will help keep me focused. And the second thing?
Dr. Abrams:	Boy, you have a good memory. Yes, the second thing. Starting with the back of your notebook, since you will be writing down your real-world issues in the front of book, I would like you to keep what I will call a "thought-feeling diary."

Let me show you (begins writing on the paper). Let's say you begin to feel really, really anxious. What I want you to do is simply write down "feeling anxious" and then under that, I would like you to describe what is happening, like "I am going over all the house bills" or "I am sitting and I began to think about all the house bills." Do you think you could do that?

Mrs. Hoshi: Yes, but I'm not sure how that will help?

Dr. Abrams: Well remember, sometimes it is not the event, like house bills, that are the cause of our anxiety, but it is how we think about that event. So maybe you are looking at the house bills or are thinking about doing the house bills, and then your thoughts go to "oh, my god, I will never be able to pay the bills. I'll have to leave the house. How will I survive?" Wow, if the issue is that you are about to be a street person, then I could see why you are maximally anxious, maybe like a 9 on a 10-point scale. But if the issue really is just trying to figure out what bills are due and how to write the checks, well, then maybe the appropriate level of anxiety would be around a 3 or 4. See, this way we can start to help you see when you are distorting the events—the real experiences or the real problems—and making them worse for you.

Mrs. Hoshi: Oh I see. Yes, I can do that, and if I get confused, I'll contact you.

Dr. Abrams: That's super. You had asked earlier what you can do, and look, you are doing it.

Mrs. Hoshi: Well, with your help, thank you.

Dr. Abrams: Mrs. Hoshi, thank you for coming in today. Thank you for sharing your story with me and working so hard in this session. Remember, if you have questions, just contact me; otherwise I will see you next week, same time?

Mrs. Hoshi: That will be great . . . and . . . Dr. Abrams, thank you.

CONCLUSION

Mrs. Ayame Hoshi is certainly a woman who is bright and capable, and has a good support network. Sadly, the ending of her marriage has completely thrown her off kilter and she was feeling overwhelmed, helpless, and depressed.

Dr. Abrams employed skills of active listening and reflection, along with conveying a genuine concern and using a nonjudgmental approach to help Mrs. Hoshi focus and share her story. Dr. Abrams, recognizing the crisis nature of this situation, attempted to be active in the session and offer strategies to provide Mrs. Hoshi with some immediate relief. He employed a cognitive model of intervention as his frame of reference and focused on helping Mrs. Hoshi separate the real facts of the divorce, as painful and as troublesome as they may be, from her exaggerated, catastrophic beliefs. His modeling of the process of challenging her catastrophic thinking helped her begin to employ that same strategy and had the effect of allowing her to experience fewer catastrophes, more control, and thus, fewer crises. Even within this one session, Dr. Abrams (1) developed a working alliance; (2) identified a number of goals for helping, including helping her control distorted thinking and begin to identify real world concerns and issues to be addressed in future sessions; and (3) engaged in real helping, moving the client from an experience of an unbearable crisis to experiencing her life as sad, and problematic, but manageable.

Through building a working alliance with effective listening skills, interventions, and identifying goals, Dr. Abrams has helped Mrs. Hoshi move from the stage of contemplation to preparation, and eventually to the stage of action.

FINAL THOUGHTS

Prior to putting a close to this text and perhaps to your first experience as a developing counselor, it would be helpful for you to take time to reflect on the three cases presented within this section. The cases are real (with all identifying information changed to protect the client anonymity) and the presentations, of course, have been adjusted to fit neatly within the confines of a chapter. But even with that limitation, it is important for you to reflect upon the following:

1. As is evident, being a helper is an awesome responsibility. Each of the people presented within these cases was coming with real-life pain, real points of concern, and real problems that could cause damage if not addressed, and each came to a helper for support and assistance.

2. While a textbook like this can talk about the elements of helping or the skills of a helper, being in the moment of a helping encounter, even if it is

vicariously through reading case presentations, reminds us of how helping is a dynamic, fluid process that requires the artful employment of a helper's knowledge and skill tailored to the uniqueness of the helpee—the issue at hand—and the nature of the helping relationship at any one moment.

3. Finally, as you read through the cases and hopefully attempted to employ your own procedural thinking to anticipate what you (or the helper in the case) should do next, we hope you felt a bit overwhelmed. It is our hope that as you read the cases, you began to realize that you have taken just the first step—a very important and valued step—but just the first of many to becoming a competent helper. It is our hope that the slight feeling of being overwhelmed or being unsure as to what you would do in any one of these cases serves as motivation for your continued education and professional development.

Epilogue

From the Authors' Chairs

Writing a textbook is part research and part experience—but mostly the articulation of the author's unique perspective on practice and profession. Each author has made personal decisions on how to organize the book and what, from the mass of information available, should be included. These decisions reflect the authors' bias, personal interest, values, and professional identity. We, as editors of the series, have invited each author to respond to the following questions as a way to provide the reader a glimpse into the person, and not just the product of the author.

However, as the editors of the series and authors of this text, we find ourselves with a bit of a dilemma, can we really interview ourselves?

Rather than present the reflections from the authors' chairs as dialogue (as is the case for the other series authors), we have simply listed the questions we have posed to others and written our own responses.

It is our hope that our brief reflections will provide a little more insight into our view of our profession—and ourselves as professionals.

—Rp/Nz

Question: Drs. Parsons and Zhang, there are certainly an abundance of insightful points found within this text. But if you were asked to identify, from all that is presented, a single point or theme that you hope will stand out and stick with the reader, what would that point or theme be?

Drs. Parsons and Zhang

We are of the same mind when responding to this question and that is, wow! Just one point?

If we were forced to identify a single point to highlight, it would be the professional nature of what we do.

Counseling is an awesome process. It is a process that has evolved through the diligent research and pursuit of knowledge of so many within our profession. It is a process that finds structure in the codes of ethics (e.g., American Counseling Association's *Code of Ethics*) developed to not only protect those whom we serve, but to give form to that which is uniquely *counseling*. It is our hope that the reader found within the chapters of this text an answer to the question which was initially posed at the opening of Chapter 1, about why students need a course on the essentials of helping—an answer grounded in the science of our profession and now in the elemental formation of the reader's own professional identity.

Question: In the text, you make reference to the dynamic nature of the counseling process. Could you share from your own experience how this may actually look in practice and what special demands it places on the counselor?

Parsons and Zhang

When we say *fluid* or *dynamic,* what we are trying to highlight is that every client, every situation—in fact, every moment—in counseling is truly the first of its kind. Granted depression or anxiety may be viewed as syndromes with standard characteristics, but we don't treat depression, we work with people, not syndromes. We approach our work with models and theories expecting a certain progression to occur, but we also approach all of our work with a sense of awe and an openness to be surprised. It is during these moments of awe and surprise that we are directed to be flexible, adaptable, and fluid at any one moment.

While counseling has a scientific core one that builds and organizes knowledge in the form of testable explanations and predictions about its practice, the application of this science invites, no, requires, some artistry. It is like singing a song or playing a piece of music. The song or the music is the same to each singer or player, but the outcome of the performance can be very different from singer to singer or player to player because of the uniqueness of each individual and the dynamic created with such uniqueness of each individual singer or player. This uniqueness includes the person's experience, training, practice, as well as the individual's understanding of the music. So, the counselor's self-cultivation including his or her training and practice determines the effectiveness of helping. This self-cultivation also means that the counselor betters him- or herself in order to be flexible enough to adapt to his or her clients.

Question: Drs. Parsons and Zhang, you are not only authors and professors, but also you are both professional practitioners. What might this book reveal about your own professional identity?

Dr. Parsons

I value and hopefully embody within all that I do, the importance of approaching counseling both as process and profession from the perspective of a reflective practitioner. Knowing what I am doing and why I am doing it helps me assess the effectiveness of my practice, be it in my clinical office or classroom. In addition to such reflection on and in practice, I value the science and art of what we are called to do. I attempt to integrate my understanding of our emerging science with the artistry that allows for adaptation of this science to the uniqueness of the person and situation with whom I am engaged. Finally, I believe that mine is a profession that demands accountability—to client and to the profession itself.

In coauthoring this text with Dr. Zhang, I was once again reminded of the concept of *intentionality* and its role in the counseling process. Ours is not an exact science and, as such, there are no fixed templates that can be employed to guide our practice. Counselors are unique—just as are clients—but one point of consistency found among all within our profession is our desire to facilitate our client's growth and well-being. With that as a beacon guiding our practice, we approach what we do with mindfulness and a sense of intentionality.

Dr. Zhang

I grew up in China but had most of my education in the United States, education in the helping profession in particular. I have seen that my worldview has gradually been transformed from the Eastern into the Western view and I exercise my values based on situations. Professionally, I always believe that counseling is a combination of science and art. Four things that I hold dear and believe are central to my professional identity are my values, passion, role, and responsibilities. I love what I'm doing—teaching, research, and practice—and I consider the roles—teacher, researcher, and practitioner—that I play to be the utmost privilege and the responsibilities that I assume exalted. I also believe that my teaching should not only be based on theories but also my own research and practice. So, much of the information I included in this text reflects my personal experience and reveals my professional identity. But this is still just the beginning. I believe as a professional counselor one must be clear about his or her professional identity and make effort to let it evolve and develop.

Index

About the Authors

Richard D. Parsons, PhD, is a Full Professor in the Department of Counseling and Educational Psychology at West Chester University of Pennsylvania. Dr. Parsons has over 32 years of university teaching in counselor preparation programs. Prior to his university teaching Dr. Parsons spent 9 years as a school counselor in an inner city high school. Dr. Parsons has been the recipient of many awards and honors, including the Pennsylvania Counselor of Year award.

Dr. Parsons has authored or co-authored over 80 professional articles and books. His most recent books include the series of 4 training texts for school counselors, *Transforming Theory Into Practice*; and individual texts: *Counseling Strategies That Work! Evidenced-based Interventions for School Counselors*; *The School Counselor as Consultant*; *Teacher as Reflective Practitioner and Action Researcher*; *Educational Psychology*; *The Ethics of Professional Practice*; *Counseling Strategies and Intervention Techniques*; and *The Skills of Helping*. In addition to these texts Dr. Parsons has authored or co-authored three seminal works in the area of psycho-educational consultation, *Mental Health Consultation in the Schools*; *Developing Consultation Skills*; and *The Skilled Consultant*.

Dr. Parsons has a private practice and serves as a consultant to educational institutions and mental health service organizations throughout the tri-state area of Pennsylvania, New Jersey, and Delaware. Dr. Parsons has served as a national consultant to the Council of Independent Colleges, Washington, D.C., providing institutions of higher education with assistance in the areas of Program Development, Student Support Services, Pedagogical Innovation and Assessment Procedures.

Naijian Zhang, PhD, is a Full Professor in the Department of Counseling and Educational Psychology at West Chester University of Pennsylvania. Dr. Zhang has over 20 years of college and university teaching in counseling, higher education/student affairs, and language programs. Dr. Zhang was also a university administrator in student affairs for 4 years. Dr. Zhang authored and coauthored over 20 articles, book chapters, and books. His most recent books include *Psychology* in 2009 and *Rentz's Student Affairs Practice in Higher Education* in 2011. He is a recipient of the Travel Award from the American Psychological Association (APA), Outstanding Research Award, and Outstanding Service

Award from the American College Personnel Association (ACPA). He has served on the editorial board of the *Journal of College Counseling*.

In addition, Dr. Zhang has practiced over 15 years and is currently a licensed psychologist in Pennsylvania. He frequently conducts counseling training workshops internationally.